FIXED INCOME AND EQUITY PORTFOLIO MANAGEMENT

CFA® Program Curriculum
2016 • LEVEL III • VOLUME 4

Photography courtesy of Hector Emanuel.

Copyright © 2015, 2014, 2013, 2012, 2011, 2010, 2009, 2008, 2007, 2006 by CFA Institute
All rights reserved.

This copyright covers material written expressly for this volume by the editor/s as well as the compilation itself. It does not cover the individual selections herein that first appeared elsewhere. Permission to reprint these has been obtained by CFA Institute for this edition only. Further reproductions by any means, electronic or mechanical, including photocopying and recording, or by any information storage or retrieval systems, must be arranged with the individual copyright holders noted.

CFA®, Chartered Financial Analyst®, AIMR-PPS®, and GIPS® are just a few of the trademarks owned by CFA Institute. To view a list of CFA Institute trademarks and the Guide for Use of CFA Institute Marks, please visit our website at www.cfainstitute.org.

This publication is designed to provide accurate and authoritative information in regard to the subject matter covered. It is sold with the understanding that the publisher is not engaged in rendering legal, accounting, or other professional service. If legal advice or other expert assistance is required, the services of a competent professional should be sought.

All trademarks, service marks, registered trademarks, and registered service marks are the property of their respective owners and are used herein for identification purposes only.

ISBN 978-1-942471-12-7 (paper)
ISBN 978-1-942471-33-2 (ebk)

10 9 8 7 6 5 4 3 2 1

Please visit our website at
www.WileyGlobalFinance.com.

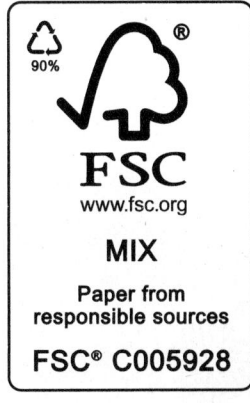

CONTENTS

How to Use the CFA Program Curriculum — v
    Curriculum Development Process — v
    Organization of the Curriculum — vi
    Features of the Curriculum — vi
    Designing Your Personal Study Program — vii
    Feedback — ix

Portfolio Management

Study Session 10   **Fixed-Income Portfolio Management (1)** — 3

Reading 20   **Fixed-Income Portfolio Management—Part I** — 5
    Introduction — 6
    A Framework for Fixed-Income Portfolio Management — 6
    Managing Funds against a Bond Market Index — 7
        Classification of Strategies — 9
        Indexing (Pure and Enhanced) — 10
        Active Strategies — 27
        Monitoring/Adjusting the Portfolio and Performance Evaluation — 29
    Managing Funds against Liabilities — 29
        Dedication Strategies — 29
        Cash Flow Matching Strategies — 48
    Summary — 52
    Practice Problems — 55
    Solutions — 61

Reading 21   **Relative-Value Methodologies for Global Credit Bond Portfolio Management** — 65
    Introduction — 65
    Credit Relative-Value Analysis — 68
        Relative Value — 70
        Classic Relative-Value Analysis — 70
        Relative-Value Methodologies — 72
    Total Return Analysis — 72
    Primary Market Analysis — 73
        The Effect of Market-Structure Dynamics — 73
        The Effect of Product Structure — 74
    Liquidity and Trading Analysis — 74
    Secondary Trade Rationales — 75
        Popular Reasons for Trading — 75
        Trading Constraints — 78
    Spread Analysis — 79
        Alternative Spread Measures — 79
        Closer Look at Swap Spreads — 80
        Spread Tools — 81

◘ indicates an optional segment

	Structural Analysis	82
	Bullets	83
	Callables	84
	Sinking Funds	85
	Putables	85
	Credit Curve Analysis	86
	Credit Analysis	87
	Asset Allocation/Sector Rotation	87
	Summary	89
	Practice Problems	91
	Solutions	98
Study Session 11	**Fixed-Income Portfolio Management (2)**	**103**
Reading 22	**Fixed-Income Portfolio Management—Part II**	**105**
	Other Fixed-Income Strategies	106
	Combination Strategies	106
	Leverage	107
	Derivatives-Enabled Strategies	111
	International Bond Investing	128
	Active versus Passive Management	129
	Currency Risk	131
	Breakeven Spread Analysis	136
	Emerging Market Debt	137
	Selecting a Fixed-Income Manager	139
	Historical Performance as a Predictor of Future Performance	140
	Developing Criteria for the Selection	140
	Comparison with Selection of Equity Managers	141
	Summary	143
	Practice Problems	145
	Solutions	153
Study Session 12	**Equity Portfolio Management**	**159**
Reading 23	**Equity Portfolio Management**	**161**
	Introduction	162
	The Role of the Equity Portfolio	163
	Approaches to Equity Investment	165
	Passive Equity Investing	166
	Equity Indices	168
	Passive Investment Vehicles	175
	Active Equity Investing	184
	Equity Styles	184
	Socially Responsible Investing	204
	Long–Short Investing	205
	Sell Disciplines/Trading	210
	Semiactive Equity Investing	211
	Managing a Portfolio of Managers	214
	Core-Satellite	217

◘ indicates an optional segment

Completeness Fund	**220**
Other Approaches: Alpha and Beta Separation	**221**
Identifying, Selecting, and Contracting with Equity Portfolio Managers	**222**
Developing a Universe of Suitable Manager Candidates	**222**
The Predictive Power of Past Performance	**222**
Fee Structures	**223**
The Equity Manager Questionnaire	**223**
Structuring Equity Research and Security Selection	**230**
Top-Down versus Bottom-Up Approaches	**230**
Buy-Side versus Sell-Side Research	**231**
Industry Classification	**231**
Summary	**232**
Practice Problems	**235**
Solutions	**242**

Glossary	**G-1**
Index	**I-1**

◘ indicates an optional segment

How to Use the CFA Program Curriculum

Congratulations on reaching Level III of the Chartered Financial Analyst (CFA®) Program. This exciting and rewarding program of study reflects your desire to become a serious investment professional. You are embarking on a program noted for its high ethical standards and the breadth of knowledge, skills, and abilities it develops. Your commitment to the CFA Program should be educationally and professionally rewarding.

The credential you seek is respected around the world as a mark of accomplishment and dedication. Each level of the program represents a distinct achievement in professional development. Successful completion of the program is rewarded with membership in a prestigious global community of investment professionals. CFA charterholders are dedicated to life-long learning and maintaining currency with the ever-changing dynamics of a challenging profession. The CFA Program represents the first step toward a career-long commitment to professional education.

The CFA examination measures your mastery of the core skills required to succeed as an investment professional. These core skills are the basis for the Candidate Body of Knowledge (CBOK™). The CBOK consists of four components:

- A broad outline that lists the major topic areas covered in the CFA Program (www.cfainstitute.org/cbok);
- Topic area weights that indicate the relative exam weightings of the top-level topic areas (www.cfainstitute.org/level_III);
- Learning outcome statements (LOS) that advise candidates about the specific knowledge, skills, and abilities they should acquire from readings covering a topic area (LOS are provided in candidate study sessions and at the beginning of each reading); and
- The CFA Program curriculum, which contains the readings and end-of-reading questions, that candidates receive upon exam registration.

Therefore, the key to your success on the CFA examinations is studying and understanding the CBOK. The following sections provide background on the CBOK, the organization of the curriculum, and tips for developing an effective study program.

CURRICULUM DEVELOPMENT PROCESS

The CFA Program is grounded in the practice of the investment profession. Beginning with the Global Body of Investment Knowledge (GBIK), CFA Institute performs a continuous practice analysis with investment professionals around the world to determine the knowledge, skills, and abilities (competencies) that are relevant to the profession. Regional expert panels and targeted surveys are conducted annually to verify and reinforce the continuous feedback from the GBIK collaborative website. The practice analysis process ultimately defines the CBOK. The CBOK reflects the competencies that are generally accepted and applied by investment professionals. These competencies are used in practice in a generalist context and are expected to be demonstrated by a recently qualified CFA charterholder.

Copyright © 2015 CFA Institute

The Education Advisory Committee, consisting of practicing charterholders, in conjunction with CFA Institute staff, designs the CFA Program curriculum in order to deliver the CBOK to candidates. The examinations, also written by charterholders, are designed to allow you to demonstrate your mastery of the CBOK as set forth in the CFA Program curriculum. As you structure your personal study program, you should emphasize mastery of the CBOK and the practical application of that knowledge. For more information on the practice analysis, CBOK, and development of the CFA Program curriculum, please visit www.cfainstitute.org.

ORGANIZATION OF THE CURRICULUM

The Level III CFA Program curriculum is organized into 10 topic areas. Each topic area begins with a brief statement of the material and the depth of knowledge expected.

Each topic area is then divided into one or more study sessions. These study sessions—18 sessions in the Level III curriculum—should form the basic structure of your reading and preparation.

Each study session includes a statement of its structure and objective and is further divided into specific reading assignments. An outline illustrating the organization of these 18 study sessions can be found at the front of each volume of the curriculum.

The readings and end-of-reading questions are the basis for all examination questions and are selected or developed specifically to teach the knowledge, skills, and abilities reflected in the CBOK. These readings are drawn from content commissioned by CFA Institute, textbook chapters, professional journal articles, research analyst reports, and cases. All readings include problems and solutions to help you understand and master the topic areas.

Reading-specific Learning Outcome Statements (LOS) are listed at the beginning of each reading. These LOS indicate what you should be able to accomplish after studying the reading. The LOS, the reading, and the end-of-reading questions are dependent on each other, with the reading and questions providing context for understanding the scope of the LOS.

You should use the LOS to guide and focus your study because each examination question is based on the assigned readings and one or more LOS. The readings provide context for the LOS and enable you to apply a principle or concept in a variety of scenarios. The candidate is responsible for the entirety of the required material in a study session, which includes the assigned readings as well as the end-of-reading questions and problems.

We encourage you to review the information about the LOS on our website (www.cfainstitute.org/programs/cfaprogram/courseofstudy/Pages/study_sessions.aspx), including the descriptions of LOS "command words" (www.cfainstitute.org/programs/Documents/cfa_and_cipm_los_command_words.pdf).

FEATURES OF THE CURRICULUM

OPTIONAL SEGMENT

Required vs. Optional Segments You should read all of an assigned reading. In some cases, though, we have reprinted an entire chapter or article and marked certain parts of the reading as "optional." The CFA examination is based only on the required segments, and the optional segments are included only when it is determined that they might help you to better understand the required segments (by seeing the required material in its full context). When an optional segment begins, you will see an icon and a dashed vertical bar in the outside margin that will continue until the optional segment ends, accompanied by another icon. *Unless the material is specifically marked as optional, you should assume it is required.* You should rely on the required segments and the reading-specific LOS in preparing for the examination.

END OPTIONAL SEGMENT

End-of-Reading Problems/Solutions *All problems in the readings as well as their solutions (which are provided directly following the problems) are part of the curriculum and are required material for the exam.* When appropriate, we have included problems within and after the readings to demonstrate practical application and reinforce your understanding of the concepts presented. The problems are designed to help you learn these concepts and may serve as a basis for exam questions. Many of these questions are adapted from past CFA examinations.

Glossary and Index For your convenience, we have printed a comprehensive glossary in each volume. Throughout the curriculum, a **bolded** word in a reading denotes a term defined in the glossary. The curriculum eBook is searchable, but we also publish an index that can be found on the CFA Institute website with the Level III study sessions.

Source Material The authorship, publisher, and copyright owners are given for each reading for your reference. We recommend that you use the CFA Institute curriculum rather than the original source materials because the curriculum may include only selected pages from outside readings, updated sections within the readings, and problems and solutions tailored to the CFA Program.

LOS Self-Check We have inserted checkboxes next to each LOS that you can use to track your progress in mastering the concepts in each reading.

DESIGNING YOUR PERSONAL STUDY PROGRAM

Create a Schedule An orderly, systematic approach to exam preparation is critical. You should dedicate a consistent block of time every week to reading and studying. Complete all reading assignments and the associated problems and solutions in each study session. Review the LOS both before and after you study each reading to ensure that you have mastered the applicable content and can demonstrate the knowledge, skill, or ability described by the LOS and the assigned reading. Use the LOS self-check to track your progress and highlight areas of weakness for later review.

As you prepare for your exam, we will e-mail you important exam updates, testing policies, and study tips. Be sure to read these carefully. Curriculum errata are periodically updated and posted on the study session page at www.cfainstitute.org. You can also sign up for an RSS feed to alert you to the latest errata update.

Successful candidates report an average of more than 300 hours preparing for each exam. Your preparation time will vary based on your prior education and experience. For each level of the curriculum, there are 18 study sessions. So, a good plan is to devote 15–20 hours per week for 18 weeks to studying the material. Use the final four to six weeks before the exam to review what you have learned and practice with topic and mock exams. This recommendation, however, may underestimate the hours needed for appropriate examination preparation depending on your individual circumstances, relevant experience, and academic background. You will undoubtedly adjust your study time to conform to your own strengths and weaknesses and to your educational and professional background.

You will probably spend more time on some study sessions than on others, but on average you should plan on devoting 15–20 hours per study session. You should allow ample time for both in-depth study of all topic areas and additional concentration on those topic areas for which you feel the least prepared.

An interactive study planner is available in the candidate resources area of our website to help you plan your study time. The interactive study planner recommends completion dates for each topic of the curriculum. Dates are determined based on study time available, exam topic weights, and curriculum weights. As you progress through the curriculum, the interactive study planner dynamically adjusts your study plan when you are running off schedule to help you stay on track for completion prior to the examination.

CFA Institute Topic Exams The CFA Institute topic exams are intended to assess your mastery of individual topic areas as you progress through your studies. After each test, you will receive immediate feedback noting the correct responses and indicating the relevant assigned reading so you can identify areas of weakness for further study. For more information on the topic tests, please visit www.cfainstitute.org.

CFA Institute Mock Exams The three-hour mock exams simulate the morning and afternoon sessions of the actual CFA examination, and are intended to be taken after you complete your study of the full curriculum so you can test your understanding of the curriculum and your readiness for the exam. You will receive feedback at the end of the mock exam, noting the correct responses and indicating the relevant assigned readings so you can assess areas of weakness for further study during your review period. We recommend that you take mock exams during the final stages of your preparation for the actual CFA examination. For more information on the mock examinations, please visit www.cfainstitute.org.

Preparatory Providers After you enroll in the CFA Program, you may receive numerous solicitations for preparatory courses and review materials. When considering a prep course, make sure the provider is in compliance with the CFA Institute Prep Provider Guidelines Program (www.cfainstitute.org/utility/examprep/Pages/index.aspx). Just remember, there are no shortcuts to success on the CFA examinations; reading and studying the CFA curriculum is the key to success on the examination. The CFA examinations reference only the CFA Institute assigned curriculum—no preparatory course or review course materials are consulted or referenced.

SUMMARY

Every question on the CFA examination is based on the content contained in the required readings and on one or more LOS. Frequently, an examination question is based on a specific example highlighted within a reading or on a specific end-of-reading question and/or problem and its solution. To make effective use of the CFA Program curriculum, please remember these key points:

1. All pages of the curriculum are required reading for the examination except for occasional sections marked as optional. You may read optional pages as background, but you will not be tested on them.

2. All questions, problems, and their solutions—found at the end of readings—are part of the curriculum and are required study material for the examination.

3. You should make appropriate use of the topic and mock examinations and other resources available at www.cfainstitute.org.

How to Use the CFA Program Curriculum

4. Use the interactive study planner to create a schedule and commit sufficient study time to cover the 18 study sessions, review the materials, and take topic and mock examinations.

5. Some of the concepts in the study sessions may be superseded by updated rulings and/or pronouncements issued after a reading was published. Candidates are expected to be familiar with the overall analytical framework contained in the assigned readings. Candidates are not responsible for changes that occur after the material was written.

FEEDBACK

At CFA Institute, we are committed to delivering a comprehensive and rigorous curriculum for the development of competent, ethically grounded investment professionals. We rely on candidate and member feedback as we work to incorporate content, design, and packaging improvements. You can be assured that we will continue to listen to your suggestions. Please send any comments or feedback to info@cfainstitute.org. Ongoing improvements in the curriculum will help you prepare for success on the upcoming examinations and for a lifetime of learning as a serious investment professional.

Portfolio Management

STUDY SESSIONS

Study Session 3	Behavioral Finance
Study Session 4	Private Wealth Management (1)
Study Session 5	Private Wealth Management (2)
Study Session 6	Portfolio Management for Institutional Investors
Study Session 7	Applications of Economic Analysis to Portfolio Management
Study Session 8	Asset Allocation and Related Decisions in Portfolio Management (1)
Study Session 9	Asset Allocation and Related Decisions in Portfolio Management (2)
Study Session 10	Fixed-Income Portfolio Management (1)
Study Session 11	Fixed-Income Portfolio Management (2)
Study Session 12	Equity Portfolio Management
Study Session 13	Alternative Investments for Portfolio Management
Study Session 14	Risk Management
Study Session 15	Risk Management Application of Derivatives
Study Session 16	Trading, Monitoring, and Rebalancing
Study Session 17	Performance Evaluation
Study Session 18	Global Investment Performance Standards

This volume includes Study Sessions 10–12.

Copyright © 2015 CFA Institute

TOPIC LEVEL LEARNING OUTCOME

The candidate should be able to prepare an appropriate investment policy statement and asset allocation; formulate strategies for managing, monitoring, and rebalancing investment portfolios; evaluate portfolio performance; and analyze a presentation of investment returns for consistency with Global Investment Performance Standards (GIPS®).

PORTFOLIO MANAGEMENT
STUDY SESSION

10

Fixed-Income Portfolio Management (1)

The elements of the investment management process, such as the consideration of risk, return, and investment constraints, are the same for a fixed-income portfolio as for any other type of portfolio. As part of the process, an appropriate benchmark is selected to serve as a reference for portfolio construction and performance evaluation. For investors taking an asset-only approach, the benchmark is typically a bond market index. For investors with a liability-based approach, performance is measured in terms of the portfolio's ability to meet a set of investor-specific liabilities. The first reading addresses these primary elements of managing fixed-income portfolios and introduces specific portfolio management strategies. The second reading discusses additional relative-value methodologies.

READING ASSIGNMENTS

Reading 20 Fixed-Income Portfolio Management—Part I
by H. Gifford Fong and Larry D. Guin, DBA, CFA

Reading 21 Relative-Value Methodologies for Global Credit Bond Portfolio Management
by Jack Malvey, CFA

Copyright © 2015 CFA Institute

READING
20

Fixed-Income Portfolio Management—Part I

by H. Gifford Fong and Larry D. Guin, DBA, CFA

H. Gifford Fong is at Gifford Fong Associates and Journal of Investment Management (USA). Larry D. Guin, DBA, CFA, is a retired professor at Murray State University (USA).

LEARNING OUTCOMES

Mastery	The candidate should be able to:
☐	a. compare, with respect to investment objectives, the use of liabilities as a benchmark and the use of a bond index as a benchmark;
☐	b. compare pure bond indexing, enhanced indexing, and active investing with respect to the objectives, advantages, disadvantages, and management of each;
☐	c. discuss the criteria for selecting a benchmark bond index and justify the selection of a specific index when given a description of an investor's risk aversion, income needs, and liabilities;
☐	d. critique the use of bond market indexes as benchmarks;
☐	e. describe and evaluate techniques, such as duration matching and the use of key rate durations, by which an enhanced indexer may seek to align the risk exposures of the portfolio with those of the benchmark bond index;
☐	f. contrast and demonstrate the use of total return analysis and scenario analysis to assess the risk and return characteristics of a proposed trade;
☐	g. formulate a bond immunization strategy to ensure funding of a predetermined liability and evaluate the strategy under various interest rate scenarios;
☐	h. demonstrate the process of rebalancing a portfolio to reestablish a desired dollar duration;
☐	i. explain the importance of spread duration;
☐	j. discuss the extensions that have been made to classical immunization theory, including the introduction of contingent immunization;

(continued)

Note: Part II of this reading is included in Study Session 11 under the title "Fixed-Income Portfolio Management—Part II."

Managing Investment Portfolios: A Dynamic Process, Third Edition, John L. Maginn, CFA, Donald L. Tuttle, CFA, Jerald E. Pinto, CFA, and Dennis W. McLeavey, CFA, editors. Copyright © 2007 by CFA Institute.

LEARNING OUTCOMES

Mastery	The candidate should be able to:
☐	k. explain the risks associated with managing a portfolio against a liability structure, including interest rate risk, contingent claim risk, and cap risk;
☐	l. compare immunization strategies for a single liability, multiple liabilities, and general cash flows;
☐	m. compare risk minimization with return maximization in immunized portfolios;
☐	n. demonstrate the use of cash flow matching to fund a fixed set of future liabilities and compare the advantages and disadvantages of cash flow matching to those of immunization strategies.

1. INTRODUCTION

Over the past 25 years, fixed-income portfolio management has moved from a sleepy backwater of the investment arena to the cutting edge of investment thought. Once, managers in the field concentrated on earning an acceptable yield to maturity and used a few relatively simple measures to control risk in the portfolio. Today, the portfolio manager has a stunning array of new tools at his disposal, capable of measuring and explaining the smallest variations in desired performance while simultaneously controlling risk with a variety of quantitative tools. This reading examines the results of that revolution in fixed-income portfolio management.

It is not our purpose to examine in great detail the analytical "tools of the trade"; these techniques are covered extensively elsewhere. Our focus is broader and emphasizes the effective construction of a fixed-income portfolio and related risk issues. The fixed-income portfolio management process and the major themes in managing the fixed-income portion of a portfolio receive the emphasis in this reading.

The reading begins with a short review in Section 2 of the framework used for managing fixed-income portfolios. A fixed-income portfolio manager may manage funds against a bond market index or against the client's liabilities. In the former approach, the chief concern is performance relative to the selected bond index; in the latter, it is performance in funding the payment of liabilities. Managing funds against a bond market index is covered in Section 3 while management against liabilities (asset/liability management or ALM) is covered in Section 4. The final section summarizes the reading.

2. A FRAMEWORK FOR FIXED-INCOME PORTFOLIO MANAGEMENT

To make our discussion easier to follow, let us revisit the four activities in the investment management process:

1. setting the investment objectives (with related constraints);
2. developing and implementing a portfolio strategy;

3 monitoring the portfolio; and

4 adjusting the portfolio.

These four steps as they apply to fixed-income portfolio management are shown in Exhibit 1. For ease of illustration, Exhibit 1 breaks the second activity (developing and implementing a portfolio strategy) into its individual parts and combines the third and fourth activities (monitoring and adjusting the portfolio).

As can be seen in Exhibit 1, the basic features of the investment management process are the same for a fixed-income portfolio as for any other type of investment. Risk, return, and constraints are considered first. If the client is a taxable investor, portfolio analysis must be done on an after-tax basis and considerations of the tax-efficient placement of fixed-income assets come to the fore. For any type of client, the fixed-income portfolio manager must agree with the client on an appropriate benchmark, based on the needs of the client as expressed in the investment policy statement or the investor's mandate to the portfolio manager.

Broadly, there are two types of investor based on investment objectives. The first type of investor does not have liability matching as a specific objective. For example, a bond mutual fund has a great deal of freedom in how to invest its funds because it does not have a set of liabilities that requires a cash flow stream to satisfy them. The fund receives money from investors and provides professional expertise in investing this money for them, but the fund is not guaranteeing investors a certain rate of return. An investor (and manager) not focused on liability matching will typically select a specific bond market index as the benchmark for the portfolio; the portfolio's objective is to either match or exceed the rate of return on that index. In other words, the bond market index serves as the benchmark for the portfolio. This approach is sometimes referred to as investing on a benchmark-relative basis. However, the investor taking this approach will generally evaluate the risk of bond holdings not only in relation to the benchmark index but also in relation to the contribution to the risk of the overall (multi-asset-class) portfolio.

The second type of investor has a liability (or set of liabilities) that needs to be met. For example, some investors create a liability by borrowing money at a stated rate of interest, thereby leveraging the portfolio. Other investors have a liability as a result of legal promises that have been made, such as the payouts under a defined-benefit pension plan. Some investors may have quasi-liabilities represented by their retirement needs, and these can be treated as liabilities in the context of portfolio management. The investor with liabilities will measure success by whether the portfolio generates the funds necessary to pay out the cash outflows associated with the liabilities. In other words, meeting the liabilities is the investment objective; as such, it also becomes the benchmark for the portfolio.

Later we will examine in detail managing funds to ensure that the investor's liabilities are met. But for now, let us concentrate on managing the portfolio against a bond market index.

MANAGING FUNDS AGAINST A BOND MARKET INDEX

This section addresses fixed-income portfolio management from the perspective of an investor who has chosen to manage the portfolio's funds against a bond market index.[1]

---

1 This section was revised by C. Mitchell Conover, CFA, CIPM.

Exhibit 1　The Fixed-Income Portfolio Management Process

Managing Funds against a Bond Market Index

A passive management strategy assumes that the market's expectations are essentially correct or, more precisely, that investors cannot add value (net of the expenses of analysis and trading) by second-guessing these expectations. By setting the portfolio's risk profile (e.g., interest rate sensitivity and credit quality) identical to the benchmark index's risk profile and pursuing a passive strategy, the investor accepts an average risk level (as defined by the index's and portfolio's risk profile) and an average rate of return (as measured by the index's and portfolio's return). Under a passive strategy, the manager does not have to make independent forecasts and the portfolio should very closely track the index.

An active management strategy essentially relies on the manager's forecasting ability. Active managers believe that they possess superior skills in interest rate forecasting, credit valuation, or in some other area that can be used to exploit opportunities in the market. The portfolio's return should increase if the manager's forecasts of the future path of the factors that influence fixed-income returns (e.g., changes in interest rates or credit spreads) are more accurate than those reflected in the current prices of fixed-income securities. The manager can create small mismatches (enhancement) or large mismatches (full-blown active management) relative to the index to take advantage of this expertise.

When the major decision to manage funds against an index has been made, the next step is to select one or more appropriate investment strategies. Strategies can be grouped along a spectrum, as explained in the next section.

3.1 Classification of Strategies

Volpert (2000, pp. 85–88) provided an excellent classification of the types of fixed-income strategies relevant to this discussion.[2] Exhibit 1, in the shaded group of boxes next to "developing a portfolio strategy" shows these five types of strategies based on a scale that ranges from totally passive to full-blown active management. The types can be explained as follows:

1 *Pure bond indexing* (or *full replication approach*).

The goal here is to produce a portfolio that is a perfect match to the index. The pure bond indexing approach attempts to duplicate the index by owning all the bonds in the index in the same percentage as the index. Full replication is typically very difficult and expensive to implement in the case of bond indices. Many issues in a typical bond index (particularly the non-Treasuries) are quite illiquid and very infrequently traded. For this reason, full replication of a bond index is rarely attempted because of the difficulty, inefficiency, and high cost of implementation. The reasons against full replication are somewhat unique to fixed income investing, and notably pure bond indexing is much less common than pure equity indexing approaches.

2 *Enhanced indexing by matching primary risk factors.*[3]

This management style uses a sampling approach in an attempt to match the primary index risk factors and achieve a higher return than under full replication. **Primary risk factors** are typically major influences on the pricing of bonds, such as changes in the level of interest rates, twists in the yield curve, and changes in the spread between Treasuries and non-Treasuries.

---

2 Note that the terms "investment style" and "investment strategy" are often used interchangeably in the investment community. In this chapter, we use the term "style" as the more general term (i.e., either active or passive). An investment style may encompass many different types of strategies, which are implementation techniques or methodologies for achieving the portfolio's objective.
3 Factor matching is considered a implementation choice for indexing by other some authorities.

A By investing in a sample of bonds rather than the whole index, the manager reduces the construction and maintenance costs of the portfolio. Although a sampling approach will usually track the index less closely than full replication, this disadvantage is expected to be more than offset by the lower expenses.

B By matching the primary risk factors, the portfolio is affected by broad market-moving events (e.g., changing interest rate levels, twists in the yield curve, spread changes) to the same degree as the index.

3 *Enhanced indexing by small risk factor mismatches.*[4]

While matching duration (interest rate sensitivity), this style allows the manager to tilt the portfolio in favor of any of the other risk factors. The manager may try to marginally increase the return by pursuing relative value in certain sectors, quality, term structure, and so on. The mismatches are small and are intended to simply enhance the portfolio's return and/or risk profile enough to overcome the difference in administrative costs between the portfolio and the index.

4 *Active management by larger risk factor mismatches.*

The difference between this style and enhanced indexing is one of degree. This style involves the readiness to make deliberately larger mismatches on the primary risk factors than in Type 3—definitely active management. The portfolio manager is now actively pursuing opportunities in the market to increase the return. The manager may overweight A rated bonds relative to AA/Aaa rated bonds, overweight corporates versus Treasuries, position the portfolio to take advantage of an anticipated twist in the yield curve, or adjust the portfolio's duration slightly away from the index's duration to take advantage of a perceived opportunity. The objective of the manager is to produce sufficient returns to overcome this style's additional transaction costs while controlling risk.

5 *Full-blown active management.*

Full-blown active management involves the possibility of aggressive mismatches on duration, sector weights, and other factors. Often, the fund manager is seeking to construct a portfolio with superior return and risk characteristics, without much day-to-day consideration of the underlying index composition.

The following sections offer further information and comments on these types of management.

3.2 Indexing (Pure and Enhanced)

We begin by asking the obvious question: "Why should an investor consider investing in an indexed portfolio?" Actually, several reasons exist for bond indexing.

- Indexed portfolios have lower fees than actively managed accounts. Advisory fees on an indexed portfolio may be only a few basis points, whereas the advisory fees charged by active managers typically range from 15 to 50 bps. Nonadvisory fees, such as custodial fees, are also much lower for indexed portfolios.

---

[4] "Small" here is used to refer to the size of the mismatch and not the level of risk.

- Outperforming a broadly based market index on a consistent basis is a difficult task, particularly when one has to overcome the higher fees and transactions costs associated with active management.
- Broadly based bond index portfolios provide excellent diversification. The most popular US bond market indices each have a minimum of 5,000 issues and a market value measured in the trillions of dollars. The indices contain a wide array of maturities, sectors, and qualities.[5] The diversification inherent in an indexed portfolio, even when using sampling, results in a lower risk for a given level of return than other less diversified portfolios.

3.2.1 Selection of a Benchmark Bond Index: General Considerations

Once the decision has been made to index, important follow-up questions remain: "Which index should I choose? Should the index have a short duration or a long duration?" "Is the index's credit quality appropriate for the role that the bond portfolio will play in my overall portfolio?" At the risk of oversimplifying, you should choose as a benchmark the index containing characteristics that match closely with the desired characteristics of your portfolio. The choice depends heavily on four factors:

1 *Market value risk.*

   The desired market value risk of the portfolio and the index should be comparable. Given a normal upward-sloping yield curve, a bond portfolio's yield to maturity increases as the maturity of the portfolio increases. Does this mean that the total return is greater on a long portfolio than on a short one? Not necessarily. Because a long duration portfolio is more sensitive to changes in interest rates, a long portfolio will likely fall more in price than a short one when interest rates rise. In other words, as the maturity and duration of a portfolio increases, the market risk increases.

2 *Income risk.*

   The chosen index should provide an income stream comparable to that desired for the portfolio. Many investors (e.g., foundations and retirees) prefer portfolios that generate a high level of income while conserving principal. Investing in a long portfolio can lock in a dependable income stream over a long period of time and does not subject the income stream to the vagaries of fluctuating interest rates. If stability and dependability of income are the primary needs of the investor, then the long portfolio is the least risky and the short portfolio is the most risky.

3 *Credit risk.*

   The average credit risk of the index should be appropriate for the portfolio's role in the investor's overall portfolio and satisfy any constraints placed on credit quality in the investor's investment policy statement. The diversification among issuers in the index should also be satisfactory to the investor.

4 *Liability framework risk.*

   This risk should be minimized. In general, it is prudent to match the investment characteristics (e.g., duration) of assets and liabilities, if liabilities play any role. The choice of an appropriate index should reflect the nature of the liabilities: Investors with long-term liabilities should select a long index.[6] Of course, bond investors that have no liabilities have much more latitude in the choice of an index because of the lack of this restriction.

---

5 "Qualities" refers to the default risk of the bonds. This can be measured by the bonds' rating, for example, Standard & Poor's/Moody's Investor Services AAA/Aaa, AA/Aa, A, BBB/Baa, and so on.
6 Management of a portfolio against liabilities is covered in detail in Section 4.

For the taxable investor, returns and risk need to be evaluated on an after-tax basis. For example, in the United States, where there are active markets in tax-exempt bonds, a taxable investor would compare the anticipated return on taxable and tax-exempt bond indices on a net-of-taxes basis.[7] In some countries, different tax rates apply to the income and capital gains components of bond returns. Furthermore, if a taxable investor can hold the bond portfolio within a taxable or a tax-deferred account, the investor can effectively view the index as having one set of return–risk characteristics in taxable account and another set in a tax-deferred account. This perspective can be helpful in a joint optimization of the asset allocation and asset location decisions. (The asset location decision is the decision concerning the account(s) in which to hold assets.)

From a macro perspective, the bond market may be separated into sectors, in which similar securities are grouped together. For example, the bond market can be divided by issuer: corporate bonds, government bonds, and asset-backed securities (ABS) and mortgage-backed securities (MBS). Or bonds can be separated by credit risk sectors: investment-grade bonds (low credit risk) and high-yield bonds (higher credit risk). Within these classifications, even finer sectors could be defined. For example, corporate bonds could be separated into industrial, utility, and financial sectors. Investment-grade bonds could be separated by the specific investment rating (e.g., AAA/Aaa, AA/Aa, A, BBB/Baa). Bonds can also be separated by other key features, such as maturity, fixed versus floating coupon rates, whether they are callable prior to maturity, and whether they are linked to inflation.

Example 1 illustrates the selection of an index as a basis for investment and the classification of the fixed-income universe by index publishers.

EXAMPLE 1

Selection of an Index as a Basis for Investment

Trustworthy Management Company specializes in managing fixed-income investments on an indexed basis. Some of the indices they consider as a basis for investing are as follows:

    BofA Merrill Lynch 1–3 Year Corporate Bond Index

    Barclays Capital Corporate High-Yield Bond Index

    Barclays Capital Corporate Intermediate Bond Index

    BofA Merrill Lynch Long-Term Corporate Bond Index

All of the above include US corporate debt, and all except Barclays Capital Corporate High-yield Bond Index include only debt issues rated investment grade, which means they are rated Baa or higher. The duration of the BofA Merrill Lynch 1–3 Year Corporate Bond Index is short, the duration of the two Barclays Capital indices is medium, and the duration of the BofA Merrill Lynch Long-term Corporate Bond Index is long.

Of the above, which index(es) would be suitable for the portfolios of the following clients?

1 A highly risk-averse investor who is sensitive to fluctuations in portfolio value.

---

[7] **Tax-exempt bonds** are bonds whose interest payments are in whole or in part exempt from taxation; they are typically issued by governmental or certain government-sponsored entities.

2. An educational endowment with a long investment horizon.
3. A life insurer that is relying on the fixed-income portfolio being managed by the Trustworthy Management Company to meet short-term claims.

Solution to 1:

Because the investor is quite risk averse, an index with a short or intermediate duration would be appropriate to limit market value risk. Of the short and intermediate duration indices listed above, the Barclays Capital Corporate High-yield Bond Index is not suitable because it invests in less-than-investment-grade bonds. Accordingly, either the BofA Merrill Lynch 1–3 Year Corporate Bond Index or the Barclays Capital Corporate Intermediate Bond Index could be selected as the index.

Solution to 2:

Given the endowment's long-term horizon, the BofA Merrill Lynch Long-term Corporate Bond Index, which has the longest duration of the indices given, is an appropriate index.

Solution to 3:

For a company issuing life insurance policies, the timing of outlay (liabilities) is uncertain. However, because the insurer is relying on the portfolio to meet short-term liabilities, stability of market value is a concern, and the insurer would desire a portfolio with a low level of market risk. Therefore, BofA Merrill Lynch 1–3 Year Corporate Bond Index, a short duration index, is an appropriate index.

3.2.2 Bond Index Investability and Use as Benchmarks

In this section, we discuss issues in index investability and the use of indices as benchmarks. As we will see, there are several reasons why many bond indices are difficult to track and are not fully investable. We begin our discussion of these issues by examining the heterogeneity and trading characteristics present in the bond universe.

The creation of a bond index requires many decisions and choices. The typical criteria used to construct a bond index concern country, credit risk, liquidity, maturity, currency, and sector classification. Furthermore, compared with equities, there are more issuers of bonds. For example, governments and government entities issue bonds but not stocks. In addition, most issuers have only one type of common stock outstanding but several bond issues of different maturity, seniority, and other features. As a result, the total market capitalization of the global bond market was almost twice as large as the global equity market, estimated as of 2011 at $93 trillion compared with $54 trillion for global equities.[8]

Compared with equities, most bond issues also have less-active secondary markets. Even in developed markets, many bond issues may not trade in the course of a typical day or their trades may not be reported because they do not trade through a centralized exchange. The most recent trade price in such cases is said to be "stale." The values of many issues constituting bond indices do not represent recent trading but are often estimated (appraised) on the basis of the inferred current market value from their characteristics (an appraisal approach known as "matrix pricing"). Delays in data on spreads used in estimated prices can cause large errors in valuation. Among the factors that explain infrequent trading are the long-term investment horizon of many bond investors, the limited number of distinct investors in many bond issues, and the limited size of many bond issues. Furthermore, corporate bond market trading

---

[8] Roxburgh, Lund, and Piotrowski (2011).

data, although improving in many markets, have typically been less readily accessible than equity trading data. As a consequence of these facts, many bond indices are not as investable as major equity indices. Because of the infrequent trading of bond issues, their heterogeneity, and often limited size, one issue with bond index investability is that a passive manager faces challenges in tracking a broad index. The full replication approach to tracking an index (buying all component securities according to their index weights) is much less common than for equity indices. The impact on price from investing in less frequently traded bonds can be substantial due to their illiquidity. To minimize problems with illiquidity, some index providers create more liquid subsets of their indices. For example, JP Morgan has created a more liquid version of its emerging market government bond index, referred to as the EMBI Global Core Index. This index is more easily and cheaply replicable by investors and has lower tracking risk than the broader EMBI Global Index.

Secondly, owing to the heterogeneity of bonds, bond indices that appear similar can often have very different composition and performance. For example, the Dow Jones Corporate Bond Index excludes bonds with sinking fund provisions, whereas the Barclays Capital Corporate Bond Index includes them. The FTSE Global Government Bond Index excludes callable and convertible bonds, whereas the Citigroup World Government Bond Index includes them in some countries.[9] Additionally, the assumptions concerning the reinvestment of coupon income are not consistent across indices because some reinvest at a short-term rate and others do not. The investor should understand the risk and return characteristics of the particular index they choose to be sure they correspond to that of the portfolio.

A third potential challenge is that the index composition tends to change frequently. Although equity indices are often reconstituted or rebalanced quarterly or annually, bond indices are usually recreated monthly. The characteristics of outstanding bonds are continually changing as maturities change, issuers sell new bonds, and issuers call in others. For example, for the year ending July 2011, the Barclays Capital US Aggregate Bond Index had over a third of its value reconstituted owing to deletion and addition of issues. As the composition of the index changes, the risk of the index can also change. For example, if the US government decreases its deficit spending, it would issue less debt, as it did in the 1990s. A shift in index weighting from government to corporate bonds would result in greater index risk. Fixed-income portfolio managers must track the effect of new issuance on sector weights and use cash flows to track such changes. Mitigating these changes is the fact that investors' portfolios tend to be affected by maturities, issuer calls, changes in issuance among sectors, and so on, in the same direction and magnitude as indices are. Nevertheless, investors tracking a bond index need to be aware of the possibility of changes in index composition.

A fourth issue is what Siegel (2003) referred to as the "bums" problem. which arises because capitalization-weighted bond indices give more weight to issuers that borrow the most (the "bums"). The bums in an index may be more likely to be downgraded in the future and experience lower returns. The bums problem is applicable to corporate as well as government issuers. With global bond indices, the countries that go the most into debt have the most weight. For example, when launched in 1999, the EMBI Global had a 66% exposure to Latin American countries. Credit risk is increasingly a concern for developed country bonds as well, given the recent difficulties in the European Union.

An index heavily weighted by bums will likely have increased risk compared with an equally weighted index. Investors tracking such indices may hold a riskier portfolio than they might otherwise desire, and the index and portfolio are unlikely to

---

[9] Amenc, Goltz, and Tang (2011, p. 46). Drenovak, Urošević, and Jelic (2012) found that apparently similar European bond indexes have significantly different performance.

be mean–variance efficient. A potential solution to this weighting problem is to use bond indices that limit the weights of component securities from particular issuers. For example, JP Morgan provides diversified versions of its emerging market bond indices, where each country's representation is capped at 10%. However, such an index is more likely to contain smaller-value securities that are difficult to trade without incurring high transaction costs, hindering its investability.

Another potential solution to the bums problem is to invest in equal-weighted indices (e.g., Dow Jones Corporate Bond Index), GDP-weighted indices (e.g., PIMCO Global Advantage Government Bond Index), fundamental-weighted indices (e.g., the Citi RAFI Sovereign Emerging Markets Local Currency Bond Index), or indices with other weighting systems.[10] However, such weighting schemes may not solve the bums problem entirely, may contain bonds that are less liquid, or may be constructed using subjective inclusion criteria.

A fifth issue is that investors may not be able to find a bond index with risk characteristics that match their portfolio's exposure. Because bonds differ in terms of credit rating, duration, prepayment risk, and other characteristics, a bond index will have a unique exposure that is unlikely to exactly match that desired for the portfolio. The risk characteristics of a bond index will reflect the bond issuers' preferences, which are not necessarily the same as those of investors. For example, if long-term interest rates are at historical lows, then many issuers will finance at the long end of the yield curve and the index will be dominated by these maturities.[11] The index will likely not be appropriate for investors desiring shorter durations. A portfolio's risk objectives depend on its risk tolerance and will not necessarily be matched by an index.

Most investors will probably want to use composites of indices and sub-indices that best reflect their portfolios' targets for those sectors and exposures. There are many specialized bond indices that allow for a closer match to the portfolio. For example, a portfolio might have a target of 10% inflation-linked and 10% high-yield bonds, corresponding to proportional positions in inflation-linked and high-yield indices.

In sum, because of the small size and heterogeneity of bond issues, their infrequent trading, and other issues, many bond indices will not be easily replicated or investable . Note that bond indices are often recommended as benchmarks for manager performance analysis, manager selection and retention, and for other performance measurement purposes. However, if bond indices are not investable, it is unrealistic and unfair to expect a manager to match its performance. As such, bond indices often do not serve as valid benchmarks.

In addition to investability, Bailey, Richards, and Tierney (2007) specify six other criteria for valid benchmarks. According to the authors, valid benchmarks will be unambiguous, measurable, appropriate, reflective of current investment opinions, specified in advance, and accountable.[12] Most bond indices are unambiguous, measurable, and specified in advance. However, they may not be appropriate if a manager's style diverges from that of an index, e.g., the index or portfolio composition changes substantially over time (the latter often the case for active managers). Additionally, they would likely not be reflective of current investment opinions if they contain unfamiliar securities. For example, many high-yield indices contain emerging market securities,

---

10 See Amenc, Goltz, and Tang (2011, pp. 51–52) for a discussion of various bond index weighting schemes.
11 Mizrach and Neely (2006) provided an example of index durations changing through time because of issuers' preferences. The US Treasury stopped issuing 30-year bonds in 2001 but started selling them again in 2006.
12 *Unambiguous* means the identities and weights of the benchmark's components are clearly defined. *Measurable* means that the benchmark's returns are readily calculable on a reasonably frequent basis. *Reflective of current investment opinions* means that the investment manager should be familiar with the benchmark's component securities. *Specified in advance* means the composition of the benchmark should be known before the evaluation period. *Accountable* (or "owned") means that the manager is willing to have his or her performance judged against the benchmark's performance.

which a developed market manager may have no knowledge of.[13] If a manager has no knowledge of index securities, they are unlikely to agree to the use of the benchmark and hence many bond indices will fail the accountable criterion.

For many investors, the typical bond index is unlikely to be replicable or serve as an optimal benchmark. In practice, the passive bond fund manager usually buys a representative subset of the index (a sampling approach). For manager performance evaluation, the use of an index as a benchmark can be problematic, especially for active managers who are not as constrained by particular indices. A custom benchmark that is constructed according to the specific characteristics of the manager's portfolio would be more likely to serve as a valid performance benchmark.[14]

EXAMPLE 2

Bond Index Investability

The Barclays Capital Emerging Markets USD Aggregate Bond Index consists of dollar-denominated, fixed and floating rate debt from sovereign, quasi-sovereign, and corporate issuers in emerging markets. Characteristics of this market value-weighted index include the following.[15]

- Principal and coupon must be denominated in US dollars.
- Emerging market status is determined through markets that meet World Bank or International Monetary Fund criteria, or investor concerns about investability. Country inclusion is evaluated annually.
- The minimum issue size is $500 million and the initial maturity must be greater than one year.
- The index is rebalanced monthly with intra-month cash flows assumed not to earn interest.
- Constituent pricing is obtained directly from third-party sources or inferred using a spread over Treasuries or a swap curve. Prices are checked using a verification process.
- There are several alternative versions of the index offered by Barclays. A country constrained version limits country weights to 10%. GDP-weighted and Fiscal Strength weighted indices, as well as tradable versions, are also available.

The index composition in 2009 and 2013 was as follows:

	2009	2013
Regional composition:		
Latin America	50.3%	37.6%
Asia	16.0%	22.8%
Europe, Middle East, and Africa	33.7%	39.6%
Sector composition:		
Corporate	13.4%	27.7%
Quasi-sovereign	17.5%	31.0%
Sovereign	69.1%	41.3%

---

13 Levine, Drucker, and Rosenthal (2010).
14 The construction of a custom benchmark is discussed in more detail in Conover, Broby, and Carino (2014).
15 Information on Barclays indexes is available at https://indices.barcap.com/show?url=Home/Guides_and_Factsheets.

Comment on the issues facing investors who would use a full replication approach for this index.

Solution:

There are several issues with the investability and replication of this index's returns, including the following:

- By definition, the index includes markets with limited investability, making it difficult for an investor to replicate the index's performance. As it is based on emerging market securities, the index also likely contains issues that are not obtainable by a developed world investor at all, or in sufficient quantity, or at favorable prices.
- The index is rebalanced monthly, which could result in frequent portfolio rebalancing and transactions costs. Transactions costs would decrease the portfolio's returns and result in its performance diverging from that of the index.
- The index assumes that no interest is earned on intra-month cash flows. The investor should be aware of this if attempting to replicate the index's performance.
- Index bond pricing is sometimes inferred using a spread over Treasuries or a swap curve. The risk and return for the portfolio will likely diverge from that reported for the index. For example, if the portfolio has to satisfy investor withdrawals, it may have to liquidate bonds at prices different than that reported by the index.
- Over time the constituents have changed, with Latin America declining in representation and Asia and Europe, the Middle East, and Africa increasing in representation. The representation of corporate and quasi-sovereign issuers has increased at the expense of sovereign issuers, who have declined in weight by almost 28%. The risk and return of the index has likely changed as a result. The changes in risk may not be suitable for the portfolio. The index may also be overweighted by the issuers who have borrowed the most, the "bums," resulting in increased risk for investors tracking the index.
- The tradable version of the index may be easier for the investor to track. Country-capped and alternative weighted versions of the index may limit exposure to "bums," but they possibly result in greater exposure to less liquid issues.
- As a performance benchmark, this emerging market index is likely to contain some issues that a developed world investor is unfamiliar with, thus not satisfying the reflective of current investment opinions or the accountable criterion for valid benchmarks of Bailey, Richards, and Tierney (2007).

3.2.3 Risk in Detail: Risk Profiles

To build an indexed portfolio, the manager begins by selecting a bond market index that will serve as the basis for the portfolio. However, as discussed above, many indices will not be investable. The manager's goal is to then construct a portfolio that mimics (closely tracks) the characteristics of the benchmark index as in Exhibit 2.

Exhibit 2   Indexing

Manager's indexed portfolio →[mimics]→ Benchmark bond market index (e.g. Barclays Capital Aggregate Bond Index) →[mimics]→ Specified bond market

The identification and measurement of risk factors will play a role both in index selection and in portfolio construction. The major source of risk for most bonds relates to the **yield curve** (the relationship between interest rates and time to maturity). Yield curve changes include (1) a parallel shift in the yield curve (an equal shift in the interest rate at all maturities), (2) a **twist** of the yield curve (movement in contrary directions of interest rates at two maturities), and (3) other curvature changes of the yield curve. Among the three, the first component (yield curve shift) typically accounts for about 90 percent of the change in value of a bond.

In assessing bond market indices as potential candidates, the manager must examine each index's **risk profile**, which is a detailed tabulation of the index's risk exposures. After all, if the portfolio manager is going to create (and invest in) a portfolio that mimics the index, the portfolio will contain the same risk exposures as the index, and those exposures should be consistent with the portfolio's objectives. The manager needs to know: "How sensitive is the index's return to changes in the level of interest rates (**interest rate risk**), changes in the shape of the yield curve (**yield curve risk**), changes in the spread between Treasuries and non-Treasuries (**spread risk**), and various other risks?"

Bonds are subject to a wide variety of risks, as illustrated in Exhibit 3.

Having obtained a clear grasp of the chosen index's risk exposures, the portfolio manager can then use the risk profile in constructing an effective indexed portfolio. A completely effective indexed portfolio will have the exact same risk profile as the selected index. The portfolio manager may use various techniques, perhaps in combination, to align the portfolio's risk exposures with those of the index.

A **cell-matching technique** (also known as **stratified sampling**) divides the index into cells that represent qualities designed to reflect the risk factors of the index. The manager then selects bonds (i.e., sample bonds) from those in each cell to represent the entire cell taking account of the cell's relative importance in the index. The total dollar amount selected from this cell may be based on that cell's percentage of the total. For example, if the A rated corporates make up 4 percent of the entire index, then A rated bonds will be sampled and added until they represent 4 percent of the manager's portfolio.

A **multifactor model technique** makes use of a set of factors that drive bond returns.[16] Generally, portfolio managers will focus on the most important or primary risk factors. These measures are described below, accompanied by practical comments.[17]

1   *Duration.*

An index's **effective duration** measures the sensitivity of the index's price to a relatively small parallel shift in interest rates (i.e., interest rate risk). (For *large* parallel changes in interest rates, a convexity adjustment is used to improve the accuracy of the index's estimated price change. A **convexity adjustment** is an estimate of the change in price that is not explained by duration.) The manager's indexed portfolio will attempt to match the duration of the index as a way of

---

[16] For a more complete coverage of how multi-factor risk models are used in portfolio construction, see Fabozzi (2004b, Chapter 3).
[17] This discussion draws heavily from Volpert (2000).

Managing Funds against a Bond Market Index

Exhibit 3 Typical Fixed-Income Portfolio Risk Exposures

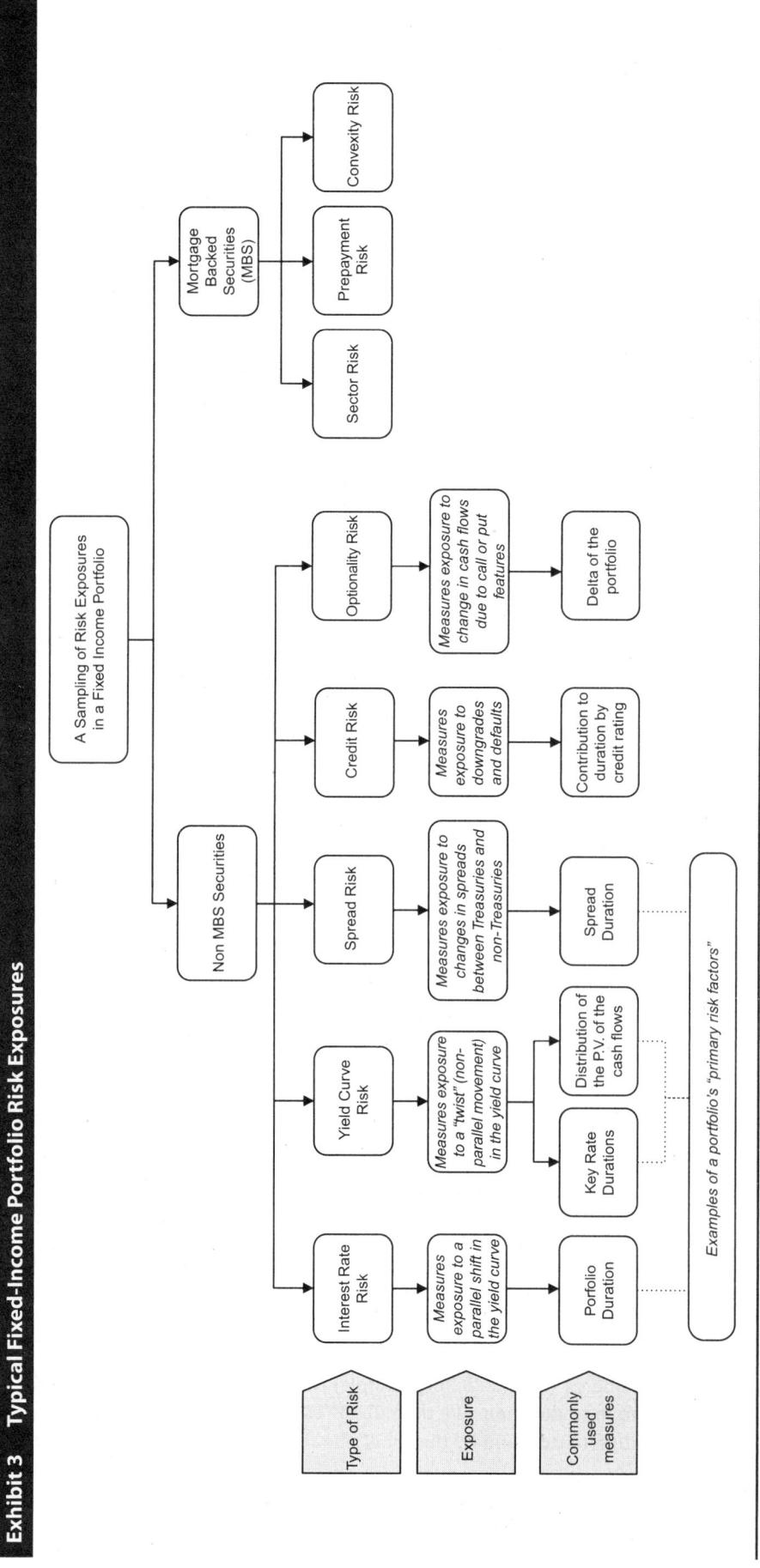

ensuring that the exposure is the same in both portfolios. Because parallel shifts in the yield curve are relatively rare, duration by itself is inadequate to capture the full effect of changes in interest rates.

2   *Key rate duration and present value distribution of cash flows.*

Nonparallel shifts in the yield curve (i.e., yield curve risk), such as an increase in slope or a twist in the curve, can be captured by two separate measures. **Key rate duration** is one established method for measuring the effect of shifts in key points along the yield curve. In this method, we hold the spot rates constant for all points along the yield curve but one. By changing the spot rate for that key maturity, we are able to measure a portfolio's sensitivity to a change in that maturity. This sensitivity is called the **rate duration**. We repeat the process for other key points (e.g., 3 years, 7 years, 10 years, 15 years) and measure their sensitivities as well. Simulations of twists in the yield curve can then be conducted to see how the portfolio would react to these changes. Key rate durations are particularly useful for determining the relative attractiveness of various portfolio strategies, such as bullet strategies with maturities focused at one point on the yield curve versus barbell strategies where maturities are concentrated at two extremes. These strategies react differently to nonparallel changes in the yield curve.

Another popular indexing method is to match the portfolio's present value distribution of cash flows to that of the index. Dividing future time into a set of non-overlapping time periods, the **present value distribution of cash flows** is a list that associates with each time period the fraction of the portfolio's duration that is attributable to cash flows falling in that time period. The calculation involves the following steps:

A   The portfolio's creator will project the cash flow for each issue in the index for specific periods (usually six-month intervals). Total cash flow for each period is calculated by adding the cash flows for all the issues. The present value of each period's cash flow is then computed and a total present value is obtained by adding the individual periods' present values. (Note that the total present value is the market value of the index.)

B   Each period's present value is then divided by the total present value to arrive at a percentage for each period. For example, the first six-month period's present value might be 3.0 percent of the total present value of cash flows, the second six-month period's present value might be 3.8 percent of the total present value, and so forth.

C   Next, we calculate the contribution of each period's cash flows to portfolio duration. Because each cash flow is effectively a zero-coupon payment, the time period is the duration of the cash flow. By multiplying the time period times the period's percentage of the total present value, we obtain the duration contribution of each period's cash flows. For example, if we show each six-month period as a fractional part of the year (0.5, 1.0, 1.5, 2.0, etc.), the first period's contribution to duration would be 0.5 × 3.0 percent, or 0.015. The second period's contribution would be 1.0 × 3.8 percent, or 0.038. We would continue for each period in the series.

D   Finally, we add each period's contribution to duration (0.015 + 0.038 + ...) and obtain a total (3.28, for example) that represents the bond index's contribution to duration. We then divide each of the individual period's contribution to duration by the total. The resulting distribution might look as follows:

period 1 = 0.46 percent

period 2 = 1.16 percent

period 3 = 3.20 percent

..., etc.

It is this distribution that the indexer will try to duplicate. If this distribution is duplicated, nonparallel yield curve shifts and "twists" in the curve will have the same effect on the portfolio and the index.

3 *Sector and quality percent.*

To ensure that the bond market index's yield is replicated by the portfolio, the manager will match the percentage weight in the various sectors and qualities of the index.

4 *Sector duration contribution.*

A portfolio's return is obviously affected by the duration of each sector's bonds in the portfolio. For an indexed portfolio, the portfolio must achieve the same duration exposure to each sector as the index. The goal is to ensure that a change in sector spreads has the same impact on both the portfolio and the index.

The manager can achieve this by matching the amount of the index duration that comes from the various sectors, i.e., the sector duration contribution.

5 *Quality spread duration contribution.*

The risk that a bond's price will change as a result of spread changes (e.g., between corporates and Treasuries) is known as spread risk. A measure that describes how a non-Treasury security's price will change as a result of the widening or narrowing of the spread is **spread duration**. Changes in the spread between qualities of bonds will also affect the rate of return. The easiest way to ensure that the portfolio closely tracks the index is to match the amount of the index duration that comes from the various quality categories.

6 *Sector/coupon/maturity cell weights.*

Because duration only captures the effect of small interest rate changes on an index's value, convexity is often used to improve the accuracy of the estimated price change, particularly where the change in rates is large. However, some bonds (such as mortgage-backed securities) may exhibit negative convexity, making the index's exposure to call risk difficult to replicate. A manager can attempt to match the convexity of the index, but such matching is rarely attempted because to stay matched can lead to excessively high transactions costs. (Callable securities tend to be very illiquid and expensive to trade.)

A more feasible method of matching the call exposure is to match the sector, coupon, and maturity weights of the callable sectors. As rates change, the changes in call exposure of the portfolio will be matched to the index.

7 *Issuer exposure.*

Event risk for a single issuer is the final risk that needs to be controlled. If a manager attempts to replicate the index with too few securities, issuer event risk takes on greater importance.

The degree of success of an indexer in mimicking index returns is measured by tracking risk.

3.2.4 Tracking Risk

Tracking risk (also known as tracking error) is a measure of the variability with which a portfolio's return tracks the return of a benchmark index. More specifically, tracking risk is defined as the standard deviation of the portfolio's active return, where the active return for each period is defined as

Active return = Portfolio's return − Benchmark index's return

Therefore,

Tracking risk = Standard deviation of the active returns

EXAMPLE 3

Exhibit 4   Calculating Tracking Risk

Period Return (1)	Portfolio Return (2)	Benchmark Return (3)	Active Return (AR) (4)	(AR − Avg. AR)² (5)
1	12.80%	12.60%	0.200%	0.00012%*
2	6.80	6.50	0.300	0.00044
3	0.80	1.20	−0.400	0.00240
4	−4.60	−5.00	0.400	0.00096
5	4.00	4.10	−0.100	0.00036
6	3.30	3.20	0.100	0.00000
7	5.40	5.10	0.300	0.00044
8	5.40	5.70	−0.300	0.00152
9	5.10	4.60	0.500	0.00168
10	3.70	3.80	−0.100	0.00036

Average active return per period: 0.090%.
Sum of the squared deviations: 0.00829(%).
Tracking risk: 0.30350%.
*For Period 1, the calculation for the 5th column is (0.200% − 0.090%)² or (0.000121%) or (0.00000121).

A portfolio's return and its benchmark's return are shown in Columns 2 and 3 of Exhibit 4. To calculate the standard deviation over the 10 periods, we calculate the active return for each period (in Column 4) and find the average active return (i.e., total return of 0.90 percent divided by 10 = 0.090 percent). We then subtract the average (or mean) active return from each period's active return and square each of the differences (Column 5). We add the values in Column 5 and divide the total by the number of sample periods minus one (i.e., 0.00829 percent/9), then take the square root of that value: $\sqrt{\dfrac{0.00829(\%)}{9}}$. The tracking risk is 0.30350 percent, or a little more than 30 bps.

Assume that the tracking risk for a portfolio is calculated to be 30 bps. Statistically, the area that is one standard deviation either side of the mean captures approximately 2/3 of all the observations if portfolio returns approximately follow a normal distribution. Therefore, a tracking risk of 30 bps would indicate that, in approximately two-thirds of the time periods, the portfolio return will be within a band of the benchmark index's return plus or minus 30 bps. The smaller the tracking risk, the more closely the portfolio's return matches, or tracks, the benchmark index's return.

Tracking risk arises primarily from mismatches between a portfolio's risk profile and the benchmark's risk profile.[18] The previous section listed seven primary risk factors that should be matched closely if the tracking risk is to be kept to a minimum. Any change to the portfolio that increases a mismatch for any of these seven items will potentially increase the tracking risk. Examples (using the first five of the seven) would include mismatches in the following:

1 *Portfolio duration.*

   If the benchmark's duration is 5.0 and the portfolio's duration is 5.5, then the portfolio has a greater exposure to parallel changes in interest rates, resulting in an increase in the portfolio's tracking risk.

2 *Key rate duration and present value distribution of cash flows.*

   Mismatches in key rate duration increase tracking risk. In addition, if the portfolio distribution does not match the benchmark, the portfolio will be either more sensitive or less sensitive to changes in interest rates at specific points along the yield curve, leading to an increase in the tracking risk.

3 *Sector and quality percent.*

   If the benchmark contains mortgage-backed securities and the portfolio does not, for example, the tracking risk will be increased. Similarly, if the portfolio overweights AAA securities compared with the benchmark, the tracking risk will be increased.

4 *Sector duration contribution.*

   Even though the sector percentages (e.g., 10 percent Treasuries, 4 percent agencies, 20 percent industrials) may be matched, a mismatch will occur if the portfolio's industrial bonds have an average duration of 6.2 and the benchmark's industrial bonds have an average duration of 5.1. Because the industrial sector's contribution to duration is larger for the portfolio than for the benchmark, a mismatch occurs and the tracking risk is increased.

5 *Quality spread duration contribution.*

   Exhibit 5 shows the spread duration for a 60-bond portfolio and a benchmark index based on sectors. The portfolio's total contribution to spread duration (3.43) is greater than that for the benchmark (2.77). This difference is primarily because of the overweighting of industrials in the 60-bond portfolio. The portfolio has greater spread risk and is thus more sensitive to changes in the sector spread than the benchmark is, resulting in a larger tracking risk.

The remaining two factors are left for the reader to evaluate.

---

18 Ignoring transaction costs and other expenses, the only way to completely eliminate tracking risk is to own all the securities in the benchmark. Even after all significant common risk factors are considered, it is possible to have some residual issue specific risk.

Exhibit 5 Contribution to Spread Duration

Sector	Portfolio % of Portfolio	Portfolio Spread Duration	Portfolio Contribution to Spread Duration	Benchmark % of Portfolio	Benchmark Spread Duration	Benchmark Contribution to Spread Duration
Treasury	22.60%	0.00%	0.00%	23.20%	0.00%	0.00%
Agencies	6.80	6.45	0.44	6.65	4.43	0.29
Financial institutions	6.20	2.87	0.18	5.92	3.27	0.19
Industrials	20.06	11.04	2.21	14.20	10.65	1.51
Utilities	5.52	2.20	0.12	6.25	2.40	0.15
Non-US credit	6.61	1.92	0.13	6.80	2.02	0.14
Mortgage	32.21	1.10	0.35	33.15	0.98	0.32
Asset backed	0.00	0.00	0.00	1.60	3.20	0.05
CMBS	0.00	0.00	0.00	2.23	4.81	0.11
Total	100.00%		3.43%	100.00%		2.77%

EXAMPLE 4

Interpreting and Reducing Tracking Risk

John Spencer is the portfolio manager of Star Bond Index Fund. This fund uses the indexing investment approach, seeking to match the investment returns of a specified market benchmark, or index. Specifically, it seeks investment results that closely match, before expenses, the Barclays Capital Global Aggregate Bond Index. This index is a market-weighted index of the global investment-grade bond market with an intermediate-term weighted average maturity, including government, credit, and collateralized securities. Because of the large number of bonds included in the Barclays Capital Global Aggregate Bond Index, John Spencer uses a representative sample of the bonds in the index to construct the fund. The bonds are chosen by John so that the fund's a) duration, b) country percentage weights, and c) sector- and quality-percentage weights closely match those of the benchmark bond index.

1 The target tracking risk of the fund is 1 percent. Interpret what is meant by this target.
2 Two of the large institutional investors in the fund have asked John Spencer if he could try to reduce the target tracking risk. Suggest some ways for achieving a lower tracking risk.

Solution to 1:

The target tracking risk of 1 percent means that the objective is that in at least two-thirds of the time periods, the return on the Star Bond Index Fund is within plus or minus 1 percent of the return on the benchmark Barclays Capital Global Aggregate Bond Index. The smaller the tracking risk, the more closely the fund's return matches the benchmark's index return.

Solution to 2:

The target tracking risk could be reduced by choosing the bonds to be included in the fund so as to match the fund's duration, country percentage weights, sector weights, and quality weights to those of the benchmark, and to minimize the following mismatches with the benchmark:

A key rate distribution and present value distribution of cash flows

B sector duration contribution

C quality spread duration contribution

D sector, coupon, and maturity weights of the callable sectors

E issuer exposure

3.2.5 Enhanced Indexing Strategies

Although there are expenses and transaction costs associated with constructing and rebalancing an indexed portfolio, there are no similar costs for the index itself (because it is, in effect, a paper portfolio). Therefore, it is reasonable to expect that a perfectly indexed portfolio will underperform the index by the amount of these costs. For this reason, the bond manager may choose to recover these costs by seeking to enhance the portfolio's return. Volpert (2000) has identified a number of ways (i.e., index enhancement strategies) in which this may be done:[19]

1 *Lower cost enhancements.*

Managers can increase the portfolio's net return by simply maintaining tight controls on trading costs and management fees. Although relatively low, expenses do vary considerably among index funds. Where outside managers are hired, the plan sponsor can require that managers re-bid their management fees every two or three years to ensure that these fees are kept as low as possible.

2 *Issue selection enhancements.*

The manager may identify and select securities that are undervalued in the marketplace, relative to a valuation model's theoretical value. Many managers conduct their own credit analysis rather than depending solely on the ratings provided by the bond rating houses. As a result, the manager may be able to select issues that will soon be upgraded and avoid those issues that are on the verge of being downgraded.

3 *Yield curve positioning.*

Some maturities along the yield curve tend to remain consistently overvalued or undervalued. For example, the yield curve frequently has a negative slope between 25 and 30 years, even though the remainder of the curve may have a positive slope. These long-term bonds tend to be popular investments for many institutions, resulting in an overvalued price relative to bonds of shorter maturities. By overweighting the undervalued areas of the curve and underweighting the overvalued areas, the manager may be able to enhance the portfolio's return.

4 *Sector and quality positioning.*

This return enhancement technique takes two forms:

A Maintaining a yield tilt toward short duration corporates. Experience has shown that the best yield spread per unit of duration risk is usually available in corporate securities with less than five years to maturity (i.e., short

---

[19] See Volpert (2000, pp. 95–98).

corporates). A manager can increase the return on the portfolio without a commensurate increase in risk by tilting the portfolio toward these securities. The strategy is not without its risks, although these are manageable. Default risk is higher for corporate securities, but this risk can be managed through proper diversification. (**Default risk** is the risk of loss if an issuer or counterparty does not fulfill contractual obligations.)

B Periodic over- or underweighting of sectors (e.g., Treasuries vs. corporates) or qualities. Conducted on a small scale, the manager may overweight Treasuries when spreads are expected to widen (e.g., before a recession) and underweight them when spreads are expected to narrow. Although this strategy has some similarities to active management, it is implemented on such a small scale that the objective is to earn enough extra return to offset some of the indexing expenses, not to outperform the index by a large margin as is the case in active management.

5 *Call exposure positioning.*

A drop in interest rates will inevitably lead to some callable bonds being retired early. As rates drop, the investor must determine the probability that the bond will be called. Should the bond be valued as trading to maturity or as trading to the call date? Obviously, there is a crossover point at which the average investor is uncertain as to whether the bond is likely to be called. Near this point, the actual performance of a bond may be significantly different than would be expected, given the bond's **effective duration**[20] (duration adjusted to account for embedded options). For example, for premium callable bonds (bonds trading to call), the actual price sensitivity tends to be less than that predicted by the bonds' effective duration. A decline in yields will lead to underperformance relative to the effective duration model's prediction. This underperformance creates an opportunity for the portfolio manager to underweight these issues under these conditions.

EXAMPLE 5

Enhanced Indexing Strategies

The Board of Directors of the Teachers Association of a Canadian province has asked its chairman, Jim Reynolds, to consider investing C$10 million of the fixed-income portion of the association's portfolio in the Reliable Canadian Bond Fund. This index fund seeks to match the performance of the Scotia Capital Universe Bond Index. The Scotia Capital Universe Bond Index represents the Canadian bond market and includes more than 900 marketable Canadian bonds with an average maturity of about nine years.

Jim Reynolds likes the passive investing approach of the Reliable Canadian Bond Fund. Although Reynolds is comfortable with the returns on the Scotia Capital Universe Bond Index, he is concerned that because of the expenses and transactions costs, the actual returns on the bond fund could be substantially lower than the returns on the index. However, he is familiar with the several index enhancement strategies identified by Volpert (2000) through which a bond index fund could minimize the underperformance relative to the index. To see if the fund follows any of these strategies, Reynolds carefully reads the fund's prospectus and notices the following.

---

[20] See Fabozzi (2004b, p. 235).

> "Instead of replicating the index by investing in over the 900 securities in the Scotia Capital Universe Bond Index, we use stratified sampling. The fund consists of about 150 securities.
>
> ... We constantly monitor the yield curve to identify segments of the yield curve with the highest expected return. We increase the holdings in maturities with the highest expected return in lieu of maturities with the lowest expected return if the increase in expected return outweighs the transactions cost. Further, the fund manager is in constant touch with traders and other market participants. Based on their information and our in-house analysis, we selectively overweight and underweight certain issues in the index."

1 Which of the index enhancement strategies listed by Volpert are being used by the Reliable Canadian Bond Fund?

2 Which additional strategies could the fund use to further enhance fund return without active management?

Solution to 1:

By investing in a small sample of 150 of over 900 bonds included in the index, the fund is trying to reduce transactions costs. Thus, the fund is following lower cost enhancements. The fund is also following yield curve positioning enhancement by overweighting the undervalued areas of the curve and underweighting the overvalued areas. Finally, the fund is following issuer selection enhancements by selectively over- and underweighting certain issues in the index.

Solution to 2:

The fund could further attempt to lower costs by maintaining tight controls on trading costs and management fees. Additional strategies that the fund could use include sector and quality positioning and call exposure positioning.

3.3 Active Strategies

In contrast to indexers and enhanced indexers, an active manager is quite willing to accept a large tracking risk, with a large positive active return. By carefully applying his or her superior forecasting or analytical skills, the active manager hopes to be able to generate a portfolio return that is considerably higher than the benchmark return.

3.3.1 Extra Activities Required for the Active Manager

Active managers have a set of activities that they must implement that passive managers are not faced with. After selecting the type of active strategy to pursue, the active manager will:

1 *Identify which index mismatches are to be exploited.*

The choice of mismatches is generally based on the expertise of the manager. If the manager's strength is interest rate forecasting, deliberate mismatches in duration will be created between the portfolio and the benchmark. If the manager possesses superior skill in identifying undervalued securities or undervalued sectors, sector mismatches will be pursued.

2 *Extrapolate the market's expectations (or inputs) from the market data.*

As discussed previously, current market prices are the result of all investors applying their judgment to the individual bonds. By analyzing these prices and yields, additional data can be obtained. For example, forward rates can be calculated from the points along the spot rate yield curve. These forward rates can provide insight into the direction and level that investors believe rates will be headed in the future.

3 *Independently forecast the necessary inputs and compare these with the market's expectations.*

For example, after calculating the forward rates, the active manager may fervently believe that these rates are too high and that future interest rates will not reach these levels. After comparing his or her forecast of forward rates with that of other investors, the manager may decide to create a duration mismatch. By increasing the portfolio's duration, the manager can profit (if he or she is correct) from the resulting drop in the yield curve as other investors eventually realize that their forecast was incorrect.

4 *Estimate the relative values of securities in order to identify areas of under- or overvaluation.*

Again, the focus depends on the skill set of the manager. Some managers will make duration mismatches while others will focus on undervalued securities. In all cases, however, the managers will apply their skills to try and exploit opportunities as they arise.

3.3.2 Total Return Analysis and Scenario Analysis

Before executing a trade, an active manager obviously needs to analyze the impact that the trade will have on the portfolio's return. What tools does the manager have in his or her tool bag to help assess the risk and return characteristics of a trade? The two primary tools are total return analysis and scenario analysis.

The **total return** on a bond is the rate of return that equates the future value of the bond's cash flows with the full price of the bond. As such, the total return takes into account all three sources of potential return: coupon income, reinvestment income, and change in price. **Total return analysis** involves assessing the expected effect of a trade on the portfolio's total return given an interest rate forecast.

To compute total return when purchasing a bond with semiannual coupons, for example, the manager needs to specify 1) an investment horizon, 2) an expected reinvestment rate for the coupon payments, and 3) the expected price of the bond at the end of the time horizon given a forecast change in interest rates. The manager may want to start with his prediction of the most likely change in interest rates.[21] The semiannual total return that the manager would expect to earn on the trade is:

$$\text{Semiannual total return} = \left(\frac{\text{Total future dollars}}{\text{Full price of the bond}}\right)^{\frac{1}{n}} - 1$$

where n is the number of periods in the investment horizon.

Even though this total return is the manager's most likely total return, this computation is for only *one* assumed change in rates. This total return number does very little to help the manager assess the risk that he faces if his forecast is wrong and rates change by some amount other than that forecast. A prudent manager will never want to rely on just one set of assumptions in analyzing the decision; instead, he or she will repeat the above calculation for different sets of assumptions or scenarios. In other words, the manager will want to conduct a **scenario analysis** to evaluate the impact of the trade on expected total return under all reasonable sets of assumptions.

---

[21] We use the term "interest rates" rather generically here. For non-Treasury issues, the manager would likely provide a more detailed breakdown, such as the change in Treasury rates, the change in sector spreads, and so on.

Scenario analysis is useful in a variety of ways:

1. The obvious benefit is that the manager is able to assess the distribution of possible outcomes, in essence conducting a risk analysis on the portfolio's trades. The manager may find that, even though the expected total return is quite acceptable, the distribution of outcomes is so wide that it exceeds the risk tolerance of the client.

2. The analysis can be reversed, beginning with a range of acceptable outcomes, then calculating the range of interest rate movements (inputs) that would result in a desirable outcome. The manager can then place probabilities on interest rates falling within this acceptable range and make a more informed decision on whether to proceed with the trade.

3. The contribution of the individual components (inputs) to the total return may be evaluated. The manager's *a priori* assumption may be that a twisting of the yield curve will have a small effect relative to other factors. The results of the scenario analysis may show that the effect is much larger than the manager anticipated, alerting him to potential problems if this area is not analyzed closely.

4. The process can be broadened to evaluate the relative merits of entire trading strategies.

The purpose of conducting a scenario analysis is to gain a better understanding of the risk and return characteristics of the portfolio before trades are undertaken that may lead to undesirable consequences. In other words, scenario analysis is an excellent risk assessment and planning tool.

3.4 Monitoring/Adjusting the Portfolio and Performance Evaluation

Details of monitoring and adjusting a fixed-income portfolio (with its related performance evaluation) are essentially the same as other classes of investments. Because these topics are covered in detail in other readings, this reading will not duplicate that coverage.

MANAGING FUNDS AGAINST LIABILITIES

We have now walked our way through the major activities in managing fixed-income investment portfolios. However, in doing so, we took a bit of a shortcut. In order to see all the steps at once, we only looked at one branch of Exhibit 1—the branch having to do with managing funds against a bond market index benchmark. We now turn our attention to the equally important second branch of Exhibit 1—managing funds against a liability, or set of liabilities.

4.1 Dedication Strategies

Dedication strategies are specialized fixed-income strategies that are designed to accommodate specific funding needs of the investor. They generally are classified as passive in nature, although it is possible to add some active management elements to them. Exhibit 6 provides a classification of dedication strategies.

Exhibit 6   Dedication Strategies

```
                    Dedication Strategies
                    /                    \
              Immunization          Cash Flow Matching
           /      |       \
  Single Period  Multiple Liability  Immunization for
  Immunization   Immunization        General Cash Flows
```

As seen in Exhibit 6, one important type of dedication strategy is immunization. **Immunization** aims to construct a portfolio that, over a specified horizon, will earn a predetermined return regardless of interest rate changes. Another widely used dedication strategy is **cash flow matching**, which provides the future funding of a liability stream from the coupon and matured principal payments of the portfolio. Each of these strategies will be more fully developed in the following sections followed by a discussion of some of the extensions based on them.

There are four typical types (or classes) of liabilities that can be identified. These are shown in Exhibit 7.

Exhibit 7   Classes of Liabilities

Amount of Liability	Timing of Liability	Example
Known	Known	A principal repayment
Known	Unknown	A life insurance payout
Unknown	Known	A floating rate annuity payout
Unknown	Unknown	Post-retirement health care benefits

Obviously, the more uncertain the liabilities, the more difficult it becomes to use a passive dedication strategy to achieve the portfolio's goals. For this reason, as liabilities become more uncertain, managers often insert elements of active management. The goal of this action is to increase the upside potential of the portfolio while simultaneously ensuring a set of cash flows that are expected to be adequate for paying the anticipated liabilities. Examples of these more aggressive strategies, such as active/passive combinations, active/immunization combinations, and contingent immunization, are discussed later.

4.1.1 Immunization Strategies

Immunization is a popular strategy for "locking in" a guaranteed rate of return over a particular time horizon. As interest rates increase, the decrease in the price of a fixed-income security is usually at least partly offset by a higher amount of reinvestment income. As rates decline, a security's price increase is usually at least partly offset by a lower amount of reinvestment income. For an arbitrary time horizon, the price and reinvestment effects generally do not exactly offset each other: The change in price may be either greater than or less than the change in reinvestment income. The purpose of immunization is to identify the portfolio for which the change in price is exactly equal to the change in reinvestment income at the time horizon of interest. If the manager can construct such a portfolio, an assured rate of return over that horizon is locked in. The implementation of an immunization strategy depends on the type of liabilities that the manager is trying to meet: a single liability (e.g., a guaranteed investment contract), multiple liabilities (a defined-benefit plan's promised payouts), or general cash flows (where the cash flows are more arbitrary in their timing).

4.1.1.1 Classical Single-Period Immunization Classical immunization can be defined as the creation of a fixed-income portfolio that produces an assured return for a specific time horizon, irrespective of any parallel shifts in the yield curve.[22] In its most basic form, the important characteristics of immunization are:

1 Specified time horizon.

2 Assured rate of return during the holding period to a fixed horizon date.

3 Insulation from the effects of interest rate changes on the portfolio value at the horizon date.

The fundamental mechanism supporting immunization is a portfolio structure that balances the change in the value of the portfolio at the end of the investment horizon with the return from the reinvestment of portfolio cash flows (coupon payments and maturing securities). That is, immunization requires offsetting price risk and reinvestment risk. To accomplish this balancing requires the management of duration. Setting the duration of the portfolio equal to the specified portfolio time horizon assures the offsetting of positive and negative incremental return sources under certain assumptions, including the assumption that the immunizing portfolio has the same present value as the liability being immunized.[23] Duration-matching is a minimum condition for immunization.

EXAMPLE 6

Total Return for Various Yields

Consider the situation that a life insurance company faces when it sells a guaranteed investment contract (GIC). For a lump sum payment, the life insurance company guarantees that a specified payment will be made to the policyholder at a specified future date. Suppose that a life insurance company sells a five-year GIC that guarantees an interest rate of 7.5 percent per year on a bond-equivalent yield basis (3.75 percent every six months for the next 10 six-month periods). Also suppose that the payment the policyholder makes is $9,642,899. The value that the life insurance company has guaranteed the policyholder five years from now is thus $13,934,413. That is, the **target value** for the manager of the portfolio of supporting assets is $13,934,413 after five years, which is the same as a target yield of 7.5 percent on a bond-equivalent basis.

Assume that the manager buys $9,642,899 face value of a bond selling at par with a 7.5 percent yield to maturity that matures in five years. The portfolio manager will not be assured of realizing a total return at least equal to the target yield of 7.5 percent, because to realize 7.5 percent, the coupon interest payments must be reinvested at a minimum rate of 3.75 percent every six months. That is, the accumulated value will depend on the reinvestment rate.

---

22 Any yield curve shift involves a change in the interest rate either up or down by the same amount at all maturities. The classical theory of immunization is set forth by Reddington (1952) and Fisher and Weil (1971).
23 See Fabozzi (2004b) for further details.

Exhibit 8 Accumulated Value and Total Return after Five Years: Five-Year, 7.5% Bond Selling to Yield 7.5%

Investment horizon (years)	5
Coupon rate	7.50%
Maturity (years)	5
Yield to maturity	7.50%
Price	100.00000
Par value purchased	$9,642,899
Purchase price	$9,642,899
Target value	$13,934,413

After Five Years

New Yield	Coupon	Interest on Interest	Bond Price	Accumulated Value	Total Return
11.00%	$3,616,087	$1,039,753	$9,642,899	$14,298,739	8.04%
10.50	3,616,087	985,615	9,642,899	14,244,601	7.96
10.00	3,616,087	932,188	9,642,899	14,191,175	7.88
9.50	3,616,087	879,465	9,642,899	14,138,451	7.80
9.00	3,616,087	827,436	9,642,899	14,086,423	7.73
8.50	3,616,087	776,093	9,642,899	14,035,079	7.65
8.00	3,616,087	725,426	9,642,899	13,984,412	7.57
7.50	3,616,087	675,427	9,642,899	13,934,413	7.50
7.00	3,616,087	626,087	9,642,899	13,885,073	7.43
6.50	3,616,087	577,398	9,642,899	13,836,384	7.35
6.00	3,616,087	529,352	9,642,899	13,788,338	7.28
5.50	3,616,087	481,939	9,642,899	13,740,925	7.21
5.00	3,616,087	435,153	9,642,899	13,694,139	7.14
4.50	3,616,087	388,985	9,642,899	13,647,971	7.07
4.00	3,616,087	343,427	9,642,899	13,602,414	7.00

Source: Fabozzi (2004b, p. 109).

To demonstrate this, suppose that immediately after investing in the bond above, yields in the market change, and then stay at the new level for the remainder of the five years. Exhibit 8 illustrates what happens at the end of five years.[24]

If yields do not change and the coupon payments can be reinvested at 7.5 percent (3.75 percent every six months), the portfolio manager will achieve the target value. If market yields rise, an accumulated value (total return) higher than the target value (target yield) will be achieved. This result follows because the coupon interest payments can be reinvested at a higher rate than the initial yield to maturity. This result contrasts with what happens when the yield declines. The accumulated value (total return) is then less than the target value (target

---

[24] For purposes of illustration, we assume no expenses or profits to the insurance company.

yield). Therefore, investing in a coupon bond with a yield to maturity equal to the target yield and a maturity equal to the investment horizon does not assure that the target value will be achieved.

Keep in mind that to immunize a portfolio's target value or target yield against a change in the market yield, a manager must invest in a bond or a bond portfolio whose 1) duration is equal to the investment horizon and 2) initial present value of all cash flows equals the present value of the future liability.

4.1.1.2 Rebalancing an Immunized Portfolio Textbooks often illustrate immunization by assuming a one-time instantaneous change in the market yield. In actuality, the market yield will fluctuate over the investment horizon. As a result, the duration of the portfolio will change as the market yield changes. The duration will also change simply because of the passage of time. In any interest rate environment that is different from a flat term structure, the duration of a portfolio will change at a different rate from time.

How often should a portfolio be rebalanced to adjust its duration? The answer involves balancing the costs and benefits of rebalancing. On the one hand, more frequent rebalancing increases transactions costs, thereby reducing the likelihood of achieving the target return. On the other hand, less frequent rebalancing causes the duration to wander from the target duration, which also reduces the likelihood of achieving the target return. Thus, the manager faces a trade-off: Some transactions costs must be accepted to prevent the duration from straying too far from its target, but some mismatch in the duration must be lived with, or transactions costs will become prohibitively high.

4.1.1.3 Determining the Target Return Given the term structure of interest rates or the yield curve prevailing at the beginning of the horizon period, the assured rate of return of immunization can be determined. Theoretically, this immunization target rate of return is defined as the total return of the portfolio, assuming no change in the term structure. This target rate of return will always differ from the portfolio's present yield to maturity unless the term structure is flat (not increasing or decreasing), because by virtue of the passage of time, there is a return effect as the portfolio moves along the yield curve (matures). That is, for an upward-sloping yield curve, the yield to maturity of a portfolio can be quite different from its immunization target rate of return while, for a flat yield curve, the yield to maturity would roughly approximate the assured target return.

In general, for an upward-sloping yield curve, the immunization target rate of return will be less than the yield to maturity because of the lower reinvestment return. Conversely, a negative or downward-sloping yield curve will result in an immunization target rate of return greater than the yield to maturity because of the higher reinvestment return.

Alternative measures of the immunization target rate of return include the yield implied by a zero coupon bond of quality and duration comparable with that of the bond portfolio and an estimate based on results of a simulation that rebalances the initial portfolio, given scenarios of interest rate change.

The most conservative method for discounting liabilities—the method resulting in the largest present value of the liabilities—involves the use of the **Treasury spot curve** (the term structure of Treasury zero coupon bonds).

A more realistic approach utilizes the yield curve (converted to spot rates) implied by the securities held in the portfolio. This yield curve can be obtained using a curve-fitting methodology.[25] Because spreads may change as well as the term structure itself, the value of the liabilities will vary over time.

4.1.1.4 Time Horizon
The **immunized time horizon** is equal to the portfolio duration. Portfolio duration is equal to a weighted average of the individual security durations where the weights are the relative amounts or percentages invested in each.

A typical immunized time horizon is five years, which is a common planning period for GICs and allows flexibility in security selection because there is a fairly large population of securities to create the necessary portfolio duration. Securities in the portfolio should be limited to high-quality, very liquid instruments, because portfolio rebalancing is required to keep the portfolio duration synchronized with the horizon date.

4.1.1.5 Dollar Duration and Controlling Positions
Dollar duration is a measure of the change in portfolio value for a 100 bps change in market yields.[26] It is defined[27] as

Dollar duration = Duration × Portfolio value × 0.01

A portfolio's dollar duration is equal to the sum of the dollar durations of the component securities.

EXAMPLE 7

Calculation of Dollar Duration

We have constructed a portfolio consisting of three bonds in equal par amounts of $1,000,000 each. The initial values and durations are shown in Exhibit 9. Note that the market value includes accrued interest.

Exhibit 9 Initial Durations of a Three-Bond Portfolio

Security	Price	Market Value	Duration	Dollar Duration
Bond #1	$104.013	$1,065,613	5.025	$53,548
Bond #2	96.089	978,376	1.232	12,054
Bond #3	103.063	1,034,693	4.479	46,343
Dollar duration				$111,945

---

[25] See Vasicek and Fong (1982).
[26] Dollar duration is a traditional term in the bond literature; the concept applies to portfolios denominated in any currency. A related concept is the price value of a basis point (PVBP), also known as the dollar value of a basis point (DV01). The PVBP is equal to the dollar duration divided by 100.
[27] The use of the term "duration" in this reading (and in the equation) is consistent with Fabozzi (2004a, p. 228), who defines it as "the approximate percentage change in price for a 100 basis point change in rates." Taking a concept known as **Macaulay duration** (the percentage change in price for a *percentage change* in yield) as a baseline calculation measure, a tradition also exists for referring to "duration" as used in the equation as "modified duration" because it is equal to Macaulay duration modified to obtain a measure of price sensitivity for a change in the *level* of yields.

In a number of ALM applications, the investor's goal is to reestablish the dollar duration of a portfolio to a desired level. This rebalancing involves the following steps:

1. Move forward in time and include a shift in the yield curve. Using the new market values and durations, calculate the dollar duration of the portfolio at this point in time.
2. Calculate the **rebalancing ratio** by dividing the desired dollar duration by the new dollar duration. If we subtract one from this ratio and convert the result to a percent, it tells us the percentage amount that each position needs to be changed in order to rebalance the portfolio.
3. Multiply the new market value of the portfolio by the desired percentage change in Step 2. This number is the amount of cash needed for rebalancing.

EXAMPLE 8

Rebalancing Based on the Dollar Duration

We now move forward one year and include a shift in the yield curve. The portfolio values at this point in time are given in Exhibit 10:

Exhibit 10 Durations of a Three-Bond Portfolio after One Year

Security	Price	Market Value	Duration	Dollar Duration
Bond #1	$99.822	$1,023,704	4.246	$43,466
Bond #2	98.728	1,004,770	0.305	3,065
Bond #3	99.840	1,002,458	3.596	36,048
				$82,579

The portfolio dollar duration has changed from $111,945 to $82,579. Our requirement is to maintain the portfolio dollar duration at the initial level. To do so, we must rebalance our portfolio. We choose to rebalance using the existing security proportions of one-third each.

To calculate the rebalancing ratio, we divide the original dollar duration by the new dollar duration:

$$\frac{\$111,945}{\$82,579} = 1.356$$

Rebalancing requires each position to be increased by 35.6 percent. The cash required for this rebalancing is calculated as

Cash required = 0.356 × ($1,023,704 + 1,004,770 + 1,002,458)
              = $1,079,012

4.1.1.6 Spread Duration Spread duration is a measure of how the market value of a risky bond (portfolio) will change with respect to a parallel 100 bps change in its spread above the comparable benchmark security (portfolio). Spread duration is an important measurement tool for the management of spread risk. Spreads do change and the portfolio manager needs to know the risks associated with such changes.

A characteristic of bonds with **credit risk** (risk of loss because of credit events such as default or downgrades in credit ratings)—sometimes called "spread product"—is that their yield will be higher than a comparable risk-free security. The large spectrum of bond products available in the marketplace leads to differing types of spread duration. The three major types are:

1 **Nominal spread**, the spread of a bond or portfolio above the yield of a certain maturity Treasury.
2 **Static spread** or zero-volatility spread, defined as the constant spread above the Treasury spot curve that equates the calculated price of the security to the market price.
3 **Option-adjusted spread (OAS)**, the current spread over the benchmark yield minus that component of the spread that is attributable to any embedded optionality in the instrument.

The spread duration of a portfolio is calculated as a market weighted average of the spread durations of the component securities. For a portfolio of non-Treasury securities, spread duration equals portfolio duration. However, because the spread duration of Treasury securities is zero, a portfolio that includes both Treasury and non-Treasury securities will have a spread duration that is different from the portfolio duration.

A bond index will have an overall spread duration as will each sector within the index. The manager can calculate the effect on the portfolio of a change in sector spreads. The effect due to a change in sector spreads is in addition to the effect that is implied by a general increase or decrease in interest rates.

EXAMPLE 9

Portfolio Immunization

The Managers of Reliable Life Insurance Company are considering hiring a consultant to advise them on portfolio immunization. Following are some of the statements that were made during these presentations:

1 A great thing about immunization is that it is a set-and-forget strategy. That is, once you have immunized your portfolio, there is no subsequent work to be done.
2 The immunization target rate of return is less than yield to maturity.
3 If a portfolio is immunized against a change in the market yield at a given horizon by matching portfolio duration to horizon, the portfolio faces no risk except for default risk.
4 The liquidity of securities used to construct an immunized portfolio is irrelevant.
5 In general, the entire portfolio does not have to be turned over to rebalance an immunized portfolio. Furthermore, rebalancing need not be done on a daily basis.

Critique the statements.

Solution to 1:

This statement is incorrect. One needs to rebalance the portfolio duration whenever interest rates change and as time elapses since the previous rebalancing.

Solution to 2:

This statement is only true if the yield curve is upward sloping. If the yield curve is downward-sloping, then this statement is not true as the immunization target rate of return would exceed the yield to maturity because of the higher reinvestment return.

Solution to 3:

The statement is incorrect. The portfolio described would be exposed to the risk of a change in interest rates that results in a change in the shape of the yield curve.

Solution to 4:

The statement is incorrect because immunized portfolios need to be rebalanced; the liquidity of securities used to construct an immunized portfolio is a relevant consideration. Illiquid securities involve high transaction costs and make portfolio rebalancing costly.

Solution to 5:

The statement is correct. The entire portfolio does not have to be turned over to rebalance it because shifting a small set of securities from one maturity range to another is generally enough. Also, to avoid excessive transactions costs, rebalancing is usually not done on a daily basis, which could involve excessive transaction costs.

4.1.2 Extensions of Classical Immunization Theory

Classical immunization theory is based on several assumptions:

1. Any changes in the yield curve are parallel changes, that is, interest rates move either up or down by the same amount for all maturities.
2. The portfolio is valued at a fixed horizon date, and there are no interim cash inflows or outflows before the horizon date.
3. The target value of the investment is defined as the portfolio value at the horizon date if the interest rate structure does not change (i.e., there is no change in forward rates).

Perhaps the most critical assumption of classical immunization techniques is the first one concerning the type of interest rate change anticipated. A property of a classically immunized portfolio is that the target value of the investment is the lower limit of the value of the portfolio at the horizon date if there are parallel interest rate changes.[28] According to the theory, if there is a change in interest rates that does not correspond to this shape-preserving shift, matching the duration to the investment horizon no longer assures immunization.[29] Non-shape-preserving shifts are the commonly observed case.

Exhibit 11 illustrates the nature of the portfolio value, given an immunized portfolio and parallel shifts in rates. The curve **aa′** represents the behavior of the portfolio value for various changes in rates, ranging from a decline to an increase as shown on the horizontal axis. Point V_0 on line **tt′** is the level of the portfolio value assuming no change in rates. As we note above, an immunized portfolio subjected to parallel shifts in the yield curve will provide at least as great a portfolio value at the horizon date as the assured target value, which thus becomes the minimum value. Therefore, if the assumptions of classical theory hold, immunization provides a minimum-risk strategy.

---

[28] See Fisher and Weil (1971) and Fabozzi (2004b).
[29] For a more complete discussion of these issues, see Cox, Ingersoll, and Ross (1979).

Exhibit 11 Changes in Portfolio Value Caused by Parallel Interest Rate Changes for an Immunized Portfolio

Exhibit 12 illustrates the relationship between the value of a classically immunized portfolio and interest rate changes when interest rates do not shift in a parallel fashion. Depending on the shape of the nonparallel shift, either the relationship shown in a) or that shown in b) will occur. This exhibit shows the possibility (in cases d and e) that the value of a classically immunized portfolio can be less than the target. The important point is that merely matching the duration of the portfolio to the investment horizon as the condition for immunization may not prevent significant deviations from the target value. As an example of the effect on accumulated value of a portfolio given nonparallel yield curve shifts, consider the return on a 6 year, 6.75 percent bond selling to yield 7.5 percent. Our horizon remains at 5 years.

Exhibit 12 Two Patterns of Changes in Portfolio Value Caused by Nonparallel Interest Rate Shifts for an Immunized Portfolio

Source: Gifford Fong Associates.

The four yield curve changes shown in Exhibit 13 are applied to the existing yield curve. For example, Scenario 1 twists the existing yield curve by reducing the 3-month rate by 50 bps and increasing the 7-year rate by 100 bps. Intermediate points on the yield curve are linearly interpolated between the end points. The total return is then calculated and displayed in Exhibit 14.

Exhibit 13 Yield Curve Changes

Exhibit 14 Total Return after Yield Curve Change

Scenario	Coupon	Interest on Interest	Price of the Bond	Accumulated Value	Total Return
Scenario 1	$3,375,000	$572,652	$9,999,376	$13,947,029	7.519%
Scenario 2	3,375,000	547,054	10,025,367	13,947,421	7.519
Scenario 3	3,375,000	679,368	9,894,491	13,948,860	7.522
Scenario 4	3,375,000	728,752	9,847,756	13,951,508	7.525

A natural extension of classical immunization theory is to extend the theory to the case of nonparallel shifts in interest rates. Two approaches have been taken. The first approach has been to modify the definition of duration so as to allow for nonparallel yield curve shifts, such as multifunctional duration (also known as **functional duration** or key rate duration). The second approach is a strategy that can handle any arbitrary interest rate change so that it is not necessary to specify an alternative duration measure. This approach, developed by Fong and Vasicek (1984), establishes a measure of immunization risk against any arbitrary interest rate change. The immunization risk measure can then be minimized subject to the constraint that the duration of the portfolio equals the investment horizon, resulting in a portfolio with minimum exposure to any interest rate movements. This approach is discussed later in the section.

A second extension of classical immunization theory applies to overcoming the limitations of a fixed horizon (the second assumption on which immunization depends). Marshall and Yawitz (1982) demonstrated that, under the assumption of parallel interest rate changes, a lower bound exists on the value of an investment portfolio at any particular time, although this lower bound may be below the value realized if interest rates do not change.

Fong and Vasicek (1984) and Bierwag, Kaufman, and Toevs (1979) extended immunization to the case of multiple liabilities. Multiple liability immunization involves an investment strategy that guarantees meeting a specified schedule of future liabilities, regardless of the type of shift in interest rate changes. Fong and Vasicek (1984) provided a generalization of the immunization risk measure for the multiple liability case. Moreover, it extends the theory to the general case of arbitrary cash flows (contributions as well as liabilities). Multiple liability immunization and the general case of arbitrary cash flows are discussed later in the reading.

In some situations, the objective of immunization as strict risk minimization may be too restrictive. The third extension of classical immunization theory is to analyze the risk and return trade-off for immunized portfolios. Fong and Vasicek (1983) demonstrated how this trade-off can be analyzed. Their approach, called "return maximization," is explained later in this reading.

The fourth extension of classical immunization theory is to integrate immunization strategies with elements of active bond portfolio management strategies. The traditional objective of immunization has been risk protection, with little consideration of possible returns. Leibowitz and Weinberger (1981) proposed a technique called **contingent immunization**, which provides a degree of flexibility in pursuing active strategies while ensuring a certain minimum return in the case of a parallel rate shift. In contingent immunization, immunization serves as a fall-back strategy if the actively managed portfolio does not grow at a certain rate.

Contingent immunization is possible when the prevailing available immunized rate of return is greater than the required rate of return. For example, if a firm has a three-year investment horizon over which it must earn 3 percent and it can immunize its asset portfolio at 4.75 percent, the manager can actively manage part or all of the portfolio until it reaches the safety net rate of return of 3 percent. If the portfolio return drops to this safety net level, the portfolio is immunized and the active management is dropped. The difference between the 4.75 percent and the 3 percent safety net rate of return is called the **cushion spread** (the difference between the minimum acceptable return and the higher possible immunized rate).

If the manager started with a $500 million portfolio, after three years the portfolio needs to grow to

$$P_I\left(1 + \frac{s}{2}\right)^{2T} = \$500\left(1 + \frac{0.03}{2}\right)^{2 \times 3} = \$546.72$$

where dollar amounts are in millions and

P_I = initial portfolio value
s = safety net rate of return
T = years in the investment horizon

At time 0, the portfolio can be immunized at 4.75 percent, which implies that the required initial portfolio amount, where dollar amounts are in millions, is

$$\frac{\text{Required terminal value}}{\left(1 + \frac{i}{2}\right)^{2T}} = \frac{\$546.72}{\left(1 + \frac{0.0475}{2}\right)^{2 \times 3}} = \$474.90$$

The manager therefore has an initial dollar safety margin of $500 million − $474.90 million = $25.10 million.

If the manager invests the entire $500 million in 4.75 percent, 10-year notes at par and the YTM (yield to maturity) immediately changes, what will happen to the dollar safety margin?

If the YTM suddenly drops to 3.75 percent, the value of the portfolio will be $541.36 million. The initial asset value required to satisfy the terminal value of $546.72 million at 3.75 percent YTM is $489.06 million so the dollar safety margin has grown to $541.36 million − $489.06 million = $52.3 million. The manager may therefore commit a larger proportion of her assets to active management.

If rates rise so that the YTM is now 5.80 percent, the portfolio value will be $460.55 million and the initial asset value required will be $460.52 million. The dollar safety margin has gone to zero, and thus the portfolio must be immunized immediately.

Another example of the use of immunization as an adjunct to active return strategies is described by Fong and Tang (1988). Based on option valuation theory, a portfolio strategy can systematically shift the proportion between an active strategy and an immunized strategy in a portfolio to achieve a predetermined minimum return while retaining the potential upside of the active strategy.

4.1.2.1 Duration and Convexity of Assets and Liabilities In order for a manager to have a clear picture of the **economic surplus** of the portfolio—defined as the market value of assets minus the present value of liabilities—the duration and convexity of both the assets and liabilities must be understood. Focusing only on the duration of a company's assets will not give a true indication of the total interest rate risk for a company.

As an example, assume that a company's assets and liabilities have the characteristics shown in Exhibit 15. We can consider two interest rate scenarios, up 100 bps and down 100 bps, with results shown in Exhibit 16 in Panels A and B, respectively. The economic surplus of the company has increased as rates rise. This increase is a result of the mismatch in duration between the assets and liabilities.

Exhibit 15 Balance Sheet Characteristics of a Company (Dollar Amounts in Millions)

	Market Value	Present Value	Economic Surplus	Duration
Assets	$500	—	$100	4
Liabilities	—	$400	—	7

Exhibit 16 Interest Rate Scenarios (Dollar Amounts in Millions)

	Approximate Market Value	Present Value	Economic Surplus
A. When Rates Increase by 100 bps			
Assets	$480	—	$108
Liabilities	—	$372	—
B. When Rates Decrease by 100 bps			
Assets	$520	—	$92
Liabilities	—	$428	—

Convexity also plays a part in changes in economic surplus. If liabilities and assets are duration matched but not convexity matched, economic surplus will be exposed to variation in value from interest rate changes reflecting the convexity mismatch.

The manager must continuously monitor the portfolio to ensure that asset and liability durations and convexities are well matched. If the duration/convexity mismatch is substantial, the portfolio should be rebalanced to achieve a closer match.

4.1.2.2 Types of Risk As the market environment changes, the portfolio manager faces the risk of not being able to pay liabilities when they come due. Three sources of this risk are interest rate risk, contingent claim risk, and cap risk.

Interest rate risk. Because the prices of most fixed-income securities move opposite to interest rates, a rising interest rate environment will adversely affect the value of a portfolio. If assets need to be sold to service liabilities, the manager may find a shortfall. Interest rate risk is the largest risk that a portfolio manager will face.

Contingent claims risk. When a security has a contingent claim provision, explicit or implicit, there is an associated risk. In a falling rate environment, the manager may have lucrative coupon payments halted and receive principal (as is the case with mortgage-backed securities when the underlying mortgages prepay principal). The loss of the coupons is bad enough but now the principal must be reinvested at a lower rate. In addition, the market value of a callable security will level out at the call price, rather than continuing upwards as a noncallable security would.

Cap risk. An asset that makes floating rate payments will typically have caps associated with the floating rate. The manager is at risk of the level of market rates rising while the asset returns are capped. This event may severely affect the value of the assets.

4.1.2.3 Risk Minimization for Immunized Portfolios The Fong and Vasicek (1984) extension of classical immunization theory produced an immunized portfolio with a minimum exposure to any arbitrary interest rate change. One way of minimizing immunization risk is shown in Exhibit 17.

Managing Funds against Liabilities

Exhibit 17　Illustration of Immunization Risk Measure

(A) High-Risk Immunized Portfolio: Portfolio A

Notes:
Portfolio duration matches horizon length.
Portfolio's cash flows dispersed.

(B) Low-Risk Immunized Portfolio: Portfolio B

Notes:
Portfolio duration matches horizon length.
Portfolio's cash flows concentrated around horizon date.

Source: Fabozzi (2004b, p. 123).

The spikes in the two panels of Exhibit 17 represent actual portfolio cash flows. The taller spikes depict the actual cash flows generated by securities at maturity, whereas the smaller spikes represent coupon payments. Both Portfolio A and Portfolio B are composed of two bonds with durations equal to the investment horizon. Portfolio A is, in effect, a **barbell portfolio**—a portfolio made up of short and long maturities relative to the horizon date and interim coupon payments. Portfolio B, however is a **bullet portfolio**—the bond maturities are very close to the investment horizon.

If both portfolios have durations equal to the horizon length, both portfolios are immune to parallel rate changes. When interest rates change in an arbitrary nonparallel way, however, the effect on the value of the two portfolios differs—the barbell portfolio is riskier than the bullet portfolio.

Suppose, for instance, short rates decline while long rates go up. Both the barbell and bullet portfolios would realize a decline of the portfolio value at the end of the investment horizon below the target investment value, because they would experience a capital loss in addition to lower reinvestment rates.

The decline would be substantially higher for the barbell portfolio, however, for two reasons. First, the barbell portfolio experiences the lower reinvestment rates longer than the bullet portfolio does. Second, more of the barbell portfolio is still outstanding at the end of the investment horizon, which means that the same rate increase causes much more of a capital loss. In short, the bullet portfolio has less exposure to changes in the interest rate structure than the barbell portfolio.

It should be clear that reinvestment risk determines immunization risk. *The portfolio that has the least reinvestment risk will have the least immunization risk.* When there is a high dispersion of cash flows around the horizon date, as in the barbell portfolio, the portfolio is exposed to high reinvestment risk. When the cash flows are concentrated around the horizon date, as in the bullet portfolio, the portfolio is subject to minimal reinvestment risk. In the case of a pure discount instrument maturing at the investment horizon, immunization risk is zero because, with no interim cash flows, reinvestment risk is absent. Moving from pure discount instruments to coupon payment instruments, the portfolio manager is confronted with the task of selecting coupon-paying securities that provide the lowest immunization risk—if the manager can construct a portfolio that replicates a pure discount instrument that matures at the investment horizon, immunization risk will be zero.

Recall that the target value of an immunized portfolio is a lower bound on the terminal value of the portfolio at the investment horizon if yields on all maturities change by the same amount. If yields of different maturities change by different amounts, the target value is not necessarily the lower bound on the investment value.

Fong and Vasicek (1984) demonstrated that if forward rates change by any arbitrary function, the relative change in the portfolio value depends on the product of two terms.[30] The first term, denoted M^2, depends solely on the structure of the investment portfolio, while the second term is a function of interest rate movement only. The second term characterizes the nature of the interest rate shock. It is an uncertain quantity and, therefore, outside the control of the manager. The first term, however, is under the control of the manager, as it depends solely on the composition of the portfolio. The first term can be used as a measure of immunization risk because when it is small, the exposure of the portfolio to any interest rate change is small. The immunization risk measure M^2 is the variance of time to payment around the horizon date, where the weight for a particular time in the variance calculation is the proportion of the instrument's total present value that the payment received at that time represents.[31] The immunization risk measure may be called the **maturity variance**; in effect, it measures how much a given immunized portfolio differs from the ideal immunized portfolio consisting of a single pure discount instrument with maturity equal to the time horizon.

Given the measure of immunization risk that is to be minimized and the constraint that the duration of the portfolio equals the investment horizon, the optimal immunized portfolio can be found using **linear programming** (optimization in which the objective function and constraints are linear). Linear programming is appropriate because the risk measure is linear in the portfolio payments.

The immunization risk measure can be used to construct approximate confidence intervals for the target return over the horizon period and the target end-of-period portfolio value. A **confidence interval** represents an uncertainty band around the target return within which the realized return can be expected with a given probability. The expression for the confidence interval is:

Confidence interval = Target return ± (k) × (Standard deviation of target return)

where k is the number of standard deviations around the expected target return. The desired confidence level determines k. The higher the desired confidence level, the larger k, and the wider the band around the expected target return.

---

[30] The Fong and Vasicek (1984) result is derived by expansion of the terminal portfolio value function into the first three terms of a Taylor series.

[31] The measure is $M^2 = \sum_{j=1}^{m}(s_j - H)^2 C_j P_0(s_j)/I_0$, where s_j is the time at which payment C_j is made, H is the horizon date, $P_0(s_j)$ is the present value of the payment(s) made at time s_j, and I_0 is initial portfolio value.

Managing Funds against Liabilities

Fong and Vasicek (1983) demonstrated that the standard deviation of the expected target return can be approximated by the product of three terms:[32] 1) the immunization risk measure, 2) the standard deviation of the variance of the one-period change in the slope of the yield curve,[33] and 3) an expression that is a function of the horizon length only.[34]

4.1.3 *Multiple Liability Immunization*

Immunization with respect to a single investment horizon is appropriate where the objective of the investment is to preserve the value of the investment at the horizon date. This objective is appropriate given that a single liability is payable at, or a target investment value must be attained by, the horizon date. More often, however, there are a number of liabilities to be paid from the investment funds and no single horizon that corresponds to the schedule of liabilities. A portfolio is said to be immunized with respect to a given liability stream if there are enough funds to pay all the liabilities when due, even if interest rates change by a parallel shift.

Bierwag, Kaufman, and Toevs (1979) demonstrate that matching the duration of the portfolio to the average duration of the liabilities is not a sufficient condition for immunization in the presence of multiple liabilities. Instead, the portfolio payment stream must be decomposable in such a way that each liability is separately immunized by one of the component streams; there may be no actual securities providing payments that individually match those of the component payment streams.

Fong and Vasicek (1984) demonstrate the conditions that must be satisfied to assure multiple liability immunization in the case of parallel rate shifts. The necessary and sufficient conditions are:

1. The present value of the assets equals the present value of the liabilities.
2. The (composite) duration of the portfolio must equal the (composite) duration of the liabilities.[35]
3. The distribution of durations of individual portfolio assets must have a wider range than the distribution of the liabilities.[36]

An implication of the second condition is that to immunize a liability stream that extends 30 years, it is not necessary to have a portfolio with a duration of 30. The condition requires that the manager construct a portfolio so that the portfolio duration matches the weighted average of the liability durations. This fact is important because in any reasonable interest rate environment, it is unlikely that a portfolio of investment-grade coupon bonds could be constructed with a duration in excess of 15. Yet for corporate pension funds retired lives, the liability stream is typically a diminishing amount. That is, liabilities in the earlier years are the greatest, and liabilities toward the 30-year end are generally lower. Taking a weighted average duration of the liabilities usually brings the portfolio duration to something manageable, say, 8 or 9.

The third condition requires portfolio payments to bracket (be more dispersed in time than) the liabilities. That is, the portfolio must have an asset with a duration equal to or less than the duration of the shortest-duration liability in order to have

---

[32] The derivation is based on the assumption that the immunization risk measure of an optimally immunized portfolio periodically rebalanced decreases in time in approximate proportion to the third power of the remaining horizon length.
[33] This term can be estimated empirically from historical yield changes.
[34] The expression for the third term for the standard deviation of the expected target return of a single-period liability immunized portfolio is $(7H)^{-1/2}$, where H is the length of the horizon.
[35] The duration of the liabilities is found as follows: $[(1) PVL_1 + (2) PVL_2 + ... + (m) PVL_m]/$(Total present value of liabilities) where PVL_t = Present value of the liability at time t and m = Time of the last liability payment.
[36] More specifically, the mean absolute deviation of the portfolio payments must be greater than or equal to the mean absolute deviation of the liabilities at each payment date.

funds to pay the liability when it is due. And the portfolio must have an asset with a duration equal to or greater than the longest-duration liability in order to avoid the reinvestment rate risk that might jeopardize payment of the longest duration. This bracketing of shortest- and longest-duration liabilities with even shorter- and longer-duration assets balances changes in portfolio value with changes in reinvestment return.

To understand why the portfolio payments have to be more spread out in time than the liabilities to assure immunization, consider the case of a single investment horizon in which immunization is achieved by balancing changes in reinvestment return on coupon payments with changes in investment value at the investment horizon. The same bracketing of each liability by the portfolio payments is necessary in the multiple liability case, which implies that the payments have to be more dispersed in time than the liabilities. Thus, managers selecting securities to be included in the portfolio must not only keep track of the matching of duration between assets and liabilities but also maintain a specified distribution for assets in the portfolio.

The three conditions for multiple liability immunization assure immunization against parallel rate shifts only. Reitano (1991) has explored the limitations of the parallel shift assumption.[37] He has also developed models that generalize the immunization of multiple liabilities to arbitrary yield curve shifts. His research indicates that classical multiple period immunization can mask the risks associated with nonparallel yield curve shifts and that a model that protects against one type of yield curve shift may expose a portfolio to other types of shifts.

Fong and Vasicek (1984) also addressed the question of the exposure of an immunized portfolio to an arbitrary interest rate change and generalize the immunization risk measure to the multiple liability case. Just as in the single investment horizon case, they find that the relative change in the portfolio value if forward rates change by any arbitrary function depends on the product of two terms: a term solely dependent on the structure of the portfolio and a term solely dependent on the interest rate movement.

An optimal immunization strategy is to minimize the immunization risk measure subject to the constraints imposed by these two conditions (and any other applicable portfolio constraints). Constructing minimum-risk immunized portfolios can then be accomplished by the use of linear programming.

Approximate confidence intervals can also be constructed in the multiple liability case. The standard deviation of the expected target return is the product of the three terms indicated in the section on risk minimization.[38]

4.1.4 Immunization for General Cash Flows

In both the single investment horizon and multiple liability cases, we have assumed that the investment funds are initially available in full. What if, instead, a given schedule of liabilities to be covered by an immunized investment must be met by investment funds that are not available at the time the portfolio is constructed?

Suppose a manager has a given obligation to be paid at the end of a two-year horizon. Only one-half of the necessary funds, however, are now available; the rest are expected at the end of the first year, to be invested at the end of the first year at whatever rates are then in effect. Is there an investment strategy that would guarantee the end-of-horizon value of the investment regardless of the development of interest rates?

---

37 See also Reitano (1992) for a detailed illustration of the relationship between the underlying yield curve shift and immunization.
38 See Fong and Vasicek (1983). The expression for the third term in the multiple liability case is a function of the dates and relative sizes of the liabilities, as well as the horizon length.

Under certain conditions, such a strategy is indeed possible. The expected cash contributions can be considered the payments on hypothetical securities that are part of the initial holdings. The actual initial investment can then be invested in such a way that the real and hypothetical holdings taken together represent an immunized portfolio.

We can illustrate this using the two-year investment horizon. The initial investment should be constructed with a duration of 3. Half of the funds are then in an actual portfolio with a duration of 3, and the other half in a hypothetical portfolio with a duration of 1. The total stream of cash inflow payments for the portfolio has a duration of 2, matching the horizon length. This match satisfies a sufficient condition for immunization with respect to a single horizon.

At the end of the first year, any decline in the interest rates at which the cash contribution is invested will be offset by a corresponding increase in the value of the initial holdings. The portfolio is at that time rebalanced by selling the actual holdings and investing the proceeds together with the new cash in a portfolio with a duration of 1 to match the horizon date. Note that the rate of return guaranteed on the future contributions is not the current spot rate but rather the forward rate for the date of contribution.

This strategy can be extended to apply to multiple contributions and liabilities, which produces a general immunization technique that is applicable to the case of arbitrary cash flows over a period. The construction of an optimal immunized portfolio involves quantifying and then minimizing the immunization risk measure. Linear programming methods can then be used to obtain the optimal portfolio.

4.1.5 Return Maximization for Immunized Portfolios

The objective of risk minimization for an immunized portfolio may be too restrictive in certain situations. If a substantial increase in the expected return can be accomplished with little effect on immunization risk, the higher-yielding portfolio may be preferred in spite of its higher risk.

Suppose that an optimally immunized portfolio has a target return of 8 percent over the horizon with a 95 percent confidence interval at ±20 bps. Thus, the minimum-risk portfolio would have a 1 in 40 chance of a realized return less than 7.8 percent. Suppose that another portfolio less well-immunized can produce a target return of 8.3 percent with a 95 percent confidence interval of ±30 bps. In all but one case out of 40, on average, this portfolio would realize a return above 8 percent compared with 7.8 percent on the minimum-risk portfolio. For many investors, the 8.3 percent target-return portfolio may be the preferred one.

The required terminal value, plus a safety margin in money terms, will determine the minimum acceptable return over the horizon period. As already mentioned, the difference between the minimum acceptable return and the higher possible immunized rate is known as the cushion spread. This spread offers the manager latitude in pursuing an active strategy. The greater the cushion spread, the more scope the manager has for an active management policy.

Fong and Vasicek's (1983) approach to the risk/return trade-off for immunized portfolios maintains the duration of the portfolio at all times equal to the horizon length. Thus, the portfolio stays fully immunized in the classical sense. Instead of minimizing the immunization risk against nonparallel rate changes, however, a trade-off between risk and return is considered. The immunization risk measure can be relaxed if the compensation in terms of expected return warrants it. Specifically, the strategy maximizes a lower bound on the portfolio return. The lower bound is defined as the lower confidence interval limit on the realized return at a given confidence level.

Linear programming can be used to solve for the optimal portfolio when return maximization is the objective. In fact, parametric linear programming can be employed to determine an efficient frontier for immunized portfolios analogous to those in the mean–variance framework.

4.2 Cash Flow Matching Strategies

Cash flow matching is an alternative to multiple liability immunization in asset/liability management. Cash flow matching is an appealing strategy because the portfolio manager need only select securities to match the timing and amount of liabilities. Conceptually, a bond is selected with a maturity that matches the last liability, and an amount of principal equal to the amount of the last liability minus the final coupon payment is invested in this bond. The remaining elements of the liability stream are then reduced by the coupon payments on this bond, and another bond is chosen for the next-to-last liability, adjusted for any coupon payments received on the first bond selected. Going back in time, this sequence is continued until all liabilities have been matched by payments on the securities selected for the portfolio. Linear programming techniques can be employed to construct a least-cost cash flow matching portfolio from an acceptable universe of bonds.

Exhibit 18 provides a simple illustration of this process for a five-year liability stream. Exhibit 19 provides a cash flow analysis of sources and application of funds of a portfolio being used to cash flow match a series of remaining liabilities falling due on 31 December of 2004 to 2018. In the first row for 2004, the previous cash balance of €0 indicates that the previous liability was exactly met by maturing principal and coupon payments. Principal payments of €1,685, coupon payments of €2,340, and €13 from an account which accumulates interest on reinvested payments, suffice to meet the liability due year-end 2004 (€1,685 + €2,340 + €13 = €4,038). (The interest account reflects interest on payments expected to be received in advance of the liability that the payments will fund.) The last column in the exhibit shows the excess funds remaining at each period, which are reinvested at an assumed 1.2 percent reinvestment rate supplied by the portfolio manager. The more excess cash, the greater the risk of the strategy, because the reinvestment rate is subject to uncertainty.

Exhibit 18 Illustration of Cash Flow Matching Process

Assume: 5-year liability stream. Cash flow from bonds is annual.

$L_1 \quad L_2 \quad L_3 \quad L_4 \quad L_5$

Liability Time: 0, 1, 2, 3, 4, 5

Step 1 – Cash flow from Bond A selected to satisfy L_5
Coupons = A_c; Principal = A_p and $A_c + A_p = L_5$

Unfunded liabilities remaining:

$L_1 - A_c \quad L_2 - A_c \quad L_3 - A_c \quad L_4 - A_c$

Unfunded liability Time: 0, 1, 2, 3, 4

Step 2 – Cash flow from Bond B selected to satisfy $L_4 - A_c$
Coupons = B_c; Principal = B_p and $B_c + B_p = L_4 - A_c$

Unfunded liabilities remaining:

$L_1 - A_c - B_c \quad L_2 - A_c - B_c \quad L_3 - A_c - B_c$

Unfunded liability Time: 0, 1, 2, 3

Step 3 – Cash flow from Bond C selected to satisfy $L_3 - A_c - B_c$
Coupons = C_c; Principal = C_p and $C_c + C_p = L_3 - A_c - B_c$

Unfunded liabilities remaining:

$L_1 - A_c - B_c - C_c \quad L_2 - A_c - B_c - C_c$

Unfunded liability Time: 0, 1, 2

Step 4 – Cash flow from Bond D selected to satisfy $L_2 - A_c - B_c - C_c$
Coupons = D_c; Principal = D_p and $D_c + D_p = L_2 - A_c - B_c - C_c$

Unfunded liabilities remaining:

$L_1 - A_c - B_c - C_c - D_c$

Unfunded liability Time: 0, 1

Step 5 – Select Bond E with a cash flow of $L_1 - A_c - B_c - C_c - D_c$

Source: Fabozzi (2004b, p. 123).

Exhibit 19 Cash Flow Analysis of Sample Portfolio for Cash Flow Matching

Year End (31 Dec)	Previous Cash Balance	Principal Payments	Coupon Payments	Interest on Reinvestment of Payments	Liability Due	New Cash Balance
2004	€0	€1,685	€2,340	€13	(€4,038)	€0
2005	0	1,723	2,165	13	(3,900)	0
2006	0	1,805	1,945	12	(3,762)	0
2007	0	1,832	1,769	23	(3,624)	0
2008	0	1,910	1,542	22	(3,474)	0
2009	0	1,877	1,443	10	(3,330)	0
2010	0	2,081	1,072	21	(3,174)	0
2011	0	2,048	950	14	(3,012)	0
2012	0	1,996	847	7	(2,850)	0
2013	0	3,683	768	9	(2,582)	1,878
2014	1,878	0	611	25	(2,514)	0
2015	0	1,730	611	5	(2,346)	0
2016	0	1,733	440	5	(2,178)	0
2017	0	1,756	233	15	(2,004)	0
2018	0	1,740	157	3	(1,900)	0

Reinvestment Rate: 1.2 percent; Evaluation Date: 31 December 2003

4.2.1 Cash Flow Matching versus Multiple Liability Immunization

If all the liability flows were perfectly matched by the asset flows of the portfolio, the resulting portfolio would have no reinvestment risk and, therefore, no immunization or cash flow match risk. Given typical liability schedules and bonds available for cash flow matching, however, perfect matching is unlikely. Under such conditions, a minimum immunization risk approach should be as good as cash flow matching and likely will be better, because an immunization strategy would require less money to fund liabilities. Two factors contribute to this superiority.

First, cash flow matching requires a relatively conservative rate of return assumption for short-term cash and cash balances may be occasionally substantial. By contrast, an immunized portfolio is essentially fully invested at the remaining horizon duration. Second, funds from a cash flow–matched portfolio must be available when (and usually before) each liability is due, because of the difficulty in perfect matching. Because the reinvestment assumption for excess cash for cash flow matching extends many years into the future, a conservative interest rate assumption is appropriate. An immunized portfolio needs to meet the target value only on the date of each liability, because funding is achieved by a rebalancing of the portfolio.

Thus, even with the sophisticated linear programming techniques used, in most cases cash flow matching will be technically inferior to immunization. Cash flow matching is easier to understand than multiple liability immunization, however; this ease of use occasionally supports its selection in dedication portfolio strategies.

4.2.2 Extensions of Basic Cash Flow Matching

In basic cash flow matching, only asset cash flows occurring prior to a liability date can be used to satisfy the liability. The basic technique can be extended to allow cash flows occurring both before and after the liability date to be used to meet a liability.[39] This technique, called **symmetric cash flow matching**, allows for the short-term borrowing of funds to satisfy a liability prior to the liability due date. The opportunity to borrow short-term so that symmetric cash matching can be employed results in a reduction in the cost of funding a liability.

A popular variation of multiple liability immunization and cash flow matching to fund liabilities is one that combines the two strategies. This strategy, referred to as **combination matching** or horizon matching, creates a portfolio that is duration-matched with the added constraint that it be cash flow–matched in the first few years, usually the first five years. The advantage of combination matching over multiple liability immunization is that liquidity needs are provided for in the initial cash flow-matched period. Also, most of the curvature of yield curves is often at the short end (the first few years). Cash flow matching the initial portion of the liability stream reduces the risk associated with nonparallel shifts of the yield curve. The disadvantage of combination matching over multiple liability immunization is that the cost to fund liabilities is greater.

4.2.3 Application Considerations

In applying dedication strategies, the portfolio manager must be concerned with universe selection, optimization, monitoring, and transaction costs.

4.2.3.1 Universe Considerations Selection of the universe for construction of a single period immunized portfolio or a dedicated portfolio is extremely important. The lower the quality of the securities considered, the higher the potential risk and return. Dedication assumes that there will be no defaults, and immunization theory further assumes that securities are responsive only to overall changes in interest rates. The lower the quality of securities, the greater the probability that these assumptions will not be met. Further, securities with embedded options such as call options or prepayments options (e.g., mortgage-backed securities) complicate and may even prevent the accurate measurement of cash flow, and hence duration, frustrating the basic requirements of immunization and cash flow matching. Finally, liquidity is a consideration for immunized portfolios, because they must be rebalanced periodically.

4.2.3.2 Optimization Optimization procedures can be used for the construction of immunized and cash flow–matched portfolios. For an immunized portfolio, optimization typically takes the form of minimizing maturity variance subject to the constraints of matching weighted average duration and having the necessary duration dispersion (in multiple-liability immunization). For cash flow matching, optimization takes the form of minimizing the initial portfolio cost subject to the constraint of having sufficient cash at the time a liability arises. Further considerations such as average quality, minimum and maximum concentration constraints, and, perhaps, issuer constraints may be included. Throughout the process, it is critical to establish realistic guidelines and objectives. Accurate pricing is important because optimization is very sensitive to the prices of the securities under consideration. Because there are many inputs and variations available, the optimization process should be approached iteratively, with a final solution that is the result of a number of trials.

---

39 See Fabozzi, Tong, and Zhu (1991).

4.2.3.3 Monitoring Monitoring an immunized or cash flow–matched portfolio requires periodic performance measurement. For a bullet portfolio, performance monitoring may take the form of regular observations of the return to date linked with the current target return and annualized. This return should fluctuate only slightly about the original target return.

The performance of a multiple liability immunized plan can be monitored most easily by comparing the current market value of the assets with the present value of the remaining liabilities. The current internal rate of return on the immunized portfolio should be used to discount the remaining liabilities. (This rate is used because it is the expected rate of return that is necessary to provide sufficient cash flow to fund the liabilities.) These two quantities should track one another closely. It may also be useful to monitor the estimated standard deviation of the terminal value of the fund to make sure that it falls more or less uniformly to zero as the horizon date approaches.

4.2.3.4 Transactions Costs Transactions costs are important in meeting the target rate for an immunized portfolio. They must be considered not only in the initial immunization (when the immunized portfolio is first created) but also in the periodic rebalancing necessary to avoid duration mismatch.

SUMMARY

The management of fixed-income portfolios is a highly competitive field requiring skill in financial and economic analysis, market knowledge, and control of costs. Among the points that have been made are the following:

- Because a benchmark is the standard with which the portfolio's performance will be compared, it should always reflect the portfolio's objective. If a portfolio has liabilities that must be met, that need is the paramount objective and thus is the most appropriate benchmark. If a portfolio has no liabilities, the most relevant standard is a bond market index that very closely matches the portfolio's characteristics.

- Bond indexing is attractive because indexed portfolios have lower fees than actively managed portfolios and broadly-based bond index portfolios provide excellent diversification.

- In selecting a benchmark index, the manager should choose an index with comparable market value risk, comparable income risk (comparable assured income stream), and minimal liability framework risk (minimal mismatch between the durations of assets and liabilities).

- Most bond indices will not be easily replicated. Issues that prevent bond index investability include the small size of bond issues, their heterogeneity, and infrequent trading. Additionally, bond indices may have unexpected risk exposures, risk that changes over time, or be overweighted by bums. Investors may also have trouble finding an index that matches the portfolio's desired risk exposures.

- For an indexed portfolio, the manager must carefully try to match the portfolio's characteristics to the benchmark's risk profile. The primary risk factors to match are the portfolio's duration, key rate duration and cash flow distribution, sector and quality percent, sector duration contribution, quality spread duration contribution, sector/coupon/maturity/cell weights, and issuer exposure.

Summary

- The indexing manager has a variety of strategies from which to choose ranging from a totally passive style to a very active style or points in between. The most popular of these strategies are pure bond indexing, enhanced indexing by matching primary risk factors, enhanced indexing by minor risk factor mismatches, active management by larger risk factor mismatches, and full-blown active management.

- Because a perfectly indexed portfolio will still underperform the benchmark by the amount of transactions costs, the manager may use a variety of techniques to enhance the return. These include lowering managerial and transactions costs, issue selection, yield curve positioning, sector and quality positioning, and call exposure positioning.

- Total return analysis and scenario analysis are methods of evaluating the impact of a trade given a change in interest rates and a range of changes in interest rates, respectively.

- The heart of a bond immunization strategy for a single liability is to match the average duration of the assets with the time horizon of the liability. However, this matching alone is not sufficient to immunize the portfolio, in general, because of the impact of twists and nonparallel changes in the yield curve. Care must be taken when designing the immunization strategy to ensure that the portfolio will remain immunized under a variety of different scenarios.

- In order to maintain the dollar duration of a portfolio, rebalancing may be necessary. Methods for achieving this include a) investing new funds (if necessary), b) changing the weight of a particular security to adjust the dollar duration, and c) using derivatives. If new funds are invested to rebalance, after an interest rate change, calculate the new dollar duration of the portfolio, calculate the rebalancing ratio, then multiply the new market value of the portfolio by the desired percentage change.

- Spread duration is a measure of how the market value of a risky bond (portfolio) will change with respect to a parallel 100 bps change in its spread above the comparable benchmark security (portfolio). Spread duration is an important factor influencing a portfolio's total return because spreads do change frequently.

- Because parallel shifts in the yield curve are rare, classical immunization will not immunize the portfolio adequately. Extensions to classical immunization provide better results. These extensions include modifying the definition of duration (to multifunctional duration), overcoming the limitations of a fixed horizon, analyzing the risk and return trade-off for immunized portfolios, and integrating immunization strategies with elements of active bond market strategies.

- Three categories that describe the risk of not being able to pay a portfolio's liabilities are interest rate risk, contingent claim, and cap risk. A rising interest rate environment (interest rate risk) comprises the largest risk that a portfolio manager will face. When a security has a contingent claim provision, the manager may have lucrative coupon payments halted (as is the case with mortgage-backed securities) or a leveling off in the market value of a callable security. An asset that makes floating rate payments will typically have caps associated with the floating rate. The manager is at risk of the level of market rates rising while the asset returns are capped.

- Multiple liabilities immunization requires the portfolio payment stream to be decomposed so that each liability is separately immunized by one of the component streams, the present value of the assets equals the present value of the liabilities, the composite duration of the portfolio must equal the composite duration of the liabilities, and the distribution of individual portfolio assets must have a wider range than the distribution of the liabilities. For general cash flows, the expected cash contributions can be considered the payments on hypothetical securities that are part of the initial holdings. The actual initial investment can then be invested in such a way that the real and hypothetical holdings taken together represent an immunized portfolio.

- Risk minimization produces an immunized portfolio with a minimum exposure to any arbitrary interest rate change subject to the duration constraint. This objective may be too restrictive in certain situations however. If a substantial increase in the expected return can be accomplished with little effect on immunization risk, the higher-yielding portfolio may be preferred in spite of its higher risk.

PRACTICE PROBLEMS

1 The table below shows the active return for six periods for a bond portfolio. Calculate the portfolio's tracking risk for the six-period time frame.

Period	Portfolio Return	Benchmark Return	Active Return
1	14.10%	13.70%	0.400%
2	8.20	8.00	0.200
3	7.80	8.00	−0.200
4	3.20	3.50	−0.300
5	2.60	2.40	0.200
6	3.30	3.00	0.300

2 The table below shows the spread duration for a 70-bond portfolio and a benchmark index based on sectors. Determine whether the portfolio or the benchmark is more sensitive to changes in the sector spread by determining the spread duration for each. Given your answer, what is the effect on the portfolio's tracking risk?

Sector	Portfolio % of Portfolio	Portfolio Spread Duration	Benchmark % of Portfolio	Benchmark Spread Duration
Treasury	22.70	0.00	23.10	0.00
Agencies	12.20	4.56	6.54	4.41
Financial institutions	6.23	3.23	5.89	3.35
Industrials	14.12	11.04	14.33	10.63
Utilities	6.49	2.10	6.28	2.58
Non-US credit	6.56	2.05	6.80	1.98
Mortgage	31.70	1.78	33.20	1.11
Asset backed	—	2.40	1.57	3.34
CMBS	—	5.60	2.29	4.67
Total	100.00		100.00	

3 You are the manager of a portfolio consisting of three bonds in equal par amounts of $1,000,000 each. The first table below shows the market value of the bonds and their durations. (The price includes accrued interest.) The second table contains the market value of the bonds and their durations one year later.

Initial Values

Security	Price	Market Value	Duration	Dollar Duration
Bond #1	$106.110	$1,060,531	5.909	?
Bond #2	98.200	981,686	3.691	?
Bond #3	109.140	1,090,797	5.843	?
		Portfolio dollar duration =		?

Practice Problems and Solutions: 1–3 taken from *Managing Investment Portfolios: A Dynamic Process*, Third Edition, John L. Maginn, CFA, Donald L. Tuttle, CFA, Jerald E. Pinto, CFA, and Dennis W. McLeavey, CFA, editors. Copyright © 2007 by CFA Institute. All other problems and solutions copyright © CFA Institute.

	After 1 year			
Security	Price	Market Value	Duration	Dollar Duration
Bond #1	$104.240	$1,042,043	5.177	?
Bond #2	98.084	980,461	2.817	?
Bond #3	106.931	1,068,319	5.125	?
		Portfolio dollar duration =		?

As manager, you would like to maintain the portfolio's dollar duration at the initial level by rebalancing the portfolio. You choose to rebalance using the existing security proportions of one-third each. Calculate:

A the dollar durations of each of the bonds.

B the rebalancing ratio necessary for the rebalancing.

C the cash required for the rebalancing.

The following information relates to Questions 4–9

The investment committee of Rojas University is unhappy with the recent performance of the fixed-income portion of their endowment and has fired the current fixed-income manager. The current portfolio, benchmarked against the Barclays Capital US Aggregate Index, is shown in Exhibit 1. The investment committee hires Alfredo Alonso, a consultant from MHC Consulting, to assess the portfolio's risks, submit ideas to the committee, and manage the portfolio on an interim basis.

Exhibit 1 Rojas University Endowment Fixed-Income Portfolio Information

	Portfolio		Index	
Sector	%	Duration*	%	Duration*
Treasuries	47.74	5.50	49.67	5.96
Agencies	14.79	5.80	14.79	5.10
Corporates	12.35	4.50	16.54	5.61
Mortgage-backed securities	25.12	4.65	19.10	4.65

*Spread durations are the same as effective durations for all sectors with spread risk.

Alonso notices that the fired manager's portfolio did not own securities outside of the index universe. The committee asks Alonso to consider an indexing strategy, including related benefits and logistical problems. Alonso identifies three factors that limit a manager's ability to replicate a bond index:

Factor #1 a lack of availability of certain bond issues

Factor #2 the limited market capitalization of the bond universe

Factor #3 differences between the bond prices used by the manager and the index provider

Alonso has done further analysis of the current US Treasury portion of the portfolio and has discovered a significant overweight in a 5-year Treasury bond ($10 million par value). He expects the yield curve to flatten and forecasts a six-month horizon

Practice Problems

price of the 5-year Treasury bond to be $99.50. Therefore, Alonso's strategy will be to sell all the 5-year Treasury bonds, and invest the proceeds in 10-year Treasury bonds and cash while maintaining the dollar duration of the portfolio. US Treasury bond information is shown in Exhibit 2.

Exhibit 2 US Treasury Bond Information

Issue Description (Term to Maturity, Ticker, Coupon, Maturity Date)	Duration	Price* ($)	Yield (%)
5-year: T 4.125% 15May2011	4.53	100.40625	4.03
10-year: T 5.25% 15May2016	8.22	109.09375	4.14

*Prices are shown per $100 par value.

4 The duration of the Rojas University fixed-income portfolio in Exhibit 1 is *closest* to:
- **A** 5.11.
- **B** 5.21.
- **C** 5.33.

5 The spread duration of the Rojas University fixed-income portfolio in Exhibit 1 is *closest* to:
- **A** 2.58.
- **B** 4.93.
- **C** 5.21.

6 Based on the data in Exhibit 1, the bond portfolio strategy used by the fired manager can *best* be described as:
- **A** pure bond index matching.
- **B** enhanced indexing/matching risk factors.
- **C** active management/larger risk factor mismatches.

7 Regarding the three factors identified by Alonso, the factor *least likely* to actually limit a manager's ability to replicate a bond index is:
- **A** #1.
- **B** #2.
- **C** #3.

8 Using Alonso's forecasted price and the bond information in Exhibit 2, the expected 6-month total return of the Treasury 4.125% 15May2011 is *closest* to (assume zero accrued interest at purchase):
- **A** −0.90%.
- **B** 1.15%.
- **C** 1.56%.

9 Using Exhibit 2, the par value of 10-year bonds to be purchased to execute Alonso's strategy is *closest* to:
- **A** $5,072,000.

B $5,489,000.

C $5,511,000.

The following information relates to Questions 10–15

The State Retirement Board (SRB) provides a defined benefit pension plan to state employees. The governors of the SRB are concerned that their current fixed-income investments may not be appropriate because the average age of the state employee workforce has been increasing. In addition, a surge in retirements is projected to occur over the next 10 years.

Chow Wei Mei, the head of the SRB's investment committee, has suggested that some of the future pension payments can be covered by buying annuities from an insurance company. She proposes that the SRB invest a fixed sum to purchase annuities in seven years time, when the number of retirements is expected to peak. Chow argues that the SRB should fund the future purchase of the annuities by creating a dedicated fixed-income portfolio consisting of corporate bonds, mortgage-backed securities, and risk-free government bonds. Chow states:

Statement #1 "To use a portfolio of bonds to immunize a single liability, and remove all risks, it is necessary only that 1) the market value of the assets be equal to the present value of the liability and 2) the duration of the portfolio be equal to the duration of the liability."

Chow lists three alternative portfolios that she believes will immunize a single, seven-year liability. All bonds in Exhibit 1 are option-free government bonds.

Exhibit 1 Alternative Portfolios for Funding an Annuity Purchase in Seven Years

Portfolio	Description	Portfolio Yield to Maturity (%)
A	Zero-coupon bond with a maturity of 7 years	4.20
B	Bond with a maturity of 6 years Bond with a maturity of 8 years	4.10
C	Bond with a maturity of 5 years Bond with a maturity of 9 years	4.15

Chow then states:

Statement #2 "Because each of these alternative portfolios immunizes this single, seven-year liability, each has the same level of reinvestment risk."

The SRB governors would like to examine different investment horizons and alternative strategies to immunize the single liability. The governors ask Chow to evaluate a contingent immunization strategy using the following assumptions:

- The SRB will commit a $100 million investment to this strategy.
- The horizon of the investment is 10 years.

Practice Problems

- The SRB will accept a 4.50 percent return (semiannual compounding).
- An immunized rate of return of 5.25 percent (semiannual compounding) is possible.

Marshall Haley, an external consultant for the SRB, has been asked by the governors to advise them on the appropriateness of its investment strategies. Haley notes that, although state employee retirements are expected to surge over the next 10 years, the SRB will experience a continual stream of retirements over the next several decades. Hence, the SRB faces a schedule of liabilities, not a single liability. In explaining how the SRB can manage the risks of multiple liabilities, Haley makes the following statements:

Statement #1   "When managing the risks of a schedule of liabilities, multiple liability immunization and cash flow matching approaches do not have the same risks and costs. Whereas cash flow matching generally has less risk of not satisfying future liabilities, multiple liability immunization generally costs less."

Statement #2   "Assuming that there is a parallel shift in the yield curve, to immunize multiple liabilities, there are three necessary conditions: i) the present value of the assets be equal to the present value of the liabilities; ii) the composite portfolio duration be equal to the composite liabilities duration; and iii) I cannot remember the third condition."

Statement #3   "Horizon matching can be used to immunize a schedule of liabilities."

10 Is Chow's Statement #1 correct?
  A Yes.
  B No, because credit risk must also be considered.
  C No, because the risk of parallel shifts in the yield curve must also be considered.

11 Is Chow's Statement #2 correct?
  A No, Portfolio B is exposed to less reinvestment risk than Portfolio A.
  B No, Portfolio B is exposed to more reinvestment risk than Portfolio C.
  C No, Portfolio C is exposed to more reinvestment risk than Portfolio B.

12 Which of the following is *closest* to the required terminal value for the contingent immunization strategy?
  A $100 million.
  B $156 million.
  C $168 million.

13 Is Haley's Statement #1 correct?
  A Yes.
  B No, because multiple liability immunization is generally less risky than cash flow matching.
  C No, because cash flow matching is generally less costly than multiple liability immunization.

14 The condition that Haley cannot remember in his Statement #2 is that the:
  A cash flows in the portfolio must be dispersed around the horizon date.
  B cash flows in the portfolio must be concentrated around the horizon date.
  C distribution of durations of individual assets in the portfolio must have a wider range than the distribution of the liabilities.

15 The *most* appropriate description of the strategy that Haley suggests in his Statement #3 is to create a portfolio that:
   A has cash flows concentrated around the horizon date.
   B is duration matched but uses cash flow matching in the later years of the liability schedule.
   C is duration matched but uses cash flow matching in the initial years of the liability schedule.

SOLUTIONS

1 The tracking risk is the standard deviation of the active returns. For the data shown in the problem, the tracking risk is 28.284 bps, as shown below:

Period	Portfolio Return	Benchmark Return	Active Return	(AR – Avg. AR)^2
1	14.10%	13.70%	0.400%	0.00090%
2	8.20	8.00	0.200	0.00010
3	7.80	8.00	−0.200	0.00090
4	3.20	3.50	−0.300	0.00160
5	2.60	2.40	0.200	0.00010
6	3.30	3.00	0.300	0.00040

Average active return per period = 0.100%

Sum of the squared deviations = 0.00400%

Tracking risk (std. dev.) = 0.28284%

2 The portfolio is more sensitive to changes in the spread because its spread duration is 3.151 compared with the benchmark's 2.834. The portfolio's higher spread duration is primarily a result of the portfolio's greater weight on agency securities. The spread duration for each can be calculated by taking a weighted average of the individual sectors' durations. Because there is a difference between the portfolio's and the benchmark's spread duration, the tracking risk will be higher than if the two were more closely matched.

	Portfolio			Benchmark		
Sector	% of Portfolio	Spread Duration	Contribution to Spread Duration	% of Portfolio	Spread Duration	Contribution to Spread Duration
Treasury	22.70	0.00	0.000	23.10	0.00	0.000
Agencies	12.20	4.56	0.556	6.54	4.41	0.288
Financial institutions	6.23	3.23	0.201	5.89	3.35	0.197
Industrials	14.12	11.04	1.559	14.33	10.63	1.523
Utilities	6.49	2.10	0.136	6.28	2.58	0.162
Non-US credit	6.56	2.05	0.134	6.80	1.98	0.135
Mortgage	31.70	1.78	0.564	33.20	1.11	0.369
Asset backed	—	2.40	0.000	1.57	3.34	0.052
CMBS	—	5.60	0.000	2.29	4.67	0.107
Total	100.00		3.151	100.00		2.834

3 Dollar duration is a measure of the change in portfolio value for a 100 bps change in market yields. It is defined as

Dollar duration = Duration × Dollar value × 0.01

A A portfolio's dollar duration is the sum of the dollar durations of the component securities. The dollar duration of this portfolio at the beginning of the period is $162,636, which is calculated as

| | Initial Values ||||
Security	Price	Market Value	Duration	Dollar Duration
Bond #1	$106.110	$1,060,531	5.909	$62,667
Bond #2	98.200	981,686	3.691	36,234
Bond #3	109.140	1,090,797	5.843	63,735
		Portfolio dollar duration =		$162,636

At the end of one year, the portfolio's dollar duration has changed to $136,318, as shown below.

| | After 1 Year ||||
Security	Price	Market Value	Duration	Dollar Duration
Bond #1	$104.240	$1,042,043	5.177	$53,947
Bond #2	98.084	980,461	2.817	27,620
Bond #3	106.931	1,068,319	5.125	54,751
		Portfolio dollar duration =		$136,318

B The rebalancing ratio is a ratio of the original dollar duration to the new dollar duration:

Rebalancing ratio = $162,636/$136,318 = 1.193

C The portfolio requires each position to be increased by 19.3 percent. The cash required for this rebalancing is calculated as:

Cash required = 0.193 × ($1,042,043 + 980,461 + 1,068,319)
= $596,529

4 B is correct. Portfolio duration is a weighted average of the component durations. In this problem, (0.4774 × 5.50) + (0.1479 × 5.80) + (0.1235 × 4.50) + (0.2512 × 4.65) = 5.20735. Round to 5.21.

5 A is correct. Spread duration is a measure of a non-Treasury security's price change as a result of a change in the spread between the security and a Treasury. The portfolio spread duration is the weighted average duration of those securities in the portfolio that have a yield above the default-free yield (i.e., non-Treasuries). In this problem, the agencies, corporates, and mortgage-backed securities have a spread. Using their original weights in the portfolio, the spread duration is (0.1479 × 5.80) + (0.1235 × 4.50) + (0.2512 × 4.65) = 2.58165. Round to 2.58.

6 C is correct. Exhibit 1 makes clear that the portfolio weights differ and for some sectors quite dramatically from those of the index and that the durations of the portfolio components differ from their respective durations in the index. Thus the manager is using active management because he had both duration and sector mismatches and not on a small scale.

7 B is correct. The market capitalization of the bond universe is large—much larger than that for equities. Alonso is incorrect in identifying this as a limiting factor. Information (data) for the other two factors can be impossible to acquire.

8 B is correct. Calculate the holding period return for the Treasury 4.125% 15 May 2011 by using the current price of 100.40625 (Exhibit 2), Alonso's forecast of 99.50, and a semi-annual coupon of 2.0625. The problem informs that there is zero accrued interest. The 6-month total return is (99.50 + 2.0625 − 100.40625)/100.40625 = 1.15%.

Solutions

9 A is correct. Alonso is not simply going to reinvest the entire proceeds of the sale into 10-year Treasuries because his stated desire is to maintain the dollar duration of the portfolio. The sale price of $10 million par value of the 5-year bond is found by multiplying $10,000,000 × 1.0040625 = $10,040,625. The dollar duration of the 5-year is 4.53 × $10,040,625 × 0.01 = $454,840.31. Now divide $454,840.31 by the product of the duration of the 10-year and its quoted price and 0.01 to get the par value of the 10-year. The result is $454,840.31/(8.22 × 1.0909375 × 0.01) = $5,072,094.

10 B is correct. Chow's statement #1 is incorrect because what she describes does not remove all risks. Credit risk destroys the immunization match; therefore, the statement is incorrect. The risk to immunization comes from non-parallel shifts in the yield curve.

11 C is correct. Portfolio A is a zero-coupon bond and thus has no reinvestment rate risk. Portfolio B has lower dispersion in maturities than Portfolio C. Therefore, Portfolio C has more reinvestment rate risk than Portfolio B.

12 B is correct. The SRB will accept (i.e., require) a return of 4.50% (semiannual compounding). Find the time ten future value of $100 million at this rate. The answer is $100,000,000 × (1 + .045/2)^{20} = $156,050,920.

13 A is correct. Haley's statement #1 defines the risk-costs tradeoffs of cash flow matching versus multiple liabilities immunization.

14 C is correct. If the distribution of the durations of the assets is wider than that of the liabilities, the durations of the assets after a parallel yield curve shift (whether up or down) will envelope the durations of the liabilities after the shift. The immunization can be maintained, although rebalancing may be necessary.

15 C is correct. Horizon matching creates a duration-matched portfolio with the added constraint that it be cash-flow-matched in the first few years. Cash flow matching the initial portion of the liability stream reduces the risk associated with nonparallel shifts of the yield curve.

READING 21

Relative-Value Methodologies for Global Credit Bond Portfolio Management

by Jack Malvey, CFA

Jack Malvey, CFA (USA).

LEARNING OUTCOMES

Mastery	The candidate should be able to:
☐	a. explain classic relative-value analysis, based on top-down and bottom-up approaches to credit bond portfolio management;
☐	b. discuss the implications of cyclical supply and demand changes in the primary corporate bond market and the impact of secular changes in the market's dominant product structures;
☐	c. explain the influence of investors' short- and long-term liquidity needs on portfolio management decisions;
☐	d. discuss common rationales for secondary market trading;
☐	e. discuss corporate bond portfolio strategies that are based on relative value.

INTRODUCTION

Corporate bonds are the second oldest and, for most asset managers, the most demanding and fascinating subset of the global debt capital markets. The label, "corporate," understates the scope of this burgeoning asset class. As commonly traded and administered within the context of an overall debt portfolio, the "corporate asset class" actually encompasses much more than pure corporate entities. Instead of the title "corporate asset class," this segment of the global bond market really should be classified as the "credit asset class," including any nonagency mortgage-backed securities (MBS), commercial mortgage-backed securities (CMBS), or asset-backed securities (ABS). Sovereigns and government-controlled entities with foreign currency debt issues thought to have more credit risk than the national government should also be included. In keeping with conventional practice in the fixed-income market, however, the application of the term "credit asset class" in this reading will pertain only to corporate bonds, sovereigns, and government-controlled entities.

Fixed Income Readings for the Chartered Financial Analyst® Program, Second Edition, edited by Frank J. Fabozzi, CFA. Copyright © 2005 by CFA Institute.

From six continents, thousands of organizations (corporations, government agencies, projects and structured pools of debt securities) with different credit "stories" have sold debt to sustain their operations and to finance their expansion. These borrowers use dozens of different types of debt instruments (first mortgage bonds, debentures, equipment trust certificates, subordinated debentures, medium-term notes, floating rate notes, private placements, preferred stock) and in multiple currencies (dollars, yen, euros, Swiss francs, pounds) from maturities ranging from one year to even a thousand years. Sometimes these debt structures carry embedded options, which may allow for full or partial redemption prior to maturity at the option of either the borrower or the investor. Sometimes, the coupon payment floats with short-term interest rates or resets to a higher rate after a fixed interval or a credit rating change.

Investors buy credit assets because of the presumption of higher long-term returns despite the assumption of credit risk. Except near and during recessions, credit products usually outperform US Treasury securities and other higher-quality "spread sectors" like US agency securities, mortgage-backed securities, and asset-backed securities. In the 30-year period since the beginning of the Lehman[1] indices (1973 through 2002), investment-grade credit outperformed US Treasuries by 30 basis points (bps) per year on average (9.42% versus 9.12%).[2] As usual, an average masks the true daily, weekly, monthly, and annual volatility of credit assets' relative performance. Looking at the rolling 5-year excess returns of US investment-grade credit from 1926 through early 2003 in Exhibit 1, one can observe extended periods of generous and disappointing returns for credit assets. Perhaps more meaningful, an examination of volatility-adjusted (Sharpe ratio) excess returns over Treasuries over a rolling 5-year period shown in Exhibit 2 further underscores the oscillations in relative credit performance.

Global credit portfolio management presents a complex challenge. Each day, hundreds of credit portfolio managers face thousands of choices in the primary (new issue) and secondary markets. In addition to tracking primary and secondary flows, investors have to keep tabs on ever-varying issuer fundamentals, credit-worthiness, acquisitions, earnings, ratings, etc. The task of global credit portfolio management is to process all of this rapidly changing information about the credit markets (issuers, issues, dealers, and competing managers) and to construct the portfolio with the best return for a given risk tolerance. This discipline combines the qualitative tools of equity analysis with the quantitative precision of fixed-income analysis. This reading provides a brief guide to methodologies that may help portfolio managers meet this formidable challenge.

---

[1] Barclays has acquired Lehman Brothers and will maintain the family of Lehman Brothers indices and the associated index calculation, publication, and analytical infrastructure and tools.
[2] Based on absolute returns of key Lehman indices from 1973.

Introduction

Exhibit 1 Rolling 5-year US Investment-Grade Credit Index Excess Returns[a] (bps) January 1926 through December 31, 2003

[a] Excess returns represent the difference, positive or negative, between the total return of all credit securities and Treasury securities along a set of key rate duration points across the term structure. This single statistic, excess return, therefore normalizes for the duration differential among debt asset classes, in this case between longer-duration credit and shorter-duration Treasuries.

Source: Data series from Ibbotson Associates prior to August 1988, Lehman Brothers data thereafter.

Exhibit 2 US Credit 5-Year Rolling Sharpe Ratio: July 1993 through December 31, 2003

Source: Lehman Brothers US Investment-Grade Credit Index.

2 CREDIT RELATIVE-VALUE ANALYSIS

Credit portfolio management represents a major subset of the multi-asset global portfolio management process illustrated in Exhibit 3. After setting the currency allocation (in this case, dollars were selected for illustration convenience) and distribution among fixed-income asset classes, bond managers are still left with a lengthy list of questions to construct an optimal credit portfolio. Some examples are:

- Should US investors add US dollar-denominated bonds of non-US issuers?
- Should central banks add high-quality euro-denominated corporate bonds to their reserve holdings?
- Should Libor-funded London-based portfolio managers buy fixed-rate US industrial paper and swap into floating-rate notes?
- Should Japanese mutual funds own euro-denominated telecommunications debt, swapped back into dollars or yen using **currency swaps**?

Credit Relative-Value Analysis

Exhibit 3 Fixed-Income Portfolio Management Process

```
Fixed Income
    |
Multi-Currency Optimization
    |
Local Currency Asset Class Optimization
    |
    ├── Governments
    │       ├── Treasuries
    │       └── Agencies
    ├── Securitized Sectors
    │       ├── MBS
    │       ├── CMBS
    │       └── ABS
    └── Credit Sectors
            ├── Investment-Grade Credit
            ├── High-Yield Credit
            └── Emerging-Market Credit
```

- Should US insurers buy perpetual floaters (i.e., floaters without a maturity date) issued by British banks and swap back into fixed-rate coupons in dollars using a currency/interest rate swap?
- When should investors reduce their allocation to the credit sector and increase allocation to governments, pursue a "strategic upgrade trade" (sell Baa/BBBs and buy higher-rated Aa/AA credit debt), rotate from industrials into utilities, switch from consumer cyclicals to non-cyclicals, overweight airlines and underweight telephones, or deploy a credit derivative (e.g., short the high-yield index or reduce a large exposure to a single issuer by buying an issuer-specific **credit default swap**) to hedge their portfolios?

To respond to such questions, managers need to begin with an analytical framework (relative-value analysis) and to develop a strategic outlook for the global credit markets.

A. Relative Value

Economists have long debated the concept and measurement of "value." But fixed-income practitioners, perhaps because of the daily pragmatism enforced by the markets, have developed a consensus about the definition of value. In the bond market, relative value refers *to the ranking of fixed-income investments by sectors, structures, issuers, and issues in terms of their expected performance during some future period of time.*

For a day trader, relative value may carry a maximum horizon of a few minutes. For a dealer, relative value may extend from a few days to a few months. For a total return investor, the relative value horizon typically runs from 1–3 months. For a large insurer, relative value usually spans a multi-year horizon. Accordingly, relative-value analysis refers to the methodologies used to generate such rankings of expected returns.

B. Classic Relative-Value Analysis

There are two basic approaches to global credit bond portfolio management—**top-down** approach and **bottom-up** approach. The top-down approach focuses on high-level allocations among broadly defined credit asset classes. The goal of top-down research is to form views on large-scale economic and industry developments. These views then drive asset allocation decisions (overweight certain sectors, underweight others). The bottom-up approach focuses on individual issuers and issues that will outperform their peer groups. Managers follow this approach hoping to outperform their benchmark due to superior security selection, while maintaining neutral weightings to the various sectors in the benchmark.

Classic relative-value analysis is a dialectical process combining the best of top-down and bottom-up approaches as shown in Exhibit 4. This process blends the macro input of chief investment officers, strategists, economists, and portfolio managers with the micro input of credit analysts, quantitative analysts, and portfolio managers. The goal of this methodology is to pick the sectors with the most potential upside, populate these favored sectors with the best representative issuers, and select the structures of the designated issuers at the yield curve points that match the investor's for the benchmark yield curve.

For many credit investors, using classic relative-value analysis provides a measure of portfolio success. Although sector, issuer, and structural analyses remain the core of superior relative-value analysis, the increased availability of information and technology has transformed the analytical process into a complex discipline. Credit portfolio managers have far more data than ever on the total returns of sectors, issuers, and structures, quantity and composition of new-issue flows, investor product

Credit Relative-Value Analysis 71

Exhibit 4 Credit Sector Portfolio Management Process: Classic, Dialectical Relative-Value Analysis

```
┌─────────────────────┐       US, European, and Asian
│ Chief Invest. Officer│       Investment-Grade Corporates
│ Strategists         │ ──►   ┌──────────────────────────┐
│ Economists          │       │ Global High Yield        │
│ Portfolio Managers  │       │ US, High Yield │ European High │ ──► Emerging
│ Quantitative Analysis│      │ Corporates     │ Yield Corporates│    Markets
└─────────────────────┘       └──────────────────────────┘
           │
           ▼
┌─────────────────────┐
│  CREDIT SECTOR      │
│  ALLOCATION         │ ◄────►
└─────────────────────┘

┌─────────────────────┐       Industrials
│ Strategists         │       Basic Industry
│ Portfolio Managers  │       Communications    Financial Institutions   Non-Corporates
│ Credit Analysis     │ ──►   Cyclical          Banks                    Sovereigns
│ Equity Analysis     │       Non-Cyclical      Brokerage         ──►    Supranationals
│ Economists          │       Energy            Finance Co.              Local Government
└─────────────────────┘       Transportation    Insurance                Agencies
           │                  Capital Goods     Real Estate
           ▼                  Technology        
┌─────────────────────┐                         Utilities
│  INTRA-SECTOR       │                         Electric
│  ALLOCATIONS        │ ◄────►                  Gas
└─────────────────────┘

┌─────────────────────┐       Volkswagen,       Citigroup,          Scottish Power,      Mexico, Canada,
│ Portfolio Managers  │ ──►   Toyota, or GM     Sumitomo,           Korea Electric  ──►  Brazil, Thailand,
│ Credit Analysis     │                         or Deutsche         Power, or            Sweden, or
└─────────────────────┘                         Bank                Texas Utilities      World Bank
           │
           ▼
┌─────────────────────┐
│  ISSUER SELECTION   │ ◄────►
└─────────────────────┘

┌─────────────────────┐       Bullets          Senior              High Coupon
│ Portfolio Managers  │ ──►   Puts             Subordinated        Low Coupon
│ Credit Analysis     │       Callables        Preferred           Floaters
│ Quantitative Analysis│      Credit Default Swaps   Convertible
└─────────────────────┘
           │
           ▼
┌─────────────────────┐
│  STRUCTURAL         │
│  SELECTION          │
└─────────────────────┘
```

demand, aggregate credit-quality movements, multiple sources of fundamental and quantitative credit analyses on individual issuers, and yield spread data to assist them in their relative-value analysis.

C. Relative-Value Methodologies

The main methodologies for credit relative-value maximization are:

- total return analysis;
- primary market analysis;
- liquidity and trading analysis;
- secondary trading rationales and constraints analysis;
- spread analysis;
- structure analysis;
- credit curve analysis;
- credit analysis;
- asset allocation/sector analysis.

In the sections that follow, we discuss each of these methodologies.

3 TOTAL RETURN ANALYSIS

The goal of global credit portfolio management for most investors is to optimize the risk-adjusted total return of their credit portfolio. The best place to start is naturally total return analysis. Accordingly, credit relative-value analysis begins with a detailed dissection of past returns and a projection of expected returns. For the entire asset class and major contributing sub-sectors (such as banks, utilities, pipelines, Baa/BBB's, etc.), how have returns been formed? How much is attributed to credit spread movements, sharp changes in the fundamental fortunes of key issuers, and yield curve dynamics? If there are macro determinants of credit returns (the total return of the credit asset class), then credit markets may display regular patterns. For instance, the macroeconomic cycle is the major determinant of overall credit spreads. During recessions, the escalation of default risk widens spreads (which are risk premiums over underlying, presumably default-free, government securities [or swaps]) and reduces credit returns relative to Treasuries. Conversely, economic prosperity reduces bankruptcies and enhances overall credit fundamentals of most issuers. Economic prosperity usually leads to tighter credit spreads and boosts credit returns relative to Treasuries. For brief intervals, noncyclical technical factors can offset fundamentals. For example, the inversion of the US Treasury yield curve in 2000 actually led to wider credit spreads and credit underperformance despite solid global economic growth and corporate profitability.

Thanks to the development of total return indices for credit debt (databases of prices, spreads, issuer, and structure composition), analyses of monthly, annual, and multi-year total returns have uncovered numerous patterns (i.e., large issue versus small issue performance variation, seasonality, election-cycle effects, and government benchmark auction effects) in the global credit market. Admittedly, these patterns do not always re-occur. But an awareness and understanding of these total-return patterns are essential to optimizing portfolio performance.

PRIMARY MARKET ANALYSIS

The analysis of primary markets centers on new issue supply and demand. Supply is often a misunderstood factor in tactical relative-value analysis. Prospective new supply induces many traders, analysts, and investors to advocate a defensive stance toward the overall corporate market as well as toward individual sectors and issuers. Yet the premise, "supply will hurt spreads," which may apply to an individual issuer, does not generally hold up for the entire credit market. Credit spreads are determined by many factors; supply, although important, represents one of many determinants. During most years, increases in issuance (most notably during the first quarter of each year) are associated with market-spread contraction and strong relative returns for credit debt. In contrast, sharp supply declines are accompanied frequently by spread expansion and a major fall in both relative and absolute returns for credit securities. For example, this counter-intuitive effect was most noticeable during the August–October 1998 interval when new issuance nearly disappeared in the face of the substantial increase in credit spreads. (This period is referred to as the "Great Spread-Sector Crash.")

In the investment-grade credit market, heavy supply often compresses spreads and boosts relative returns for credit assets as new primary valuations validate and enhance secondary valuations. When primary origination declines sharply, secondary traders lose reinforcement from the primary market and tend to reduce their bids, which will increase the spread. Contrary to the normal supply-price relationship, relative credit returns often perform best during periods of heavy supply. For example, 2001 will be recalled for both the then all-time record for new credit origination as well as the best relative performance for US credit securities in nearly two decades.

A. The Effect of Market-Structure Dynamics

Given their immediate focus on the deals of the day and week, portfolio managers often overlook short-term and long-term market-structure dynamics in making portfolio decisions. Because the pace of change in market structure is often gradual, market dynamics have less effect on short-term tactical investment decision-making than on long-term strategy.

The composition of the global credit bond market has shifted markedly since the early 1980s. Medium-term notes (MTN) dominate issuance in the front end of the credit yield curve. Structured notes and swap products have heralded the introduction of derivative instruments into the mainstream of the credit market. The high-yield corporate sector has become an accepted asset class. Global origination has become more popular for US government agencies, supranationals (e.g., the World Bank), sovereigns, and large corporate borrowers.

Although the ascent of derivatives and high-yield instruments stands out during the 1990s, the true globalization of the credit market was the most important development. The rapid development of the Eurobond market since 1975, the introduction of many non-US issuers into the dollar markets during the 1990s, and the birth of the euro on January 1, 1999, have led to the proliferation of truly transnational credit portfolios.

These long-term structural changes in the composition of the global credit asset class arise due to the desire of issuers to minimize funding costs under different yield curve and yield spread, as well as the needs of both active and asset/liability bond managers to satisfy their risk and return objectives. Portfolio managers will adapt their portfolios either in anticipation of or in reaction to these structural changes across the global credit markets.

B. The Effect of Product Structure

Partially offsetting this proliferation of issuers since the mid-1990s, the global credit market has become structurally more homogeneous. Specifically, bullet and intermediate-maturity structures have come to dominate the credit market. A bullet maturity means that the issue is not callable, putable, or sinkable prior to its scheduled final maturity. The trend toward bullet securities does not pertain to the high-yield market, where callables remain the structure of choice. With the hope of credit-quality improvement, many high-yield issuers expect to refinance prior to maturity at lower rates.

There are three strategic portfolio implications for this structural evolution. First, the dominance of bullet structures translates into scarcity value for structures with embedded call and put features. That is, credit securities with embedded options have become rare and therefore demand a premium price. Typically, this premium (price) is not captured by option-valuation models. Yet, this "scarcity value" should be considered by managers in relative-value analysis of credit bonds.

Second, bonds with maturities beyond 20 years are a small share of outstanding credit debt. This shift reduced the effective duration of the credit asset class and cut aggregate sensitivity to interest-rate risk. For asset/liability managers with long time horizons, this shift of the maturity distribution suggests a rise in the value of long credit debt and helps to explain the warm reception afforded, initially at least, to most new offerings of issues with 100-year maturities in the early and mid-1990s.

Third, the use of credit derivatives has skyrocketed since the early 1990s. The rapid maturation of the credit derivative market will lead investors and issuers to develop new strategies to match desired exposures to credit sectors, issuers, and structures.

5 LIQUIDITY AND TRADING ANALYSIS

Short-term and long-term liquidity needs influence portfolio management decisions. Citing lower expected liquidity, some investors are reluctant to purchase certain types of issues such as small-sized issues (less than $1.0 billion), private placements, MTNs, and non-local corporate issuers. Other investors gladly exchange a potential liquidity disadvantage for incremental yield. For investment-grade issuers, these liquidity concerns often are exaggerated.

The liquidity of credit debt changes over time. Specifically, liquidity varies with the economic cycle, credit cycle, shape of the yield curve, supply, and the season. As in all markets, unknown shocks, like a surprise wave of defaults, can reduce credit debt liquidity as investors become unwilling to purchase new issues at any spread and dealers become reluctant to position secondary issues except at very wide spreads. In reality, these transitory bouts of illiquidity mask an underlying trend toward heightened liquidity across the global credit asset class. With a gentle push from regulators, the global credit asset class is well along in converting from its historic "over-the-counter" domain to a fully transparent, equity/US Treasury style marketplace. In the late 1990s, new technology led to creating ECNs (electronic communication networks), essentially electronic trading exchanges. In turn, credit bid/ask spreads generally have trended lower for very large, well-known corporate issues. This powerful twin combination of technological innovation and competition promises the rapid development of an even more liquid and efficient global credit market during the early 21st century.

SECONDARY TRADE RATIONALES

Capital market expectations constantly change. Recessions may arrive sooner rather than later. The yield curve may steepen rather than flatten. The auto and paper cycles may be moving down from their peaks. Higher oil and natural gas prices may benefit the credit quality of the energy sector. An industrial may have announced a large debt-financed acquisition, earning an immediate ratings rebuke from the rating agencies. A major bank may plan to repurchase 15% of its outstanding common stock (great for shareholders but leading to higher financial leverage for debtholders). In response to such daily information flows, portfolio managers amend their holdings. To understand trading flows and the real dynamics of the credit market, investors should consider the most common rationales of whether to trade and not to trade.

A. Popular Reasons for Trading

There are dozens of rationales to execute secondary trades when pursuing portfolio optimization. Several of the most popular are discussed below. The framework for assessing secondary trades is the total return framework.

1 Yield/Spread Pickup Trades

Yield/spread pickup trades represent the most common secondary transactions across all sectors of the global credit market. Historically, at least half of all secondary swaps reflect investor intentions to add additional yield within the duration and credit-quality constraints of a portfolio. If 5-year, Baa1/BBB General Motors paper trades at 150 bps, 10 bps more than 5-year, Baa1/BBB– Ford Motor, some investors will determine the rating differential irrelevant and purchase General Motors bond and sell the Ford Motor (an issue swap) for a spread gain of 10 bps per annum.

This "yield-first psychology" reflects the institutional yield need of long-term asset/liability managers. Despite the passage of more than three decades, this investor bias toward yield maximization also may be a methodological relic left over from the era prior to the introduction and market acceptance of total-return indices in the early 1970s. Yield measures have limitations as an indicator of potential performance. The total return framework is a superior framework for assessing potential performance for a trade.

2 Credit-Upside Trades

Credit-upside trades take place when the debt asset manager expects an upgrade in an issuer's credit quality that is not already reflected in the current market yield spread. In the illustration of the General Motors and Ford Motor trade described above, some investors may swap based on their view of potential credit-quality improvement for General Motors. Obviously, such trades rely on the credit analysis skills of the investment management team. Moreover, the manager must be able to identify a potential upgrade before the market, otherwise the spread for the upgrade candidate will already exhibit the benefits of a credit upgrade.

Credit-upside trades are particularly popular in the crossover sector—securities with ratings between Ba2/BB and Baa3/BBB—by two major rating agencies. In this case, the portfolio manager is expressing an expectation that an issue of the highest speculative grade rating (Ba1/BB+) has sufficiently positive credit fundamentals to be upgraded to investment grade (i.e., Baa3/BBB–). If this upgrade occurs, not only would the issue's spread narrow based on the credit improvement (with an accompanying increase in total return, all else equal), but the issue also would benefit from improved liquidity, as managers prohibited from buying high-yield bonds could then purchase that issue. Further, the manager would expect an improvement in the portfolio's overall risk profile.

3 Credit-Defense Trades

Credit-defense trades become more popular as geopolitical and economic uncertainty increase. Secular sector changes often generate uncertainties and induce defensive positioning by investors. In anticipating greater competition, in the mid-1990s some investors reduced their portfolio exposures to sectors like electric utilities and telecommunications. As some Asian currencies and equities swooned in mid-1997, many portfolio managers cut their allocation to the Asian debt market. Unfortunately because of yield-maximization needs and a general reluctance to realize losses by some institutions (i.e., insurers), many investors reacted more slowly to credit-defensive positioning. But after a record number of "fallen angels" in 2002, which included such major credit bellwether issuers as WorldCom, investors became more quick to jettison potential problem credits from their portfolios. Ironically once a credit is downgraded by the rating agencies, internal portfolio guidelines often dictate security liquidation immediately after the loss of single-A or investment-grade status. This is usually the worst possible time to sell a security and maximizes losses incurred by the portfolio.

4 New Issue Swaps

New issue swaps contribute to secondary turnover. Because of perceived superior liquidity, many portfolio managers prefer to rotate their portfolios gradually into more current and usually larger sized on-the-run issues. This disposition, reinforced by the usually superior market behavior of newer issues in the US Treasury market (i.e., the on-the-run issues), has become a self-fulfilling prophecy for many credit issues. In addition, some managers use new issue swaps to add exposure to a new issuer or a new structure.

5 Sector-Rotation Trades

Sector-rotation trades, within credit and among fixed-income asset classes, have become more popular since the early 1990s. In this strategy, the manager shifts the portfolio from a sector or industry that is expected to underperform to a sector or industry which is believed will outperform on a total return basis. With the likely development of enhanced liquidity and lower trading transaction costs across the global bond market in the early 21st century, sector-rotation trades should become more prevalent in the credit asset class.

Such intra-asset class trading already has played a major role in differentiating performance among credit portfolio managers. For example, as soon as the Fed launched its preemptive strike against inflation in February 1994, some investors correctly exchanged fixed-rate corporates for floating-rate corporates. In 1995, the specter of US economic weakness prompted some investors in high-yield corporates to rotate from consumer-cyclical sectors like autos and retailing into consumer non-cyclical sectors like food, beverage, and healthcare. Anticipating slower US economic growth in 1998 induced a defensive tilt by some portfolio managers away from other cyclical groups like paper and energy. The resurrection of Asian and European economic growth in 1999 stimulated increased portfolio interest in cyclicals, financial institutions, and energy debt. Credit portfolio managers could have avoided a great deal of portfolio performance disappointment in 2002 by underweighting utilities and many industrial sectors.

6 Curve-Adjustment Trades

Yield curve-adjustment trades, or simply, curve-adjustment trades are taken to reposition a portfolio's duration. For most credit investors, their portfolio duration is typically within a range from 20% below to 20% above the duration of the benchmark index. If credit investors could have predicted US, euro, and yen yield curve movements perfectly in 2002, then they would have increased their credit portfolio duration at the beginning of 2002 in anticipation of a decrease in interest rates. Although most fixed-income investors prefer to alter the duration of their aggregate portfolios in the more-liquid Treasury market, strategic portfolio duration tilts also can be implemented in the credit market.

This is also done with respect to anticipated changes in the credit term structure or credit curve. For example, if a portfolio manager believes credit spreads will tighten (either overall or in a particular sector), with rates in general remaining relatively stable, they might shift the portfolio's exposure to longer spread duration issues in the sector.

7 Structure Trades

Structure trades involve swaps into structures (e.g., callable structures, bullet structures, and putable structures) that are expected to have better performance given expected movements in volatility and the shape of the yield curve. Here are some examples of how different structures performed in certain periods in the 1990s.

- During the second quarter of 1995, the rapid descent of the US yield curve contributed to underperformance of high-coupon callable structures because of their negative convexity property.
- When the yield curve stabilized during the third quarter of 1995, investors were more willing to purchase high-quality callable bonds versus high-quality bullet structures to earn an extra 35 bps of spread.
- The sharp downward rotation of the US yield curve during the second half of 1997 contributed to poor relative performance by putable structures. The yield investors had sacrificed for protection against higher interest rates instead constrained total return as rates fell.
- The plunge in US interest rates and escalation of yield-curve volatility during the second half of 1998 again restrained the performance of callable structures compared to bullet structures.
- The upward rebound in US interest rates and the fall in interest-rate volatility during 1999 contributed to the relative outperformance of callable structures versus bullet structures.

These results follow from the price/yield properties of the different structures. Structural analysis is also discussed in Section 8 of this reading.

8 Cash Flow Reinvestment

Cash flow reinvestment forces investors into the secondary market on a regular basis. During 2003, the sum of all coupon, maturity, and partial redemptions (via tenders, sinking funds, and other issuer prepayments) equaled approximately 100% of all new gross issuance across the dollar bond market. Before the allocation of any net new investment in the bond market, investors had sufficient cash flow reinvestment to absorb nearly all new bond supply. Some portfolio cash inflows occur during interludes in the primary market or the composition of recent primary supply may not be compatible with portfolio objectives. In these periods, credit portfolio managers must shop the secondary market for investment opportunities to remain fully invested or temporarily replicate the corporate index by using financial futures. Portfolio managers who incorporate analysis of cash flow reinvestment into their valuation of the credit market can position their portfolios to take advantage of this cash flow reinvestment effect on spreads.

B. Trading Constraints

Portfolio managers also should review their main rationales for not trading. Some of the best investment decisions are not to trade. Conversely, some of the worst investment decisions emanate from stale views based on dated and anachronistic constraints (e.g., avoid investing in bonds rated below Aa/AA). The best portfolio managers retain very open minds, constantly self-critiquing both their successful and unsuccessful methodologies.

1 Portfolio Constraints

Collectively, portfolio constraints are the single biggest contributor to the persistence of market inefficiency across the global credit market. Here are some examples:

- Because many asset managers are limited to holding securities with investment-grade ratings, they are forced to sell immediately the debt of issuers who are downgraded to speculative-gradings (Ba1/BB+ and below). In turn, this selling at the time of downgrade provides an opportunity for investors with more flexible constraints to buy such newly downgraded securities at a temporary discount (provided, of course, that the issuer's credit-worthiness stabilizes after downgrade).
- Some US state employee pension funds cannot purchase credit securities with ratings below A3/A– due to administrative and legislative guidelines.
- Some US pension funds also have limitations on their ownership of MTNs and non-US corporate issues.
- Regulators have limited US insurance companies' investment in high-yield corporates.
- Many European investors are restricted to issues rated at least single-A and sometimes Aa3/AA– and above, created originally in annual-pay Eurobond form.
- Many investors are confined to their local currency market—yen, sterling, euro, US dollar. Often, the same issuer, like Ford, will trade at different spreads across different geographic markets.
- Globally, many commercial banks must operate exclusively in the floating-rate realm: all fixed-rate securities, unless converted into floating-rate cash flows via an interest rate swap, are prohibited.

2 "Story" Disagreement

"Story" disagreement can work to the advantage or disadvantage of a portfolio manager. Traders, salespersons, sell-side analysts and strategists, and buy-side credit researchers have dozens of potential trade rationales that supposedly will benefit portfolio performance. The proponents of a secondary trade may make a persuasive argument, but the portfolio manager may be unwilling to accept the "shortfall risk"[3] if the investment recommendation does not provide its expected return. For example in early 1998, analysts and investors alike were divided equally on short-term prospects for better valuations of Asian sovereign debt. After a very disappointing 1997 for

---

[3] Shortfall risk is the probability that the outcome will have a value less than the target return.

Asian debt performance, Asia enthusiasts had little chance to persuade pessimists to buy Asian debt at the beginning of 1998. Technically, such lack of consensus in the credit market signals an investment with great outperformance potential. Indeed, most Asian debt issues recorded exceptional outperformance over the full course of 1998 and 1999. After a difficult 2002, the same "rebound effect" was observed in electric utilities during 2003. Of course, "story" disagreement can also work in the other direction. For example, Enron was long viewed as a very solid credit before its sudden bankruptcy in late 2001. An asset manager wedded to this long-term view might have been reluctant to act on the emergence of less favorable information about Enron in the summer of 2001.

3 Buy-and-Hold

Although many long-term asset/liability managers claim to have become more total return focused in the 1990s, accounting constraints (cannot sell positions at a loss compared with book cost or take too extravagant a gain compared with book cost) often limit the ability of these investors to trade. Effectively, these investors (mainly insurers) remain traditional "buy-and-hold" investors. Some active bond managers have converged to quasi-"buy-and-hold" investment programs at the behest of consultants to curb portfolio turnover. In the aftermath of the "Asian Contagion" in 1997–1998, this disposition toward lower trading turnover was reinforced by the temporary reduction in market liquidity provided by more wary bond dealers. As shown in 2000–2002, however, a buy-and-hold strategy can gravely damage the performance of a credit portfolio. At the first signs of credit trouble for an issuer, many credit portfolios would have improved returns by reducing their exposure to a deteriorating credit.

4 Seasonality

Secondary trading slows at month ends, more so at quarter ends, and the most at the conclusion of calendar years. Dealers often prefer to reduce their balance sheets at fiscal year-end (November 30, December 31, or March 31 [Japan]). Also, portfolio managers take time to mark their portfolios, prepare reports for their clients, and chart strategy for the next investment period. During these intervals, even the most compelling secondary offerings can languish.

SPREAD ANALYSIS

By custom, some segments of the high-yield and emerging (EMG) debt markets still prefer to measure value by bond price or bond yield rather than spread. But for the rest of the global credit market, nominal spread (the yield difference between corporate and government bonds of similar maturities) has been the basic unit of both price and relative-value analysis for more than two centuries.

A. Alternative Spread Measures

Many US practitioners prefer to value investment-grade credit securities in terms of option-adjusted spreads (OAS) so they can be more easily compared to the volatility ("vol") sectors (mortgage-backed securities and US agencies).[4] But given the rapid reduction of credit structures with embedded options since 1990 (see structural

---

[4] These sectors are referred to as "vol" sectors because the value of the securities depends on expected interest rate volatility. These "vol" securities have embedded call options and the value of the options, and hence the value of the securities, depends on expected interest rate volatility.

discussion above), the use of OAS in primary and secondary pricing has diminished within the investment-grade credit asset class. Moreover, the standard one-factor binomial models[5] do not account for credit spread volatility. Given the exclusion of default risk in OAS option-valuation models, OAS valuation has seen only limited extension into the higher-risk markets of the quasi-equity, high-yield corporate, and EMG-debt asset classes.

Starting in Europe during the early 1990s and gaining momentum during the late 1990s, interest rate swap spreads have emerged as the common denominator to measure relative value across fixed- and floating-rate note credit structures. The US investment-grade and high-yield markets eventually may switch to swap spreads to be consistent with Europe and Asia.

Other US credit spread calculations have been proposed, most notably using the US agency benchmark curve. These proposals emanate from the assumption of a persistent US budgetary surplus and significant liquidation of outstanding US Treasury securities during the first decade of the 21st century. As again demonstrated by 2002, history teaches that these budget assumptions may unfortunately prove to be faulty. Although some practitioners may choose to derive credit-agency spreads for analytical purposes, this practice will be unlikely to become standard market convention.

Credit-default swap spreads have emerged as the latest valuation tool during the great stresses in the credit markets of 2000–2002. Most likely, credit-default swap spreads will be used as a companion valuation reference to nominal spreads, OAS, and swap spreads. The market, therefore, has an ability to price any credit instrument using multiple spread references. These include nominal spread, static or zero-volatility spread, OAS, credit-swap spreads (or simply swap spreads), and credit default spreads. The spread measures used the Treasury yield curve or Treasury spot rate curve as the benchmark. Given the potential that swap spreads will become the new benchmark, these same measures can be performed relative to swaps rather than relative to US Treasuries. However, using swap rates as a benchmark has been delayed by the decoupling of traditional credit spreads (credit yield minus government yield) from swap spreads over 2000–2002. Effectively, credit risk during a global recession and its aftermath superseded the countervailing influence of strong technical factors like lower and steeper yield curves which affected the interest rate swap market differently.

B. Closer Look at Swap Spreads

Swap spreads became a popular valuation yardstick for credit debt in Europe during the 1990s. This practice was enhanced by the unique nature of the European credit asset class. Unlike its American counterpart, the European credit market has been consistently homogeneous. Most issuance was of high quality (rated Aa3/AA– and above) and intermediate maturity (10 years and less). Consequently, swap spreads are a good proxy for credit spreads in such a uniform market. Most issuers were financial institutions, natural swappers between fixed-rate and floating-rate obligations. And European credit investors, often residing in financial institutions like commercial banks, have been much more willing to use the swap methodology to capture value discrepancies between the fixed- and floating-rate markets.

Structurally, the Asian credit market more closely resembles the European than the US credit market. As a result, the use of swap spreads as a valuation benchmark also became common in Asia.

---

[5] The model is referred to as a one-factor model because only the short-term rate is the factor used to construct the tree.

The investment-grade segment of the US credit market may well be headed toward an embrace of swap spreads. The US MBS, CMBS, agency, and ABS sectors (accounting for about 55% of the US fixed-income market) made the transition to swap spreads as a valuation benchmark during the second half of the 1990s. Classical nominal credit spreads derived directly from the US Treasury yield curve were distorted by the special effects of US fiscal surpluses and buybacks of US Treasury securities in 2000 and 2001. Accordingly, many market practitioners envision a convergence to a single global spread standard derived from swap spreads.

Here is an illustration of how a bond manager can use the interest rate swap spread framework. Suppose that a hypothetical Ford Motor Credit 7 1/2's of 2008 traded at a bid price (i.e., the price at which a dealer is willing to buy the issue) of 113 bps over the 5-year US Treasury yield of 6.43%. This equates to a yield-to-maturity of 7.56% (6.43% + 113 bps). On that date, 5-year swap spreads were 83 bps (to the 5-year US Treasury). Recall that swaps are quoted where the fixed-rate payer pays the yield on a Treasury with a maturity equal to the initial term of the swap plus the swap spread. The fixed-rate payer receives Libor flat—that is, no increment over Libor. So, if the bond manager invests in the Ford Motor Credit issue and simultaneously enters into this 5-year swap, the following would result:

	Receive from Ford Motor Credit (6.43% + 113 bps)	7.56%
−	Pay on swap (6.43% + 83 bps)	7.26%
+	Receive from swap	Libor
	Net	Libor + 30 bps

Thus, a bond manager could exchange this Ford Motor Credit bond's fixed coupon flow for Libor + 30 bps. On the trade date, Libor was 6.24%, so that the asset swapper would earn 6.54% (= 6.24% + 30 bps) until the first reset date of the swap. A total return manager would want to take advantage of this swap by paying fixed and receiving floating if he expects interest rates to increase in the future.

The swaps framework allows managers (as well as issuers) to more easily compare securities across fixed-rate and floating-rate markets. The extension of the swap spread framework may be less relevant for speculative-grade securities, where default risk becomes more important. In contrast to professional money managers, individual investors are not comfortable using bond valuation couched in terms of swap spreads. The traditional nominal spread framework is well understood by individual investors, has the advantages of long-term market convention, and works well across the entire credit-quality spectrum from Aaa's to B's. However, this nominal spread framework does not work very well for investors and issuers when comparing the relative attractiveness between the fixed-rate and floating-rate markets.

C. Spread Tools

Investors should also understand how best to evaluate spread levels in their decision-making. Spread valuation includes mean-reversion analysis, quality-spread analysis, and percent yield spread analysis.

1 *Mean-Reversion Analysis*

The most common technique for analyzing spreads among individual securities and across industry sectors is mean-reversion analysis. The "mean" is the average value of some variable over a defined interval (usually one economic cycle for the credit market). The term "mean-reversion" refers to the tendency for some variable's value to revert (i.e., move towards) its average value. Mean-reversion analysis is a form of relative-value analysis based on the assumption that the spread between two sectors or two issuers will revert back to its historical average. This would lead investors to buy a sector or issuer identified as "cheap" because historically the spread has been tighter and will eventually revert back to that tighter spread. Also, this would lead investors to sell a sector or issuer identified as "rich" because the spread has been wider and is expected to widen in the future.

Mean-reversion analysis involves the use of statistical analysis to assess whether the current deviation from the mean spread is significant. For example, suppose the mean spread for an issuer is 80 basis points over the past six months and the standard deviation is 12 basis points. Suppose that the current spread of the issuer is 98 basis points. The spread is 18 basis points over the mean spread or equivalently 1.5 standard deviations above the mean spread. The manager can use that information to determine whether or not the spread deviation is sufficient to purchase the issue. The same type of analysis can be used to rank a group of issuers in a sector.

Mean-reversion analysis can be instructive as well as misleading. The mean is highly dependent on the interval selected. There is no market consensus on the appropriate interval and "persistence" frequents the credit market, meaning cheap securities, mainly a function of credit uncertainty, often tend to become cheaper. Rich securities, usually high-quality issues, tend to remain rich.

2 Quality-Spread Analysis

Quality-spread analysis examines the spread differentials between low- and high-quality credits. For example, portfolio managers would be well advised to consider the "credit upside trade" discussed in Section 6 when quality-spreads collapse to cyclical troughs. The incremental yield advantage of lower-quality products may not compensate investors for lower-quality spread expansion under deteriorating economic conditions. Alternatively, credit portfolio managers have long profited from overweighting lower-quality debt at the outset of an upward turn in the economic cycle.

3 Percent Yield Spread Analysis

Dating from the early 20th century, percent yield spread analysis (the ratio of credit yields to government yields for similar duration securities) is another popular technical tool used by some investors. This methodology has serious drawbacks that undermine its usefulness. Percent yield spread is more a derivative than an explanatory or predictive variable. The usual expansion of credit percent yield spreads during low-rate periods like 1997, 1998, and 2002 overstates the risk as well as the comparative attractiveness of credit debt. And the typical contraction of credit percent yield spreads during upward shifts of the benchmark yield curve does not necessarily signal an imminent bout of underperformance for the credit asset class. Effectively, the absolute level of the underlying benchmark yield is merely a single factor among many factors (demand, supply, profitability, defaults, etc.) that determine the relative value of the credit asset class. These other factors can offset or reinforce any insights derived from percent yield spread analysis.

8 STRUCTURAL ANALYSIS

As explained earlier in this reading, there are bullet, callable, putable, and sinking fund structures. Structural analysis is simply analyzing the performance of the different structures discussed throughout this reading. While evaluating bond structures was extremely important in the 1980s, it became less influential in credit bond market since the mid-1990s for several reasons. First, the European credit bond market almost exclusively features intermediate bullets. Second, as can be seen in Exhibit 5, the US credit and the global bond markets have moved to embrace this structurally homogeneous European bullet standard. Plenty of structural diversity still resides within the US high yield and EMG debt markets, but portfolio decisions in these speculative-grade sectors understandably hinge more on pure credit differentiation than the structural diversity of the issue-choice set.

Exhibit 5   Changing Composition of the US Investment-Grade Credit Markets

	1990 (%)	2003 (%)
Bullets	24	94
Callables	72	3
Sinking Funds	32	1
Putables	5	2
Zeros	4	N/A

Note: Figures in table do not add to 100% given that some structures may have contained multiple options (e.g., a callable corporate bond may also have a sinking fund and put provision).
Source: Lehman Brothers US Investment-Grade Credit Index.

Still, structural analysis can enhance risk-adjusted returns of credit portfolios. Leaving credit aside, issue structure analysis and structural allocation decisions usually hinge on yield curve and volatility forecasts as well as interpretation of option-valuation model outputs (see the discussion below). This is also a key input in making relative value decisions among structured credit issues, mortgage-backed securities, and asset-backed securities. In the short run and assuming no change in the perceived credit-worthiness of the issuer, yield curve and volatility movements will largely influence structural performance. Investors should also take into account long-run market dynamics that affect the composition of the market and, in turn, credit index benchmarks.

Specifically, callable structures have become rarer in the US investment-grade credit bond market with the exception of the 2000 inversion. This is due to an almost continuously positively-sloped US term structure since 1990 and the yield curve's intermittent declines to approximately multi-decade lows in 1993, 1997, 1998, and 2002. As a result, the composition of the public US corporate bond market converged toward the intermediate-bullet Eurobond and euro-denominated bond market. To see this, we need only look at the structure composition of Lehman's US Investment-Grade Credit Bond Index. Bullets increased from 24% of this index at the start of 1990 to 94% (principal value basis) by 2003. Over this interval, callables declined at a remarkable rate from 72% to just a 3% index share. Sinking-fund structures, once the structural mainstay of natural-gas pipelines and many industrial sectors, are on the "structural endangered species list" with a drop from 32% of the public bond market in 1990 to only 1% in 2003. Despite several brief flurries of origination in the mid-1990s and the late-1990s introduction of callable/putable structures, putable structure market share fell from 5% in 1990 to 2% by 2003. Pure corporate zeros are in danger of extinction with a fall from 4% market share in 1990 to negligible by 2003.

A. Bullets

Here is a review of how different types of investors are using bullet structures with different maturities.

Front-end bullets (i.e., bullet structures with 1- to 5-year maturities) have great appeal for investors who pursue a "barbell strategy" in which both the short and long end of the barbell are US Treasury securities. There are "barbellers" who use credit securities at the front or short-end of the curve and Treasuries at the long-end of the yield curve. There are non-US institutions who convert short bullets into floating-rate products by using interest rate swaps. The transactions are referred to as "asset swaps," and the investors who employ this transaction are referred to as "asset swappers."

Intermediate credit bullets (5- to 12-year maturities), especially the 10-year maturity sector, have become the most popular segment of the US and European investment-grade and high-yield credit markets. Fifteen-year maturities, benchmarked off the 10-year bellwether Treasury, are comparatively rare and have been favored by banks that occasionally use them for certain types of swaps. Because new 15-year structures take five years to descend along a positively sloped yield curve to their underlying 10-year bellwether, 15-year maturities hold less appeal for many investors in search of return through price appreciation emanating from benchmark rolldown. In contrast, rare 20-year structures have been favored by many investors. Spreads for these structures are benched off the 30-year Treasury. With a positively sloped yield curve, the 20-year structure provides higher yield than a 10-year or 15-year security and less vulnerability (lower duration) than a 30-year security.

The 30-year maturity is the most popular form of long-dated security in the global credit market. In 1992, 1993, late 1995, and 1997, there was a minor rush to issue 50-year (half-centuries) and 100-year (centuries) securities in the US credit bond market. These longer-dated securities provide investors with extra positive convexity for only a modest increase in effective (or modified-adjusted) duration.[6] In the wake of the "Asian Contagion" and especially the "Great Spread-Sector Crash" of August 1998, the cyclical increases in risk aversion and liquidity premiums greatly reduced both issuer and investor interest in these ultra-long maturities.

B. Callables

Typically after a 5-year or 10-year wait (longer for some rare issues), credit structures are callable at the option of the issuer at any time. Call prices usually are set at a premium above par (par + the initial coupon) and decline linearly on an annual basis to par by 5–10 years prior to final scheduled maturity. The ability to refinance debt in a potentially lower-interest rate environment is extremely valuable to issuers. Conversely, the risk of earlier-than-expected retirement of an above-current market coupon is bothersome to investors.

In issuing callables, issuers pay investors an annual spread premium (about 20 bps to 40 bps for high-quality issuers) for being long (from an issuer's perspective) the call option. Like all security valuations, this call premium varies through time with capital market conditions. Given the higher chance of exercise, this call option becomes much more expensive during low rate and high volatility periods. Since 1990, this call premium has ranged from approximately 15 bps to 50 bps for investment-grade issuers. Callables significantly underperform bullets when interest rates decline because of their negative convexity. When the bond market rallies, callable structures do not fully participate given the upper boundary imposed by call prices. Conversely, callable structures outperform bullets in bear bond markets as the probability of early call diminishes.

---

6 The longer the maturity, the greater the convexity.

Structural Analysis

C. Sinking Funds

A sinking fund structure allows an issuer to execute a series of partial calls (annually or semiannually) prior to maturity. Issuers also usually have an option to retire an additional portion of the issue on the sinking fund date, typically ranging from 1 to 2 times the mandatory sinking fund obligation. Historically, especially during the early 1980s, total return investors favored the collection of sinking fund structures at sub-par prices. These discounted sinking funds retained price upside during interest rate rallies (provided the indicated bond price remained below par), and, given the issuers' requirement to retire at least annually some portion of the issue at par, the price of these sinking fund structures did not fall as much compared to callables and bullets when interest rates rose. It should be noted that astute issuers with strong liability management skills can sometimes satisfy such annual sinking fund obligations in whole or in part through prior open market purchases at prices below par. Nonetheless, this annual sinking fund purchase obligation by issuers does limit bond price depreciation during periods of rising rates.

D. Putables

Conventional put structures are simpler than callables. Yet in trading circles, put bond valuations often are the subject of debate. American-option callables grant issuers the right to call an issue at any time at the designated call price after expiration of the non-callable or non-redemption period. Put bonds typically provide investors with a one-time, one-date put option (European option) to demand full repayment at par. Less frequently, put bonds include a second or third put option date. A very limited number of put issues afford investors the privilege to put such structures back to the issuers at par in the case of rating downgrades (typically to below investment-grade status).

Thanks to falling interest rates, issuers shied away from new put structures as the 1990s progressed. Rather than incur the risk of refunding the put bond in 5 or 10 years at a higher cost, many issuers would prefer to pay an extra 10 bps to 20 bps in order to issue a longer-term liability.

Put structures provide investors with a partial defense against sharp increases in interest rates. Assuming that the issuer still has the capability to meet its sudden obligation, put structures triggered by a credit event enable investors to escape from a deteriorating credit. Perhaps because of its comparative scarcity, the performance and valuation of put structures have been a challenge for many portfolio managers. Unlike callable structures, put prices have not conformed to expectations formed in a general volatility-valuation framework. Specifically, the implied yield volatility of an option can be computed from the option's price and a valuation model. In the case of a putable bond, the implied volatility can be obtained using a valuation model such as the binomial model. The implied volatility should be the same for both puts and calls, all factors constant. Yet, for putable structures, implied volatility has ranged between 4%–9% since 1990, well below the 10%–20% volatility range associated with callable structures for the same time period. This divergence in implied volatility between callables (high) and putables (low) suggests that asset managers, often driven by a desire to boost portfolio yield, underpay issuers for the right to put a debt security back to the issuer under specified circumstances. In other words, the typical put bond should trade at a lower yield in the market than is commonly the case.

Unless put origination increases sharply, allowing for greater liquidity and the creation of more standardized trading conventions for this rarer structural issue, this asymmetry in implied volatility between putable and callable structures will persist. Meanwhile, this structure should be favored as an outperformance vehicle only by those investors with a decidedly bearish outlook for interest rates.

9 CREDIT CURVE ANALYSIS

The rapid growth of credit derivatives since the mid-1990s has inspired a groundswell of academic and practitioner interest in the development of more rigorous techniques to analyze the term structure (1–100 years) and credit structure (Aaa/AAA through B2/B's) of credit spread curves (higher risk higher-yield securities trade on a price rather than a spread basis).

Credit curves, both term structure and credit structure, are almost always positively sloped. In an effort to moderate portfolio risk, many portfolio managers take credit risk in short and intermediate maturities and to substitute less-risky government securities in long-duration portfolio buckets. This strategy is called a credit barbell strategy. Accordingly, the application of this strategy diminishes demand for longer-dated credit risk debt instruments by many total return, mutual fund, and bank portfolio bond managers. Fortunately for credit issuers who desire to issue long maturities, insurers and pension plan sponsors often meet long-term liability needs through the purchase of credit debt with maturities that range beyond 20 years.

Default risk increases non-linearly as credit-worthiness declines. The absolute risk of issuer default in any one year remains quite low through the investment-grade rating categories (Aaa/AAA to Baa3/BBB–). But investors constrained to high-quality investments often treat downgrades like quasi-defaults. In some cases like a downgrade from single-A to the Baa/BBB category, investors may be forced to sell securities under rigid portfolio guidelines. In turn, investors justifiably demand a spread premium for the increased likelihood of potential credit difficulty as rating quality descends through the investment-grade categories.

Credit spreads increase sharply in the high-yield rating categories (Ba1/BB+ through D). Default, especially for weak single-Bs and CCCs, becomes a major possibility. The credit market naturally assigns higher and higher risk premia (spreads) as credit and rating risk escalate. Exhibit 6 shows the credit curve for two credit sectors (Baa and single-A industrials) and also illustrates a higher spread is required as maturity lengthens.

Exhibit 6 Illustration of Two Typical US Investment-Grade Credit Curves

Years to maturity	Baa Industrial	Single-A Industrial
2-Year	110	75
5-Year	125	98
10-Year	165	143
30-Year	225	190

Spread over on-the-run US Treasuries (bps)

Source: Lehman Brothers US Investment-Grade Credit Index, based on average corporate curves 1990–2003.

In particular, the investment-grade credit market has a fascination with the slope of issuer credit curves between 10-year and 30-year maturities. Like the underlying Treasury benchmark curve, credit spread curves change shape over the course of economic cycles. Typically, spread curves steepen when the bond market becomes more wary of interest rate and general credit risk. Spread curves also have displayed a minor propensity to steepen when the underlying benchmark curve flattens or inverts. This loose spread curve/yield curve linkage reflects the diminished appetite for investors to assume both curve and credit risk at the long end of the yield curve when higher total yields may be available in short and intermediate credit products.

CREDIT ANALYSIS 10

In the continuous quest to seek credit upgrades and contraction in issuer/issue spread resulting from possible upgrades and, more importantly, to avoid credit downgrades resulting in an increase in issuer/issue spread, superior credit analysis has been and will remain the most important determinant of credit bond portfolio relative performance. Credit screening tools tied to equity valuations, relative spread movements, and the internet (information available tracking all related news on portfolio holdings) can provide helpful supplements to classic credit research and rating agency opinions. But self-characterized credit models, relying exclusively on variables like interest-rate volatility and binomial processes imported from option-valuation techniques, are not especially helpful in ranking the expected credit performance of individual credits like IBM, British Gas, Texas Utilities, Pohang Iron & Steel, Sumitomo, and Brazil.

Credit analysis is both non-glamorous and arduous for many top-down portfolio managers and strategists, who focus primarily on macro variables. Genuine credit analysis encompasses actually studying issuers' financial statements and accounting techniques, interviewing issuers' managements, evaluating industry issues, reading indentures and charters, and developing an awareness of (not necessarily concurrence with) the views of the rating agencies about various industries and issuers.

Unfortunately, the advantages of such analytical rigor may clash with the rapid expansion of the universe of issuers of credit bonds. There are approximately 5,000 different credit issuers scattered across the global bond market. With continued privatization of state enterprises, new entrants to the high-yield market, and expected long-term growth of the emerging-debt markets, the global roster of issuers could swell to 7,500 by 2010. The sorting of this expanding roster of global credit issues into outperformers, market performers, and underperformers demands establishing and maintaining a formidable credit-valuation function by asset managers.

ASSET ALLOCATION/SECTOR ROTATION 11

Sector rotation strategies have long played a key role in equity portfolio management. In the credit bond market, "macro" sector rotations among industrials, utilities, financial institutions, sovereigns, and supranationals also have a long history. During the last quarter of the 20th century, there were major variations in investor sentiment toward these major credit sectors. Utilities endured market wariness about heavy supply and nuclear exposure in the early-to-mid 1980s. US and European financial institutions coped with investor concern about asset quality in the late 1980s and early 1990s. Similar investor skittishness affected demand for Asian financial institution debt in the late 1990s. Industrials embodied severe "event risk" in the mid-to-late

1980s, recession vulnerability during 1990–1992, a return of event risk in the late 1990s amid a general boom in corporate mergers and acquisitions, and a devastating series of accounting and corporate governance blows during 2001–2002. Sovereigns were exposed to periodic market reservations about the implications of independence for Quebec, political risk for various countries (i.e., Russia), the effects of the "Asian Contagion" during 1997–1998, and outright defaults like Argentina (2001).

In contrast, "micro" sector rotation strategies have a briefer history in the credit market. A detailed risk/return breakdown (i.e., average return and standard deviation) of the main credit sub-sectors (i.e., banks, brokerage, energy, electrics, media, railroads, sovereigns, supranationals, technology) was not available from credit index providers until 1993 in the United States and until 1999 in Europe. Beginning in the mid-1990s, these "micro" sector rotation strategies in the credit asset class have become much more influential as portfolio managers gain a greater understanding of the relationships among intra-credit sectors from these statistics.

Exhibit 7 illustrates the main factors bearing on sector rotation and issuer selection strategies. For example, an actual or perceived change in rating agency philosophy toward a sector and a revision in profitability expectations for a particular industry represent just two of many factors that can influence relative sectoral performance.

Exhibit 7   Some Outperformance Methodologies

- Economic Expectations
  - GDP
  - Interest Rates
  - Exchange Rates
- Credit-Quality Fundamentals
  - Earnings/Cash Flow Growth
  - Financial Leverage
  - Rating Agency Philosophy
- Technicals
  - Market Risk Premiums (spreads)
  - Origination Expectations
  - Dealer Positioning
  - Investor Demand
- Structural Factors
  - Issuer Industries
  - Asset Management Industry
  - Investment Banking Industry
  - Academic Developments

→ Sector Rotation
→ Issuer Selection

- Portfolio Characteristics
  - Liquidity
  - Availability
  - Duration
  - Convexity
  - Senior vs. Junior Obligations

→ Issue and Structural Selection

- Seasonality: Quarter Ends, "First" and "Fourth Quarter Effects"
- Treasury Auction Effects
- Political Cycles
- Futures
- Credit Derivatives
- Geographic Extensions
- Credit-Quality Constraint Relaxation
- Asset Swaps
- Credit Barbells
- Current Coupon Rotations

→ Portfolio Enhancements

Common tactics to hopefully enhance credit portfolio performance are also highlighted in Exhibit 7. In particular, seasonality deserves comment. The annual rotation toward risk aversion in the bond market during the second half of most years contributes to a "fourth-quarter effect"—that is, there is underperformance of lower-rated credits, B's in high-yield and Baa's in investment-grade, compared to higher-rated credits. A fresh spurt of market optimism greets nearly every New Year. Lower-rated credit outperforms higher-quality credit—this is referred to as the "first-quarter effect." This pattern suggests a very simple and popular portfolio strategy: underweight low-quality credits and possibly even credit products altogether until the mid-third quarter of each year and then move to overweight lower-quality credits and all credit product in the fourth quarter of each year.

SUMMARY

- Superior credit analysis has been and will remain the most important determinant of the relative performance of credit bond portfolios, allowing managers to identify potential credit upgrades and to avoid potential downgrades.
- The "corporate asset class" includes more than pure corporate entities; this segment of the global bond market is more properly called the "credit asset class," including sovereigns, supranationals, agencies of local government authorities, nonagency mortgage-backed securities, commercial mortgage-backed securities, and asset-backed securities.
- Relative value refers to the ranking of fixed-income investments by sectors, structures, issuers, and issues in terms of their expected performance during some future interval.
- Relative-value analysis refers to the methodologies used to generate expected return rankings.
- Within the global credit market, classic relative-value analysis combines top-down and bottom-up approaches, blending the macro input of chief investment officers, strategists, economists, and portfolio managers with the micro input of credit analysts, quantitative analysts, and portfolio managers.
- The objective of relative value analysis is to identify the sectors with the most potential upside, populate these favored sectors with the best representative issuers, and select the structures of the designated issuers at the yield curve points that match the investor's outlook for the benchmark yield curve.
- The main methodologies for credit relative-value maximization are total return analysis, primary market analysis, liquidity and trading analysis, secondary trading rationales and constraints analysis, spread analysis, structure analysis, credit curve analysis, credit analysis, and asset allocation/sector analysis.
- Credit relative-value analysis starts with a detailed decomposition of past returns and a projection of expected returns.
- Primary market analysis refers to analyzing the supply and demand for new issues.
- The global credit market has become structurally more homogeneous, with intermediate maturity (5 to 10 years) bullet structure (noncallable issues) coming to dominate the investment-grade market.
- The trend toward bullet securities does not pertain to the high-yield market, where callable structures dominate the market.
- Short-term and long-term liquidity influence portfolio management decisions.
- Credit market liquidity changes over time, varying with the economic cycle, credit cycle, shape of the yield curve, supply, and the season.
- Despite the limitations of yield measures, yield/spread pickup trades account for the most common secondary market trades across all sectors of the global credit market.
- Credit-upside trades seek to capitalize on expectations of issues that will be upgraded in credit quality with such trades particularly popular in the crossover sector (securities with ratings between Ba2/BB and Baa3/BBB− by a major rating agency).
- Credit-defense trades involve trading up in credit quality as economic or geopolitical uncertainty increases.

- Sector-rotation trades involve altering allocations among sectors based on relative-value analysis; such strategies can be used within the credit bond market (intra-asset class sector rotation) and among fixed-income asset classes.
- Sector-rotation trades are not as popular in the bond market as in the equity market because of less liquidity and higher costs of trading; however, with the expected development of enhanced liquidity and lower trading transaction costs in the future, sector-rotation trades should become more prevalent in the credit asset class.
- Trades undertaken to reposition a portfolio's duration are called yield curve-adjustment trades, or simply, curve-adjustment trades.
- Structure trades involve swaps into structures (e.g., callable structures, bullet structures, and put structures) that are expected to have better performance given anticipated movements in volatility and the shape of the yield curve.
- Portfolio managers should review their main rationales for not trading.
- Portfolio constraints are the single biggest contributor to the persistence of market inefficiency across the global credit bond market.
- Many US practitioners prefer to cast the valuations of investment-grade credit securities in terms of option-adjusted spreads (OAS), but given the rapid reduction of credit structures with embedded options since 1990, the use of OAS in primary and secondary pricing has diminished within the investment-grade credit asset class.
- Swap spreads have become a popular valuation yardstick for European credit, Asian credit, and US MBS, CMBS, agency, and ABS sectors.
- In the global credit bond market, nominal spread (the yield difference between credit and government bonds of similar maturities) has been the basic unit of relative-value analysis.
- Mean-reversion analysis is the most common technique for analyzing spreads among individual securities and across industry sectors.
- Mean-reversion analysis can be misleading because the mean or average value is highly dependent on the time period analyzed.
- In quality-spread analysis, a manager examines the spread differentials between low- and high-quality credits.
- Structural analysis involves analyzing different structures' performance on a relative-value basis.
- Put structures provide investors with a partial defense against sharp increases in interest rates: this structure should be favored as an outperformance vehicle only by those investors with a decidedly bearish outlook for interest rates.
- Credit curves, both term structure and credit structure, are almost always positively sloped.
- In credit barbell strategies, many portfolio managers choose to take credit risk in short and intermediate maturities and to substitute less risky government securities in long-duration portfolio buckets.
- Like the underlying Treasury benchmark curve, credit spread curves change shape over the course of economic cycles; typically, spread curves steepen when the bond market becomes more wary of interest rate and general credit risk.

PRACTICE PROBLEMS

1. What is meant by relative value in the credit market?

2. **A** What is the dominant type of structure in the investment-grade credit market?

   B What are the strategic portfolio implications of the dominant structure answer in Part (A)?

   C What is the dominant structure in the high-yield corporate bond market and why is it not the same structure as discussed in Part (A)?

3. The following quote is from Lev Dynkin, Peter Ferket, Jay Hyman, Erik van Leeuwen, and Wei Wu, "Value of Security Selection versus Asset Allocation in Credit Markets," Fixed Income Research, Lehman Brothers, March 1999, p. 3:

   > Most fixed income investors in the United States have historically remained in a single-currency world. Their efforts to outperform their benchmarks have focused on yield curve placement, sector and quality allocations, and security selection. The style of market participants is expressed in the amount of risk assumed along each of these dimensions (as measured by the deviation from their benchmarks), and their research efforts are directed accordingly.

   A What is meant by "yield curve placement, sector and quality allocations, and security selection"?

   B What is meant by the statement: "The style of market participants is expressed in the amount of risk assumed along each of these dimensions (as measured by the deviation from their benchmarks)"?

4. The following two passages are from Peter J. Carril, "Relative Value Concepts within the Eurobond Market," Chapter 29 in Frank J. Fabozzi (ed.), *The Handbook of Corporate Debt Instruments* (New Hope, PA: Frank J. Fabozzi Associates, 1998), p. 552.

   A In discussing Eurobond issuers, Carril wrote: "Many first time issuers produce tighter spreads than one may anticipate because of their so called scarcity value." What is meant by scarcity value?

   B In describing putable bonds Carril wrote: "Much analytical work has been devoted to the valuation of the put's option value, especially in the more mature US investment-grade market." However, he states that in the high-yield market the overriding concern for a putable issue is one of credit concern. Specifically, he wrote: "traditional analysis used to quantify the option value which the issuer has granted the investor is overridden by the investor's specific view of the credit-worthiness of the issuer at the time of first put." Explain why.

5. In describing the approaches to investing in emerging markets credits, Christopher Taylor wrote the following in "Challenges in the Credit Analysis of Emerging Market Corporate Bonds," Chapter 16 in Frank J. Fabozzi (ed.), *The Handbook of Corporate Debt Instruments* (New Hope, PA: Frank J. Fabozzi Associates, 1998), p. 311:

Practice Problems and Solutions 1–20 taken from *Fixed Income Readings for the Chartered Financial Analyst® Program*, Second Edition, edited by Frank J. Fabozzi, CFA. Copyright © 2005 by CFA Institute. All other problems and solutions copyright © CFA Institute.

> There traditionally have been two approaches to investing in emerging market corporate bonds: top-down and bottom-up.... The *top-down approach* essentially treats investing in corporates as "sovereign-plus." The *bottom-up approach* sometimes has a tendency to treat emerging market corporate as "US credits-plus."

What do you think Mr. Taylor means by "sovereign-plus" and "US credits-plus"?

6 Chris Dialynas in "The Active Decisions in the Selection of Passive Management and Performance Bogeys" (in Frank J. Fabozzi (ed.), *Perspectives on Fixed Income Portfolio Management*, Volume 2) wrote:

> Active bond managers each employ their own methods for relative value analysis. Common elements among most managers are historical relations, liquidity considerations, and market segmentation. Market segmentation allegedly creates opportunities, and historical analysis provides the timing cure.

A What is meant by "historical relations, liquidity considerations, and market segmentation" that Chris Dialynas refers to in this passage?

B What is meant by: "Market segmentation allegedly creates opportunities, and historical analysis provides the timing cure?"

7 The following passages are from Leland Crabbe "Corporate Spread Curve Strategies," Chapter 28 in Frank J. Fabozzi (ed.), *The Handbook of Corporate Debt Instruments* (New Hope, PA: Frank J. Fabozzi Associates, 1998).

> In the corporate bond market, spread curves often differ considerably across issuers...

> Most fixed income investors understand the relation between the term structure of interest rates and implied forward rates. But some investors overlook the fact that a similar relation holds between the term structure of corporate spreads and forward corporate spreads. Specifically, when the spread curve is steep, the forward spreads imply that spreads will widen over time. By contrast, a flat spread curve gives rise to forwards that imply stability in corporate spreads. Essentially the forward spread can be viewed as a breakeven spread...

> Sometimes, investors may disagree with the expectations implied by forward rates, and consequently they may want to implement trading strategies to profit from reshapings of the spread curve.

A What is meant by "spread curves" and in what ways do they differ across issuers?

B Consider the relationship between the term structure of interest rates and implied forward rates (or simply forward rates). What is a "forward spread" that Mr. Crabbe refers to and why can it be viewed as a breakeven spread?

C How can implied forward spreads be used in relative-value analysis?

8 What is the limitation of a yield-pickup trade?

9 Increases in investment-grade credit securities new issuance have been observed with contracting yield spreads and strong relative bond returns. In contrast, spread expansion and a major decline in both relative and absolute returns usually accompanies a sharp decline in the supply of new credit issues. These outcomes are in stark contrast to the conventional wisdom held by many portfolio managers that supply hurts credit spreads. What reason can be offered for the observed relationship between new supply and changes in credit spreads?

Practice Problems

10 A What is meant by the "crossover sector of the bond market"?

   B How do portfolio managers take advantage of potential credit upgrades in the crossover sector?

11 When would a portfolio manager consider implementing a credit-defense trade?

12 What is the motivation for portfolio managers to trade into more current and larger sized "on-the-run" issues?

13 A Why has the swap spread framework become a popular valuation yardstick in Europe for credit securities?

   B Why might US managers embrace the swap spread framework for the credit asset class?

   C Compare the advantages/disadvantage of the nominal spread framework to the swap spread framework.

14 An ABC Corporate issue trades at a bid price of 120 bps over the 5-year US Treasury yield of 6.00% at a time when Libor is 5.70%. At the same time, 5-year Libor-based swap spreads equal 100 bps (to the 5-year US Treasury).

   A If a manager purchased the ABC Corporate issue and entered into a swap to pay fixed and receive floating, what spread over Libor is realized until the first swap reset date?

   B Why would a total return manager buy the issue and then enter into a swap to pay fixed and receive floating?

15 The following was reported in the "Strategies" section of the January 3, 2000 issue of *BondWeek* ("Chicago Trust to Move Up in Credit Quality," p. 10):

> The Chicago Trust Co. plans to buy single-A corporate bonds with intermediate maturities starting this quarter, as the firm swaps out of lower-rated, triple B rated paper to take advantage of attractive spreads from an anticipated flood of single-A supply....

The portfolio manager gave the following reasoning for the trade:

> ... he says a lack of single-A corporate offerings during the fourth quarter has made the paper rich, and he expects it will result in a surge of issuance by single-A rated companies this quarter, blowing out spreads and creating buying opportunities. Once the issuance subsides by the end of the quarter, he expects spreads on the single-A paper will tighten.

   A What type of relative value analysis is the portfolio manager relying on in making this swap decision and what are the underlying assumptions? (Note: When answering this question, keep the following in mind. The manager made the statement at either the last few days of December 1999 or the first two days in January 2000. So, reference to the fourth quarter means the last quarter in 1999. When the statement refers to the end of the quarter or to "this quarter" it is meant the first quarter of 2000.)

   B Further in the article, it was stated that the portfolio manager felt that on an historical basis the corporate market as a whole was cheap. The portfolio manager used new cash to purchase healthcare credits, doubling the portfolio's allocation to the healthcare sector. The portfolio manager felt that the issuers in the healthcare sector he purchased for the portfolio had fallen out of favor with investors as a result of concerns with healthcare reform. He thought that the cash flows for the issuers purchased were strong and the concerns regarding reform were "overblown." Discuss the key elements to this strategy.

16 The following was reported in the "Strategies" section of the January 3, 2000 issue of *BondWeek* ("... Even as Wright Moves Down." p. 10):

> Wright Investors Services plans to buy triple B-rated corporate paper in the industrial sector and sell higher rated corporate paper on the view that stronger-than-anticipated economic growth will allay corporate bond investor fears.

In the article, the following was noted about the portfolio manager's view:

> spreads on higher rated investment grade paper already have come in some from last summer's wides, but he believes concerns over year-end and rising rates have kept investors from buying lower rated corporate paper, keeping spreads relatively wide.

Discuss the motivation for this strategy and the underlying assumptions.

17 The following appeared in the "Strategies" section of the September 27, 1999 issue of *BondWeek* ("Firm Sticks to Corps, Agencies," p. 6):

> The firm, which is already overweight in corporates, expects to invest cash in single A corporate paper in non-cyclical consumer non-durable sectors, which should outperform lower-quality, cyclicals as the economy begins to slow.

Discuss this strategy and its assumptions.

18 A Suppose that a manager believes that credit spreads are mean reverting. Below are three issues along with the current spread, the mean (average) spread over the past six months, and the standard deviation of the spread. Assuming that the spreads are normally distributed, which issue is the most likely to be purchased based on mean-reversion analysis?

Issue	Current Spread	Mean Spread for Past 6 Months	Standard Deviation of Spread
A	110 bps	85 bps	25 bps
B	124	100	10
C	130	110	15

B What are the underlying assumptions in using mean-reversion analysis?

19 Ms. Xu is the senior portfolio manager for the Solid Income Mutual Fund. The fund invests primarily in investment-grade credit and agency mortgage-backed securities. For each quarterly meeting of the board of directors of the mutual fund, Ms. Xu provides information on the characteristics of the portfolio and changes in the composition of the portfolio since the previous board meeting. One of the board members notices two changes in the composition of the portfolio. First, he notices that while the percentage of the portfolio invested in credit was unchanged, there was a sizeable reduction in callable credit relative to noncallable credit bonds. Second, while the portfolio had the same percentage of mortgage passthrough securities, there was a greater percentage of low-coupon securities relative to high-coupon securities.

When Ms. Xu was asked why she changed the structural characteristics of the securities in the portfolio, she responded that it was because the management team expects a significant drop in interest rates in the next quarter and the new structures would benefit more from declining interest rates than the structures held in the previous quarter. One of the directors asked why. How should Ms. Xu respond?

20 Ms. Smith is the portfolio manager of the Good Corporate Bond Fund, which invests primarily in investment-grade corporate bonds. The fund currently has an overweight within the retail industrial sector bonds of retailers. Ms. Smith is concerned that increased competition from internet retailers will negatively affect the earnings and cash flow of the traditional retailers. The fund is also currently underweighted in the US dollar-denominated bonds of European issuers placed in the United States, which she believes should benefit from increased opportunities afforded by European Union. She believes that many of these companies may come to market with new US dollar issues to fund some of their expansion throughout Europe.

Formulate and support a strategy for Ms. Smith that will capitalize on her views about the retail and European corporate sectors of her portfolio. What factors might negatively impact this strategy?

The following information relates to Questions 21–26 and is based on "Fixed-Income Portfolio Management—Part I" and this reading

Coughlin Fixed Income Funds is a family of mutual funds with assets totaling $4 billion, comprised primarily of US corporate bonds. Hanover-Green Life Insurance Company has just under $1 billion in total assets primarily invested in US corporate bonds. The two companies are considering combining their research and analysis units into one entity. They are also looking at possible synergies from consolidating their trading desks and/or back-office operations. Over a longer horizon, the companies also are open to the possibility of merger.

Gaven Warren is a senior portfolio manager with Hanover-Green. He has been asked to review the prospectuses for the various Coughlin funds and make recommendations regarding how the two companies might combine operations. Specifically, Warren is reviewing three of Coughlin's funds—The Select High-Performance Fund, the Yield Curve Plus Fund, and the Index Match Fund. Highlights of the investment objectives of the three funds are shown below:

> The Select High-Performance Fund relies on the superior skills of its analyst team to discover hidden values among a wide range of corporate fixed-income securities. The fund will be approximately 95 percent invested in US dollar denominated corporate bonds with medium-term to long-term maturities and Standard & Poors ratings of B or higher. The fund may use options, futures, and other derivative products to enhance returns. The primary goal of the fund is to maximize total return. The fund's annual total return target is to exceed the Lehman Brothers US Corporate Bond Index total return by 200 basis points.

> The Yield Curve Plus Fund uses selected investments at key points along the yield curve to enhance portfolio returns. The fund will be approximately 95 percent invested in US dollar denominated corporate bonds with medium-term to long-term maturities and Standard & Poors ratings of BBB or higher. The fund may use options, futures, and other derivative products to enhance returns. The primary goal of the fund is to outperform the Lehman Brothers US Corporate Bond Index by analyzing the yield curve appropriate to pricing corporate bonds, identifying key rate durations for the bonds held in the portfolio, and positioning the portfolio to benefit from anticipated shifts in the slope and shape of the yield curve.

The Index Match Fund seeks to match the return on the Lehman Brothers US Corporate Bond Index. The fund will be approximately 98 percent invested in US dollar denominated corporate bonds with medium-term to long-term maturities and Standard & Poors ratings of BBB or higher. The fund may use options, futures, and other derivative products to match the Lehman Brothers US Corporate Bond Index returns.

As is typical of life insurance companies, Hanover-Green has estimated its liabilities using standard actuarial methods. The weighted-average duration of Hanover-Green's liabilities is about 12 years. The long-term focus of Hanover-Green means they can tolerate low liquidity in their portfolio. The primary management technique used by Hanover-Green has been contingent immunization. Because Warren anticipates a discussion with Coughlin regarding contingent immunization, he has prepared the following statements as part of a presentation.

Statement 1   "Contingent immunization requires the prevailing immunized rate of return to exceed the required rate of return."

Statement 2   "When interest rates fall, contingent immunization switches to more active management because the dollar safety margin is higher."

Although the Lehman Brothers US Corporate Bond Index is the benchmark for the Coughlin funds, Warren is not certain that the index is appropriate for Hanover-Green. He compiled the data given in Exhibit 1 as a step toward deciding what index might be the best benchmark for Hanover-Green.

Exhibit 1   Selected Characteristics, Bond Indexes

Index	Effective Duration	YTM (%)	Average Coupon (%)	Number of Securities	Weighting
Long-Term US Corporate Bond Index	8.65	5.75	5.25	558	Value
Global Government Bond Index	5.15	6.30	5.85	520	Value
Selected Municipal Bonds Index	4.65	4.87	4.75	20	Value
Equal-Weighted Corporate Bond Index	4.70	5.19	5.75	96	Equal

Hanover-Green is considering a more active style for a small part of its portfolio. Warren is investigating several relative value methodologies. Two approaches are of particular interest—primary market analysis and spread analysis. Warren is worried that the primary market is about to enter a period where the supply of new issues will increase causing spreads to tighten, and furthermore, that most of the new issues will not be callable.

Regarding spread analysis, Hanover-Green is considering the addition of mortgage-backed securities (MBS) to its portfolio. Warren has investigated the MBS market and found that MBS analysis emphasizes the option-adjusted spread (OAS). Warren is

Practice Problems

considering using OAS to measure the risk of the corporate bonds in Hanover-Green's portfolio. Specifically, he wants to analyze the risks involved in holding several bonds whose credit ratings have deteriorated to speculative status.

21 The strategy used by the Yield Curve Plus Fund *most likely* attempts to enhance portfolio returns by taking advantage of:
   A changes in credit spreads.
   B changes in the level of interest rates.
   C nonparallel changes in the yield curve.

22 The contingent immunization technique that Hanover-Green currently uses in managing their fixed-income portfolio is *best* described as:
   A a passive management strategy similar to that of the Index Match Fund.
   B an active management strategy similar to that of the Select High-Performance Fund.
   C a mix of active and passive management strategies similar to that of the Yield Curve Plus Fund.

23 Are Warren's statements regarding contingent immunization *most likely* correct or incorrect?

	Statement 1	Statement 2
A	Correct	Correct
B	Correct	Incorrect
C	Incorrect	Correct

24 Based solely on the information in Exhibit 1, which index is the *most* appropriate benchmark for Hanover-Green's portfolio?
   A Global Government Bond Index.
   B Long-Term US Corporate Bond Index.
   C Equal-Weighted Corporate Bond Index.

25 Consider Warren's expectations regarding the supply of new issues in the primary market. Given recent research into primary markets, is Warren *most likely* correct or incorrect regarding the effect on spreads and the probability of the bonds being callable?

	Effect on Spreads	Bonds Being Callable
A	Correct	Correct
B	Correct	Incorrect
C	Incorrect	Correct

26 Which of the following statements *most* accurately evaluates the use of the option-adjusted spread (OAS) to analyze the bonds held in Hanover-Green's portfolio?
   A OAS excludes default risk from its calculation; therefore OAS has limited applicability to the analysis of speculative grade bonds.
   B OAS uses Monte Carlo simulation to factor out default risk from the spread; therefore OAS is not well suited to the analysis of speculative grade bonds.
   C OAS is often used to evaluate bonds other than mortgage-backed securities. It is a very useful tool, especially appropriate for high-risk positions such as speculative grade bonds.

SOLUTIONS

Note: Many of the questions are conceptual in nature. The solutions offered are one interpretation, and there may be other valid views.

1. Relative value refers to ranking credit sectors, bond structures, issuers, and issues in terms of their expected performance over some future time period.

2. **A** The dominant structure in the investment-grade credit market is the bullet structure with an intermediate maturity.

   B There are three strategic portfolio implications of the bullet structure with an intermediate maturity:

   i. The dominance of bullet structures creates a scarcity value for structures with embedded call and put features, resulting in premium price for bonds with embedded call options. This "scarcity value" should be considered by managers in relative-value analysis of credit bonds.

   ii. Because long-dated maturities have declined as a percentage of outstanding credit debt, there is a lower effective duration of all outstanding credit debt and, as a result, a reduction in the aggregate sensitivity to interest-rate risk.

   iii. There will be increased use of credit derivatives, whether on a stand-alone basis or embedded in structured notes, so that investors and issuers can gain exposure to the structures they desire.

   C High-yield issuers will continue to issue callable bond structures in order to have the opportunity to refinance at a lower credit spread should credit quality improve.

3. **A** Yield curve placement is simply the positioning of a portfolio with respect to duration and yield curve risk. Trades involving yield curve placement are referred to as curve adjustment trades in the reading. Sector and quality allocations refer to allocations based on relative value analysis of the different bond market sectors and quality sectors. Security selection involves the purchase or avoidance of individual issues based on some relative value basis.

   B For a manager who is evaluated relative to some bond index, the deviation of the portfolio from the benchmark in terms of yield curve exposure, sector exposure, quality exposure, and exposure to individual issues is the appropriate way to measure risk.

4. **A** Scarcity value means that an issue will trade at a premium price due to a lack of supply (relative to demand) for that issue. This is the same as saying that the issue will trade at a narrower spread. If investors want exposure to a first-time issuer, the spread can be narrower than otherwise comparable issuers.

   B Analytical models for valuing bonds with embedded put options assume the issuer will fulfill the obligation to repurchase an issue if the bondholder exercises the put option. For high-yield issuers, there is the credit risk associated with the potential inability to satisfy the put obligation. Thus for high-yield issuers, the credit risk may override the value for a putable issue derived from a valuation model.

5. In general, the top-down approach involves beginning with a macroeconomic outlook and making allocation decisions to sectors based on that outlook. With respect to credit in emerging markets, the top-down approach begins with the assessment of the economic outlook for emerging market countries and then

Solutions

basing the allocation of funds across emerging market credit issuers in different countries on that macroeconomic outlook. This is what Mr. Taylor means by "sovereign plus." The bottom-up approach focuses on the selection of corporate issuers in emerging market countries that are expected to outperform US credit issuers. This is what Mr. Taylor means by "US credits-plus."

6 A Historical relations help a portfolio manager identify opportunities when current spreads are out of line and relative-value opportunities may be available. Liquidity considerations affect spreads and the ability to trade. Market segmentation means factors affecting supply and demand within sectors of the bond market due to impediments or restrictions on investors from reallocating funds across those bond sectors.

B Market segmentation may create relative value opportunities when spreads get out of line due to obstructions that prevent or impede investors from allocating funds to certain sectors due to regulatory constraints and asset/liability constraints. Market segmentation may affect the supply of bonds in a sector for the same reasons. In pursuit of the optimal timing to move into or out of a sector (industry category, maturity neighborhood, or structure) or individual issuer, historical analysis of spreads, based on mean-reversion analysis can help identify when spreads might revert to some "normal" equilibrium.

7 A Spread curves show the relationship between spreads and maturity. They differ by issuer or sector in terms of the amount of the spread and the slope of the spread curve.

B Forward rates are derived from spot rates using arbitrage arguments. A forward spread, or an implied forward spread, can be derived in the same way. Also, forward rates were explained as basically hedgeable or breakeven rates—rates that will make an investor indifferent between two alternatives. For example, for default-free instruments a 2-year forward rate 3 years from now is a rate that will make an investor indifferent between investing in a 5-year zero-coupon default-free instrument or investing in a 3-year zero-coupon default-free instrument and reinvesting the proceeds for two more years after the 3-year instrument matures.

A forward spread can be interpreted in the same way. For example, a 2-year forward spread 3 years from now is the credit spread that will make an investor indifferent to investing in a 5-year zero-coupon instrument of an issuer or investing in a 3-year zero-coupon instrument of the same issuer and reinvesting the proceeds from the maturing instrument in a 2-year zero-coupon instrument of the same issuer.

The forward spread is a breakeven spread because it is the spread that would make the investor indifferent between two alternative investments with different maturities over a given investment horizon.

C Because a forward spread is one that will make an investor indifferent between two alternatives, a manager must compare his or her expectations relative to the forward spread. Relative-value analysis involves making this comparison between expected spread and what is built into market prices (i.e., forward spread).

8 Yield measures are poor indicators of total return realized by holding a security to maturity or over some investment horizon. Thus, an asset manager does not know what a yield pickup of, say, 20 basis points means for subsequent total return. A bond manager can pick up yield on a trade (holding credit quality constant), but on a relative value basis underperform an alternative issue with a lower yield over the manager's investment horizon.

An example of this would be if at the beginning of the month, a portfolio manager sold the 5-year Ford issue at a spread of 140 basis points and purchased the 5-year General Motors issue at a spread of 150 basis points, for a yield pickup of 10 basis points. If the spread on the Ford issue continued to tighten throughout the month, while the General Motors issue's spread remained constant, the Ford issue would outperform the General Motors issue on a total return basis.

9 The reason suggested as to why heavy supply of new investment-grade credit issues will help spreads contract and enhance returns is that new primary bond valuations validate and enhance secondary valuations. In contrast, when new issuance declines sharply, secondary traders lose confirmation from the primary market and tend to require higher spreads.

10 A The crossover sector refers to the sector with issuers whose ratings are between Ba2/BB and Baa3/BBB– by a major rating agency. These issuers are on the border between investment grade and high yield.

B A manager can purchase a below-investment grade issue which he believes will be upgraded to investment grade. If the manager is correct, then the issue will outperform due to spread narrowing resulting from the upgrade and also from increased liquidity as it becomes available to a broader class of investors.

11 A portfolio manager would consider implementing a credit-defense trade when the manager became increasingly concerned about geopolitical risk, the general economy, sector risk, or specific-issuer risk which could lead to widening credit spreads.

12 The motivation is to increase portfolio liquidity.

13 A The European credit market has been consistently homogeneous, having mostly high quality (rated Aa3/AA– and above) and intermediate maturity issues. So swap spreads were a good proxy for credit spreads. Because of the homogeneous character of the credit market in Europe, the swaps framework allows managers as well as issuers to more easily compare securities across fixed- and floating-rate markets. Moreover, in Europe, financial institutions such as commercial banks have been much more willing to use swap methodology to capture value discrepancies between the fixed- and floating-rate markets.

B US managers have embraced swap spreads for the MBS, CMBS, agency, and ABS sectors. This may gradually occur in the US credit markets as well to help facilitate relative value comparisons across non-US and non-credit sectors to US credit securities.

C Individual investors understand the traditional nominal spread framework as a market convention. Moreover despite its limitations, this framework can be used across the entire credit-quality spectrum from Aaa's to B's. The disadvantage is that the nominal spread framework does not work very well for investors and issuers in comparing the relative attractiveness between the fixed- and floating-rate markets. This is the advantage of using the swap framework.

14 A By buying ABC Corporation issue and entering into a 5-year swap to pay fixed and receive floating, the spread over Libor until the first reset date for the swap is:

	Receive from ABC Corp. (6.00% + 120 bps)	7.20%
−	Pay on swap (6.00% + 100 bps)	7.00%
+	Receive from swap	Libor
	Net	Libor + 20 bps

Since Libor is 5.70%, the manager is locking in a rate of 5.90% (= 5.70% + 20 basis points) until the first reset date.

B If the manager expects that interest rates will increase, total return performance will be better using the swap.

15 A The manager is relying on primary market analysis. The manager believes that one of the reasons why the spread on single-A rated issues may be out of line in the fourth quarter of 1999 is due to the lack of single-A rated issues coming to market in that quarter. The manager expects that in the first quarter of 2000, there will be a surge of single-A rated issues that will come to market, resulting in a widening of spreads and thereby providing an opportunity to purchase single-A rated issues relatively cheaply versus BBB issues.

The assumption is that the attractive level of the corporate spread for single-A rated issuers is driven principally by new issuance and not any structural issue or other factor that determines corporate spreads. Furthermore, it is assumed that once the market is cleared of the increase in supply of single-A rated issuers, the spread will narrow and provide better performance relative to BBB rated issuers.

B The keys to this strategy are 1) that the cash flows will in fact remain strong, 2) that the spread for these health care issuers are not justified by the strong cash flow despite concerns with healthcare reform, and 3) that investors in the bond market will recognize this (by some time period), resulting in a decline in the credit spread for these issuers.

16 The motivation for this strategy is that while investment-grade issues may decline due to stronger-than-anticipated economic growth, a good amount of spread reduction has already occurred in above BBB rated sectors. Thus, on a relative basis, the decline in corporate spreads on investment grade bonds due to stronger-than-anticipated growth will be primarily in BBB rated sectors. The assumption is that spreads will contract more in the BBB rated sector.

17 This relative value strategy has two elements to it. First, there appears to be an allocation to single-A rated corporates versus lower-quality corporates. Hence, it appears to be a credit-defense trade because of a concern with the economy slowing down. Moreover, there is an allocation within the single-A rated corporates to a sector—non-cyclical consumer non-durables—that is expected to outperform an alternative sector—cyclicals—should the economy slow down.

18 A One can use mean-reversion analysis in this question as follows. For each issue, the number of standard deviations that the current spread is above the historical average (the mean spread for the past six months) is computed as:

Issue	Number of Standard Deviations Above Mean
A	(110 – 85)/25 = 1.0
B	(124 – 100)/10 = 2.4
C	(130 – 110)/15 = 1.3

Issue B has the largest deviation above the mean and is therefore the one more likely to contract. Actually, based on a normal distribution, the probability associated with realizing a specified number of standard deviation above the mean can be determined.

B The assumptions are that 1) the spreads will revert back to their historic means and 2) there have been no structural changes in the market that would render the historical mean and standard deviation useless for the analysis.

19 Ms. Xu should first explain that callable bonds exhibit negative convexity when interest rates decline, while noncallable bonds exhibit positive convexity. This means that when rates decline, the price appreciation for a callable bond will not be as great as an otherwise noncallable bond. Since the management team expects a significant drop in interest rates in the next quarter, to better participate in the rise in bond prices, there was a shift to noncallable credit securities.

All mortgage passthrough securities exhibit negative convexity. However, low-coupon issues exhibit less negative convexity than high-coupon issues. That is, there will be greater price appreciation for low-coupon issues when rates decline. Given the anticipated decline in interest rates, the low-coupon issues will appreciate more and hence the reason for the shift to such issues.

20 Ms. Smith could sell retail issues and use the proceeds to purchase US dollar-denominated corporate bonds of European issuers. This would be consistent with her expectation of underperformance of the retail sector and outperformance of the European corporate sector. She could make her purchases in the new issue market, if she believes new issues will be attractively priced.

Ms. Smith should use credit analysis to select which issues to buy or sell within each sector. She must consider the possibility of a risk premium in the European corporate sector, as some managers cannot purchase bonds in that sector. Seasonality may also be a factor, depending on the timing of her purchases/sales.

21 C is correct. The Yield Curve Plus Fund is using key rate duration to enhance portfolio returns. Key rate duration attempts to profit from non-parallel shifts in the yield curve.

22 C is correct. Contingent immunization is a mix of the passive and active styles. Therefore, it is closest to the Yield Curve Plus Fund.

23 A is correct. Both statements regarding contingent immunization are correct.

24 B is correct. The Long-Term US Corporate Bond Index's duration is closest to that of Hanover-Green's liabilities and reflects the corporate bonds that form the bulk of their assets.

25 A is correct. Warren is most likely correct regarding the effect on spreads and the probability of the bonds being callable. During most years, increases in issuance are associated with market-spread contraction. Bullet structures without call, put, or sinking fund options have come to dominate the credit market.

26 A is correct. OAS has limited use in the analysis of speculative grade bonds because default risk is excluded from the calculation.

PORTFOLIO MANAGEMENT
STUDY SESSION

11

Fixed-Income Portfolio Management (2)

Study Session 11 builds on the fundamentals of fixed-income portfolio management to address international and emerging market strategies and the use of derivatives to manage interest rate and credit risks.

READING ASSIGNMENTS

Reading 22   Fixed-Income Portfolio Management—Part II
by H. Gifford Fong and Larry D. Guin, DBA, CFA

READING 22

Fixed-Income Portfolio Management—Part II

by H. Gifford Fong and Larry D. Guin, DBA, CFA

H. Gifford Fong is at Gifford Fong Associates and Journal of Investment Management (USA). Larry D. Guin, DBA, CFA, is a retired professor at Murray State University (USA).

LEARNING OUTCOMES	
Mastery	The candidate should be able to:
☐	a. evaluate the effect of leverage on portfolio duration and investment returns;
☐	b. discuss the use of repurchase agreements (repos) to finance bond purchases and the factors that affect the repo rate;
☐	c. critique the use of standard deviation, target semivariance, shortfall risk, and value at risk as measures of fixed-income portfolio risk;
☐	d. demonstrate the advantages of using futures instead of cash market instruments to alter portfolio risk;
☐	e. formulate and evaluate an immunization strategy based on interest rate futures;
☐	f. explain the use of interest rate swaps and options to alter portfolio cash flows and exposure to interest rate risk;
☐	g. compare default risk, credit spread risk, and downgrade risk and demonstrate the use of credit derivative instruments to address each risk in the context of a fixed-income portfolio;
☐	h. explain the potential sources of excess return for an international bond portfolio;
☐	i. evaluate 1) the change in value for a foreign bond when domestic interest rates change and 2) the bond's contribution to duration in a domestic portfolio, given the duration of the foreign bond and the country beta;
☐	j. recommend and justify whether to hedge or not hedge currency risk in an international bond investment;

(continued)

Note: Part I of this reading is included in Study Session 10 under the title "Fixed-Income Portfolio Management—Part I."

Managing Investment Portfolios: A Dynamic Process, Third Edition, John L. Maginn, CFA, Donald L. Tuttle, CFA, Jerald E. Pinto, CFA, and Dennis W. McLeavey, CFA, editors. Copyright © 2007 by CFA Institute.

LEARNING OUTCOMES	
Mastery	The candidate should be able to:
☐	k. describe how breakeven spread analysis can be used to evaluate the risk in seeking yield advantages across international bond markets;
☐	l. discuss the advantages and risks of investing in emerging market debt;
☐	m. discuss the criteria for selecting a fixed-income manager.

5 OTHER FIXED-INCOME STRATEGIES

Whether managing against a bond market index or against a pool of liabilities, there are a range of combinations and alternatives that fixed-income managers might pursue in search of enhanced performance.

5.1 Combination Strategies

Although we have explained a number of basic portfolio strategies, the range of portfolio strategies really represents a continuum. At various phases during an interest rate cycle, a particular strategy may be most appropriate, but more often than not, a mix of alternatives is best for part or all of the cycle.

When decision makers have strong convictions, a one-strategy approach may be optimal; in the more likely case of uncertainty, strategy combinations may produce the best expected risk/return trade-off. A trade-off, for example, might be to tie a portion of the portfolio's risk and return to some baseline portfolio whose performance over the long term should provide satisfactory results, and actively manage the remaining portion. Retaining an active component preserves the opportunity for superior performance.

Two of the most popular combination strategies are active/passive and active/immunization. An **active/passive combination** allocates a core component of the portfolio to a passive strategy and the balance to an active component. The passive strategy would replicate an index or some sector of the market. In the active portion, the manager is free to pursue a return maximization strategy (at some given level of risk). A large pension fund might have a large allocation to a core strategy, consisting of an indexed portfolio, with additional active strategies chosen on the margin to enhance overall portfolio returns.

An **active/immunization combination** also consists of two component portfolios: The immunized portfolio provides an assured return over the planning horizon while the second portfolio uses an active high-return/high-risk strategy. The immunized portfolio is intended to provide an assured absolute return source. An example of an active immunization strategy is a surplus protection strategy for a fully funded pension plan in which the liabilities are immunized and the portion of assets equal to the surplus is actively managed.

5.2 Leverage

Frequently, a manager is permitted to use leverage as a tool to help increase the portfolio's return. In fact, the whole purpose of using leverage is to magnify the portfolio's rate of return. As long as the manager can earn a return on the investment of the borrowed funds that is greater than the interest cost, the portfolio's rate of return will be magnified. For example, if a manager can borrow €100 million at 4 percent (i.e., €4 million interest per year) and invest the funds to earn 5 percent (i.e., €5 million return per year), the difference of 1 percent (or €1 million) represents a profit that increases the rate of return on the entire portfolio. When a manager leverages a bond portfolio, however, the interest rate sensitivity of the equity in the portfolio usually increases, as will be discussed shortly.

5.2.1 Effects of Leverage

As we have just seen, the purpose of using leverage is to potentially magnify the portfolio's returns. Let us take a closer look at this magnification effect with the use of an example.

EXAMPLE 9

The Use of Leverage

Assume that a manager has $40 million of funds to invest. The manager then borrows an additional $100 million at 4 percent interest in the hopes of magnifying the rate of return on the portfolio. Further assume that the manager can invest all of the funds at a 4.5 percent rate of return. The return on the portfolio's components will be as follows:

	Borrowed Funds	Equity Funds
Amount Invested	$100,000,000	$40,000,000
Rate of Return @4.5%	4,500,000	1,800,000
Less Interest Expense @4.0%	4,000,000	0
Net Profitability	500,000	1,800,000
Rate of Return on Each Component	$\frac{\$500,000}{\$100,000,000} = 0.50\%$	$\frac{\$1,800,000}{\$40,000,000} = 4.50\%$

Because the profit on the borrowed funds accrues to the equity, the rate of return increases from 4.5 percent in the all-equity case to 5.75 percent when leverage is used:

$$\frac{\$1,800,000 + \$500,000}{\$40,000,000} = 5.75\%$$

Even though the net return on the borrowed funds is only 50 bps, the return on the portfolio's equity funds is increased by 125 bps (5.75 percent − 4.50 percent) because of the large amount of funds borrowed. The larger the amount of borrowed funds, the larger the magnification will be.

Leverage cuts both ways, however. If the manager cannot invest the borrowed money to earn at least the rate of interest, the leverage will serve as a drag on profitability. For example, in the illustration above, if the manager can only earn a 3.50 percent rate on the portfolio, the portfolio's net return will be 2.25 percent, which is 125 bps less than the unleveraged return. Exhibit 20 shows the portfolio return at various yields on the invested funds (and for varying levels of borrowed funds).

Exhibit 20   Portfolio Returns at Various Yields

Borrowed Funds	Annual Rate of Return on Portfolio's Equity Funds				
	2.50%	3.50%	4.50%	5.50%	6.50%
$60,000,000	0.25%	2.75%	5.25%	7.75%	10.25%
80,000,000	−0.50	2.50	5.50	8.50	11.50
100,000,000	−1.25	2.25	5.75	9.25	12.75
120,000,000	−2.00	2.00	6.00	10.00	14.00
140,000,000	−2.75	1.75	6.25	10.75	15.25

Two relationships can be seen in the above exhibit:

1 The larger the amount of borrowed funds, the greater the variation in potential outcomes. In other words, the higher the leverage, the higher the risk.

2 The greater the variability in the annual return on the invested funds, the greater the variation in potential outcomes (i.e., the higher the risk).

Let us now examine the expressions for the returns on borrowed and equity components of a portfolio with leverage. Let us also develop the expression for the overall return on this portfolio. Suppose that

E = Amount of equity
B = Amount of borrowed funds
k = Cost of borrowing
r_F = Return on funds invested
R_B = Return on borrowed funds
    = Profit on borrowed funds/Amount of borrowed funds
    = $B \times (r_F - k)/B$
    = $r_F - k$

As expected, R_B equals the return on funds invested less the cost of borrowing.

R_E = Return on equity
    = Profit on equity/Amount of equity
    = $E \times r_F / E$
    = r_F

As expected, R_E equals the return on funds invested.

R_p = Portfolio rate of return
    = (Profit on borrowed funds + Profit on equity)/Amount of equity
    = $\left[B \times (r_F - k) + E \times r_F\right]/E$
    = $r_F + (B/E) \times (r_F - k)$

For example, assume equity is €100 million and €50 million is borrowed at a rate of 6 percent per year. If the investment's return is 6.5 percent, portfolio return is 6.5 percent + (€50/€100)(6.5 percent − 6.0 percent) = 6.75 percent.

Other Fixed-Income Strategies

Besides magnification of returns, the second major effect of leveraging a bond portfolio is on the duration of the investor's equity in the portfolio. That duration is typically higher than the duration of an otherwise identical, but unleveraged, bond portfolio, given that the duration of liabilities is low relative to the duration of the assets they are financing. The expression for the duration of equity reflects the durations of assets and liabilities and their market values. With D_A denoting the duration of the assets (the bond portfolio) and D_L the duration of the liabilities (borrowings), the duration of equity, D_E, is given by[1]

$$D_E = \frac{D_A A - D_L L}{E}$$

In the above expression, A and L represent the market value of assets and liabilities, respectively.

To illustrate the calculation using the data from Example 9, suppose the $140 million bond portfolio (A = $140 million) has a duration of 4.00 (D_A = 4.00). However, $100 million of the value of the portfolio is borrowed (L = $100 million; $E = A - L$ = $40 million). Let us assume that the duration of the liabilities is 1.00 (D_L = 1.00). Then, stating quantities in millions of dollars,

$$D_E = \frac{4.00(\$140) - 1.00(\$100)}{\$40}$$

$$= \frac{\$460}{\$40}$$

$$= 11.50$$

Duration at 11.50 is almost three times larger than the duration of the unleveraged bond portfolio, 4.00.

As will be discussed later, derivatives such as interest rate futures are another means by which duration can be increased (or decreased, according to the investor's needs).

5.2.2 Repurchase Agreements

Managers may use a variety of financial instruments to increase the leverage of their portfolios. Among investment managers' favorite instruments is the repurchase agreement (also called a repo or RP). A **repurchase agreement** is a contract involving the sale of securities such as Treasury instruments coupled with an agreement to repurchase the same securities on a later date. The importance of the repo market is suggested by its colossal size, which is measured in trillions of dollars of transactions per year.

Although a repo is legally a sale and repurchase of securities, the repo transaction functions very much like a collateralized loan. In fact, the difference in selling price and purchase price is referred to as the "interest" on the transaction.[2] For example, a manager can borrow $10 million overnight at an annual interest rate of 3 percent by selling Treasury securities valued at $10,000,000 and simultaneously agreeing to repurchase the same notes the following day for $10,000,833. The payment from the initial sale represents the principal amount of the loan; the excess of the repurchase price over the sale price ($833) is the interest on the loan.

In effect, the repo market presents a low-cost way for managers to borrow funds by providing Treasury securities as collateral. The market also enables investors (lenders) to earn a return above the risk-free rate on Treasury securities without sacrificing liquidity.

---

1 See Saunders and Cornett (2003), Chapter 9, for related expressions.
2 The repo "interest" should not be confused with the interest that is accruing on the security being used as loan collateral. The borrower is entitled to receive back the security that was put up as collateral as well as any interest paid or accrued on this instrument.

Term to maturity. RP agreements typically have short terms to maturity, usually overnight or a few days, although longer-term repos of several weeks or months may be negotiated. If a manager wants to permanently leverage the portfolio, he may simply "roll over" the overnight loans on a permanent basis by entering the RP market on a daily basis.

Transfer of securities (with related costs). Obviously, the buyer of the securities would like to take possession (or delivery) of the securities. Otherwise, complications may arise if the seller defaults on the repurchase of the securities. Also, if delivery is not insisted on, the potential exists for an unscrupulous seller to sell the same securities over and over again to a variety of buyers. Transfer agreements take a variety of forms:

- Physical delivery of the securities. Although this arrangement is possible, the high cost associated with physical delivery may make this method unworkable, particularly for short-term transactions.
- A common arrangement is for the securities to be processed by means of credits and debits to the accounts of banks acting as clearing agents for their customers (in the United States, these would be credit and debits to the banks' Federal Reserve Bank accounts). If desired, the banking system's wire transfer system may be used to transfer securities electronically in book-entry form from the seller (the borrower of funds) to the buyer (or lender of funds) and back later. This arrangement may be cheaper than physical delivery, but it still involves a variety of fees and transfer charges.
- Another common arrangement is to deliver the securities to a custodial account at the seller's bank. The bank takes possession of the securities and will see that both parties' interests are served; in essence, the bank acts as a trustee for both parties. This arrangement reduces the costs because delivery charges are minimized and only some accounting entries are involved.
- In some transactions, the buyer does not insist on delivery, particularly if the transaction is very short term (e.g., overnight), if the two parties have a long history of doing business together, and if the seller's financial standing and ethical reputation are both excellent.

Default risk and factors that affect the repo rate. Notice that, as long as delivery is insisted on, a repo is essentially a secured loan and its interest rate does not depend on the respective parties' credit qualities. If delivery is not taken (or is weakly secured), the financial stability and ethical characteristics of the parties become much more important.

A variety of factors will affect the repo rate. Among them are:

1 *Quality of the collateral.*

   The higher the quality of the securities, the lower the repo rate will be.

2 *Term of the repo.*

   Typically, the longer the maturity, the higher the rate will be. The very short end of the yield curve typically is upward sloping, leading to higher yields being required on longer-term repos.

3 *Delivery requirement.*

   If physical delivery of the securities is required, the rate will be lower because of the lower default risk; if the collateral is deposited with the bank of the borrower, the rate is higher; if delivery is not required, the rate will be still higher. As with all financial market transactions, there is a trade-off between risk and return: The greater control the repo investor (lender) has over the collateral, the lower the return will be.

4 *Availability of collateral.*

Other Fixed-Income Strategies

Occasionally, some securities may be in short supply and difficult to obtain. In order to acquire these securities, the buyer of the securities (i.e., the lender of funds) may be willing to accept a lower rate. This situation typically occurs when the buyer needs securities for a short sale or to make delivery on a separate transaction. The more difficult it is to obtain the securities, the lower the repo rate.

5 *Prevailing interest rates in the economy.*

The federal funds rate is often used to represent prevailing interest rates in the United States on overnight loans.[3] As interest rates in general increase, the rates on repo transactions will increase. In other words, the higher the federal funds rate, the higher the repo rate will be.

6 *Seasonal factors.*

Although minor compared with the other factors, there is a seasonal effect on the repo rate because some institutions' supply of (and demand for) funds is influenced by seasonal factors.

The sections above demonstrate the motivation for managers to borrow money and discuss a major instrument used to raise this money—the repurchase agreement. Borrowed money often constitutes a single liability and, therefore, a single benchmark. Other managers are faced with multiple liabilities—managers of defined-benefit plans, for example. Regardless of whether the benchmark is single or multiple, a variety of investment strategies are available to the manager to satisfy the goal of generating cash flows to meet these liabilities. Let us now examine some of those strategies.

5.3 Derivatives-Enabled Strategies

Fixed-income securities and portfolios have sensitivities to various factors. These sensitivities are associated with return and risk characteristics that are key considerations in security selection and portfolio management. Factors include duration and convexity as well as additional factors for some securities such as liquidity and credit. We can call these sensitivities "factor exposures," and they provide a basis for understanding the return and risk characteristics of an investment.

The use of derivatives can be thought of as a means to create, reduce, or magnify the factor exposures of an investment. This modification can make use of basic derivatives such as futures and options in addition to combinations of factor exposures such as structured products.

In the following sections, we will review interest risk measurement and control and some of the most common derivatives used for such purposes, such as interest rate futures, interest rate swaps, credit options, credit swaps, and collateralized debt obligations.

5.3.1 Interest Rate Risk

The typical first-order source of risk for fixed-income portfolios is the duration or sensitivity to interest rate change. Conveniently, portfolio duration is a weighted average of durations of the individual securities making up the portfolio:

$$\text{Portfolio duration} = \frac{\sum_{i=1}^{n} D_i \times V_i}{V_p}$$

---

[3] The federal funds rate is the interest rate on an unsecured overnight loan (of excess reserves) from one bank to another bank.

where

D_i = duration of security i
V_i = market value of security i
V_p = market value of the portfolio

In the course of managing a portfolio, the portfolio manager may want to replace one security in the portfolio with another security while keeping portfolio duration constant. To achieve this, the concept of dollar duration or the duration impact of a one dollar investment in a security can be used. Dollar duration is calculated using

$$\text{Dollar duration} = \frac{D_i \times V_i}{100}$$

where V_i = market value of the portfolio position if held; the price of one bond if not held.

To maintain the portfolio duration when one security is being exchanged for another, the dollar durations of the securities being exchanged must be matched. This matching can be accomplished by comparing the dollar durations of each side and thereby determining the necessary par value of the new bond. Specifically,

$$\text{New bond market value} = \frac{DD_O}{D_N} \times 100$$

where

DD_O = dollar duration of old bond
D_N = duration of new bond

EXAMPLE 10

Maintaining Portfolio Duration in Changing Portfolio Holdings

A portfolio manager wants to exchange one bond issue for another that he believes is undervalued. The existing position in the old bond has a market value of 5.5 million dollars. The bond has a price of $80 and a duration of 4. The bond's dollar duration is therefore 5.5 million × 4/100 or $220,000.

The new bond has a duration of 5 and a price of $90, resulting in a dollar duration of 4.5 ($90 × 5/100) per bond. What is the par value of the new bond needed to keep the duration of the portfolio constant?

Solution:

The market value of the new bond issue would be ($220,000/5)100 = $4,400,000. The bond is trading at $90 per $100 of par. The par value of this issue would be $4,400,000/0.9 = $4.889 million. This can also be calculated as $4.889 million ($220,000/4.5 × 100).

Although duration is an effective tool for measuring and controlling interest rate sensitivity, it is important to remember that there are limitations to this measure. For example, the accuracy of the measure decreases as the magnitude of the amount of interest rate change increases.

Duration is one measure of risk, related to sensitivity to interest rate changes. The following sections address statistical risk measures.

5.3.2 Other Risk Measures

The risk of a portfolio can be viewed as the uncertainty associated with the portfolio's future returns. Uncertainty implies dispersion of returns but raises the question, "What are the alternatives for measuring the dispersion of returns?"

If one assumes that portfolio returns have a normal (bell-shaped) distribution, then standard deviation is a useful measure. For a normal distribution, standard deviation has the property that plus and minus one standard deviation from the mean of the distribution covers 68 percent of the outcomes; plus and minus two standard deviations covers 95 percent of outcomes; and, plus and minus three standard deviations covers 99 percent of outcomes. The standard deviation squared (multiplied by itself) results in the variance of the distribution.

Realistically, the normality assumption may not be descriptive of the distribution, especially for portfolios having securities with embedded options such as puts, call features, prepayment risks, and so on.

Alternative measures have been used because of the restrictive conditions of a normal distribution. These have focused on the quantification of the undesirable left hand side of the distribution—the probability of returns less than the mean return. However, each of these alternatives has its own deficiency.

1 **Semivariance** measures the dispersion of the return outcomes that are below the target return.

   Deficiency: Although theoretically superior to the variance as a way of measuring risk, semivariance is not widely used in bond portfolio management for several reasons:[4]

   - It is computationally challenging for large portfolios.
   - To the extent that investment returns are symmetric, semivariance is proportional to variance and so contains no additional information. To the extent that returns may not be symmetric, return asymmetries are very difficult to forecast and may not be a good forecast of future risk anyway. Plus, because we estimate downside risk with only half the data, we lose statistical accuracy.

2 **Shortfall risk** (or risk of loss) refers to the probability of not achieving some specified return target. The focus is on that part of the distribution that represents the downside from the designated return level.

   Deficiency: Shortfall risk does not account for the magnitude of losses in money terms.

3 **Value at risk (VAR)** is an estimate of the loss (in money terms) that the portfolio manager expects to be exceeded with a given level of probability over a specified time period.

   Deficiency: VAR does not indicate the magnitude of the very worst possible outcomes.

Unfortunately, a universal and comprehensive risk measure does not exist. Each alternative has its merits and limitations. It is important to keep in mind that the portfolio will have multiple risk exposures (factors) and the appropriate risk measures will vary with the particular requirements of the portfolio.

---

[4] See Kahn (1997).

5.3.3 Bond Variance versus Bond Duration

The expected return of a portfolio is the weighted average of the expected returns of each individual security in the portfolio. The weight is calculated as the market value of each security as a percentage of the market value of the portfolio as a whole. The variance of a portfolio is determined by the weight of each security in the portfolio, the variance of each security, and the covariance between each pair of securities.

Two major problems are associated with using the variance or standard deviation to measure bond portfolio risk:

1 The number of the estimated parameters increases dramatically as the number of the bonds considered increases. The total number of variances and covariances that needs to be estimated can be found as follows:

Number of bonds × (Number of bonds + 1)/2

If a portfolio has 1,000 bonds, there would be 500,500 [i.e., 1,000 × (1,000 + 1) / 2] different terms to be estimated.

2 Accurately estimating the variances and covariances is difficult. Because the characteristics of a bond change as time passes, the estimation based on the historical bond data may not be useful. For instance, a bond with five years to maturity has a different volatility than a four-year or six-year bond. Besides the time to maturity factor, some securities may have embedded options, such as calls, puts, sinking fund provisions, and prepayments. These features change the security characteristics dramatically over time and further limit the use of historical estimates.

Because of the problems mentioned above, it is difficult to use standard deviation to measure portfolio risk.

We now turn our attention to a variety of strategies based on derivatives products. A number of these derivatives products are shown in Exhibit 21 and are explained in the following sections.

Exhibit 21 Derivatives-Enabled Strategies

Products Used in Derivatives-Enabled Strategies:
- Interest Rate Futures
- Interest Rate Swaps
- Interest Rate Options (Options on Physicals and Options on Futures)
  - Credit Options
  - Credit Forward Contracts
  - Credit Derivatives
  - Credit Default Swaps
- Structured Products (MBS, ABS, & CDOs)

5.3.4 Interest Rate Futures

A **futures contract** is an enforceable contract between a buyer (seller) and an established exchange or its clearinghouse in which the buyer (seller) agrees to take (make) delivery of something at a specified price at the end of a designated period of time. The "something" that can be bought or sold is called the **underlying** (as in *underlying asset* or *underlying instrument*). The price at which the parties agree to exchange the underlying in the future is called the **futures price**. The designated date at which the parties must transact is called the **settlement date** or delivery date.

When an investor takes a new position in the market by buying a futures contract, the investor is said to be in a long position or to be long futures. If, instead, the investor's opening position is the sale of a futures contract, the investor is said to be in a short position or to be short futures.

Interest rate futures contracts are traded on short-term instruments (for example, Treasury bills and the Eurodollars) and longer-term instruments (for example, Treasury notes and bonds). Because the Treasury futures contract plays an important role in the strategies we discuss below, it is worth reviewing the nuances of this contract. The government bond futures of a number of other countries, such as Japan and Germany, are similar to the US Treasury futures contract.

The 30-year Treasury bond and 10-year US Treasury note futures contracts are both important contracts. The 30-year contract is an important risk management tool in ALM; the 10-year US Treasury note futures contract has become more important than the 30-year contract in terms of liquidity. The US Treasury ceased issuing its 30-year bond in 2002 but reintroduced it in 2006. The following discussion focuses on the 30-year bond futures contract, which shares the same structure as the 10-year note futures contract.

The underlying instrument for the Treasury bond futures contract is $100,000 par value of a hypothetical 30-year, 6 percent coupon bond. Although price and yield of the Treasury bond futures contract are quoted in terms of this hypothetical Treasury bond, the seller of the futures contract has the choice of several actual Treasury bonds that are acceptable to deliver. The Chicago Board of Trade (CBOT) allows the seller to deliver any Treasury bond that has at least 15 years to maturity from the date of delivery if not callable; in the case of callable bonds, the issue must not be callable for at least 15 years from the first day of the delivery month. To settle the contract, an acceptable bond must be delivered.

The delivery process for the Treasury bond futures contract makes the contract interesting. In the settlement month, the seller of a futures contract (the short) is required to deliver to the buyer (the long) $100,000 par value of a 6 percent, 30-year Treasury bond. No such bond exists, however, so the seller must choose from other acceptable deliverable bonds that the exchange has specified.

To make delivery equitable to both parties, and to tie cash to futures prices, the CBOT has introduced **conversion factors** for determining the invoice price of each acceptable deliverable Treasury issue against the Treasury bond futures contract. The conversion factor is determined by the CBOT before a contract with a specific settlement date begins trading. The conversion factor is based on the price that a deliverable bond would sell for at the beginning of the delivery month if it were to yield 6 percent. The conversion factor is constant throughout the trading period of the futures contract. The short must notify the long of the actual bond that will be delivered one day before the delivery date.

In selecting the issue to be delivered, the short will select, from all the deliverable issues and bond issues auctioned during the contract life, the one that is least expensive. This issue is referred to as the **cheapest-to-deliver** (CTD). The CTD plays a key role in the pricing of this futures contract.

In addition to the option of which acceptable Treasury issue to deliver, sometimes referred to as the **quality option** or swap option, the short position has two additional options granted under CBOT delivery guidelines. The short position is permitted to decide when in the delivery month actual delivery will take place—a feature called the **timing option**. The other option is the right of the short position to give notice of intent to deliver up to 8:00 p.m. Chicago time after the closing of the exchange (3:15 p.m. Chicago time) on the date when the futures settlement price has been fixed. This option is referred to as the **wild card option**. The quality option, the timing option, and the wild card option (referred to in sum as the **delivery options**) mean that the long position can never be sure which Treasury bond will be delivered or when it will be delivered.

Modeled after the Treasury bond futures contract, the underlying for the Treasury note futures contract is $100,000 par value of a hypothetical 10-year, 6 percent Treasury note. Several acceptable Treasury issues may be delivered by the short. An issue is acceptable if the maturity is not less than 6.5 years and not greater than 10 years from the first day of the delivery month. The delivery options granted to the short position are the same as for the Treasury bond futures contract.

5.3.4.1 Strategies with Interest Rate Futures The prices of an interest rate futures contract are negatively correlated with the change in interest rates. When interest rates rise, the prices of the deliverable bonds will drop and the futures price will decline; when interest rates drop, the price of the deliverable bonds will rise and the futures price will increase. Therefore, buying a futures contract will increase a portfolio's sensitivity to interest rates, and the portfolio's duration will increase. On the other hand, selling a futures contract will lower a portfolio's sensitivity to interest rates and the portfolio's duration will decrease.

There are a number of advantages to using futures contracts rather than the cash markets for purposes of portfolio duration control. Liquidity and cost-effectiveness are clear advantages to using futures contracts. Furthermore, for duration reduction, shorting the contract (i.e., selling the contract) is very effective. In general, because of the depth of the futures market and low transaction costs, futures contracts represent a very efficient tool for timely duration management.

Various strategies can use interest rate futures contracts and other derivative products, including the following.

Duration Management A frequently used portfolio strategy targets a specific duration target such as the duration of the benchmark index. In these situations, futures are used to maintain the portfolio's duration at its target value when the weighted average duration of the portfolio's securities deviate from the target. The use of futures permits a timely and cost-effective modification of the portfolio duration.

More generally, whenever the current portfolio duration is different from the desired portfolio duration, interest rate futures can be an effective tool. For example, interest rate futures are commonly used in interest rate anticipation strategies, which involve reducing the portfolio's duration when the expectation is that interest rates will rise and increasing duration when the expectation is that interest rates will decline.

To change a portfolio's dollar duration so that it equals a specific target duration, the portfolio manager needs to estimate the number of future contracts that must be purchased or sold.

Portfolio's target dollar duration = Current portfolio's dollar duration without futures + Dollar duration of the futures contracts

Dollar duration of futures = Dollar duration per futures contract × Number of futures contracts

Other Fixed-Income Strategies

The number of futures contracts that is needed to achieve the portfolio's target dollar duration then can be estimated by:

$$\text{Approximate number of contracts} = \frac{(D_T - D_I)P_I}{\text{Dollar duration per futures contract}}$$

$$= \frac{(D_T - D_I)P_I}{D_{CTD}P_{CTD}} \times \frac{D_{CTD}P_{CTD}}{\text{Dollar duration per futures contract}}$$

$$= \frac{(D_T - D_I)P_I}{D_{CTD}P_{CTD}} \times \text{Conversion factor for the CTD bond}$$

where

D_T = target duration for the portfolio
D_I = initial duration for the portfolio
P_I = initial market value of the portfolio
D_{CTD} = the duration of the cheapest-to-deliver bond
P_{CTD} = the price of the cheapest-to-deliver bond

Notice that if the manager wishes to increase the duration, then D_T will be greater than D_I and the equation will have a positive sign. Thus, futures contracts will be purchased. The opposite is true if the objective is to shorten the portfolio duration. It should be kept in mind that the expression given is only an approximation.

An expanded definition of D_{CTD} would be the duration of the cheapest-to-deliver bond to satisfy the futures contract. Whenever phrasing similar to the following is used, "a futures contract priced at y with a duration of x," what x actually represents is the duration of the cheapest-to-deliver bond to satisfy the futures contract.

EXAMPLE 11

Duration Management with Futures

A UK-based pension fund has a large portfolio of British corporate and government bonds. The market value of the bond portfolio is £50 million. The duration of the portfolio is 9.52. An economic consulting firm that provides economic forecasts to the pension fund has advised the fund that the chance of an upward shift in interest rates in the near term is greater than the market currently perceives. In view of this advice, the pension fund has decided to reduce the duration of its bond portfolio to 7.5 by using a futures contract priced at £100,000 that has a duration of 8.47. Assume that the conversion factor for the futures contract is 1.1.

1 Would the pension fund need to buy futures contracts or sell?
2 Approximately, how many futures contracts would be needed to change the duration of the bond portfolio?

Solution to 1:

Because the pension fund desires to reduce the duration, it would need to sell futures contracts.

> **Solution to 2:**
>
> D_T = target duration for the portfolio = 7.5
> D_I = initial duration for the portfolio = 9.52
> P_I = initial market value of the portfolio = £50 million
> D_{CTD} = the duration of the cheapest-to-deliver bond = 8.47
> P_{CTD} = the price of the cheapest-to-deliver bond = £100,000
>
> Conversion factor for the cheapest-to-deliver bond = 1.1
> Approximate number of contracts
>
> $$= \frac{(D_T - D_I)P_I}{D_{CTD}P_{CTD}} \times \text{Conversion factor for the CTD bond}$$
>
> $$= \frac{(7.5 - 9.52) \times 50{,}000{,}000}{8.47 \times 100{,}000} \times 1.1 = -131.17.$$
>
> Thus, the pension fund would need to sell 131 futures contracts to achieve the desired reduction in duration.

Duration Hedging Fixed-income portfolios are commonly used for purposes of asset/liability management in which portfolio assets are managed to fund a specified set of liabilities. In the case of immunization, the use of duration is critical. The matching of the portfolio duration to the duration of liabilities to be funded by the portfolio is a form of hedging. Offsetting (reducing) the interest rate exposure of a cash position in a portfolio is also a form of hedging. Whenever an interest rate exposure must be reduced, futures can be used to accomplish the hedge. The following discussion reviews several important issues in hedging an existing bond position.

Hedging with futures contracts involves taking a futures position that offsets an existing interest rate exposure. If the hedge is properly constructed, as cash and futures prices move together any loss realized by the hedger from one position (whether cash or futures) will be offset by a profit on the other position.

In practice, hedging is not that simple. The outcome of a hedge will depend on the relationship between the cash price and the futures price both when a hedge is placed and when it is lifted. The difference between the cash price and the futures price is called the **basis**. The risk that the basis will change in an unpredictable way is called **basis risk**.

In some hedging applications, the bond to be hedged is not identical to the bond underlying the futures contract. This kind of hedging is referred to as cross hedging. There may be substantial basis risk in cross hedging, that is, the relationship between the two instruments may change and lead to a loss. An unhedged position is exposed to **price risk**, the risk that the cash market price will move adversely. A hedged position substitutes basis risk for price risk.

Conceptually, cross hedging requires dealing with two additional complications. The first complication is the relationship between the cheapest-to-deliver security and the futures contract. The second is the relationship between the security to be hedged and the cheapest-to-deliver security.

The key to minimizing risk in a cross hedge is to choose the right **hedge ratio**. The hedge ratio depends on exposure weighting, or weighting by relative changes in value. The purpose of a hedge is to use gains or losses from a futures position to offset any difference between the target sale price and the actual sale price of the asset.

Other Fixed-Income Strategies

Accordingly, the hedge ratio is chosen with the intention of matching the volatility (specifically, the dollar change) of the futures contract to the volatility of the asset. In turn, the factor exposure drives volatility. Consequently, the hedge ratio is given by:

$$\text{Hedge ratio} = \frac{\text{Factor exposure of the bond (portfolio) to be hedged}}{\text{Factor exposure of hedging instrument}}$$

As the formula shows, if the bond to be hedged has greater factor exposure than the hedging instrument, more of the hedging instrument will be needed.

Although it might be fairly clear why factor exposure is important in determining the hedge ratio, "exposure" has many definitions. For hedging purposes, we are concerned with exposure in absolute money terms. To calculate the dollar factor exposure of a bond (portfolio), one must know the precise time at which exposure is to be calculated as well as the price or yield at which to calculate exposure (because higher yields generally reduce dollar exposure for a given yield change).

The relevant point in the life of the bond for calculating exposure is the point at which the hedge will be lifted. Exposure at any other point is essentially irrelevant, because the goal is to lock in a price or rate only on that particular day. Similarly, the relevant yield at which to calculate exposure initially is the target yield. Consequently, the "factor exposure of the bond to be hedged" referred to in the formula is the dollar duration of the bond on the hedge lift date, calculated at its current implied forward rate. The dollar duration is the product of the price of the bond and its duration.

The relative price exposures of the bonds to be hedged and the cheapest-to-deliver bond are easily obtained from the assumed sale date and target prices. In the formula for the hedge ratio, we need the exposure not of the cheapest-to-deliver bond, but of the hedging instrument, that is, of the futures contract. Fortunately, knowing the exposure of the bond to be hedged relative to the cheapest-to-deliver bond and the exposure of the cheapest-to-deliver bond relative to the futures contract, the relative exposures that define the hedge ratio can be easily obtained as follows:

$$\text{Hedge ratio} = \frac{\text{Factor exposure of bond to be hedged}}{\text{Factor exposure of futures contract}}$$

$$= \frac{\text{Factor exposure of bond to be hedged}}{\text{Factor exposure of CTD bond}}$$

$$\times \frac{\text{Factor exposure of CTD bond}}{\text{Factor exposure of futures contract}}$$

Considering only interest rate exposure and assuming a fixed yield spread between the bond to be hedged and the cheapest-to-deliver bond, the hedge ratio is

$$\text{Hedge ratio} = \frac{D_H P_H}{D_{CTD} P_{CTD}} \times \text{Conversion factor for the CTD bond}$$

where D_H = the duration of the bond to be hedged and P_H = the price of the bond to be hedged. The product of the duration and the price is the dollar duration.

Another refinement in the hedging strategy is usually necessary for hedging nondeliverable securities. This refinement concerns the assumption about the relative yield spread between the cheapest-to-deliver bond and the bond to be hedged. In the discussion so far, we have assumed that the yield spread is constant over time. In practice, however, yield spreads are not constant over time. They vary with the maturity of the instruments in question and the level of rates, as well as with many unpredictable factors.

A hedger can use regression analysis to capture the relationship between yield levels and yield spreads. For hedging purposes, the variables are the yield on the bond to be hedged and the yield on the cheapest-to-deliver bond. The regression equation takes the form:

Yield on bond to be hedged = $a + b$(Yield on CTD bond) + Error term

The regression procedure provides an estimate of b, called the **yield beta**, which is the expected relative change in the two bonds. The error term accounts for the fact that the relationship between the yields is not perfect and contains a certain amount of noise. The regression will, however, give an estimate of a and b so that, over the sample period, the average error is zero. Our formula for the hedge ratio assumes a constant spread and implicitly assumes that the yield beta in the regression equals 1.0.

The formula for the hedge ratio can be revised to incorporate the impact of the yield beta by including the yield beta as a multiplier.

$$\text{Hedge ratio} = \frac{D_H P_H}{D_{CTD} P_{CTD}} \times \text{Conversion factor for the CTD bond} \times \text{Yield beta}$$

The effectiveness of a hedge may be evaluated after the hedge has been lifted. The analysis of hedging error can provide managers with meaningful insights that can be useful subsequently.

The three major sources of hedging error are incorrect duration calculations, inaccurate projected basis values, and inaccurate yield beta estimates. A good valuation model is critical to ensure the correct calculation of duration, especially for portfolios containing securities with embedded options.

5.3.5 Interest Rate Swaps

An **interest rate swap** is a contract between two parties (counterparties) to exchange periodic interest payments based on a specified dollar amount of principal (**notional principal amount**). The interest payments on the notional principal amount are calculated by multiplying the specified interest rate times the notional principal amount. These interest payments are the only amounts exchanged; the notional principal amount is only a reference value.

The traditional swap has one party (**fixed-rate payer**) obligated to make periodic payments at a fixed rate in return for the counter party (**floating-rate payer**) agreeing to make periodic payments based on a benchmark floating rate.

The benchmark interest rates used for the floating rate in an interest rate swap are those on various money market instruments: Treasury bills, the London Interbank Offered Rate (Libor), commercial paper, bankers' acceptances, certificates of deposit, the federal funds rate, and the prime rate.

5.3.5.1 Dollar Duration of an Interest Rate Swap
As with any fixed-income contract, the value of a swap will change as interest rates change and dollar duration is a measure of interest-rate sensitivity. From the perspective of the party who pays floating and receives fixed, the interest rate swap position can be viewed as

Long a fixed-rate bond + Short a floating-rate bond

This means that the dollar duration of an interest rate swap from the perspective of a floating-rate payer is just the difference between the dollar duration of the two bond positions that make up the swap:

Dollar duration of a swap = Dollar duration of a fixed-rate bond − Dollar duration of a floating-rate bond

The dollar duration of the fixed-rate bond chiefly determines the dollar duration of the swap because the dollar duration of a floating-rate bond is small.

Other Fixed-Income Strategies

5.3.5.2 Applications of a Swap to Asset/Liability Management An interest rate swap can be used to alter the cash flow characteristics of an institution's assets or liabilities so as to provide a better match between assets and liabilities. More specifically, an institution can use interest rate swaps to alter the cash flow characteristics of its assets or liabilities: changing them from fixed to floating or from floating to fixed. In general, swaps can be used to change the duration of a portfolio or an entity's surplus (the difference between the market value of the assets and the present value of the liabilities).

Instead of using an interest rate swap, the same objectives can be accomplished by taking an appropriate position in a package of forward contracts or appropriate cash market positions. The advantage of an interest rate swap is that it is, from a transaction costs standpoint, a more efficient vehicle for accomplishing an asset/liability objective. In fact, this advantage is the primary reason for the growth of the interest rate swap market.

5.3.6 Bond and Interest Rate Options

Options can be written on cash instruments or futures. Several exchange-traded option contracts have underlying instruments that are debt instruments. These contracts are referred to as **options on physicals**. In general, however, **options on futures** have been far more popular than options on physicals. Market participants have made increasingly greater use of over-the-counter options on Treasury and mortgage-backed securities.

Besides options on fixed-income securities, there are OTC options on the shape of the yield curve or the yield spread between two securities (such as the spread between mortgage passthrough securities and Treasuries or between double-A rated corporates and Treasuries). A discussion of these option contracts, however, is beyond the scope of this section.

An option on a futures contract, commonly referred to as a futures option, gives the buyer the right to buy from or sell to the writer a designated futures contract at the strike price at any time during the life of the option. If the futures option is a call option, the buyer has the right to purchase one designated futures contract at the strike price. That is, the buyer has the right to acquire a long futures position in the designated futures contract. If the buyer exercises the call option, the writer of the call acquires a corresponding short position in the futures contract.

A put option on a futures contract grants the buyer the right to sell one designated futures contract to the writer at the strike price. That is, the option buyer has the right to acquire a short position in the designated futures contract. If the buyer exercises the put option, the writer acquires a corresponding long position in the designated futures contract.

5.3.6.1 Bond Options and Duration The price of a bond option will depend on the price of the underlying instrument, which depends in turn on the interest rate on the underlying instrument. Thus, the price of a bond option depends on the interest rate on the underlying instrument. Consequently, the interest-rate sensitivity or duration of a bond option can be determined.

The duration of an option can be calculated with the following formula:

Duration for an option = Delta of option × Duration of underlying instrument × (Price of underlying)/ (Price of option instrument)

As expected, the duration of an option depends on the duration of the underlying instrument. It also depends on the price responsiveness of the option to a change in the underlying instrument, as measured by the option's **delta**. The leverage created by a position in an option comes from the last ratio in the formula. The higher the price of the underlying instrument relative to the price of the option, the greater the leverage (i.e., the more exposure to interest rates for a given level of investment).

The interaction of all three factors (the duration of the underlying, the option delta, leverage) affects the duration of an option. For example, all else equal, a deep out-of-the-money option has higher leverage than a deep in-the-money option, but the delta of the former is less than that of the latter.

Because the delta of a call option is positive, the duration of a bond call option will be positive. Thus, when interest rates decline, the value of a bond call option will rise. A put option, however, has a delta that is negative. Thus, duration is negative. Consequently, when interest rates rise, the value of a put option rises.

5.3.6.2 Hedging with Options The most common application of options is to hedge a portfolio. There are two hedging strategies in which options are used to protect against a rise in interest rates: **protective put** buying and **covered call** writing. The protective put buying strategy establishes a minimum value for the portfolio but allows the manager to benefit from a decline in rates. The establishment of a floor for the portfolio is not without a cost. The performance of the portfolio will be reduced by the cost of the put option.

Unlike the protective put strategy, covered call writing is not entered into with the sole purpose of protecting a portfolio against rising rates. The covered call writer, believing that the market will not trade much higher or much lower than its present level, sells out-of-the-money calls against an existing bond portfolio. The sale of the calls brings in premium income that provides partial protection in case rates increase. The premium received does not, of course, provide the kind of protection that a long put position provides, but it does provide some additional income that can be used to offset declining prices. If, on the other hand, rates fall, portfolio appreciation is limited because the short call position constitutes a liability for the seller, and this liability increases as rates go down. Consequently, there is limited upside potential for the covered call writer. Covered call writing yields best results if prices are essentially going nowhere; the added income from the sale of options would then be obtained without sacrificing any gains.

Options can also be used by managers seeking to protect against a decline in reinvestment rates resulting from a drop in interest rates. The purchase of call options can be used in such situations. The sale of put options provides limited protection in much the same way that a covered call writing strategy does in protecting against a rise in interest rates.

Interest rate **caps**—call options or series of call options on an interest rate to create a cap (or ceiling) for funding cost—and interest rate **floors**—put options or series of put options on an interest rate—can create a minimum earning rate. The combination of a cap and a floor creates a **collar**.

Banks that borrow short term and lend long term are usually exposed to short-term rate fluctuation. Banks can use caps to effectively place a maximum interest rate on short-term borrowings; specifically, a bank will want the **cap rate** (the exercise interest rate for a cap) plus the cost of the cap to be less than its long-term lending rate. When short-term rates increase, a bank will be protected by the ceiling created by the cap rate. When short-term rates decline, the caps will expire worthless but the bank is better off because its cost of funds has decreased. If they so desire, banks can reduce the cost of purchasing caps by selling floors, thereby giving up part of the potential benefit from a decline in short-term rates.

On the opposite side, a life insurance company may offer a guaranteed investment contract that provides a guaranteed fixed rate and invest the proceeds in a floating-rate instrument. To protect itself from a rate decline while retaining the benefits from an interest rate increase, the insurance company may purchase a floor. If the insurance company wants to reduce the costs of purchasing a floor, it can sell a cap and give up some potential benefit from the rate increase.

5.3.7 Credit Risk Instruments

A given fixed-income security usually contains several risks. The interest rate may change and cause the value of the security to change (interest rate risk); the security may be prepaid or called (option risk); and the value of the issue may be affected by the risk of defaults, credit downgrades, and widening credit spreads (credit risk). In this section, we will focus on understanding and hedging credit risk.

Credit risk can be sold to another party. In return for a fee, another party will accept the credit risk of an underlying financial asset or institution. This party, called the **credit protection seller**, may be willing to take on this risk for several reasons. Perhaps the credit protection seller believes that the credit of an issuer will improve in a favorable economic environment because of a strong stock market and strong financial results. Also, some major corporate events, such as mergers and acquisitions, may improve corporate ratings. Finally, the corporate debt refinancing caused by a friendlier interest rate environment and more favorable lending rates would be a positive credit event.

There are three types of credit risk: default risk, credit spread risk, and downgrade risk. Default risk is the risk that the issuer may fail to meet its obligations. **Credit spread risk** is the risk that the spread between the rate for a risky bond and the rate for a default risk-free bond (like US treasury securities) may vary after the purchase. **Downgrade risk** is the risk that one of the major rating agencies will lower its rating for an issuer, based on its specified rating criteria.

5.3.7.1 Products That Transfer Credit Risk Credit risk may be represented by various types of credit events, including a credit spread change, a rating downgrade, or default. A variety of derivative products, known as **credit derivatives**, exist to package and transfer the credit risk of a financial instrument or institution to another party. The first type of credit derivative we examine is credit options.

Credit Options Unlike ordinary debt options that protect investors against interest rate risk, credit options are structured to offer protection against credit risk. The triggering events of credit options can be based either on 1) the value decline of the underlying asset or 2) the spread change over a risk-free rate.

1 *Credit Options Written on an Underlying Asset*: **Binary credit options** provide payoffs contingent on the occurrence of a specified negative credit event.

   In the case of a binary credit option, the negative event triggering a specified payout to the option buyer is default of a designated reference entity. The term "binary" means that there are only two possible scenarios: default or no default. If the credit has not defaulted by the maturity of the option, the buyer receives nothing. The option buyer pays a premium to the option seller for the protection afforded by the option.

   The payoff of a binary credit option can also be based on the credit rating of the underlying asset. A credit put option pays for the difference between the strike price and the market price when a specified credit event occurs and pays nothing if the event does not occur. For example, a binary credit put option may pay the option buyer $X - V(t)$ if the rating of Bond A is below investment-grade and pay nothing otherwise, where X is the strike price and $V(t)$ is the market value of Bond A at time t. The strike price could be a fixed number, such as $200,000, or, more commonly, expressed as a spread (**strike spread**) that is used to determine the strike price for the payoff when the credit event occurs.

> ## EXAMPLE 12
>
> ### Binary Credit Option
>
> The manager of an investment-grade fixed-income fund is concerned about the possibility of a rating downgrade of Alpha Motors, Inc. The fund's holding in this company consists of 5,000 bonds with a par value of $1,000 each. The fund manager doesn't want to liquidate the holdings in this bond, and instead decides to purchase a binary credit put option on the bond of Alpha Motors. This option expires in six months and pays the option buyer if the rating of Alpha Motors' bond on expiration date is below investment grade (Standard & Poor's/Moody's BB/Ba or lower). The payoff, if any, is the difference between the strike price ($1,000) and the value of the bond at expiration. The fund paid a premium of $130,000 to purchase the option on 5,000 bonds.
>
> 1 What would be the payoff and the profit if the rating of Alpha Motors' bond on expiration date is below investment grade and the value of the bond is $870?
>
> 2 What would be the payoff and the profit if the rating of Alpha Motors' bond on expiration date is investment grade and the value of the bond is $980?
>
> ### Solution to 1:
>
> The option is in the money at expiration because the bond's rating is below investment grade. The payoff on each bond is $1,000 − $870 = $130. Therefore, the payoff on 5,000 bonds is 5,000 × $130 = $650,000. The profit is $650,000 − $130,000 = $520,000.
>
> ### Solution to 2:
>
> The option is out of the money at expiration because the bond's rating is above investment grade. The payoff on each bond is zero. The premium paid of $130,000 is the loss.

2 *Credit Spread Options*: Another type of credit option is a call option in which the payoff is based on the spread over a benchmark rate. The payoff function of a credit spread call option is as follows:

Payoff = Max[(Spread at the option maturity − K) × Notional amount × Risk factor, 0]

where K is the strike spread, and the risk factor is the value change of the security for a one basis point change in the credit spread. Max[A, B] means "A or B, whichever is greater."

Credit Forwards **Credit forwards** are another form of credit derivatives. Their payoffs are based on bond values or credit spreads. There are a buyer and a seller for a credit forward contract. For the buyer of a credit forward contract, the payoff functions as follows:

Payoff = (Credit spread at the forward contract maturity − Contracted credit spread) × Notional amount × Risk factor

Other Fixed-Income Strategies

If a credit forward contract is symmetric, the buyer of a credit forward contract benefits from a widening credit spread and the seller benefits from a narrowing credit spread. The maximum the buyer can lose is limited to the payoff amount in the event that the credit spread becomes zero. In a credit spread option, by contrast, the maximum that the option buyer can lose is the option premium.

Example 13 illustrates the payoff of credit spread forward, and Example 14 contrasts binary credit options, credit spread options, and credit spread forwards.

EXAMPLE 13

Evaluating the Payoff of a Credit Spread Forward

The current credit spread on bonds issued by Hi-Fi Technologies relative to same maturity government debt is 200 bps. The manager of Stable Growth Funds believes that the credit situation of Hi-Fi Technologies will deteriorate over the next few months, resulting in a higher credit spread on its bonds. He decides to buy a six-month credit spread forward contract with the current spread as the contracted spread. The forward contract has a notional amount of $5 million and a risk factor of 4.3.

1. On the settlement date six months later, the credit spread on Hi-Fi Technologies' bonds is 150 bps. How much is the payoff to Stable Growth Funds?
2. How much would the payoff to Stable Growth Funds be if the credit spread on the settlement date is 300 bps?
3. How much is the maximum possible loss to Stable Growth Funds?
4. How much would the payoffs in Parts 1, 2, and 3 above be to the party that took the opposite side of the forward contract?

Solutions:

The payoff to Stable Growth Funds would be:

$$\text{Payoff} = (\text{Credit spread at the forward contract maturity} - 0.020) \times \$5 \text{ million} \times 4.3$$

1. Payoff = (0.015 − 0.020) × $5 million × 4.3 = −$107,500, a loss of $107,500.
2. Payoff = (0.030 − 0.020) × $5 million × 4.3 = $215,000.
3. Stable Growth Funds would have the maximum loss in the unlikely event of the credit spread at the forward contract maturity being zero. So, the worst possible payoff would be (0.000 − 0.020) × $5 million × 4.3 = −$430,000, a loss of $430,000.
4. The payoff to party that took the opposite side of the forward contract, that is, the party that took the position that credit spread would decrease, would be:

$$\text{Payoff} = (0.020 - \text{Credit spread at the forward contract maturity}) \times \$5 \text{ million} \times 4.3$$

The payoffs to this party would be the opposite of the payoffs to Stable Growth Fund. So, the payoffs would be a gain of $107,500 in Part 1, a loss of $215,000 in Part 2, and a maximum possible gain of $430,000 in Part 3. Because there is no limit to the increase in credit spread, the maximum possible loss for this party is limitless.

EXAMPLE 14

Binary Credit Option, Credit Spread Option, and Credit Spread Forward

The portfolio manager of a fixed-income fund is concerned about possible adverse developments in three of the bond holdings of the fund. The reason for his concern is different for the three bond holdings. In particular, he is concerned about the possibility of a credit rating downgrade for Company X, the possibility of a credit default by Company Y, and the possibility of a widening credit spread for Company Z. The portfolio manager contacts a credit derivative dealer. The dealer tells him that his firm offers several credit instruments, some of which are given on the next page.

For each of the following, indicate if it could be used to cover one or more of the three risks the portfolio manager is concerned about.

1. A binary credit put option with the credit event specified as a default by the company on its debt obligations.
2. A binary credit put option with the credit event specified as a credit rating downgrade.
3. A credit spread put option where the underlying is the level of the credit spread.
4. A credit spread call option where the underlying is the level of the credit spread.
5. A credit spread forward, with the credit derivative dealer firm taking a position that the credit spread will decrease.

Solution to 1:

The fixed-income fund could purchase this put option to cover the risk of a credit default by Company Y.

Solution to 2:

The fixed-income fund could purchase this put option to cover the risk of a credit rating downgrade for Company X.

Solution to 3:

This option is not useful to cover any of the three risks. A credit spread put option where the underlying is the level of the credit spread is useful if one believes that credit spread will decline.

Solution to 4:

The fixed-income fund could purchase this credit spread call option where the underlying is the level of the credit spread to cover the risk of an increased credit spread for Company Z.

> **Solution to 5:**
> The fixed-income fund could enter into this forward contract to cover the risk of an increased credit spread for Company Z. The dealer firm would take a position that the credit spread will decrease, while the fixed-income fund would take the opposite position.

Credit Swaps A number of different products can be classified as credit swaps, including credit default swaps, asset swaps, total return swaps, credit-linked notes, synthetic collateralized bond obligations, and basket default swaps. Among all credit derivative products, the **credit default swap** is the most popular and is commonly recognized as the basic building block of the credit derivative market. Therefore, we focus our discussion on credit default swaps.

A credit default swap is a contract that shifts credit exposure of an asset issued by a specified **reference entity** from one investor (protection buyer) to another investor (protection seller). The protection buyer usually makes regular payments, the swap premium payments (default swap spread), to the protection seller. For short-dated credit, investors may pay this fee up front. In the case of a **credit event**, the protection seller compensates the buyer for the loss on the investment, and the settlement by the protection buyer can take the form of either physical delivery or a negotiated cash payment equivalent to the market value of the defaulted securities. The transaction can be schematically represented as in Exhibit 22.

Exhibit 22 Credit Default Swap

```
                  Swap Premium (default swap spread)
 Protection Buyer  ◄──────────────────────────────►  Protection Seller
                  Contingent Payment on Credit Event
```

Credit default swaps can be used as a hedging instrument. Banks can use credit default swaps to reduce credit risk concentration. Instead of selling loans, banks can effectively transfer credit exposures by buying protections with default swaps. Default swaps also enable investors to hedge nonpublicly traded debts.

Credit default swaps provide great flexibility to investors. Default swaps can be used to express a view on the credit quality of a reference entity. The protection seller makes no upfront investment to take additional credit risk and is thus able to leverage credit risk exposure. In most cases, it is more efficient for investors to buy protection in the default swap market than selling or shorting assets. Because default swaps are negotiated over the counter, they can be tailored specifically toward investors' needs.

> **EXAMPLE 15**
>
> ## Credit Default Swap
>
> We Deal, Inc., a dealer of credit derivatives, is quite bullish on the long-term debt issued by the governments of three countries in South America. We Deal decides to sell protection in the credit default swap market on the debt issued by these countries. The credit event in these transactions is defined as the failure by the borrower to make timely interest and/or principal payments. A few months later, the government of Country A defaults on its debt obligations, the rating of debt issued by Country B is lowered by Moody's from Baa to Ba because of adverse economic developments in that country, and the rating of debt issued by

> Country C is upgraded by Moody's from Baa to A in view of favorable economic developments in that country. For each of the countries, indicate whether We Deal suffers a loss.
>
> **Solution:**
>
> In the protection sold by the dealer, the credit event was defined as the failure by the borrower to make timely interest and/or principal payments. This credit event occurred only in the case of Country A. Therefore, the dealer is likely to have suffered a loss only in the protection sold for Country A.

In the next section we broaden our view of fixed-income portfolio management by examining selected issues in international bond investing.

6. INTERNATIONAL BOND INVESTING

The motivation for international bond investing (i.e., investing in nondomestic bonds) includes portfolio risk reduction and return enhancement compared with portfolios limited to domestic fixed-income securities. In the standard Markowitz mean–variance framework, the risk reduction benefits from adding foreign-issued bonds to a domestic bond portfolio result from their less-than-perfect correlation with domestic fixed-income assets. Exhibit 23 illustrates historical correlations among a selection of developed fixed-income markets.

Exhibit 23 Correlation Coefficients of Monthly Total Returns between International Government Bond Indices 1989–2003

In US$

	Aus	Can	Fra	Ger	Jap	Net	Swi	UK	US
Australia	1.00								
Canada	0.57	1.00							
France	0.27	0.26	1.00						
Germany	0.27	0.26	0.97	1.00					
Japan	0.16	0.12	0.43	0.46	1.00				
Netherlands	0.28	0.31	0.97	0.95	0.43	1.00			
Switzerland	0.20	0.14	0.88	0.90	0.49	0.86	1.00		
United Kingdom	0.24	0.33	0.67	0.66	0.35	0.69	0.58	1.00	
United States	0.27	0.49	0.43	0.42	0.19	0.41	0.37	0.48	1.00

In Local Currency

	Aus	Can	Fra	Ger	Jap	Net	Swi	UK	US
Australia	1.00								
Canada	0.70	1.00							
France	0.45	0.46	1.00						
Germany	0.48	0.52	0.86	1.00					
Japan	0.25	0.27	0.20	0.29	1.00				
Netherlands	0.43	0.42	0.86	0.74	0.12	1.00			

Exhibit 23 (Continued)

	In Local Currency								
	Aus	Can	Fra	Ger	Jap	Net	Swi	UK	US
Switzerland	0.34	0.35	0.61	0.68	0.27	0.55	1.00		
United Kingdom	0.51	0.59	0.67	0.71	0.24	0.58	0.53	1.00	
United States	0.63	0.71	0.56	0.62	0.26	0.46	0.47	0.57	1.00

The highest correlation was observed among the European markets because of the common monetary policy of the European Central Bank and introduction of the euro in 1999, which resulted in a larger, more liquid, and integrated European bond market. The correlation coefficients are the lowest among countries with the weakest economic ties to each other. When returns are converted to US dollars, the correlation coefficients reflect the impact of currency exchange rates on international investment. For example, the correlation coefficient between US and UK returns is 0.57 in local currency terms and only 0.48 in US dollar terms.

Overall, local currency correlations tend to be higher than their US dollar equivalent correlations. Such deviations are attributed to currency volatility, which tends to reduce the correlation among international bond indices when measured in US dollars.

In summary, the low-to-moderate correlations presented in Exhibit 23 provide historical support for the use of international bonds for portfolio risk reduction. Expanding the set of fixed-income investment choices beyond domestic markets should reveal opportunities for return enhancement as well.

If the investor decides to invest in international fixed-income markets, what directions and choices may be taken? Clearly, certain issues in international bond investing, such as the choice of active or passive approaches, as well as many fixed-income tools (e.g., yield curve and credit analysis), are shared with domestic bond investing. However, international investing raises additional challenges and opportunities and, in contrast to domestic investing, involves exposure to **currency risk**—the risk associated with the uncertainty about the exchange rate at which proceeds in the foreign currency can be converted into the investor's home currency. Currency risk results in the need to formulate a strategy for currency management. The following sections offer an introduction to these topics.

6.1 Active versus Passive Management

As a first step, investors in international fixed-income markets need to select a position on the passive/active spectrum. The opportunities for active management are created by inefficiencies that may be attributed to differences in tax treatment, local regulations, coverage by fixed-income analysts, and even to differences in how market players respond to similar information. The active manager seeks to add value through one or more of the following means: bond market selection, currency selection, duration management/yield curve management, sector selection, credit analysis of issuers, and investing outside the benchmark index.

- *Bond market selection.*

  The selection of the national market(s) for investment. Analysis of global economic factors is an important element in this selection that is especially critical when investing in emerging market debt.

- *Currency selection.*

This is the selection of the amount of currency risk retained for each currency, in effect, the currency hedging decision. If a currency exposure is not hedged, the return on a nondomestic bond holding will depend not only on the holding's return in local currency terms but also on the movement of the foreign/domestic exchange rate. If the investor has the ability to forecast certain exchange rates, the investor may tactically attempt to add value through currency selection. Distinct knowledge and skills are required in currency selection and active currency management more generally. As a result, currency management function is often managed separately from the other functions.

- *Duration management/yield curve management.*

    Once a market is chosen and decisions are made on currency exposures, the duration or interest rate exposure of the holding must be selected. Duration management strategies and positioning along the yield curve within a given market can enhance portfolio return. Duration management can be constrained by the relatively narrow selection of maturities available in many national markets; however, growing markets for fixed-income derivatives provide an increasingly effective means of duration and yield curve management.

- *Sector selection.*

    The international bond market now includes fixed-income instruments representing a full range of sectors, including government and corporate bonds issued in local currencies and in US dollars. A wide assortment of coupons, ratings, and maturities opens opportunities for attempting to add value through credit analysis and other disciplines.

- *Credit analysis of issuers.*

    Portfolio managers may attempt to add value through superior credit analysis, for example, analysis that identifies credit improvement or deterioration of an issuer before other market participants have recognized it.

- *Investing in markets outside the benchmark.*

    For example, benchmarks for international bond investing often consist of government-issued bonds. In such cases, the portfolio manager may consider investing in nonsovereign bonds not included in the index to enhance portfolio returns. This tactic involves a risk mismatch created with respect to the benchmark index; therefore, the client should be aware of and amenable to its use.

Relative to duration management, the relationship between duration of a foreign bond and the duration of the investor's portfolio including domestic and foreign bonds deserves further comment. As defined earlier, portfolio duration is the percentage change in value of a bond portfolio resulting from a 100 bps change in rates. Portfolio duration defined this way is meaningful only in the case of a domestic bond portfolio. For this duration concept to be valid in the context of international bond investments, one would need to assume that the interest rates of every country represented in the portfolio simultaneously change by 100 bps. International interest rates are not perfectly correlated, however, and such an interpretation of international bond portfolio duration would not be meaningful.

The duration measure of a portfolio that includes domestic and foreign bonds must recognize the correlation between the movements in interest rates in the home country and each nondomestic market. Thomas and Willner (1997) suggest a methodology for computing the contribution of a foreign bond's duration to the duration of a portfolio.

The Thomas–Willner methodology begins by expressing the change in a bond's value in terms of a change in the foreign yields, as follows:

$$\text{Change in value of foreign bond} = -\text{Duration} \times \text{Change in foreign yield} \times 100$$

International Bond Investing

From the perspective of a Canadian manager, for example, the concern is the change in value of the foreign bond when domestic (Canadian) rates change. This change in value can be determined by incorporating the relationship between changes in domestic (Canadian) rates and changes in foreign rates as follows:

$$\text{Change in value of foreign bond} = -\text{Duration} \times \text{Change in foreign yield given a change in domestic yield} \times 100$$

The relationship between the change in foreign yield and the change in Canadian yield can be estimated empirically using monthly data for each country. The following relationship is estimated:

$$\Delta y_{\text{foreign}} = \alpha + \beta \Delta y_{\text{domestic}}$$

where

$\Delta y_{\text{foreign}}$ = change in a foreign bond's yield in month t
$\Delta y_{\text{domestic}}$ = change in domestic (Canadian) yield in month time t
β = correlation($\Delta y_{\text{foreign},t}$, $\Delta y_{\text{domestic},t}$) × $\sigma_{\text{foreign}}/\sigma_{\text{domestic}}$

The parameter β is called the **country beta**. The duration attributed to a foreign bond in the portfolio is found by multiplying the bond's country beta by the bond's duration in local terms, as illustrated in Example 16.

EXAMPLE 16

The Duration of a Foreign Bond

Suppose that a British bond portfolio manager wants to invest in German government 10-year bonds. The manager is interested in the foreign bond's contribution to the duration of the portfolio when domestic interest rates change.

The duration of the German bond is 6 and the country beta is estimated to be 0.42. The duration contribution to a British domestic portfolio is 2.52 = 6 × 0.42. For a 100 bps change in UK interest rates, the value of the German bond is expected to change by approximately 2.52 percent.

Because a portfolio's duration is a weighted average of the duration of the bonds in the portfolio, the contribution to the portfolio's duration is equal to the adjusted German bond duration of 2.52 multiplied by its weight in the portfolio.

6.2 Currency Risk

For the investor in international bonds, fluctuations in the exchange rate between domestic and foreign currencies may decrease or increase the value of foreign investments when converted into the investor's local currency. In particular, when a foreign currency depreciates against the investor's home currency (i.e., a given amount of the foreign currency buys less of the home currency) a currency loss occurs, but when it appreciates, a currency gain occurs. Currency risk is often substantial relative to interest rate risk in its effects on the returns earned on international bond portfolios.

In order to protect the value of international investments from adverse exchange rate movements, investors often diversify currency exposures by having exposure to several currencies. To the extent depreciation of one currency tends to be associated with appreciation of another—i.e., currency risks are less than perfectly correlated—a multi-currency portfolio has less currency risk than a portfolio denominated in a single currency.

The standard measure of the currency risk effect on foreign asset returns involves splitting the currency effect into 1) the expected effect captured by the **forward discount** or forward premium (the forward rate less the spot rate, divided by the spot rate; called the forward discount if negative) and 2) the unexpected effect, defined as the unexpected movement of the foreign currency relative to its forward rate. Every investor in the foreign markets can either remain exposed to this currency risk or hedge it. The investor may also have access to and may consider investing in **currency-hedged instruments**, which neutralize the currency exposure while maintaining the exposure to local bond price changes.

The bond investor should be aware of a basic result in economics concerning the forward discount/premium called covered interest rate parity as it suggests an approach to comparing (fully) hedged returns across international bond markets.

6.2.1 Interest Rate Parity

Interest rate parity (IRP) states that the forward foreign exchange rate discount or premium over a fixed period should equal the risk-free interest rate differential between the two countries over that period to prevent the opportunity for arbitrage profits using spot and forward currency markets plus borrowing or lending. Furthermore, as the interest rate differential between two countries changes, so should the forward discount or premium. To explain further, let the forward discount or premium, f, be given by

$$f = (F - S_0)/S_0$$

where

F = forward exchange rate (stated as domestic currency/foreign currency)
S_0 = spot exchange rate (stated as domestic currency/foreign currency)

The currency quotation convention used—domestic currency/foreign currency—called **direct quotation**, means that from the perspective of an investor in a foreign asset an increase in the spot exchange rate is associated with a currency gain from holding the foreign asset. According to IRP,[5]

$$f \approx i_d - i_f$$

where i_d and i_f are, respectively, the domestic and foreign risk-free interest rates over the time horizon associated with the forward exchange rate. For example, suppose the investor is based in the Eurozone and the available 1-year risk-free interest rate, at i_d = 3.0 percent, is lower than the 1-year US risk-free interest rate, at i_f = 4.5 percent. Thus, the interest rate differential is $i_d - i_f$ = 3.0 percent – 4.5 percent = –1.5 percent. The spot exchange range is €0.8000 per dollar. According to IRP, the no-arbitrage forward exchange rate is €0.7880 per dollar because the resulting forward discount is (0.7880 – 0.8000)/0.8000 = –1.5 percent. If the Eurozone investor makes a US dollar bank deposit, the higher interest earned is offset by a currency loss.

6.2.2 Hedging Currency Risk

The decision on how much currency risk to hedge—from none to all—is important because currency movements can have a dramatic effect on the investor's return from international bond holdings. To illustrate the issue, Exhibit 24 shows the fluctuations in the US–Australian dollar exchange rate over the period January 1993 to January 2004.

---

[5] For more details, including an explanation of the approximation, see Solnik and McLeavey (2004), Chapters 1 and 2.

Exhibit 24   US Dollars per Australian Dollars

During the period of a falling Australian dollar (1997 to mid-2001), hedged Australian investment positions generated higher returns in terms for US investors than similar unhedged positions. From mid-2001 to the start of 2004, the trend reversed—the Australian currency appreciated—and hedged investments underperformed. Hedged and unhedged international investments with Australian dollar exposure generated drastically different returns in 2000 and 2003. Therefore, investors must carefully examine the decision to hedge and be familiar with hedging methods.

The three main methods of currency hedging are:

- forward hedging;
- proxy hedging; and
- cross hedging.

Forward hedging involves the use of a forward contract between the bond's currency and the home currency. **Proxy hedging** involves using a forward contract between the home currency and a currency that is highly correlated with the bond's currency. The investor may use proxy hedging because forward markets in the bond's currency are relatively undeveloped, or because it is otherwise cheaper to hedge using a proxy. In the context of currency hedging, cross hedging refers to hedging using two currencies other than the home currency and is a technique used to convert the currency risk of the bond into a different exposure that has less risk for the investor. The investment policy statement often provides guidance on permissible hedging methods.

The most popular hedging approach is forward hedging. For example, a German investor may be holding a position in Canadian bonds that is expected to pay C$5 million at maturity in nine months. Forward contracts are used to lock in the current value of a currency for future delivery. To hedge this position, therefore, the investor enters a forward agreement to purchase euros nine months from today at a forward rate of €1.20 per Canadian dollar. By entering the forward agreement and arranging the receipt of €6 million = C$5 million × 1.20€/C$ nine months from now, the investor is hedging against fluctuations in the euro/Canadian dollar exchange rate over the next nine months.

Currency exposures associated with investments with variable cash flows, such as variable coupon bonds or collateralized debt obligations, cannot be hedged completely because forward contracts only cover the expected cash flows.[6] The actual investment payoff may differ from the expected, resulting in an over- or underhedged portfolio, in which case, the currency may have to be exchanged at the future spot rate.

---

6 A **collateralized debt obligation** is a securitized pool of fixed-income assets.

This reading can only briefly introduce the subject of hedging currency risk, and the perspective taken will be tactical. A first, basic fact is that a foreign bond return stated in terms of the investor's home currency, the **unhedged return** (R), is approximately equal to the foreign bond return in local currency terms, r_l, plus the **currency return**, e, which is the percentage change in the spot exchange rate stated in terms of home currency per unit of foreign currency (direct quotation, as before):

$$R \approx r_l + e$$

If the investor can hedge fully with forward contracts, what return will the investor earn? The (fully) **hedged return**, HR, is equal to the sum of r_l plus the forward discount (premium) f, which is the price the investor pays (receives) to hedge the currency risk of the foreign bond. That is,

$$HR \approx r_l + f$$

If IRP holds, f is approximately equal to the interest rate differential, so that

$$HR \approx r_l + f \approx r_l + (i_d - i_f) = i_d + (r_l - i_f)$$

In other words, the hedged bond return can be viewed as the sum of the domestic risk-free interest rate (i_d) plus the bond's local risk premium (its excess return in relation to the local risk-free rate) of the foreign bond. If we compare the fully hedged return of international bond issues from different national markets, the expected difference in their fully hedged returns will reflect only the differences in their local risk premia. This idea provides an easy way to compare the hedged yields of bonds in different markets, as illustrated in Example 17.

EXAMPLE 17

Comparing Hedged Returns across Markets

Suppose a UK investor is making a choice between same maturity (and credit risk) Japanese and Canadian government bonds. Currently, 10-year yields on government bonds in Japan and in Canada are 2.16 percent and 3.40 percent, respectively. Short-term interest rates are 1.25 percent and 1.54 percent in Japan and Canada, respectively. Assume that IRP holds. Contrast the expected fully hedged returns on 10-year Japanese and Canadian government bonds.

Solution:

The Japanese government bond's local risk premium is 0.91 percent = 2.16 percent − 1.25 percent, and the Canadian government bond's local risk premium is 1.86 percent = 3.40 percent − 1.54 percent. Because the local risk premium on the Canadian bond is higher, its expected fully hedged return will be higher as well.

Example 17 contrasted the hedged yields of two bonds. In Example 18, the investor chooses hedging with forwards over leaving an investment unhedged based on a comparison of the interest rate differential with the expected currency return.

EXAMPLE 18

To Hedge or Not with a Forward Contract (1)

A US fixed-income fund has substantial holdings in euro-denominated German bonds. The portfolio manager of the fund is considering whether to leave the fund's exposure to the euro unhedged or fully hedge it using a dollar–euro forward contract. Assume that the short-term interest rates are 4 percent in the

International Bond Investing

United States and 3.2 percent in Germany. The fund manager expects the euro to appreciate against the dollar by 0.6 percent. Assume that IRP holds. Explain which alternative has the higher expected return based on the short-term interest rates and the manager's expectations about exchange rates.

Solution:

The interest rate differential between the dollar and the euro is 4 − 3.2 = 0.8 percent. Because this differential is greater than the expected return on euro of 0.6 percent, a forward hedged investment is expected to result in a higher return than an unhedged position.

Example 19 examines the tactical decision to hedge or not based on the expected **excess currency return**, which is defined as the expected currency return in excess of the forward premium or discount.

EXAMPLE 19

To Hedge or Not with a Forward Contract (2)

David Marlet is the portfolio manager of a French fund that has substantial holdings in the UK pound-denominated British government bonds. Simon Jones is the portfolio manager of a British fund that has large holdings in euro-denominated French government bonds. Both the portfolio managers are considering whether to hedge their portfolio exposure to the foreign currency using a forward contract or leave the exposure unhedged. Assume that the short-term interest rates are 3.2 percent in France and 4.7 percent in the United Kingdom and that the forward discount on the pound is 4.7 − 3.2 = 1.5 percent. Marlet and Jones believe that the UK pound, the currency associated with the higher interest rate, will depreciate less relative to the euro than what the forward rate between the two currencies would indicate assuming interest rate parity.

1. Should Marlet use a forward contract to hedge the fund's exposure to the British pound?
2. Should Jones use a forward contract to hedge the fund's exposure to the euro?

Solutions:

Both portfolio managers expect that the pound will depreciate less than 1.5 percent.

1. If Marlet were to hedge using a forward contract, he would be locking in a currency return of −1.5 percent; that is, a 1.5 percent loss on currency. By remaining unhedged, however, he expects the loss on currency to be less than 1.5 percent. Based on expected returns alone, he should not hedge the currency risk using a forward contract.
2. The situation of Jones, the portfolio manager of the British fund, is exactly the opposite of the portfolio manager of the French fund. If Jones were to hedge using a forward contract, he would be locking in a currency return of 1.5 percent, that is, a 1.5 percent gain on currency. Jones expects the gain on currency to be less than 1.5 percent if he does not hedge.

Therefore, Jones should hedge the currency risk. Because Jones's anticipated return on currency (less than 1.5 percent) is below the interest rate differential (1.5 percent), the currency risk should be hedged.

6.3 Breakeven Spread Analysis

One consideration in active international bond portfolio selection is bond and country yield advantages. Breakeven spread analysis can be used to quantify the amount of spread widening required to diminish a foreign yield advantage. Breakeven spread analysis does not account for exchange rate risk, but the information it provides can be helpful in assessing the risk in seeking higher yields. Yield relationships can change because of a variety of factors. Furthermore, even a constant yield spread across markets may produce different returns. One reason is that prices of securities that vary in coupon and maturity respond differently to changes in yield: Duration plays an important role in breakeven spread analysis. Also, the yield advantage of investing in a foreign country may disappear if domestic yields increase and foreign yields decline.

EXAMPLE 20

Breakeven Spread Analysis

Suppose the spread between Japanese and French bonds is 300 bps, providing Japanese investors who purchased the French bond with an additional yield income of 75 bps per quarter. The duration of the Japanese bond is 7. Let W denote the spread widening.

With a duration of 7, the price change for the Japanese bond will be seven times the change in yield. (For 100 bps change yield in yield, the price change for the Japanese bond will be 7 percent.)

Change in price = 7 × Change in yield

Change in price = 7 × W

Assuming that the increase in price caused by the spread widening will be 0.75 percent, the yield advantage of French bonds would be:

0.75 percent = 7 × W

Solving for the spread widening, W,

W = 0.1071 percent = 10.71 bps

Thus, a spread widening of 10.71 bps because of a decline in the yields in Japan would wipe out the additional yield gained from investing in the French bond for that quarter. A change in interest rates of only 10.71 bps in this case would wipe out the quarterly yield advantage of 75 bps.

Note that the breakeven spread widening analysis must be associated with an investment horizon (3 months in Example 20) and must be based on the higher of the two countries' durations. The analysis ignores the impact of currency movements.

The ability to choose individual sectors and/or securities varies considerably across the globe. For the developed countries, the same type of analysis for each of the respective fixed-income markets is appropriate. For the developing countries, such external influences as specific country or worldwide economic factors are relatively more important.

Emerging market security selection is especially limited. The resulting liquidity variation must be taken into account, which results in many countries limiting the choice to benchmark government bonds. In all cases, the details on settlements, taxation, and regulatory issues are important. Finally, as one builds a portfolio, the effects of currency positions add a critical dimension. Use of derivative products has enabled more flexibility but is usually available only at notional amounts in the tens of millions of dollars at a minimum.

6.4 Emerging Market Debt

Emerging markets comprise those nations whose economies are considered to be developing and are usually taken to include Latin America, Eastern Europe, Africa, Russia, the Middle East, and Asia excluding Japan. Emerging market debt (EMD) includes sovereign bonds (bonds issued by a national government) as well as debt securities issued by public and private companies in those countries.

Over the past 10 years, emerging market debt has matured as an asset class and now frequently appears in many strategic asset allocations. Because of its low correlation with domestic debt portfolios, EMD offers favorable diversification properties to a fixed-income portfolio. EMD has played an important role in **core-plus** fixed-income portfolios. Core-plus is a label for fixed-income mandates that permit the portfolio manager to add instruments with relatively high return potential, such as EMD and high-yield debt, to core holdings of investment-grade debt.[7]

6.4.1 *Growth and Maturity of the Market*

Although emerging market governments have always borrowed to meet their needs, the modern emerging markets debt sector originated in the 1980s when the Mexican financial crisis led to the creation of a secondary market in loans to that country. The Brady plan, which followed soon thereafter, allowed emerging country governments to securitize their outstanding external bank loans. A liquid market for these securities (called Brady bonds) soon followed. As a result of debt securitization, the majority of emerging market debt risk has now shifted from the banks to the private sector. The market has grown rapidly to its current substantial size—the International Monetary Fund (2005, p. 268) estimates the total size of the emerging external debt market in 2006 to be approximately $3.3 trillion.

The proportion of emerging market countries that are rated as investment grade has risen to about 40 percent of the countries represented in the emerging market indices. Mexico, for example, can now borrow almost as cheaply as the US government. The quality of emerging market sovereign bonds has increased to the point that they now have frequencies of default, recovery rates, and ratings transition probabilities similar to corporate bonds as well as similar ratings. As a result, the spread of emerging market debt over risk-free rates has narrowed considerably.

The EMD market has also shown remarkable resiliency. During the Asian crisis of the late 1990s, the price of Asian debt fluctuated over wide ranges, but the market rebounded impressively, offering rates of return that exceeded those of many developed countries' equity markets in the post-crisis period. The market has dealt with crises in Latin America, Southeast Asia, and Russia with relatively little damage to investors, with the notable exception of the large Russian default in 1998.

---

[7] For example, a core-plus manager might be officially benchmarked to the Lehman Aggregate Bond Index, but invest a fraction of the portfolio (perhaps up to 25 percent) outside the benchmark.

Since 1992, the standard index in emerging markets has been the Emerging Markets Bond Index Plus (EMBI+). Although the index emphasizes the inclusion of highly liquid bonds, its main disadvantage is the lack of diversification in the securities that make up the index. An overwhelming percentage of the index (58 percent) is in Latin American securities, with Brazil and Mexico making up 37 percent of the total.

6.4.2 Risk and Return Characteristics

Emerging market debt frequently offers the potential for consistent, attractive rates of return. Sovereign emerging market governments possess several advantages over private corporations. They can react quickly to negative economic events by cutting spending and raising taxes and interest rates (actions that may make it more difficult for private corporations in these countries to service their own debt). They also have access to lenders on the world stage, such as the International Monetary Fund and the World Bank. Many emerging market nations also possess large foreign currency reserves, providing a shock absorber for bumps in their economic road. Using these resources, any adverse situation can be rapidly addressed and reversed.

Risks do exist in the sector however—volatility in the EMD market is high. EMD returns are also frequently characterized by significant negative skewness. Negative skewness is the potential for occasional very large negative returns without offsetting potential on the upside. An instance of an extreme negative event is the massive market sell-off that occurred from August 1997 to September 1998.

Other risks abound. Emerging market countries frequently do not offer the degree of transparency, court-tested laws, and clear regulations that developed market countries do. The legal system may be less developed and offer less protection from interference by the executive branch than in developed countries. Also, developing countries have tended to over borrow, which can damage the position of existing debt. If a default of sovereign debt occurs, recovery against sovereign states can be very difficult. Also, little standardization of covenants exists among various emerging market issuers. Sovereign debt also typically lacks an enforceable seniority structure, in contrast to private debt.

6.4.3 Analysis of Emerging Market Debt

Just as with any credit analysis, an investor in EMD securities must determine the willingness and ability of the issuers to pay their debt obligations. This analysis begins with a look at the country's fundamentals: the source of government revenues, fiscal and monetary policies, current debt levels, and willingness of the country's citizens to accept short-term sacrifices in order to strengthen the country's long-term economic situation. For example, consider the Russian default in 1998. A great deal of money was lent to Russia before its economic and financial collapse. Yet, even a cursory examination would have shown that the country had no experience in collecting taxes, had an extremely weak economic infrastructure, and was dependent on a single commodity (energy) for its revenues. Investors either forgot the fundamentals or chose to ignore them. Historically, the largest returns have come from countries with strong fundamentals, usually characterized by an export-oriented economy and a high savings rate.

In evaluating EMD, the risk of default remains a critical consideration, particularly when private debt is concerned. Investors should not simply accept a bond rating as the final measure of the issue's default risk. In some countries, the financial strength of a large company may be greater than that of the sovereign government. The underlying assets for the company can be quite valuable and may justify a high credit rating. However, the credit rating for the company debt will not be higher than that of sovereign debt. This restriction on private debt ratings creates opportunities for astute investors to purchase high-quality debt at prices below fair market value.

Whether investing in established or emerging markets, investment in foreign assets, while providing diversification benefits, carries the same types of risk of domestic investments plus some additional risks associated with converting the foreign investment cash flows into domestic currency. Political risk and currency risk are major sources of uncertainty for portfolios with international exposures. And, changes in liquidity and taxation may be additional sources of risk.

Political risk or geopolitical risk includes the risk of war, government collapse, political instability, expropriation, confiscation, and adverse changes in taxation. A common political risk is the uncertainty that investors will be able to convert the foreign currency holdings into their home currency as a result of constraints imposed by foreign government policies or political actions of any sort.

Sovereign governments may impose restrictions on capital flows, change rules, revise taxes, liberalize bankruptcy proceedings, modify exchange rate regimes, and create new market regulations, all of which add an element of uncertainty to financial markets by affecting the performance and liquidity of investments in those countries.

Political crises during the 1990s in Europe, Southeast Asia, Russia, Latin America, and the Middle East highlight the increasing global links among political risks. Today's political risks are often subtle, arising not only from legal and regulatory changes and government transitions but also from environmental issues, foreign policies, currency crises, and terrorism. Nevertheless, diversification among international securities is one means to controlling the effect of political risk on the investment performance. However, investments in countries with close economic and political links would afford less than investments in countries with looser links.

Investors in EMD face default risk as does any investor in debt. Sovereign EMD bears greater credit risk than developed market sovereign debt, reflecting less-developed banking and financial market infrastructure, lower transparency, and higher political risk in developing countries. Rating agencies issue sovereign ratings that indicate countries' ability to meet their debt obligations. Standard & Poor's investment-grade sovereign rating of BBB– and Moody's Baa3 are given to the most credit-worthy emerging markets countries. Increased transparency and availability of reliable foreign market data are valued in the marketplace and directly linked to foreign capital inflow. For example, some evidence indicates that US investors in the early 2000s moved out of smaller markets and markets with low and declining credit ratings to countries with more transparent financial markets, open economies, and better inflation performance.[8]

In the next section, we turn our attention to the final topic of this reading, selecting a fixed-income portfolio manager.

SELECTING A FIXED-INCOME MANAGER

When funds are not managed entirely in-house, a search for outside managers must be conducted. Because the average institutional fixed-income portfolio has approximately 85 percent of the assets managed actively and 15 percent indexed, we focus our attention here on the selection of an active manager.

Active return and active risk (tracking risk) are intricately linked. The typical range for tracking risk in large fixed-income institutional portfolios is between 40 and 120 bps with the upper end of the range typically including a high-yield component and

---

[8] See Burger and Warnock (2003).

the lower end being more typical for core managers. Because active management fees typically range from 15 to 50 bps (plus custodial fees), it is clear that outperforming the benchmark on a net-of-fees basis is a challenging and difficult task.

The due diligence for selection of managers is satisfied primarily by investigating the managers' investment process, the types of trades the managers are making, and the manager's organizational strengths and weaknesses. The key to better performance is to find managers who can produce consistent positive style-adjusted alphas. Then, the portfolio can be constructed by optimizing the combination of managers in order to maximize the variety of styles and exposures contributed by each manager.

7.1 Historical Performance as a Predictor of Future Performance

Is a fixed-income manager's historical performance a good predictor of future performance? Studies indicate some evidence of persistence of outperformance by some managers relative to their peers over short periods of time. However, over long periods of time (15 years or more) and when fund fees and expenses are factored in, the realized alpha of fixed-income managers has averaged very close to zero and little evidence of persistence exits. So it is clear that selecting a manager purely on the basis of historical performance is not a good approach to manager selection.

7.2 Developing Criteria for the Selection

The value of due diligence is found in the details; a fundamental analysis of the manager's strategy must be conducted. Here are some of the factors that should be considered:

1 *Style analysis.*

   In large part, the active risk and return are determined by the extent to which the portfolio differs from the benchmark's construction—particularly with regard to overweighting of sectors and duration differences. An analysis of the manager's historical style may prove helpful in explaining how the types of biases and quality of the views reflected in the portfolio weighting have affected a portfolio's overall performance.

   For example, consider a style analysis of an individual core-plus manager. The analysis may demonstrate a significant style weight to MBS and high-yield bonds (consistent with the core-plus strategy), coupled with a persistent and large underweighting of investment-grade securities (relative to the Lehman Aggregate). Also, the manager may make consistent duration bets across the portfolio by investing in bonds with a longer duration than the benchmark. Under the right conditions, this approach could certainly lead to larger returns, but it will also likely lead to higher active risk. A close examination of the results should yield some insight into the manager's skill in using this approach.

2 *Selection bets.*

   If an active manager believes that she possesses superior credit or security analysis skills, she may frequently deviate from the weights in the normal portfolio. By forecasting changes in relative credit spreads and identifying undervalued securities, the manager may attempt to increase the active return of the portfolio. The manager's skill in this approach may be measured by decomposing the portfolio's returns.

3 *The organization's investment process.*

Selecting a Fixed-Income Manager

The investor needs to be intimately familiar with the investment process of the manager's organization. What research methods are used by the organization? What are the main drivers of alpha? How are decisions regarding changes in the portfolio made? A manager is often only as good as the support staff. Before selection, the plan sponsor needs to spend quite a bit of time asking questions of several key people in the organization.

4 *Correlation of alphas.*

The historical correlations of alpha across managers should also be examined. Many managers exhibit similarities in their management of a portfolio. If multiple managers are to be used, obviously the plan sponsor will prefer low to high correlation among managers' alphas to control portfolio risk.

7.3 Comparison with Selection of Equity Managers

Selecting a fixed-income manager has both similarities with and differences from the selection of an equity manager.

1 In both cases, a consultant is frequently used to identify a universe of suitable manager candidates (because of the consultants' large databases).

2 In both sectors, the available evidence indicates that past performance is not a reliable guide to future results.

3 The same qualitative factors are common to both analyses: philosophy of the manager and organization, market opportunity, competitive advantages, delegation of responsibility, experience of the professionals, and so on.

4 Management fees and expenses are vitally important in both areas, because they often reduce or eliminate the alpha that managers are able to earn gross of expenses. If anything, fees are more important in the fixed-income area, because fixed-income funds have a higher ratio of fees to expected outperformance. There is some evidence that fixed-income managers with the highest fees have the lowest information ratios (i.e., ratio of expected alpha to volatility of alpha), so the avoidance of high fees is clearly a defensible strategy.

Although limited space prevents discussion for all the relevant items here, Example 21 illustrates some of the key areas that should be investigated in a complete due diligence analysis.

EXAMPLE 21

Due Diligence Questionnaire for a US Fixed-Income Portfolio

When conducting a search for managers, organizations will typically ask portfolio managers to submit answers to a wide variety of questions as part of the due diligence process. The following questionnaire illustrates the types of information typically asked of candidate managers:

1 Organization
   a history (key events and date)
   b structure
   c ownership
   d number of employees (last three years)
   e awards/ratings

    f flagship products and core competencies
    g timeline of products/product development
    h total assets, total fixed-income assets, and total core-plus assets
    i significant client additions/withdrawals in last three years
    j current lawsuits for investigations
    k policy on market timing, excessive trading, and distribution fee arrangements
    l Form ADV, Parts 1 and 2

2 Product (provide information based on a similar or composite portfolio)
    a inception date
    b investment philosophy
    c nonbenchmark sectors and exposure to these sectors via commingled fund or direct investment
    d return objective
    e gross and net-of-fee performance versus the Lehman Brothers Aggregate Bond Index
- annualized returns for the quarter, year-to-date, 1 year, 3 years, 5 years, 10 years, and since inception
- annual returns for 1 through 10 years
- monthly returns for 1 through 5 years

    f quantitative analysis—metrics such as:
- volatility, tracking risk, information ratio, Sharpe ratio, and so on

    g sector allocation versus the Lehman Brothers Aggregate Bond Index, quarterly for the past three years
    h portfolio characteristics versus the Lehman Brothers Aggregate Bond Index, quarterly for the past three years
- duration, average quality, average maturity, average yield, and so on

    i permitted security types, including a statement on the use of short positions, derivative products, and leveraging
    j description of any constraints/limits
- frequency of subscription/redemption
- cash limits

    k average number of total holdings
    l total management fees and additional fees, if any
    m asset value data provider
    n administrator, custodian, auditor, advisers for commingled funds, if any
    o growth of assets under management of this product
    p top clients by assets under management utilizing this product
    q three current client references

3 Risk Management
    a philosophy and process
    b portfolio risk monitoring
    c limits on single positions, regions/countries, industries/sectors, and so on

4 Investment Personnel
  - **a** structure of investment team
  - **b** responsibilities
  - **c** biographies of key personnel
  - **d** significant team departures in last five years
  - **e** additional products managed by same manager or management team
  - **f** compensation structure of investment team
  - **g** tenure of investment team
  - **h** a description of the client service resources that will be made available

5 Investment Process
  - **a** decisions by committee or by manager
  - **b** quantitative or fundamental analysis
  - **c** top-down or bottom-up approach
  - **d** use of internal and external research
  - **e** universal securities
  - **f** main alpha drivers/sources of value added
  - **g** significant changes in investment process over last 10 years or since inception
  - **h** process driven or people driven fund management
  - **i** sell discipline
  - **j** best execution trading policy

6 Reporting Capabilities
  - **a** sample monthly and quarterly reports
  - **b** online reporting/download capability

SUMMARY

The management of fixed-income portfolios is a highly competitive field requiring skill in financial and economic analysis, market knowledge, and control of costs. Among the points that have been made are the following:

- Standard deviation, target semivariance, shortfall risk, and value at risk have all been proposed as appropriate measures of risk for a portfolio. However, each has its own deficiency. For example, standard deviation (or variance) assumes that risk has a normal distribution (which may not be true). Semivariance often provides little extra information if returns are symmetric. Shortfall risk is expressed as a probability, not as a currency amount. Value at risk does not indicate the magnitude of the very worst possible outcomes.

- A repurchase agreement is subject to a variety of credit risks, including:
  - **a** *Quality of the collateral.* The higher the quality of the securities, the lower the repo rate will be.
  - **b** *Term of the repo.* Typically, the longer the maturity, the higher the rate will be.

- **c** *Delivery requirement*. If physical delivery of the securities is required, the rate will be lower because of the lower credit risk.
- **d** *Availability of collateral*. The buyer of the securities may be willing to accept a lower rate in order to obtain securities that are in short supply.
- **e** *Prevailing interest rates in the economy*. As interest rates increase, the rates on repo transactions will generally increase.
- **f** *Seasonal factors*. A seasonal effect may exist because some institutions' supply of funds varies by the season.

- The primary advantages to using futures to alter a portfolio's duration are increased liquidity and cost-effectiveness.

- Futures contracts can be used to shorten or lengthen a portfolio's duration. The contracts may also be used to hedge or reduce an existing interest rate exposure. As such, they may be combined with traditional immunization techniques to improve the results.

- Unlike ordinary bond options that protect against interest rate risk, credit options are structured to offer protection against credit risk. Binary credit option and binary credit option based on a credit rating are the two types of credit options written on an underlying asset. The former pays the option buyer in the event of default; otherwise nothing is paid. The latter pays the difference between the strike price and the market price when the specified credit rating event occurs and pays nothing if the event does not occur.

- Credit options are structured to offer protection against both default risk and credit spread risk, credit forwards offer protection against credit spread risk, and credit default swaps help in managing default risk.

- The sources of excess return for an international bond portfolio include bond market selection, currency selection, duration management/yield curve management, sector selection, credit analysis, and investing in markets outside the benchmark index.

- Emerging market debt has matured as an asset class. The spread of EMD over risk-free rates has narrowed considerably as the quality of sovereign bonds has increased to the point that they now have similar frequencies of default, recovery rates, and ratings transition probabilities compared with corporate bonds with similar ratings.

- Emerging market debt is still risky, however, and is characterized by high volatility and returns that exhibit significant negative skewness. Moreover, emerging market countries frequently do not offer the degree of transparency, court tested laws, and clear regulations found in established markets.

- For a change in domestic interest rates, the change in a foreign bond's value may be found by multiplying the duration of the foreign bond times the country beta. Because a portfolio's duration is a weighted average of the duration of the bonds in the portfolio, the contribution to the portfolio's duration is equal to the adjusted foreign bond duration multiplied by its weight in the portfolio.

- Breakeven spread analysis is used to estimate relative values between markets by quantifying the amount of spread widening required to reduce a foreign bond's yield advantage to zero. The breakeven spread can be found by dividing the yield advantage by the bond's duration.

- When funds are not managed entirely in-house, a search for outside managers must be conducted. The due diligence for selection of managers is satisfied primarily by investigating the managers' investment process, the types of trades the managers are making, and the organizational strengths.

PRACTICE PROBLEMS

1 Your client has asked you to construct a £2 million bond portfolio. Some of the bonds that you are considering for this portfolio have embedded options. Your client has specified that he may withdraw £25,000 from the portfolio in six months to fund some expected expenses. He would like to be able to make this withdrawal without reducing the initial capital of £2 million.

   A Would shortfall risk be an appropriate measure of risk while evaluating the portfolios for your client?

   B What are some of the shortcomings of the use of shortfall risk?

2 The market value of the bond portfolio of a French investment fund is €75 million. The duration of the portfolio is 8.17. Based on the analysis provided by the in-house economists, the portfolio manager believes that the interest rates are likely to have an unexpected decrease over the next month. Based on this belief, the manager has decided to increase the duration of its entire bond portfolio to 10. The futures contract it would use is priced at €130,000 and has a duration of 9.35. Assume that the conversion factor for the futures contract is 1.06.

   A Would the fund need to buy futures contracts or sell?

   B Approximately, how many futures contracts would be needed to change the duration of the bond portfolio?

3 The trustees of a pension fund would like to examine the issue of protecting the bonds in the fund's portfolio against an increase in interest rates using options and futures. Before discussing this with their external bond fund manager, they decide to ask four consultants about their recommendations as to what should be done at this time. It turns out that each of them has a different recommendation. Consultant A suggests selling covered calls, Consultant B suggests doing nothing at all, Consultant C suggests selling interest rate futures, and Consultant D suggests buying puts. The reason for their different recommendations is that although all consultants understand the pension fund's objective of minimizing risk, they differ with one another in regards to their outlook on future interest rates. One of the consultants believes interest rates are headed downward, one has no opinion, one believes that the interest rates would not change much in either direction, and one believes that the interest rates are headed upward. Based on the consultants' recommendations, could you identify the outlook of each consultant?

4 The current credit spread on bonds issued by Great Foods Inc. is 300 bps. The manager of More Money Funds believes that Great Foods' credit situation will improve over the next few months, resulting in a smaller credit spread on its bonds. She decides to enter into a six-month credit spread forward contract taking the position that the credit spread will decrease. The forward contract has the current spread as the contracted spread, a notional amount of $10 million, and a risk factor of 5.

   A On the settlement date six months later, the credit spread on Great Foods bonds is 250 bps. How much is the payoff to More Money Funds?

   B How much would the payoff to More Money Funds be if the credit spread on the settlement date is 350 bps?

C How much is the maximum possible gain for More Money Funds?

5 Consider a collateralized debt obligation (CDO) that has a $250 million structure. The collateral consists of bonds that mature in seven years, and the coupon rate for these bonds is the seven-year Treasury rate plus 500 bps. The senior tranche comprises 70 percent of the structure and has a floating coupon of Libor plus 50 bps. There is only one junior tranche that comprises 20 percent of the structure and has a fixed coupon of seven-year Treasury rate plus 300 bps. Compute the rate of return earned by the equity tranche in this CDO if the seven-year Treasury rate is 6 percent and the Libor is 7.5 percent. There are no defaults in the underlying collateral pool. Ignore the collateral manager's fees and any other expenses.

6 Assume that the rates shown in the table below accurately reflect current conditions in the financial markets.

Dollar/Euro Spot Rate	1.21
Dollar/Euro 1-Year Forward Rate	1.18
1-Year Deposit Rate:	
Euro	3%
US	2%

In the table, the one-year forward dollar/euro exchange rate is mispriced, because it doesn't reflect the interest rate differentials between the United States and Europe.

A Calculate the amount of the current forward exchange discount or premium.

B Calculate the value that the forward rate would need to be in order to keep riskless arbitrage from occurring.

7 Assume that a US bond investor has invested in Canadian government bonds. The duration of a 12-year Canadian government bond is 8.40, and the Canadian country beta is 0.63. Interest rates in the United States are expected to change by approximately 80 bps. How much can the US investor expect the Canadian bond to change in value if US rates change by 80 bps?

8 Assume that the spread between US and German bonds is 300 bps, providing German investors who purchase a US bond with an additional yield income of 75 bps per quarter. The duration of the German bond is 8.3. If German interest rates should decline, how much of a decline is required to completely wipe out the quarterly yield advantage for the German investor?

9 A portfolio manager of a Canadian fund that invests in the yen-denominated Japanese bonds is considering whether or not to hedge the portfolio's exposure to the Japanese yen using a forward contract. Assume that the short-term interest rates are 1.6 percent in Japan and 2.7 percent in Canada.

A Based on the in-house analysis provided by the fund's currency specialists, the portfolio manager expects the Japanese yen to appreciate against the Canadian dollar by 1.5 percent. Should the portfolio manager hedge the currency risk using a forward contract?

B What would be your answer if the portfolio manager expects the Japanese yen to appreciate against the Canadian dollar by only 0.5 percent?

10 A British fixed-income fund has substantial holdings in US dollar-denominated bonds. The fund's portfolio manager is considering whether to leave the fund's exposure to the US dollar unhedged or to hedge it using a UK pound–US dollar forward contract. Assume that the short-term interest rates are 4.7 percent

Practice Problems

in the United Kingdom and 4 percent in the United States. The fund manager expects the US dollar to appreciate against the pound by 0.4 percent. Assume IRP holds. Explain which alternative has the higher expected return based on the short-term interest rates and the manager's expectations about exchange rates.

The following information relates to Questions 11–16

Sheila Ibahn, a portfolio manager with TBW Incorporated, is reviewing the performance of L.P. Industries' $100 million fixed-income portfolio with Stewart Palme from L.P. Industries. TBW Incorporated employs an active management strategy for fixed-income portfolios. Ibahn explains to Palme that the portfolio return was greater than the benchmark return last year and states:

> "We outperformed our benchmark by using inter-sector allocation and individual security selection strategies rather than a duration management strategy. However, at this point in the interest rate cycle, we believe we can add relative return by taking on additional interest rate risk across the portfolio."

Ibahn recommends purchasing additional bonds to adjust the average duration of the portfolio. After reviewing the portfolio recommendations, Palme asks Ibahn:

> "How can we adjust the portfolio's duration without contributing significant funds to purchase additional bonds in the portfolio?"

Ibahn responds:

Ibahn 1   We could employ futures contracts to adjust the duration of the portfolio, thus eliminating the need to purchase more bonds.

Ibahn 2   We could lever the portfolio by entering into either an overnight or 2-year term repurchase agreement [repo] and use the repo funds to purchase additional bonds that have the same duration as the current portfolio. For example, if we use funds from a $25 million overnight repo agreement to purchase bonds in addition to the current $100 million portfolio, the levered portfolio's change in value for a 1% change in interest rates would equal $5,125,000 while giving you the portfolio duration you require. Unfortunately the current cost of the repo is high because the repo collateral is "special collateral" but the margin requirement is low because the collateral is illiquid.

After listening to Ibahn, Palme agrees to use a repo to lever the portfolio but leaves the repo term decision to Ibahn's discretion. Because the yield curve is inverted, the cost of both the overnight and the 2-year term repo is higher than the yield on the levered portfolio. As Ibahn and Palme discuss the repo term, Palme asks two final questions:

Palme 1   "What is the effect of leverage on a portfolio's range of returns if interest rates are expected to change?"

Palme 2   "If interest rates are unchanged over a six-month period, what is the effect on the levered portfolio return compared to the unlevered portfolio return?"

11 Given Ibahn's recommendation, which of the following interest rate forecasts is TBW Incorporated *most likely* using?

- **A** A flattening of the yield curve.
- **B** An upward parallel shift in the yield curve.
- **C** A downward parallel shift in the yield curve.

12 Referring to Ibahn's first response to Palme, which of the following best describes TBW's *most likely* course of action?
- **A** Sell interest rate futures contracts to increase portfolio duration.
- **B** Buy interest rate futures contracts to increase portfolio duration.
- **C** Buy interest rate futures contracts to decrease portfolio duration.

13 Referring to Ibahn's second response to Palme, the levered portfolio would have:
- **A** the same duration if either the overnight repo or the 2-year term repo is used.
- **B** a longer duration if the overnight repo is used instead of the 2-year term repo.
- **C** a shorter duration if the overnight repo is used instead of the 2-year term repo.

14 In Ibahn's second response to Palme, the duration of the sample leveraged portfolio is *closest* to:
- **A** 4.10.
- **B** 5.13.
- **C** 6.83.

15 Is Ibahn's second response to Palme regarding the cost and margin requirements for the repo *most likely* correct?

	High Repo Cost	Low Margin Requirement
A	No	No
B	Yes	Yes
C	Yes	No

16 In response to Palme's two final questions, the levered portfolio's range of returns and six-month return when compared to the unlevered portfolio *most likely* would be:

	Levered Portfolio Range of Returns	Levered Portfolio Six-month Return
A	narrower	lower
B	narrower	higher
C	wider	lower

The following information relates to Questions 17–22 and is based on "Fixed-Income Portfolio Management—Part I" and this reading

The investment committee of the US-based Autónoma Foundation has been dissatisfied with the performance of the fixed-income portion of their endowment and has recently fired the fixed-income manager.

Practice Problems

The investment committee has hired a consultant, Julia Santillana, to oversee the portfolio on an interim basis until the search for a new manager is completed. She is also expected to assess the portfolio's risks and propose investment ideas to the committee.

Total Return Analysis and Scenario Analysis

During a meeting between Santillana and members of the committee, a member asks her to discuss the use of total return analysis and scenario analysis before executing bond trades. In her response, Santillana states:

- "To compute total return, the manager needs a set of assumptions about the investment horizon, the expected reinvestment rate, and the expected change in interest rates."
- "If the manager wants to evaluate how the individual assumptions affect the total return computation, she can use scenario analysis."
- "Scenario analysis can lead to rejection of a strategy that is acceptable from a total return perspective."

Use of Repurchase Agreements

During the meeting, Santillana reviews with the investment committee a hypothetical transaction in which leverage is used. A manager with $2 million of funds to invest purchases corporate bonds with a market value of $7 million. To partially finance the purchase, the manager enters into a 30-day repurchase agreement with the bond dealer for $5 million. The 30-day term repo rate is assumed to be 4.20 percent per year. At the end of the 30 days, when the transaction expires, the corporate bonds are assumed to have increased in value by 0.30 percent. Santillana uses this information to demonstrate the effects of leverage on portfolio returns.

Responding to a question asked by a committee member, Santillana explains: "The quality of collateral as well as short sellers' positions affect the repo rate."

International Bond Investing and Hedging

Santillana also mentions to the investment committee that the Foundation's current portfolio does not include international bonds. She describes the benefits of investing in international bonds and answers the committee's questions. Exhibit 1 displays information she uses during the meeting to clarify her answers. The 1-year interest rate is used as a proxy for the risk-free rate.

Exhibit 1   Summary Information Relevant to International Bond Investing

	UK	Japan	Germany	Singapore	US
1-year interest rate (percent)	6.24	0.97	4.69	2.09	5.30
Yield on 10-year government bond/note (percent)	5.04	1.67	4.36	2.74	4.62
Expected one-year currency appreciation in percent (USD per local currency)	0.10	0.50	0.95	1.60	N/A
10-year bond duration	7.34	9.12	7.72	8.19	7.79

The committee is persuaded by Santillana's presentation and decides to invest in international bonds. As a result, Santillana considers whether she should recommend currency hedging using forward contracts, assuming that interest rate parity holds.

During the discussion on international bond investing, a member comments that investors in Japan and Singapore in particular should be investing in the United States because of the difference in bond yields. Santillana agrees but explains that investors should also perform a breakeven spread analysis when investing internationally.

17 Is Santillana correct in her statements about total return analysis *and* scenario analysis?

   A Yes.

   B No, because scenario analysis cannot evaluate how individual assumptions affect the total return computation.

   C No, because scenario analysis cannot lead to a rejection of a strategy with an acceptable expected total return.

18 The 30-day rate of return on the hypothetical leveraged portfolio of corporate bonds is *closest* to:

   A −0.05 percent.

   B 0.05 percent.

   C 0.18 percent.

19 Is Santillana correct in her explanation of factors affecting the repo rate?

   A Yes.

   B No, only the quality of collateral is correct.

   C No, only the short sellers' position is correct.

20 Based on Exhibit 1 and assuming interest rates remain unchanged, which bond will have the *highest* hedged return?

   A UK 10-year.

   B Japan 10-year.

   C Germany 10-year.

21 Based on Exhibit 1 and assuming interest rates remain unchanged, which bond will have the *highest* expected unhedged return?

   A UK 10-year.

   B Germany 10-year.

   C Singapore 10-year.

22 Based on Exhibit 1, for investors that purchased 10-year US notes, the spread widening in basis points that will wipe out the additional yield gained for a quarter is *closest* to:

   A 6.03 in Singapore.

   B 8.09 in Japan.

   C 13.48 in the United Kingdom.

Practice Problems

The following information relates to Questions 23–28 and is based on "Fixed-Income Portfolio Management—Part I" and this reading

Salvatore Choo, the Chief Investment Officer at European Pension Fund (EPF), wishes to maintain the fixed-income portfolio's active management but recognizes that the portfolio must remain fully funded. The portfolio is run by World Asset Management, where Jimmy Ferragamo, a risk manager, is analyzing the portfolio (shown in Exhibit 1), whose benchmark has a duration of 5.6. None of the bonds in the portfolio have embedded options. However, EPF's liability has a duration of 10.2, creating an asset liability mismatch for the pension fund.

Exhibit 1   EPF Portfolio

Maturity	Market Value (000)	Duration
2-year bond	€421,000	1.8
5-year bond	€1,101,000	4.8
10-year bond	€1,540,000	8.4
Total	€3,062,000	6.2

Choo is utilizing a contingent immunization (CI) approach to achieve better returns for the fund, so by his understanding of CI, he can use the entire fixed-income portfolio for active management until the portfolio drops below the safety net level or the terminal value.

Ferragamo runs the following risk statistics on the EPF portfolio to ensure that they are not outside the EPF trustee guidelines. He has the following comment:

> "The portfolio value at risk, as opposed to shortfall risk and standard deviation, determines the most the portfolio can lose in any month."

Ferragamo has collected the following data on the bund (German Bond) future, which has a conversion factor of 1.1, and the cheapest to deliver bond is priced at €100,000 and has a duration of 8.2.

In addition to his CIO responsibilities, Choo is also responsible for managing the funding liabilities for a new wing at the local hospital, which is currently fully funded utilizing a standard immunization approach with noncallable bonds. However, he is concerned about the various risks associated with the liabilities including interest rate risk, contingent claim risk, and cap risk.

Choo is interested in using cash flow matching rather than immunization to fund a liability for the new wing. The liability is denominated in euros and will be a lump sum payment in five years. The term structure of interest rates is currently a steep upward-sloping yield curve.

23 Given the term structure of interest rates and the duration mismatch between EPF's benchmark and its pension liability, the plan should be *most concerned* about a:
   A flattening of the yield curve.
   B steepening of the yield curve.
   C large parallel shift up in the yield curve.

24 Choo's understanding of contingent immunization (CI) is:

A   correct.
   B   incorrect, because CI does not use a terminal value.
   C   incorrect, because CI does not allow for active management.

25 Is Ferragamo's comment correct?
   A   Yes.
   B   No, because shortfall risk would provide this information.
   C   No, because value at risk does not indicate the magnitude of the very worst possible outcomes.

26 Based on the data Ferragamo collected on the bund and Exhibit 1, Choo can adjust the EPF portfolio duration to match the benchmark duration by selling:
   A   2,240 contracts.
   B   2,406 contracts.
   C   2,465 contracts.

27 Are Choo's concerns regarding various risks of funding the hospital liability correct?
   A   Yes.
   B   No, because interest rate risk is not a factor.
   C   No, because contingent claim risk is not a factor.

28 Which of the following would best immunize the hospital liability?
   A   A five-year euro coupon bond.
   B   A five-year euro zero-coupon bond.
   C   Equal investment in three- and seven-year euro zero-coupon bonds.

The following problem is based on "Fixed-Income Portfolio Management—Part I" and this reading

29 A portfolio manager decided to purchase corporate bonds with a market value of €5 million. To finance 60 percent of the purchase, the portfolio manager entered into a 30-day repurchase agreement with the bond dealer. The 30-day term repo rate was 4.6 percent per year. At the end of the 30 days, the bonds purchased by the portfolio manager have increased in value by 0.5 percent and the portfolio manager decided to sell the bonds. No coupons were received during the 30-day period.
   A   Compute the 30-day rate of return on the equity and borrowed components of the portfolio.
   B   Compute the 30-day portfolio rate of return.
   C   Compute the 30-day portfolio rate of return if the increase in value of the bonds was 0.3 percent instead of 0.5 percent.
   D   Use your answers to parts B and C above to comment on the effect of the use of leverage on the portfolio rate of return.
   E   Discuss why the bond dealer in the above example faces a credit risk even if the bond dealer holds the collateral.

SOLUTIONS

1 A Because you are considering bonds with embedded options, the returns of portfolios are unlikely to be normally distributed. Because shortfall risk is not based on normality assumption, however, it may be used as a risk measure. Furthermore, because the client has specified a minimum target return (£25,000/£2,000,000 or 1.25 percent over the next six months), shortfall risk could be a useful measure to look at.

B One of the shortcomings of shortfall risk is that it is not as commonly used as standard deviation, and there is relatively less familiarity with shortfall risk. Also, its statistical properties are not well known. Unlike VAR, it does not take the form of a dollar amount. Finally, the shortfall risk gives the probability of the returns from the portfolio falling below the specified minimum target return, but it does not provide any information about the extent to which the return may be below the specified minimum target.

2 A Because the fund desires to increase the duration, it would need to buy futures contracts.

B D_T = target duration for the portfolio = 10

D_I = initial duration for the portfolio = 8.17

P_I = initial market value of the portfolio = €75 million

D_{CTD} = the duration of the cheapest-to-deliver bond = 9.35

P_{CTD} = the price of the cheapest-to-deliver bond = €130,000

Conversion factor for the cheapest-to-deliver bond = 1.06

$$\text{Approximate number of contracts} = \frac{(D_T - D_I)P_I}{D_{CTD}P_{CTD}} \times \text{Conversion factor for the CTD bond}$$

$$= \frac{(10.0 - 8.17) \times 75,000,000}{9.35 \times 130,000} \times 1.06 = 119.69.$$

Thus, the pension fund would need to buy 119 futures contracts to achieve the desired increase in duration.

3 Covered call writing is a good strategy if the rates are not going to change much from their present level. The sale of the calls brings in premium income that provides partial protection in case rates increase. The additional income from writing calls can be used to offset declining prices. If rates fall, portfolio appreciation is limited because the short call position is a liability for the seller, and this liability increases as rates go down. Consequently, there is limited upside potential for the covered call writer. Overall, this drawback does not have negative consequences if rates do not change because the added income from the sale of calls would be obtained without sacrificing any gains. Thus, Consultant A, who suggested selling covered calls, probably believes that the interest rates would not change much in either direction.

Doing nothing would be a good strategy for a bondholder if he believes that rates are going down. The bondholder could simply gain from the increasing bond prices. Thus, Consultant B, who suggested doing nothing, likely believes that the interest rates would go down.

If one has no clear opinion about the interest rate outlook but would like to avoid risk, selling interest rate futures would be a good strategy. If interest rates were to increase, the loss in value of bonds would be offset by the gains from futures. Thus, Consultant C, who suggested selling interest rate futures, is likely the one who has no opinion.

Paying the premium for buying the puts would not be a bad idea if a bondholder believes that interest rates are going to increase. Thus, Consultant D is likely the one who believes that the interest rates are headed upward.

4 The payoff to More Money Funds would be:

Payoff = (0.030 − Credit spread at maturity) × $10 million × 5

A Payoff = (0.030 − 0.025) × $10 million × 5 = $250,000.

B Payoff = (0.030 − 0.035) × $10 million × 5 = $250,000, or a loss of $250,000.

C The maximum gain would be in the unlikely event of credit spread at the forward contract maturity being zero. So, the best possible payoff is (0.030 − 0.000) × $10 million × 5 = $1,500,000.

5 First, let us compute the amount in each of the three tranches in the CDO. The senior tranche is 70 percent of $250 million = $175 million. The junior tranche is 20 percent of $250 million = $50 million. The rest is the equity tranche = $250 million − $175 million − $50 million = $25 million.

Now let us compute the amount that would be received by the equity tranche. Annual interest generated by the collateral would be 6 + 5 = 11 percent of $250 million = $27.5 million. Annual interest received by the senior tranche would be 7.5 + 0.5 = 8 percent of $175 million = $14 million. Annual interest received by the junior tranche would be 6 + 3 = 9 percent of $50 million = $4.5 million. So, the amount to be received by the equity tranche is 27.5 − 14 − 4.5 = $9 million. This amount represents a return of 9/25 = 0.36 or 36 percent.

6 The mispricing occurs because the forward rate doesn't conform to the covered interest rate parity theorem.

A The current discount rate is −2.48 percent [i.e., ($1.18 − $1.21)/$1.21]

B The covered interest rate parity theorem states that the forward foreign exchange rate for a fixed period must be equal to the interest rate differentials between the two countries.

Forward rate = Spot rate × (1 + Domestic interest rate) / (1 + Foreign interest rate)

Substituting into the formula:

Forward rate = $1.21(1 + 0.02)/(1 + 0.03)

Forward rate = $1.198

7 The investor can evaluate the change in value of the Canadian bond if US rates change by 80 bps as follows:

Δ in value of Canadian bond = Candian bond's duration × Canada country beta × Δ in US rates

Δ in value of Canadian bond = 8.40 × 0.63 × 0.80 percent

Δ in value of Canadian bond = 4.23 percent

8 Let W denote the spread widening.

Change in price = Duration × Change in yield

Change in price = 8.3 × W

Assuming the increase in price caused by the spread widening will be 0.75 percent

$$0.75 \text{ percent} = 8.3 \times W$$

Solving for the spread widening, W,

$$W = 0.0904 \text{ percent} = 9.04 \text{ bps}$$

Thus, a spread widening of 9.04 bps would wipe out the additional yield gained from investing in the US bond. The 0.0904 percent change in rates would wipe out the quarterly yield advantage of 75 bps.

9   The forward premium on the Japanese yen is 2.7 – 1.6 = 1.1 percent. So, the portfolio manager should hedge using a forward contract if the anticipated return on yen is less than 1.1 percent.

   A   Because the anticipated return on yen of 1.5 percent is greater than 1.1 percent, the portfolio manager should not hedge.

   B   Because the anticipated return on yen of 0.5 percent is less than 1.1 percent, the portfolio manager should hedge.

10 The interest rate differential between the UK pound and the US dollar is 4.7 – 4.0 = 0.7 percent. Because this differential is greater than the 0.4 percent return on the US dollar expected by the fund manager, the forward hedged position has a higher expected return than the unhedged position.

11 C is correct. TBW is most likely forecasting a decrease in interest rates based on the desire to take on additional interest rate risks. Based on the recommendation to adjust the average duration across the portfolio, rather than key rate duration adjustments, it conveys the expectation of a parallel yield curve shift.

12 B is correct. Because Ibahn wants to take on additional interest rate risk in the portfolio, she would extend duration. To extend duration, Ibahn would need to purchase interest rate futures contracts.

13 B is correct. The 2-year term leverage would shorten the total duration of the levered portfolio relative to overnight repo by the dollar duration of the 2-year liability. The levered portfolio duration would be longer using overnight repo because its proceeds are being invested in bonds to have the same duration as the unlevered portfolio—thus the net effect is a longer duration because the overnight repo duration is zero.

14 B is correct. The duration of the sample leveraged portfolio = (Total dollar duration/Investors' equity in the original portfolio) × 100 = ($5,125,000/100,000,000) × 100 = 5.13

15 A is correct. The cost of a repo on special collateral is actually lower than the standard cost of a repo because those needing that collateral are willing to lend funds at a lower cost to obtain that "special" collateral. The illiquidity of the collateral actually increases the margin requirement for the repo as those lending funds want more margin to offset the risk of them having to liquidate the collateral in the event of a borrower default (the entity using the repo to obtain the funds).

16 C is correct. The effect of leverage on a portfolio is that the distribution of returns widens, both to the upside and the downside. In this case, the cost of carry versus the yield on the portfolio causes the return on the levered portfolio to be lower than the return on the unlevered portfolio when interest rates are unchanged.

17 A is correct. Scenario analysis can help evaluate the contribution of individual assumptions (inputs, like the reinvestment rate assumption) to the total return computation. Also, the distribution of outcomes from a scenario analysis may be so wide that it exceeds a client's risk tolerance, even if the expected return is acceptable.

18 C is correct.

	Borrowed Funds	Equity Funds
Amount Invested	$5,000,000	$2,000,000
Rate of Return (0.30% increase in value)	$15,000	$6,000
Less Interest expense at 4.2% (4.2/12 = 0.35% per 30 day)	$17,500	
Net Profitability	–$2,500	$6,000
Rate of Return on Each Component	–0.05% (–2,500/5,000,000)	0.30%
Rate of Return	0.175% [(–2,500 + 6,000)/2,000,000]	

19 A is correct. The quality of the collateral affects the repo rate. Short sellers' needs can affect the demand/availability of the collateral, and hence the repo rate, when the lender of the funds needs the collateral for a short sale.

20 B is correct. The hedged return is equal to the sum of the domestic risk-free interest rate i_d plus the bond's local risk premium of the foreign bond $r_l - i_f$. The local risk premium of 0.70% on the Japanese bond (1.67 – 0.97) is higher than the local risk premium in any of the other countries.

21 B is correct. The unhedged return is approximately equal to the foreign bond return in local currency terms plus the currency return, which is the percentage change in the spot exchange rate stated in terms of home currency per unit of foreign currency. The expected unhedged return on the German bond is the bond yield of 4.36% plus the expected local currency appreciation of 0.95%, for a total of 5.31%.

22 B is correct. The spread widening equals the additional yield income per quarter (4.62 – 1.67)/4 = 0.7375% for Japan, divided by the higher of the two countries' durations, that is, 73.75/9.12 = 8.09.

23 A is correct. Given the mismatch in the liability and the benchmark they are running against, a flattening of the yield curve would cause the liability to increase faster than the asset.

24 A is correct. Contingent immunization does utilize the entire portfolio for active management.

25 C is correct. Value at risk does not indicate the magnitude of the very worst possible outcomes.

26 C is correct. (5.6 – 6.2) × 3,062,000,000/8.2/100,000 × 1.1 = –2,465, or sell 2,465 contracts.

27 A is correct. Cap risk, interest rate risk, and contingent claim risk are all risks the portfolio manager faces.

28 B is correct. A five-year zero-coupon bond best matches the liability of five years.

29 A Equity = E = 40 percent of €5 million = €2 million

Borrowed funds = B = 60 percent of €5 million = €3 million

k = Cost of borrowed funds = 4.6 percent per year = 4.6/12 or 0.3833 percent per 30 days

r_F = Return on funds invested = 0.5 percent

Therefore,

R_E = Return on equity = r_F = 0.5 percent

R_B = Return on borrowed funds = $r_F - k$ = 0.5 − 0.3833

= 0.1167 percent

B R_P = Portfolio rate of return = (Profit on borrowed funds + Profit on equity)/Amount of equity = $[B \times (r_F - k) + E \times r_F]/E$ = [€3 million × (0.5 − 0.3833) + €2 million × 0.5]/€2 million = 0.6750 percent.

C R_P = Portfolio rate of return = (Profit on borrowed funds + Profit on equity)/Amount of equity = $[B \times (r_F - k) + E \times r_F]/E$ = [€3 million × (0.3 − 0.3833) + €2 million × 0.3]/€2 million = 0.1751 percent.

D If the return on funds invested exceeds the cost of borrowing, then leverage magnifies the portfolio rate of return. This condition holds for the case in Part B, where the return on funds of 0.5 percent exceeds the cost of borrowing of 0.3833 percent, and therefore, the portfolio return (0.6750 percent) is greater than the return on funds.

If the return on funds invested is less than the cost of borrowing, then leverage is a drag on the portfolio rate of return. This condition holds for the case in Part C, where the return on funds of 0.3 percent is less than the cost of borrowing of 0.3833 percent, and therefore, the portfolio return (0.1751 percent) is less than the return on funds.

E The bond dealer faces a credit risk even if he holds the collateral. The reason is that the value of the collateral may decline to such an extent that its market value falls below the amount lent. In such a situation, if the borrower defaults, the market value of the collateral will be insufficient to cover the amount lent.

PORTFOLIO MANAGEMENT
STUDY SESSION

12

Equity Portfolio Management

Because equity securities represent a significant portion of many investment portfolios, equity portfolio management is often an important component of overall investment success. This study session focuses on the role of equities in an investment portfolio, three major approaches used to manage equity portfolios, and the evaluation of equity managers.

READING ASSIGNMENT

Reading 23   Equity Portfolio Management
by Gary L. Gastineau, Andrew R. Olma, CFA, and Robert G. Zielinski, CFA

Copyright © 2015 CFA Institute

READING 23

Equity Portfolio Management

by Gary L. Gastineau, Andrew R. Olma, CFA, and Robert G. Zielinski, CFA

Gary L. Gastineau is at ETFconsultants.com, Inc. (USA). Andrew R. Olma, CFA (USA). Robert G. Zielinski, CFA, is at Charlotte Cattle Company (USA).

LEARNING OUTCOMES

Mastery	The candidate should be able to:
☐	a. discuss the role of equities in the overall portfolio;
☐	b. discuss the rationales for passive, active, and semiactive (enhanced index) equity investment approaches and distinguish among those approaches with respect to expected active return and tracking risk;
☐	c. recommend an equity investment approach when given an investor's investment policy statement and beliefs concerning market efficiency;
☐	d. distinguish among the predominant weighting schemes used in the construction of major equity market indices and evaluate the biases of each;
☐	e. compare alternative methods for establishing passive exposure to an equity market, including indexed separate or pooled accounts, index mutual funds, exchange-traded funds, equity index futures, and equity total return swaps;
☐	f. compare full replication, stratified sampling, and optimization as approaches to constructing an indexed portfolio and recommend an approach when given a description of the investment vehicle and the index to be tracked;
☐	g. explain and justify the use of equity investment–style classifications and discuss the difficulties in applying style definitions consistently;
☐	h. explain the rationales and primary concerns of value investors and growth investors and discuss the key risks of each investment style;

(continued)

Managing Investment Portfolios: A Dynamic Process, Third Edition, John L. Maginn, CFA, Donald L. Tuttle, CFA, Jerald E. Pinto, CFA, and Dennis W. McLeavey, CFA, editors. Copyright © 2007 by CFA Institute.

LEARNING OUTCOMES

Mastery	The candidate should be able to:
☐	i. compare techniques for identifying investment styles and characterize the style of an investor when given a description of the investor's security selection method, details on the investor's security holdings, or the results of a returns-based style analysis;
☐	j. compare the methodologies used to construct equity style indices;
☐	k. interpret the results of an equity style box analysis and discuss the consequences of style drift;
☐	l. distinguish between positive and negative screens involving socially responsible investing criteria and discuss their potential effects on a portfolio's style characteristics;
☐	m. compare long–short and long-only investment strategies, including their risks and potential alphas, and explain why greater pricing inefficiency may exist on the short side of the market;
☐	n. explain how a market-neutral portfolio can be "equitized" to gain equity market exposure and compare equitized market-neutral and short-extension portfolios;
☐	o. compare the sell disciplines of active investors;
☐	p. contrast derivatives-based and stock-based enhanced indexing strategies and justify enhanced indexing on the basis of risk control and the information ratio;
☐	q. recommend and justify, in a risk-return framework, the optimal portfolio allocations to a group of investment managers;
☐	r. explain the core-satellite approach to portfolio construction and discuss the advantages and disadvantages of adding a completeness fund to control overall risk exposures;
☐	s. distinguish among the components of total active return ("true" active return and "misfit" active return) and their associated risk measures and explain their relevance for evaluating a portfolio of managers;
☐	t. explain alpha and beta separation as an approach to active management and demonstrate the use of portable alpha;
☐	u. describe the process of identifying, selecting, and contracting with equity managers;
☐	v. contrast the top-down and bottom-up approaches to equity research.

1 INTRODUCTION

Equities constitute a significant part of many investment portfolios' value. For numerous investors, the decision of how to invest the equity allocation among competing investment approaches ranks second in importance only to the decision of how much of the portfolio to allocate to equities in the first place.

This reading presents a broad overview of equity portfolio management organized as follows: Section 2 summarizes the role of equities in investors' portfolios. Sections 3 through 6 introduce and discuss three broad approaches to equity investing and their subdisciplines. Section 7 discusses managing a portfolio of managers so that the overall equity allocation achieves the investor's purposes. Section 8 presents the important subject of identifying, selecting, and contracting with equity portfolio managers. Section 9 discusses structuring equity research and security selection, and the final section summarizes the reading.

THE ROLE OF THE EQUITY PORTFOLIO

Equities represent a significant source of wealth in the world today. As of 31 March 2011, the aggregate market value of the equities in the Morgan Stanley Capital International All Country World Index (MSCI ACWI) was more than $34 trillion, of which more than half represented markets outside the United States.[1] Furthermore, over 10 percent of the $34 trillion total represented emerging markets.

This vast pool of equity assets is held in both individual and institutional portfolios. As an example of the latter, the allocations of pension funds to equities and other assets are shown for seven major markets in Exhibit 1. On average, equities are 47 percent of portfolio allocations, which is a larger allocation that that for bonds, cash, or real estate and alternative assets. However, the allocation to equity varies considerably, from 28 percent of the portfolio in Switzerland to over half the portfolio, 55 percent in the United Kingdom. Pensions in the United Kingdom, United States, and Australia are relatively heavily weighted in equities while Japan, the Netherlands, and Switzerland are relatively lightly weighted in them. These differences reflect, at least in part, differences in investment constraints, risk aversion, and traditions of equity holding.

Exhibit 1   Pensions' Equity Allocations (Selected Major Markets)

	Equity	Bonds	Real Estate and Alternative Assets	Cash
Australia	49%	14%	25%	12%
Canada	41	36	21	2
Japan	37	56	4	3
Netherlands	33	50	16	1
Switzerland	28	35	29	8
United Kingdom	55	35	7	3
United States	49	27	24	0
Average	47	33	19	1

Source: Towers Watson Global Pension Asset Study 2011, available at www.towerswatson.com.

Most investors worry about inflation, and inflation hedging ability is a sought-after characteristic. Informally, an asset is an **inflation hedge** if its returns are sufficient on average to preserve purchasing power during periods of inflation. More formally stated, an inflation hedge's nominal returns tend to be highly correlated with inflation

---

[1] As of May 2011, this index covers 45 developed and emerging markets and represents approximately 98 percent of global equity market value.

rates. As residual real claims on businesses, common equities should offer superior protection against unanticipated inflation compared with conventional bonds. This phenomenon is so because companies' earnings tend to increase with inflation, whereas payments on conventional bonds are fixed in nominal terms. Nevertheless, companies do face challenges in coping with inflation. Reported earnings often overstate their real economic value to varying degrees. Corporate income taxes and capital gains tax rates are typically not inflation indexed, so inflation can cut into investors' after-tax real returns unless share prices fully reflect (through lower prices) the interaction of inflation and taxation. Furthermore, individual equities differ in their sensitivities to inflation because of industry, competitive, and other types of factors. Companies' abilities to raise output prices and revenues to keep pace with increases in input prices vary inversely with the amount of price competition in their markets. Yet the historical record indicates that the very long-run real return on stocks in the United States has been relatively insensitive to realized inflation rates, in contrast to bonds, whose returns have been negatively related to inflation.[2] Evidence from many markets indicates that using long measurement periods (longer than annual), equities on average do have value as an inflation hedge.[3] That fact has been an argument for equity investment not only for investors with general inflation concerns but also for defined-benefit plan sponsors, which may be exposed through the terms of the pension benefit formula to increasing nominal wage and salary costs.

Finally, equities' comparatively high historical long-term real rates of return have been important in establishing the widely held perspective that they play a growth role in a portfolio. Exhibit 2, showing historical real rates of return on equity, is taken from a Dimson, Marsh, and Staunton (2011) survey of capital market returns internationally. Their analysis shows that during the 111 years from 1900 to 2010, the long-term real rates of return to equities have exceeded that of bonds in all 19 countries listed in Exhibit 2.[4]

For all the reasons discussed, many successful long-term investors have had an equity bias in their asset allocation, diversifying with instruments such as bonds to obtain an acceptable level of risk and/or income. In the next sections we discuss how investors approach equity investment.

Exhibit 2   Equity Real Rates of Return, 1900–2010

Country	Geometric Mean	Standard Deviation
Australia	7.7%	18.2%
Belgium	2.5	23.6
Canada	5.9	17.2
Denmark	5.1	20.9
Finland	5.4	30.3
France	3.1	23.5
Germany (excludes 1922–23)	3.1	32.2
Ireland	3.8	23.2
Italy	2.0	29.0

---

[2] See Siegel (2008), p. 199. Siegel examined 30-year holding periods from 1871 to 2006. Equities have not been effective inflation hedges, however, for the short-term (Siegel 2008).

[3] See Boudoukh and Richardson (1993), focusing on US data; Ely and Robinson (1997) for an international focus; and Luintel and Paudyal (2006), focusing on UK data. More recently, Bekaert and Wang (2010) find that stocks are poor short-term inflation hedges in industrialized countries, but are better hedges at longer horizons and in high-inflation economies.

[4] See Dimson, Marsh, and Staunton (2011) for data on historical bond returns.

Exhibit 2 (Continued)

Country	Geometric Mean	Standard Deviation
Japan	3.8	29.8
The Netherlands	5.0	21.8
New Zealand	5.8	19.7
Norway	4.2	27.4
South Africa	7.3	22.6
Spain	3.6	22.3
Sweden	6.3	22.9
Switzerland	4.2	19.8
United Kingdom	5.3	20.0
United States	6.3	20.3
World	5.5	17.7

Source: Credit Suisse Global Investment Returns Yearbook 2011. Dimson, Marsh, and Staunton (2011).

APPROACHES TO EQUITY INVESTMENT

There are a number of different approaches to managing equity portfolios, each of which we will discuss in more detail later in this reading.

In **passive management**, the investor does not attempt to reflect his investment expectations through changes in security holdings. The dominant passive approach is **indexing**, which involves investing in a portfolio that attempts to match the performance of some specified benchmark. Although passive in the sense of not incorporating the investor's expectations concerning securities, indexed portfolios are anything but passive in implementation. When a stock is added to or dropped from an index, or when the weight of a given stock changes because of a corporate action (such as a share buyback, or a **secondary offering**—an offering after the initial public offering of securities), the portfolio must be adjusted. Pioneered in the 1970s, indexing has quickly grown to the point that the United States alone has more than $1 trillion in institutional indexed equities. Today, indexed portfolios often function as the core holding in an investor's overall equity allocation.

Another approach is **active management**, which historically is the principal way that investors have managed equity portfolios. An active manager seeks to outperform a given benchmark portfolio (the portfolio against which the manager's performance will be evaluated). The manager does this by identifying which stocks she thinks will perform comparatively well versus the benchmark portfolio, buying or holding those, and avoiding stocks she believes will underperform the benchmark. Despite indexing's growing popularity during the last few decades, active equity management still accounts for the overwhelming majority of equity assets managed.

The final approach is **semiactive management** (also called enhanced indexing or risk-controlled active management) and is in reality a variant of active management. In a semiactive portfolio, the manager seeks to outperform a given benchmark, as do active managers in general. A semiactive portfolio manager, however, worries more about tracking risk than an active manager does and will tend to build a portfolio whose performance will have very limited volatility around the benchmark's returns.

Exhibit 3 compares the typical expected active return, tracking risk, and information ratio for successful (first-quartile) practitioners of these three different approaches. **Active return** is the portfolio's return in excess of the return on the portfolio's benchmark. **Tracking risk**, the annualized standard deviation of active returns, measures **active risk** (risk relative to the portfolio's benchmark).[5]

The **information ratio** equals a portfolio's mean active return divided by tracking risk and represents the efficiency with which a portfolio's tracking risk delivers active return.[6] What can we infer from Exhibit 3 about how an investor in each of these categories views equity market informational efficiency? Investors who believe that an equity market is efficient will usually favor indexing because they think that equity research will not provide a sufficient increment in return to overcome their research and transaction costs. Active investors believe that the equity market is often inefficient and that good research will allow them to outperform the market net of all costs. Enhanced indexers fall somewhere between the two, believing that they can extract information about companies that has not been embedded in stock prices, but attempting to do so in a way that limits tracking risk.

Exhibit 3 Indexing, Enhanced Indexing, and Active Approaches: A Comparison

	Indexing	Enhanced Indexing	Active
Expected active return	0%	1%–2%	2%+
Tracking risk	<1%	1%–2%	4% + r
Information ratio[a]	0	0.75	0.50

[a] Estimated values expected of first-quartile portfolio managers.
Source: Authors' estimates.

Within any of these three broad investment approaches, the investor needs to define the investment universe from which to select common stock. Considerations such as fund size and investment horizon affect the desired minimal level of holdings' liquidity. Tax concerns particularly concern individual and taxable corporate investors. Social concerns (e.g., corporate performance in matters such as governance and ethics, environment, workplace conditions, product safety and impact, and human rights) may matter to any type of investor. The mandates that clients give their investment managers will reflect these constraints.

4 PASSIVE EQUITY INVESTING

Passive investment philosophy has its roots in the history of equity indexing. The first indexed portfolio, launched in 1971 by Wells Fargo, was created for a single pension fund client. In 1973, Wells Fargo organized a commingled index fund for trust accounts. In 1976, Wells Fargo combined the funds, using capitalization-weighted

---

[5] Tracking risk has also been called tracking error and tracking error volatility.
[6] An information ratio (IR) of 0.50 is frequently viewed as distinguishing top-quartile active equity managers. For a summary of empirical results, see Grinold and Kahn (2000), p. 131. Jorion (2002), Table 4, finds that the first quartile of enhanced index funds is close to 0.75. Bossert, Füss, Rindler, and Schneider (2010) find that the IR that distinguishes a top-quartile manager changes over time and across equity style. However, the average threshold IR for equity managers in their Exhibit 2 is 0.36.

S&P 500 Index as the template for the combined portfolios. By 1981, Wells Fargo had established a fund designed to track the broader market of companies outside the S&P 500. By holding these two funds in market cap weights, an investor could effectively capture the return of the US equity market. Indexed investments became available for individual investors too. John Bogle at The Vanguard Group, Inc., launched the first broad-market index fund for retail investors in 1975.

Several early advocates of indexing were influential in establishing indexing as a major investment approach. Burton Malkiel called for "A New Investment Instrument" in the first edition of his best seller, *A Random Walk Down Wall Street* (1973). He wrote, "What we need is a no-load, minimum-management-fee mutual fund that simply buys the hundreds of stocks making up the broad stock-market averages and does no trading from security to security in an attempt to catch the winners." Other early advocates included Paul Samuelson (1974) and Charles D. Ellis in "The Loser's Game" (1975), one of the most widely cited papers in the literature of both finance and tennis. Ellis marshaled some simple facts illustrating that the institutionalization of the equity markets in the 1960s and early 1970s had made it probable that the *average* institutional investment manager would typically underperform the market as measured by a representative index. According to Ellis, the increased institutional share of the market left too little stock in the hands of nonprofessional investors for amateurs to fill the ranks of underperformers by themselves. Given the costs of trading, administrative expenses, and management fees as well, average active institutional investors inevitably would underperform the unmanaged market indices over time. In his classic article "The Arithmetic of Active Management," William F. Sharpe (1991) explains why the average investor cannot hope to beat a comprehensive equity index. His argument is unassailably clear and simple: "If 'active' and 'passive' management styles are defined in sensible ways, it *must* be the case that:

- before costs, the return on the average actively managed dollar will equal the return on the average passively managed dollar; and
- after costs, the return on the average actively managed dollar will be less than the return on the average passively managed dollar."

History has generally proven Ellis and Sharpe right. Appropriately designed performance studies have generally found that the *average* active institutional portfolio fails to beat the relevant comparison index after expenses.[7] Frequently, the difference in performance has been found to be close to the average expense disadvantage of active management.[8] Therefore, compared with the average actively managed fund that has similar objectives, a well-run indexed fund's major advantage is expected superior long-term net-of-expenses performance because of relatively low portfolio turnover and management fees (often 0.10 percent of assets or less). For tax-sensitive investors, indexing's often relatively high tax efficiency (i.e., post-tax returns that are close to pre-tax returns) is appealing. That tax efficiency comes from turnover that is usually low compared with active investing.

Indexing has advantages in a broad range of equity market segments. The relatively high informational efficiency of prices in large-cap equity markets favors indexing. In typically less efficient market segments, such as small cap, the supply of active investment opportunities may be larger but transaction costs are higher. Indexing

---

[7] Equity mutual funds have been perhaps the most intensively and rigorously researched institutional equity segment. See Daniel, Grinblatt, Titman, and Wermers (1997) and the references therein for equity mutual funds for empirical findings, as well as Ennis (2005). Lewellen (2011) finds that for institutional investors in general, portfolio managers do not earn significantly positive alpha.
[8] See Daniel et al.

is also a logical choice to gain exposure to markets with which an investor may be unfamiliar (e.g., an overseas market), because active investing when one may be at an informational disadvantage is usually ill-advised.

To thoroughly understand the implementation of indexing, we need to discuss the construction and maintenance of equity indices. The way indices are created, selected, and used may be passive investing's weakest link.

4.1 Equity Indices

Investment performance is undeniably important to an equity portfolio manager, whether he takes an active or passive investment approach. It makes little difference how well a manager can identify great companies, make long-term earnings estimates, or forecast the economy if his investment performance is consistently inferior. Equity portfolio managers frequently evaluate their performance against equity benchmark indices designed to show how the overall stock market or some subsector of the market has performed.[9]

The benchmark is not just about measuring asset-class performance. A well-chosen benchmark index for a portfolio manager also represents that manager's investment "neighborhood." If a manager's benchmark is the S&P 500, he is unlikely to be investing in Russian stocks. Investors find it easier to manage their aggregate portfolios if an index well captures the investment universe of their investment managers, and to compartmentalize managers for the purposes of comparison with peers.

In addition to their role as portfolio management benchmarks, stock indices are also used to measure the returns of a market or market segment, as the basis for creating an index fund, to study factors that influence share price movements, to perform technical analysis, and to calculate a stock's systematic risk (or beta).

Four choices determine a stock index's characteristics: the boundaries of the index's universe, the criteria for inclusion in the index, how the stocks are weighted, and how returns are calculated. The first choice, the boundaries of the stock index's universe, is important in determining how well the index represents a specific population of stocks. The greater its number of stocks and the more diversified by industry and size, the better the index will measure broad market performance. A narrower universe will measure performance of a specific group of stocks. The second choice, the criteria for inclusion, establishes any specific characteristics desired for stocks within the selected universe. The third, the weighting of the stocks, is usually a choice among price weighting, value (or float) weighting, or equal weighting. The fourth choice, computational method, includes variations such as price only and total return series that include the reinvestment of dividends. Only total return series capture the two sources of equity returns, capital appreciation and dividends.

4.1.1 Index Weighting Choices

Probably the greatest differences among indices covering similar universes lie in how the index components are weighted. The three basic index weighting methods are price weighting, value (or float) weighting, and equal weighting.

- **Price weighted**. In a price-weighted index, each stock in the index is weighted according to its absolute share price. In other words, the index is simply the sum of the share prices divided by the adjusted number of shares in the index (adjustments are for the purpose of ensuring that the index value does not change merely because of stock splits or changes in index components since

---

[9] See the reading on performance evaluation for details and alternative approaches to evaluation.

the base or launch date of the index). *The performance of a price-weighted index represents the performance of a portfolio that simply bought and held one share of each index component.*

- **Value weighted** (or market-capitalization weighted). In a value-weighted index (also called a market-capitalization weighted index or a market capitalization index), each stock in the index is weighted according to its market cap (share price multiplied by the number of shares outstanding). *The performance of a value-weighted index would represent the performance of a portfolio that owns all the outstanding shares of each index component.* A given percentage change in a value-weighted index is equal to the change in the total value of all included companies. A value-weighted index self-corrects for stock splits, reverse stock splits, and dividends because such actions are directly reflected in the number of shares outstanding and price per share for the company affected.

  A subcategory of the value-weighted method involves adjustment of market cap weights for each issue's **floating supply of shares** or free float—the number of shares outstanding that are actually available to investors. The resulting index is called a free float–adjusted market capitalization index, or float-weighted index for short. Float adjustments usually exclude corporate cross-holdings, large holdings by founding shareholders, and government holdings of shares in partly privatized companies.[10] The weight of a stock in a float-weighted index equals its market-cap weight multiplied by a free-float adjustment factor (a number between 0 and 1 representing the fraction of shares that float freely). A float-weighted index is concerned with the *investable* market values of equity issues—the market values actually available to be held by the public. *The performance of a float-weighted index represents the performance of a portfolio that buys and holds all the shares of each index component that are available for trading.* Thus, the (total) return of a float-weighted index will represent the return to the average dollar invested passively in the index's securities (ignoring costs). If the index securities are the manager's investment universe, such a float-weighted index represents a plausible performance benchmark for him. With the changeover of Standard & Poor's principal US indices (the S&P 500, the S&P MidCap 400 Index, and the S&P SmallCap 600 Index) and the principal Japanese index (TOPIX) to float weighting, all major value-weighted indices are now free-float adjusted.

  For brevity, in the reading we will use "value-weighted/float-weighted indices" to refer to value-weighted indices without float adjustment (sometimes called for emphasis *full* market-cap indices) and value-weighted indices with float adjustment as a group.

- **Equal weighted**. In an equal-weighted index, each stock in the index is weighted equally. *The performance of an equal-weighted index represents the performance of a portfolio in which the same amount of money is invested in the shares of each index component.* Equal-weighted indices must be rebalanced periodically (e.g., monthly, quarterly, or annually) to reestablish the equal weighting, because varying individual stock returns will cause stock weights to drift from equal weights.

These different weighting schemes can lead to a number of biases. A price-weighted index is biased toward the highest-priced share. For example, a stock with a price of €50 will have twice the weight in a price-weighted index as a stock with a price of

---

10 For instance, in Example 1 given later, two stocks (Wal-Mart and Microsoft) have substantial free-float adjustments. In both cases, substantial shareholdings of founding executives, their heirs, or foundations that they established are expected never to be liquidated.

€25. Therefore, a 10 percent increase in the higher-priced stock will have the same effect on the index as a 20 percent increase in the lower-priced stock. The absolute level of a share price is an arbitrary figure, however, because a company can change its share price through a stock split, a stock dividend, or a reverse split. It makes no sense to invest money merely in proportion to an absolute share price, which is what such an index would dictate. Some price-weighted averages, such as the Nikkei 225 for Japanese equities, systematically reduce the weighting of very high-priced stocks to minimize such arbitrary distortion of the index by very high-priced shares.

A price-weighted index's main advantage lies in the simplicity of its construction. Straightforwardly, the share prices are added up and then divided by the number of shares in the index adjusted to maintain continuity in the series, taking account of stock splits and additions/deletions of components. Stock price data series are also easier to obtain historically than market value series. Consequently, price-weighted index series can go back far into the past. Price-weighted indices can be created with a rich, if sometimes hypothetical, history. The oldest and most widely followed equity index, the Dow Jones Industrial Average, is calculated this way. When that index was first published in 1896, the weighting choices most index users prefer today were impractical.

A value-weighted index is biased toward the shares of companies with the largest market capitalizations. In other words, a 10 percent share price increase for a large-cap company would affect the index more than would a 10 percent share price increase for a smaller company. Such an index excels at conveying the effect of a change in companies' total value, or aggregate investor wealth. Float adjustments to capitalization weights exclude shares that are unavailable to investors, making float-weighted indices most representative of the range of securities and weights that public investors as a group can buy and hold. The bias toward large market cap issues in value-weighted/float-weighted indices, however, means that such indices will tend to be biased toward:

- large and probably mature companies, and
- overvalued companies, whose share prices have already risen the most.

Arnott (2005) argues that even if pricing errors are random, the largest-cap stocks are more likely to incorporate positive pricing errors than negative pricing errors. Arnott, Hsu, and Moore (2005) have suggested the weighting of component securities by fundamentals (adjusting the market cap of components downward or upward when price-to-fundamentals metrics such as P/Es are high or low, respectively) as a means of addressing such biases.[11] Another criticism of value-weighted/float-weighted indices is that a portfolio based on such an index may be concentrated in relatively few issues and, hence, less diversified than most actively managed portfolios.[12] Furthermore, because of regulatory or other restrictions on maximum holdings, indexing to some concentrated indices may be infeasible. Although controversy exists (as on many investment issues), floatweighting is generally regarded as today's gold standard for indexing portfolios because it facilitates the minimization of tracking risk and portfolio turnover, and because it results in indices that well represent asset-class performance.

In an equal-weighted index, all stocks are treated the same. Small companies have the same weight in the index as very large companies. An equal-weighting methodology introduces a small-company bias because such indices include many more small companies than large ones. Moreover, to maintain equal weighting, this type of index must be rebalanced periodically. Frequent rebalancing can lead to high transaction

---

[11] More recently, Clark, Hessel, Wang, and Zhang (2010) find superior performance from using portfolios weighted by share repurchases and total payout, relative to other fundamentally weighted portfolios.
[12] See Bernstein (2003).

Passive Equity Investing

costs in a portfolio tracking such an index. Another limitation of equal-weighted indices as indexing benchmarks is that not all components in such an index may have sufficiently liquid markets to absorb the demand of indexers.

Example 1 contrasts the various types of indices.

EXAMPLE 1

A Problem of Benchmark Index Selection

Stephen Alcorn is a portfolio manager at Amanda Asset Management, Inc. (AAM). In March 2010, a wealthy client engaged Alcorn to manage $10,000,000 for one year in an active focused (concentrated) equity style. The investment management contract specified a symmetric incentive fee of $10,000 per 100 basis points (bps) of capital appreciation relative to that of an index of the stocks selected for investment.[13] (*Symmetric* means that the incentive fee will reduce the investment management fee if benchmark-relative performance is negative.) In an oversight, the contract leaves open the method by which the benchmark index will be calculated. Alcorn invests in shares of the Exxon Corporation, McDonald's Corporation, Intel Corporation, Merck & Co., Wal-Mart Stores, and Microsoft Corporation, achieving a 6.5 percent price return for the year. Exhibit 4 gives information on the six stocks.

Exhibit 4 Equity Market Data for the Shares of Six Companies

	Share Price 31–Mar-10	Share Price 31–Mar-11	Price Change	Market Value of Shares 31-Mar-10 (Millions)	Market Value of Shares 31-Mar-11 (Millions)	Free Float Factor
Exxon	$67.00	$84.11	25.5%	$316,231	$396,988	1
McDonald's	66.68	76.13	14.2	71,788	81,962	1
Intel	15.57	20.20	29.7	123,130	159,745	1
Merck	37.43	33.03	−11.8	116,357	102,679	1
Wal-Mart	55.60	52.10	−6.3	209,001	195,844	0.51
Microsoft	29.30	25.40	−13.3	256,865	222,675	0.88
Total				$1,093,372	$1,159,893	

Using only the information given, address the following:

1. For each of the six shares, explain the price-only return calculation on the following indices for the period 31 March 2010 to 31 March 2011:
   i. price-weighted index
   ii. value-weighted index
   iii. float-weighted index
   iv. equal-weighted index
2. Recommend the appropriate benchmark index for calculating the performance incentive fee on the account and determine the amount of that fee.

---

[13] To simplify the calculations, the problem is stated in terms of capital appreciation. In practice, the incentive fee would usually be stated in terms of total return.

Solution to 1:

i. As Exhibit 5 illustrates, the value of the price-weighted index on 31 March 2010 is found by adding the six share prices as of that date and dividing by 6: 271.58/6 = 45.26. As of 31 March 2011, the value of the index is 290.97/6 = 48.50. Thus the one-year return is (48.50 − 45.26)/45.26 = 0.071, or 7.1 percent. At 31 March 2010, the index gives a 67.00/271.58 = 24.67 percent weight to Exxon and a 66.68/271.58 = 24.55 percent weight to McDonald's, the highest-priced shares.

Exhibit 5 Price-Weighted Index

	Share Price 31-Mar-10	Share Price 31-Mar-11	Price Change	Percentage of index 31-Mar-10	Contribution to Return
Exxon	$67.00	$84.11	25.5%	24.67%	6.30%
McDonald's	66.68	76.13	14.2	24.55	3.48
Intel	15.57	20.20	29.7	5.73	1.70
Merck	37.43	33.03	−11.8	13.78	−1.62
Wal-Mart	55.60	52.10	−6.3	20.47	−1.29
Microsoft	29.30	25.40	−13.3	10.79	−1.44
Total	$271.58	$290.97	7.1%	100%	7.1%
Index	$45.26	$48.50			

ii. A value-weighted index is calculated by multiplying the share price by the number of shares outstanding to arrive at each company's market value, then summing these values to create an index. As Exhibit 6 shows, such an index would have risen by 6.1 percent by March 2011, which is less than the 7.1 percent return for the price-weighted index. This is because the weighting of the stocks is different under the two methods. For example, under the price-weighted index, McDonald's was weighted by 24.55 percent because its price was second highest. Under the value-weighted index, it is weighted the lowest at 6.57 percent. Hence, McDonald's positive return of 14.2 percent is weighted less under the value-weighted index methodology.

Note that for real world value-weighted indices, if X is the total market values of the index components, the index vendor will normalize X by dividing it by the total market value as of some baseline date, and multiply that result by some value such as 100 to represent the starting index value. In the case of Exhibit 6 data, for example, if 31 March 2010 were chosen as the starting date and 100 as the beginning value, then an index vendor would give the index value as of 31 March 2010 as 100, and its value as of 31 March 2011 as (1,159,893/1,093,372) × 100 = 106.10.

Exhibit 6 Value-Weighted Index

	Market Value of Shares 31-Mar-10 (Millions)	Market Value of Shares 31-Mar-11 (Millions)	Value Change	Percentage of index 31-Mar-10	Contribution to Return
Exxon	$316,231	$396,988	25.5%	28.92%	7.39
McDonald's	71,788	81,962	14.2	6.57	0.93
Intel	123,130	159,745	29.7	11.26	3.35
Merck	116,357	102,679	−11.8	10.64	−1.25
Wal-Mart	209,001	195,844	−6.3	19.12	−1.20
Microsoft	256,865	222,675	−13.3	23.49	−3.13
Index	$1,093,372	$1,159,893	6.1%	100%	6.1%

iii. A float-weighted index is calculated the same way as a value-weighted index, except that the market value is adjusted by a float factor that represents the fraction of shares outstanding actually available to investors. As shown in Exhibit 7, the market values are identical to those given in Exhibit 6 for the value-weighted index except for Wal-Mart and Microsoft, which have free-float factors below 1.0 (provided in Exhibit 4). A free-float index would have risen by 8.0 percent by March 2011, or almost 2 percentage points more than a simple value-weighted index. The pickup results from the fact that the effect of Wal-Mart and Microsoft's relatively poor performance becomes less important because of their smaller weights after adjusting for free float.

Exhibit 7 Float-Weighted Index

	Market Value of Shares 31-Mar-10 (Millions)	Market Value of Shares 31-Mar-11 (Millions)	Value Change	Percentage of index 31-Mar-10	Contribution to Return
Exxon	$316,231	$396,988	25.5%	32.94%	8.41%
McDonald's	71,788	81,962	14.2	7.48	1.06
Intel	123,130	159,745	29.7	12.82	3.81
Merck	116,357	102,679	−11.8	12.12	−1.42
Wal-Mart	106,591	99,881	−6.3	11.10	−0.70
Microsoft	226,041	195,954	−13.3	23.54	−3.13
Index	$960,138	$1,037,208	8.0%	100.00%	8.0%

iv. An equal-weighted index assumes an equal investment in each of the six stocks. Its performance would be the average performance of the six stocks over the year, or 6.35 percent. In Exhibit 8, the base value of each of the six components on 31 March 2010 is 100/6 = 16.67. The value of a component shown for 31 March 2011 is found by multiplying its 31 March 2010 value by 1 plus the return over the year. For example, Exxon's 31 March 2011 value is 16.67(1 + 0.255) = 20.92. The weights of the components would then be rebalanced to 16.67 to reestablish equal weighting.

Exhibit 8 Equal-Weighted Index

	Index 31-Mar-10	Index 31-Mar-11	Price Change	Percentage of Index 31-Mar-10	Contribution to Return
Exxon	16.67	20.92	25.5%	16.67%	4.26%
McDonald's	16.67	19.03	14.2	16.67	2.36
Intel	16.67	21.62	29.7	16.67	4.96
Merck	16.67	14.71	−11.8	16.67	−1.96
Wal-Mart	16.67	15.62	−6.3	16.67	−1.05
Microsoft	16.67	14.45	−13.3	16.67	−2.22
Index	100	106.35	6.35%	100%	6.35%

Solution to 2:

A float-weighted index of the six shares is the recommended benchmark index because it represents the return to the average dollar invested passively in the six stocks, reflecting the supply of shares actually available to the public. Because the portfolio underperformed that index by 150 basis points, AAM management fees should be reduced by (150/100) × $10,000 = $15,000. Exhibit 9 summarizes the dispersion of active returns for the various ways in which the benchmark index might be calculated. The manager just outperformed a value-weighted index and an equal-weighted index of the six shares and underperformed price-weighted and float-weighted indices.

Exhibit 9 Summary of Weighting Method Results

Weighting Method	Index Return	Active Return to Benchmark
Price-weighted	7.1%	-0.6%
Value-weighted	6.1	0.4
Float-weighted	8.0	−1.5
Equal-weighted	6.4	0.1

4.1.2 Equity Indices: Composition and Characteristics of Major Indices

A large number of stock price indices exist for measuring share performance on a global, regional, country, and sector basis. The sector category includes indices designed to reflect results for large stocks, small stocks, growth stocks, value stocks, and specific industries.

Exhibit 10 compares some of the major stock market indices. The exhibit first gives facts on indices within the currently very small group of major price-weighted and equal-weighted equity indices. The list of important value-weighted/float-weighted indices is very long: even giving summary facts on them would run to many pages. Exhibit 10 thus covers indices that are discussed in text examples, examples from six of the world's largest equity markets (in alphabetical order: Canada, France, Germany, Japan, the United Kingdom, and the United States), and an example of a global index family.

The first entry is the oldest equity index, the Dow Jones Industrial Average. Interestingly, the DJIA consists of only 30 companies, but since its creation in 1896 it has had a total of more than 100 different constituents. As leading companies of their time go into decline, they are routinely taken out of the index. Many disappeared long ago. General Electric is the only one of the original 12 constituents in the DJIA currently in the index, and it has been in and out of the DJIA a few times over the years. One moral of DJIA's story for equity investors is that if an investor holds a single stock long enough, he is about as likely to lose most or all of his money as to accumulate great wealth. The history of changes in the Dow's composition is one of the best arguments for diversification.

An indexer's choice of index to track has important consequences. Committee-determined indices tend to have lower turnover than those reconstituted regularly according to an algorithm. Thus indexing on the former type of index may have transaction cost and tax advantages. On the other hand, indices (and index funds based on them) that are not reconstituted regularly may drift away from the market segment they are intended to cover. The indexer should also be aware of liquidity differences among the component securities of the various indices that cover the same market segment. For example, liquidity and relatively adequate float are criteria for selection to the S&P SmallCap 600 Index but not the Russell 2000 Index. On the other hand, investing in less liquid shares may allow the indexer to capture an illiquidity premium. In choosing the index to replicate, a fund must evaluate the trade-off between differences in transaction costs and differences in return premiums among the indices.

4.2 Passive Investment Vehicles

Having described the array of equity indices, in the following sections we describe specific passive investment vehicles. The major choices are:

- investment in an indexed portfolio;
- a long position in cash plus a long position in futures contracts on the underlying index, when such markets are available and adequately liquid; and
- a long position in cash plus a long position in a swap on the index. (That is, in the swap the investor pays a fixed rate of interest on the swap's notional principal and in return receives the return on the index.)

4.2.1 Indexed Portfolios

The three most important categories of indexed portfolios are:

- conventional index mutual funds;
- exchange-traded funds (ETFs), which are based on benchmark index portfolios; and
- separate accounts or pooled accounts, mostly for institutional investors, designed to track a benchmark index.

The most obvious difference between conventional index mutual funds and ETFs is that shareholders in mutual funds usually buy shares from the fund and sell them back to the fund at a net asset value determined once a day at the market close.[14] ETF

---

[14] A few funds in the United States and all funds in some countries make more-frequent net asset value calculations: once an hour in some cases, and almost continuously in others.

Exhibit 10 Some Representative Equity Indices Worldwide

	Representing	Number of Stocks	Weighting of Index	Special Characteristics	Drawbacks/Comments
Dow Jones Industrial Average	US blue chip companies	30	Price-weighted	The oldest and most widely followed US equity index	30 stocks chosen by *Wall Street Journal* editors; large, mature blue chip companies
Nikkei Stock Average	Japanese blue chip companies	225	Modified price-weighted	Originally formulated by Dow Jones & Company, using essentially the same method as the DJIA	Also known as the Nikkei 225. There is a huge variation in share price levels of the component companies, and some high-priced shares are weighted at a fraction of their share price. Some component stocks are illiquid.
Value Line Arithmetic Composite Index	Equities traded in US markets	Approximately 1,700	Equal-weighted	Represents the performance of the stocks covered in the *Value Line Investment Survey*	A well-known equal-weighted index. The Value Line Geometric Composite Index is based on the same stocks but calculates index changes using a geometric rather than arithmetic mean.
S&P TSX Composite	Broad market cap stocks listed on the Toronto Stock Exchange	Varies	Float-weighted	Very comprehensive index	Widely used Canadian equities benchmark
CAC 40	French blue chip companies	40	Float-weighted	Chosen from the 100 largest market cap stocks on the Paris Bourse (Euronext Paris)	
DAX 30	German blue chip companies	30	Float-weighted	Published by the Frankfurt Stock Exchange	Widely used German equities benchmark
TOPIX	All listed companies on the Tokyo Stock Exchange 1st Section	Varies	Value-weighted[a]	Includes all stocks listed on the TSE 1st Section, which represents about 93% of the market value of all equities in Japan	The index contains a large number of very small, illiquid stocks, making it difficult to replicate exactly.
FTSE 100	The 100 largest publicly traded stocks on the London Stock Exchange	100	Float-weighted	A large-cap index, pronounced "Footsie 100"	There are also a FTSE Mid 250 for mid-cap stocks and a small-cap index.
Russell 3000	The 3,000 largest stocks in the United States by market cap	3,000 selected on the last trading day of May. The new composition becomes effective on the last Friday in June.	Float-weighted and value-weighted available	Very comprehensive index	The Russell indices are reconstituted annually based on market cap data as of the last day of May. Widely used institutional benchmark.

Exhibit 10   (Continued)

	Representing	Number of Stocks	Weighting of Index	Special Characteristics	Drawbacks/Comments
Russell 1000	The 1,000 largest stocks in the Russell 3000	1,000 on the day the new composition is determined	Float-weighted	A large-cap index	Competes with the S&P 500 as a large-cap benchmark.
Russell 2000	The smallest 2,000 stocks in the Russell 3000	2,000 on the day the new composition is determined	Float-weighted	A small-cap index	The many US small-cap index funds tracking this index and the consequent annual reconstitution costs and possible tax consequences make this a relatively high-cost benchmark for a US small-cap index fund.
S&P 500	Predominantly large-cap companies representative of the US stock market	500	Float-weighted	Membership determined by a committee of S&P employees	Its popularity with indexers causes new components to earn average positive abnormal returns on the announcement that they are joining the index.[b]
MSCI Index Family	Separate series for individual developed and emerging markets; regions; world developed markets—MSCI World; and All Country World (developed and emerging markets)—MSCI ACWI	Varies	Float-weighted	Most widely used global index family. The MSCI World ex US, ex Japan (MSCI Kokusai), ex UK, and ex EMU, are some indices used as benchmarks for nondomestic equities in various markets.	Other major families of global benchmark indices are published by FTSE, Dow Jones, and S&P/Citigroup.

[a] The TOPIX became float-weighted in three stages: October 2005, February 2006, and June 2006.
[b] See Lynch and Mendenhall (1997) and Malkiel and Radisich (2001), and Zhou (2011) for more information and a discussion of competing explanations for this phenomenon.

shareholders buy and sell shares in public markets anytime during the trading day. Dealers can create and redeem ETF shares with in-kind deposits and withdrawals at each day's market close.

The principal difference between index mutual funds and exchange-traded funds on the one hand, and indexed institutional portfolios, on the other hand, is cost. Indexed institutional portfolios managed as separate accounts with a single shareholder or, increasingly, as pooled accounts, are extremely low-cost products. Depending on the nature of the securities used in the portfolio, total annual expenses may be as low as a few basis points. Occasionally, where securities with an active lending market are involved, the revenue from securities lending can equal or exceed total portfolio management and custody expenses.[15]

Conventional index mutual funds can vary greatly in their cost structure and returns. Elton, Gruber, and Busse (2004) examined and compared the expenses and performance of S&P 500 mutual funds from 1996 to 2001. A large part of the difference in performance among these funds came from differences in the funds' expense ratios. However, differences in expenses may be expected to narrow the more such funds compete for investors' money. The results from Wahal and Wang (2011) indicates that management fees do decline as more index funds enter a market, and also that fund industry competition has increased since the late 1990s.

Other fund differences affect performance as well. For example, funds use securities lending as a source of income to varying degrees. In the Elton et al. study the difference between the best-performing S&P 500 fund and the worst-performing fund for that six-year period was an average of 209 bps (2.09 percent) a year. Clearly, S&P 500 index funds and index portfolio managers are sometimes not the "commodities" they are often thought to be.

Other differences among index funds become apparent when exchange-traded funds are added to the range of choices. At least four economically significant differences separate conventional index mutual funds from indexed exchange-traded funds:[16]

1 Shareholder accounting at the fund level can be a significant expense for conventional mutual funds in some markets, but ETFs do not have fund level shareholder accounting.

2 Exchange-traded funds generally pay much higher index license fees than conventional funds.

3 Exchange-traded funds are often much more tax-efficient than conventional funds in many markets, including the United States.

4 Users of exchange-traded funds pay transaction costs including commissions to trade them, but for their ongoing shareholders, ETFs provide inherently better protection from the cost of providing liquidity to shareholders who are selling fund shares.

To the extent that a fund has a large number of small shareholders, shareholder record-keeping will be a significant cost reflected in the fund's expense ratio. Some funds attempt to cope with this cost and to allocate it to the shareholders who are responsible for it by charging a maintenance fee for accounts below a certain size and/or by offering funds with a lower expense ratio to very large investors. For example,

---

[15] Securities lending is a common practice in most equity and fixed-income markets around the world. The securities lender typically receives cash equal or slightly greater in value than the securities lent. The lender invests this cash and typically shares the interest with the securities borrower. In some cases, when a security has great value in the lending market because it is popular with short sellers, the securities lender may keep all the interest and even receive an additional premium for lending the securities.

[16] When first introduced, all ETFs in the United States were index funds. In the late-2000s, actively managed ETFs were introduced in the United States. There are now actively managed equity, bond, and currency ETFs. There is a longer history of actively managed ETFs outside the United States.

Vanguard charges lower fees on its Admiral class shares than it does for its Investor class shares, which have a lower minimum investment.[17] Exchange-traded funds have no shareholder accounting at the fund level, so their expense ratios are typically lower than conventional mutual fund expense ratios for funds linked to comparable indices. Brokers who carry these shares for investors may levy inactivity fees on ETF shareholders if they trade rarely, and of course there are transaction costs associated with buying and selling ETF shares in the marketplace.

Another important difference between index mutual funds and exchange-traded funds is that, at least in the United States, exchange-traded funds are usually more tax efficient in the sense that they are less likely than mutual funds to make taxable capital gains distributions. At the investor level, mutual fund buyers are affected by a fund's cost basis for its positions, which may differ quite a bit from the positions' current values. As a result, at the time of purchase an investor may buy into a potential tax liability if the positions show a gain.

At the fund level, the most significant tax difference between conventional funds and ETFs is in the process by which fund shares are redeemed. A traditional mutual fund will usually experience a tax event from selling portfolio securities when holders of a significant number of shares redeem their positions for cash. Unlike a traditional mutual fund that will ordinarily sell stocks inside the fund and pay cash to a fund shareholder who is redeeming shares, the redemption mechanism for an exchange-traded fund is usually "in kind" in the sense of being an exchange of shares. The fund typically delivers a basket of the fund's portfolio stocks to a redeeming dealer who has turned in shares of the fund for this exchange. In the United States, this transaction is not taxable from the fund's perspective, and there is no distributable gain on the redemption. Occasionally, a conventional fund—particularly a non-index fund—will deliver stock in kind to a large redeeming shareholder; but most conventional funds offer limited opportunities to redeem fund shares by delivering portfolio stock in kind. The in-kind creation and redemption process of ETFs also insulates long-term ETF shareholders from the costs of supplying liquidity to traders, a persistent problem with mutual funds in a number of markets.[18]

Turning to indexed institutional portfolios, a relatively small number of quantitatively oriented investment management organizations manage the majority of the money in such indexed accounts. The same organization may manage institutional portfolios, conventional funds, and ETFs. Management of these different portfolios may be assigned to separate groups of managers or integrated, with the portfolio management and trading functions consolidated in a single indexing group. Investment management firms' aggressiveness in implementing index composition changes varies, and in fact may vary from one type of account to another within the same firm. Indeed, index fund managers have sometimes come under scrutiny for failing to implement anticipated index composition changes aggressively because of their concern for minimizing tracking risk. The issue arises because changes to indices are often predictable or announced in advance of the effective date, but index funds may not effect the forthcoming changes as soon as they are foreseeable because of a concern with minimizing tracking risk relative to the current index components. In the interim, arbitrageurs may trade on the basis of the anticipated changes, affecting prices and causing an implicit loss to index fund investors.[19]

If an index contains less than, say, 1,000 stocks, and the stocks are liquid, the index fund manager will usually attempt to manage the portfolio with **full replication** of the index—that is, every issue in the index will be represented in the portfolio, and

---

17 Vanguard and other managers also offer even lower expense ratio share classes to "institutional" investors.
18 In the United States, the inconsistent application of deadlines for accepting mutual fund buy and sell orders has been a related problem for long-term mutual fund shareholders.
19 See Chen, Noronha, and Singal (2006) and Petajisto (2011).

each portfolio position will have approximately the same weight in the fund as in the index. As the number of issues in the index passes 1,000, it is increasingly likely that the manager will construct the portfolio using either **stratified sampling** (also called representative sampling) or **optimization**. In some cases, the preferred method depends on portfolio size and the availability of active trading in an index basket by means of portfolio trades. For example, an indexer may use full replication for a large fund (e.g., an ETF) tracking the Russell 2000, making use of standard Russell 2000 basket trades, but may choose optimization for smaller, separately managed accounts indexed to the same index.

Full replication, where the number and liquidity of the issues permit using it, should result in minimal tracking risk. Apart from minimizing tracking risk, a full replication portfolio based on a value-weighted (or float-weighted) index has the advantage of being self-rebalancing because the stock weights in the portfolio will mirror changes in the index weights resulting from constantly changing stock prices. Self-rebalancing is a desirable characteristic because it implies that trading is needed only for the reinvestment of dividends and to reflect changes in index composition. Full replication is the most common procedure for indices such as the S&P 500 that are composed of highly liquid securities. Typically, the return on a full replication index fund may be less than the index return by an amount equal to the sum of:

- the cost of managing and administering the fund;
- the transaction costs of portfolio adjustments to reflect changes in index composition;
- the transaction costs of investing and disinvesting cash flows; and
- in upward-trending equity markets, the drag on performance from any cash positions.[20]

Attempting to fully replicate an index containing a large proportion of illiquid stocks will usually result in an index portfolio that underperforms the index.[21] This phenomenon occurs because indices do not have to bear transaction costs but a real portfolio does. These transaction costs include brokerage commissions, bid–offer spreads, taxes, and the market impact of trades (the effect of large trades on the market price).[22] There are two ways to build an index-tracking portfolio using a subset of stocks in the index: stratified sampling and optimization. Skillful use of these techniques should permit a portfolio manager to index successfully to even a very broad index containing illiquid securities.

Using stratified sampling, a portfolio manager divides the index along a number of dimensions (e.g., market capitalization, industry, value, and growth), creating multidimensional cells. Each index stock is placed into the cell that best describes it. For instance, a simple cell structure could focus on market cap and industry. A manager trying to build a portfolio mimicking the TOPIX index would then place a stock such as Toyota into a cell that is defined by automobile stocks with a market cap greater than ¥5 trillion. Next, she would characterize all stocks in the index in this way and determine the weight of each cell in the index by totaling the market cap for all stocks in that cell. The manager would then build a portfolio by selecting a random sample of stocks from each cell and ensuring that the sum of the weights of the stocks purchased from each cell corresponds to the cell's weight in the index.

---

[20] In the long run, we expect equity returns to exceed the returns on cash, justifying the inclusion of this factor.

[21] Nevertheless, superior tax reclaims (of withheld taxes) on large international index funds can deliver a significant boost to performance relative to most international indices, which use conservative assumptions on tax reclaims.

[22] Taxes are levied on transactions in some countries. For example, a stamp duty of 0.50% is paid on the value of each stock purchase in the United Kingdom.

Passive Equity Investing

For example, suppose that a cell contains 2 percent of the weight of the index and that two stocks chosen to represent the cell have index weights of 0.3 percent and 0.5 percent, leaving a balance of 2.0% − 0.8% = 1.2%. By overweighting each security by 1.2%/2 = 0.6 percentage points (i.e., holding them in weights of 0.3% + 0.6% = 0.9% and 0.5% + 0.6% = 1.1%), the index fund can achieve the same exposure to the cell factors as the index.[23] Stratified sampling allows the manager to build a portfolio that retains the basic characteristics of the index without having to buy all of the stocks in the index. Generally speaking, the greater the number of dimensions and the finer the divisions, the more closely the portfolio will resemble the index.

Sometimes an index with relatively few components or with a few heavily weighted components is not naturally compliant with regulatory requirements for fund diversification (which often place maximums on how much of the portfolio may be invested in any one issuer). In such cases, stratified sampling techniques may be used to create an index fund variation loosely based on the non-diversification-compliant index. In the United States, the relevant diversification requirements are the rules for Regulated Investment Company (RIC) diversification in Sub-Chapter M of the Internal Revenue Code. In the European Union, the appropriate rules cover Undertakings for Collective Investment in Transferable Securities (UCITS), which was passed in 2009 for implementation in 2011. UCITS rules allow index funds with an EU passport (approved for offering in all EU jurisdictions) to hold up to 20 percent of assets in one security if the index called for such.[24] Increasingly, ETF issuers and index publishers who develop indices specifically for the ETF market are designing indices to be inherently RIC-compliant in the United States and UCITS-compliant in Europe. If the fund can replicate the index and comply with local diversification requirements simultaneously, a fund analyst can better evaluate the fund's portfolio manager and the fund management process.

Another technique commonly used to build portfolios containing only a subset of an index's stocks is optimization. Optimization is a mathematical approach to index fund construction involving the use of:

- a multifactor risk model, against which the risk exposures of the index and individual securities are measured, and
- an objective function that specifies that securities be held in proportions that minimize expected tracking risk relative to the index subject to appropriate constraints.

The multifactor model might include factors such as market capitalization, beta, and industry membership, as well as macroeconomic factors such as interest rate levels. The objective function seeks to match the portfolio's risk exposures to those of the index being tracked. An advantage of optimization compared with stratified sampling is that optimization takes into account the covariances among the factors used to explain the return on stocks. The stratified sampling approach implicitly assumes the factors are mutually uncorrelated.

Optimization has several drawbacks as an approach to indexation. First, even the best risk models are likely to be imperfectly specified. That is, it is virtually impossible to create a risk model that exactly captures the risk associated with a given stock, if only because risks change over time and risk models are based on historical data. Furthermore, the optimization procedure seeks to maximally exploit any risk differences among securities, even if they just reflect sampling error (this is the problem

---

[23] This simple approach to weight adjustment has been used in practice. A more precise approach would be to increase the securities weights so as to maintain their relative proportion of 0.3/0.5 = 0.6: weights of 0.75 percent and 1.25 percent for the first and second securities, respectively (0.75%/1.25% = 0.60 and 0.75% + 1.25% = 2%).

[24] EU member states could increase the limit to 35 percent under exceptional market circumstances.

known as overfitting the data). Even in the absence of index changes and dividend flows, optimization requires periodic trading to keep the risk characteristics of the portfolio lined up with those of the index being tracked. As a result of these limitations, the predicted tracking risk of an optimization-based portfolio will typically understate the actual tracking risk. That said, indexers have found that the results of an optimization approach frequently compare well with those of a stratified sampling approach, particularly when replication is attempted using relatively few securities. With either stratified sampling or optimization, the indexer may fully replicate (purchase in index-weight proportions) the largest stocks and create an optimized/sampled portfolio for the rest.

> **EXAMPLE 2**
>
> ### Passive Portfolio Construction Methods
>
> An investment manager has been given a mandate for managing a Russell 2000 index fund for a moderate-size foundation. The manager must choose either full replication or optimization for managing the portfolio. Recommend the most appropriate method for constructing this index portfolio.
>
> ### Solution:
>
> Optimization is the most appropriate method. Each of the techniques for building an index portfolio has strengths and weaknesses. Generally, when the index contains highly liquid stocks, full replication is usually the preferred index construction method. Apart from minimizing tracking risk, a full replication portfolio has the advantage of being self-rebalancing (given that it is based on a value- or float-weighted index). That said, the Russell 2000 is dominated by smaller-cap companies, and replication may not be the most cost-effective choice given the costs of transacting in small-cap issues.
>
> Stratified sampling and optimization are preferred when a portfolio manager wishes to track an index containing a large number of stocks, particularly stocks that are more difficult and costly to trade. In this case, however, stratified sampling is not under consideration. Therefore, the pension plan should use optimization to construct the index portfolio.

4.2.2 Equity Index Futures

Institutional indexed portfolios and conventional indexed mutual funds, which date back to the 1970s, are the earliest index products and are probably the most familiar to investors. In the 1980s, two additional indexing products, **portfolio trades** (also known as basket trades or program trades) and **stock index futures**, arrived. These products grew in tandem because they were closely related; the success of each was closely linked to the success of the other. A portfolio trade is simply a basket of securities traded as a basket or unit, whereas a traditional security trade is done one share issue at a time. A portfolio trade is made when all of the stocks in the basket—most commonly, the components of an index—are traded together under relatively standardized terms.

In the United States, the most popular trading basket by far is the S&P 500 basket. In the early 1980s, trading in such baskets increased dramatically in conjunction with the introduction of S&P 500 index futures contracts on the Chicago Mercantile Exchange (CME). By the end of that decade, trading in S&P 500 portfolios accounted for a growing share of trading in US securities, and the notional value of trading in the S&P 500 futures contract regularly surpassed the notional value of trading in the underlying securities. The e-mini S&P 500 futures contract, with a notional value of

50 times the value of the S&P 500 (compared with 250 times for the standard S&P 500 contract), became a very liquid vehicle favored by traders in the early 2000s.[25] Trading in these index instruments interacted and found a variety of applications. Trading index securities as a basket and exchanging the stock basket for the futures contract on the index—a transaction called an Exchange of Futures for Physicals—permits sharp reductions in transaction costs.[26] Using an EFP, a futures position can be translated into a portfolio position. The product interchangeability through the EFP process facilitates risk-management transactions for many participants in the securities markets.

Although the S&P 500 portfolios are still the largest such standardized portfolios, trading in a variety of other index baskets and futures contracts has grown significantly throughout the world. Among the most liquid stock index futures contracts are those on the FTSE 100, the Nikkei 225, the CAC 40, and DAX 30.[27]

The limited life of a futures contract and the fact that the most active trading in the futures market is in the nearest expiration contract means that a futures position must be rolled over periodically to maintain appropriate market exposure. Trading a basket of stocks can be relatively cumbersome at times, particularly on the short side where any uptick rule historically impeded basket transactions in US markets. (**Uptick rules** require that a short sale must not be on a downtick relative to the last trade at a different price.)[28] Exchange-traded funds historically have been exempt from the uptick rule for short sales. This fact, and their lack of an expiration date, has made ETFs instruments of choice for many indefinite-term portfolio hedging and risk management applications.

4.2.3 *Equity Total Return Swaps*

Conceptually, equity swaps resemble the more widely known fixed-income and currency swaps. The distinct feature of an equity swap is that at least one side of the transaction receives the total return of either an equity instrument or, more commonly, an equity index portfolio. The other side can be either another equity instrument or index or an interest payment. The most common nonequity swap counter payments are US dollar Libor for equity swaps based on US securities, or Libor in the appropriate currency for equity swaps based on non-US stocks.

Equity swaps enjoyed a brief and intense popularity in the United States as a way for high-tax bracket investors to achieve diversification, by exchanging the return on a single stock or an undiversified stock basket for the return on a broad stock market index. Changes in US tax law, however, sharply curtailed this application. Today, most equity swap applications are motivated by differences in the tax treatment of shareholders domiciled in different countries or by the desire to gain exposure to an asset class in asset allocation. The tax-oriented applications focus primarily on differences in tax treatment accorded domestic and international recipients of corporate dividends in many countries. Dividend withholding taxes, and an often cumbersome process for obtaining appropriate relief from part of the withholding tax, give many cross-border investors an incentive to use an equity total return swap. They receive the total return

---

[25] The e-mini futures contracts trade on CME's Globex electronic trading system.
[26] In an EFP, one party buys cash market assets and sells futures contracts, and the opposite party sells the cash market assets and buys futures contracts. For example, a long position in equity futures can be exchanged for a long position in a portfolio of securities representative of the index composition. The counterparties privately set the prices, quantities, and other terms of the transaction.
[27] The CME launched futures on equity style indices in 1995. See Hill (2003). As of 2011, the CME continues to offer mid-cap, small-cap, value, and growth equity futures contracts.
[28] A **tick** is the smallest possible price movement of a security. Uptick and downtick in this context refer to any up- or down-price change, whatever the size. In 2007, the US uptick rule was repealed, but in 2010 an alternative uptick rule was enacted that prevented short-selling when a stock fell by more than 10% from the previous close.

of a nondomestic equity index in return for an interest payment to a counterparty that holds the underlying equities more tax-efficiently. Although many crossborder tax differences have been reduced, as long as tax differences persist, equity swaps can provide significant tax-saving opportunities to many large crossborder investors.

Equity swaps have another important application: asset allocation transactions. A manager can use equity swaps to rebalance portfolios to the strategic asset allocation. Total costs to rebalance by trading the underlying securities may exceed the cost of an equity swap. Consequently, effecting the asset allocation change with a swap is often more efficient. Equity swaps are used in tactical asset allocation for similar reasons.

5 ACTIVE EQUITY INVESTING

The active equity portfolio manager's primary job is to deliver the best possible performance relative to the benchmark's performance working within the risk and other constraints specified in the client's mandate. To add value, the active manager must sharpen information, investment insights, and investment tools to the point at which he has a distinct competitive advantage over his peers. Investment tools include the area of equity valuation models, a subject of study in itself.[29] The following sections on active investing focus on macro choices of orientation and strategy that distinguish the different approaches to active equity investing.

Indexing, discussed earlier, sprang from the efficient markets theory initiated in academia during the 1960s. In the subsequent three decades, however, academic and practitioner research identified a variety of possible opportunities for active management. These developments have reinvigorated active management, allowing portfolio managers to justify the higher expenses of active management compared with passive management. Furthermore, demand for performance in excess of broad market averages has been and probably will continue to be a regular feature of both the individual and institutional investor landscape. That said, many investment managers offer a range of equity investment products from active to passive to suit the differing interests of a broad spectrum of investors.

5.1 Equity Styles

To understand the landscape of active equity portfolio management today, we must discuss the concept of equity styles. Most broadly, an **investment style** is a natural grouping of investment disciplines that has some predictive power in explaining the future dispersion of returns across portfolios.[30] As we will discuss in detail later, a traditional equity style contrast is between **value** (focused on paying a relatively low share price in relation to earnings or assets per share) and growth (focused on investing in high-earnings-growth companies) disciplines. **Market oriented** is often specified as an intermediate grouping for investment disciplines that cannot be clearly categorized as value or growth. Furthermore, the market-capitalization segment(s) in which an equity investor operates is frequently specified in describing an investor's style.

Style plays roles in both risk management and performance evaluation. If an equity portfolio manager adopts a specific style and is evaluated relative to a benchmark that reflects that style, then investors who hire the manager can readily determine whether she is talented or is just earning the generic returns to a style, which might be more

---

29 See Pinto, Henry, Robinson, and Stowe (2010).
30 See Brown and Goetzmann (1997) and Ferson (2010) for a discussion of mutual fund style and performance evaluation in general.

inexpensively obtained by indexing on an appropriate equity **style index** (an index intended to reflect the average returns to a given style). Certain categories of stocks (e.g., value stocks) can outperform the overall market for years. A mediocre value stock investor might be beating a broad market benchmark consistently while actually underperforming his chosen style as represented by a benchmark for a value style.

Identifying true talent became an important issue with the emergence of the pension fund consultant in the 1980s. Pension fund consultants are hired to identify good portfolio managers, track their performance, and recommend their replacement if necessary. To accomplish this, the consultants partition managers according to the style that each follows. In this environment, an active equity portfolio manager who claims he follows no definable style automatically excludes himself from consideration by many pension funds and other institutional accounts.

The groundbreaking work in style and performance measurement was done by Nobel Laureate William F. Sharpe (1988, 1992). Sharpe set out to explain US equity mutual funds' returns in terms of their exposures to the four asset classes into which he divided the US institutional equity universe: large-cap value, large-cap growth, medium cap, and small cap. Exhibit 11 reproduces Sharpe's original diagram. The horizontal lines divide total market cap into the fraction accounted for by large-cap, mid-cap, and small-cap equities; the vertical line divides large-cap equities into equal halves of large-cap value and large-cap growth.

Exhibit 11 Composition of Four Domestic Equity Classes

Source: Sharpe (1992).

Sharpe's purpose was to define style to facilitate performance measurement and to reflect the distinct and useful differences in the way active portfolio managers structured their portfolios. As he observed in 1992,

> Much has been written about both the small-stock and the value/growth phenomena. While the terms "value" and "growth" reflect common usage in the investment profession, they serve only as convenient names for stocks that tend to be similar in several respects. As is well known, across securities there is significant positive correlation among: book/price, earnings/price, low earnings growth, dividend yield and low return on equity. Moreover, the industry compositions of the value and growth groups differ (e.g., companies with high research budgets tend to have low book values relative to their stock prices).

Thus style distinctions recognize the similarities and differences among active equity managers. The contrast between value and growth stocks is fuzzy, however, particularly when we categorize stocks in a forward-looking sense rather than using historical data. Almost any stock can be categorized as cheap or expensive depending on one's expectations for the future. Fuzziness in the growth-value contrast coincides with a movement in some quarters to give portfolio managers greater flexibility to use a wide range of techniques and instruments to add value wherever they perceive it lies.[31]

> **EXAMPLE 3**
>
> ### Same Stock, Different Opinions
>
> Value and growth investors have opposite views on the best way to invest, and they thus tend to reach different conclusions about a stock. In 2011, one example was the Microsoft Corporation, a leading provider of computer software and services. Because of its rapid growth in the 1990s, Microsoft became a member of the DJIA in 1999.
>
> For much of its history, Microsoft was a growth company. It dominated its only real rival in personal computer operating software, the Apple Corporation, maintaining a more than 90 percent share. It also had a dominant market share in word processing, spreadsheet, and presentation software. Microsoft's earnings and cash flow were strong throughout its history. However, the company was less successful in its attempts to diversify into phones, internet-based software, and internet-based services. In recent years, its sales and earnings growth lagged behind that of Google and other internet firms. In October 2011, its share price traded at less than half of its December 1999 peak.
>
> A growth investor might dismiss Microsoft's stock as a potential investment. The company's share price has been relatively stagnant for over a decade and it was recently surpassed in market capitalization by Apple and IBM. It could have a difficult time transitioning from a software firm to higher growth industries. Most of the personal computer sales in the future will likely come from the emerging markets, where software piracy is often more prevalent and selling prices tend to be low. These developments could reduce Microsoft's pricing power and earnings growth. Furthermore, web-based software will likely grow in popularity, limiting Microsoft's ability to sell its application software.
>
> A value investor, however, would point to the fact that Microsoft was trading with a P/E of 9.98, less than half Google's 19.37 and less than Apple's 15.39. Microsoft recently recorded cash of more than $50 billion, operating cash flow of $26 billion, and debt of just $12 billion. Furthermore, it has one of the strongest brand names in the world, similar in public recognition to those of Coca-Cola and Sony. Although Microsoft has struggled to make the transition to the cell phone and internet industry, it is a technologically advanced company with a great deal of intellectual capital. For a value investor, Microsoft might be a buy.

In the following sections, we examine the major types of investment styles.

---

[31] Bernstein (2003). Sensoy (2009) finds that about one-third of actively managed, diversified US equity mutual funds use a benchmark index that does not match the fund's actual style. These mismatches appear to be to the result of funds attempting to attract investment capital.

5.1.1 Value Investment Styles

All else being equal, value investors are more concerned about buying a stock that is deemed relatively cheap in terms of the purchase price of earnings or assets than about a company's future growth prospects. They may make several possible arguments to justify buying such stocks. One is that companies' earnings may have a tendency to revert to a mean value; if valuation multiples for a set of stocks are depressed because of recent earnings problems, an investor in those stocks may benefit from reversion to the mean in earnings accompanied by expansion in P/Es. The flip side of the argument is that investments in stocks that are relatively expensive expose the investor to the risk of contractions in multiples and in earnings. Value investors often believe that investors inherently overpay for "glamour" stocks—those seen as having particularly good growth prospects—while neglecting those with less favorable prospects.

All of these arguments presume that investors as a whole do not accurately judge forward-looking risk and return prospects, and so this line of thinking relates closely to the behavioral argument that investors overreact to bad news and thus provide opportunities for value investors. In contrast, Fama and French (1996) suggest that stocks that are cheap in terms of assets—in particular, stocks having a relatively high ratio of book value of equity to market value of equity (equivalent to a *low* price-to-book ratio, or P/B)—have a higher risk of financial distress and thus offer higher expected returns as fair compensation for that risk.[32] Empirically, most studies have found that in the long run a value style may earn a positive return premium relative to the market.[33] Evidence on this phenomenon is still evolving, however. For example, Phalippou (2008) found that the extra return to value is concentrated in the smallest 7 percent of equities by market value. That segment is relatively illiquid. Various commentators have suggested that, in general, value investors may earn a return premium for supplying liquidity to the market, buying when short-term excess supply causes shares to decline.

The main risk for a value investor is that he has misinterpreted a stock's cheapness. The stock may be cheap for a very good economic reason that the investor does not fully appreciate. Value investors also face the risk that the perceived undervaluation will not be corrected within the investor's investment time horizon. Questions that the value investor should ask include the following:

- How long is it expected to take for price to rise to reflect the shares' perceived higher intrinsic value?
- What catalyst (triggering event or change) will make the price rise?
- Is the expected timeframe for the price to correct acceptable?

The value investing style has at least three substyles: **low P/E**, **contrarian**, and **high yield**.[34] A low P/E investor will look for stocks that sell at low prices to current or normal earnings. Such stocks are generally found in industries categorized as defensive, cyclical, or simply out-of-favor. The investor buys on the expectation that the P/E will at least rise as the stock or industry recovers. A contrarian investor will look for stocks that have been beset by problems and are generally selling at low P/Bs, frequently below 1. Such stocks are found in very depressed industries that may have virtually no current earnings. The investor buys on the expectation of a cyclical rebound that drives up product prices and demand. A yield investor focuses on stocks

---

[32] They postulate that distress risk is highly correlated across firms so that it is nondiversifiable and commands a premium. Some support for a risk-based explanation is provided by Kapadia (2011), who finds that higher rates of business failures are associated with higher returns for distressed stocks. He also finds that the Fama–French factors for value/growth are associated with a financial distress factor.
[33] See Bodie, Kane, and Marcus (2010).
[34] See Christopherson, Cariño, and Ferson (2009), chapter 24, for this classification.

that offer high dividend yield with prospects of maintaining or increasing the dividend, knowing that in the long run, dividend yield has generally constituted a major portion of the total return on equities.[35]

5.1.2 Growth Investment Styles

In contrast to value investors, who are more concerned with price, growth investors are more concerned with earnings. Their underlying assumption is that if a company can deliver future growth in earnings per share and its P/E does not decline, then its share price will appreciate at least at the rate of EPS growth. Growth investors generally will pay above-market earnings multiples for companies that have superior growth rates. They also tend to invest in companies in growth industries, such as technology, health care, and consumer products. Growth stocks have high sales growth relative to the overall market and tend to trade at high P/Es, P/Bs, and price-to-sales ratios (P/Ss). The major risk facing growth investors is that the forecasted EPS growth does not materialize as expected. In that event, P/E multiples may contract at the same time as EPS, amplifying the investor's losses.

The growth style has at least two substyles: **consistent growth** and **earnings momentum**. Companies with consistent growth have a long history of unit-sales growth, superior profitability, and predictable earnings. They tend to trade at high P/Es and be the leaders in consumer-oriented businesses. An example of such a growth stock as of 2011 is Becton, Dickinson & Co., a US manufacturer and distributor of medical products. Companies with earnings momentum have high quarterly year-over-year earnings growth (e.g., EPS for the first quarter of 2011 represents a large increase over EPS for the first quarter of 2010). Such companies may have higher potential earnings growth rates than consistent growth companies, but such growth is likely to be less sustainable. Some growth investors also include price momentum indicators such as relative strength indicators in their investment disciplines, relying on possible patterns of price persistence for certain (usually relatively short) time horizons.[36] (**Relative strength indicators** compare a stock's performance during a specific period either to its own past performance or to the performance of some group of stocks.)

The growth investor who buys a stock at a premium to the overall market is counting on the market to continue paying a premium for the earnings growth that a company has been providing and may continue to deliver. During an economic expansion, earnings growth is abundant—even in the depressed stocks preferred by a value investor—which *may* cause this premium to above-average growth to shrink or vanish. By contrast, when companies with positive earnings momentum become scarce, as in a slowing economy, earnings growth becomes a scarce resource commanding a higher price, and growth investors may do relatively well.[37]

5.1.3 Other Active Management Styles

Market-oriented investors do not restrict themselves to either the value or growth philosophies. The term "market-oriented style" (also sometimes called a blend or core style) gathers an eclectic group of approaches, with the common element that the valuation metrics of market-oriented portfolios resemble those of a broad market

---

[35] See Siegel (2008) for a popular account and details of these substyles focused on the US experience.
[36] See Chan, Jegadeesh, and Lakonishok (1999) for a discussion of price persistence and reversal. At the index level, Malin and Bornholt (2010) find that momentum strategies are profitable in developed and emerging markets.
[37] See Bernstein (1995), pp. 61–62. Similarly, the results for French stocks in Eser (2010) support a "flight-to-quality" effect where investors favor growth stocks when a recession is expected because growth stocks provide a hedge against losses in wealth.

index more than those of a value or growth index, averaged over a full market cycle.[38] Market-oriented investors may be willing to buy stocks no matter where they fall on the growth/value spectrum, provided they can buy a stock below its perceived intrinsic value. They might use a discounted cash flow model or other discipline to estimate intrinsic value. Market-oriented style investors might buy a stock with a high P/E provided the price can be justified through future growth expected in EPS. They might also buy a depressed cyclical issue provided that they foresee some recovery in product pricing in the future. The potential drawback of a market-oriented active style is that if the portfolio achieves only market-like returns, indexing or enhanced indexing based on a broad equity market index will likely be the lower-cost and thus more effective alternative.

Among the recognized subcategories of market-oriented investors are market-oriented with a value bias, market-oriented with a growth bias, growth-at-a-reasonable-price, and style rotators. As the names imply, value bias and growth bias investors tilt their portfolios toward value and growth respectively, but not so distinctively as to clearly identify them as value or growth investors. They typically hold well-diversified portfolios. Growth-at-a-reasonable-price investors favor companies with above-average growth prospects that are selling at relatively conservative valuation levels compared with other growth companies. Their portfolios are typically somewhat less well diversified than those of other growth investors. Style rotators invest according to the style that they believe will be favored in the marketplace in the relatively near term.

Another characteristic often used in describing the style of equity investors is the typical market capitalization of the issues they hold. Small-capitalization equity investors (also called small-cap or small-stock investors) focus on the lowest market-capitalization stocks in the countries in which they invest. (Micro-cap is sometimes used to characterize investors in the lowest capitalization range within the small-cap segment.) The underlying premise of this style is that more opportunity exists to find mispriced stocks through research in the small-cap universe than in the less numerous and more intensely researched universe of large-cap blue chip firms.[39] Another rationale is that smaller companies tend to have better growth prospects (if their business model is sound) because their business is starting from a smaller base and their product line tends to be more focused. Also, the chance of earning a very high rate of return on one's money is much better if the starting market capitalization is small. Small-cap investors can also focus on value, growth, or market-orientation within the small-cap universe.

In some equity markets, mid-cap equity investors have defined an investment segment focusing on middle-capitalization equities; in the United States, such investors typically focus on stocks that are between the 200th and 1,000th largest by market cap, which typically constitutes 20 to 30 percent of US stock market capitalization.[40] Mid-cap investors argue that the companies in this segment may be less well researched than the largest-cap companies but financially stronger and less volatile than small-cap companies.

Large-cap equity investors focus on large-cap equities. Such investors favor the relative financial stability of large-cap issues and believe that they can add value through superior analysis and insight.

---

38 Many investors use "core" in the sense of *playing a central role in the portfolio*, as in the *core-satellite* approach to managing a portfolio of managers discussed later. A "market-oriented" portfolio may be appropriate for a central role but is not absolutely required for it. Because *core* adds a connotation of role unnecessarily, rather than focusing on characteristics, we prefer the more descriptive term "market oriented."
39 Kritzman and Page (2003). However, Ibbotson, Chen, and Hu (2011) find that that the least liquid micro-cap stocks have the highest returns, suggesting that the returns to micro-cap stocks may be partly a risk premium for illiquidity.
40 See Christopherson, Cariño, and Ferson (2009), chapter 24.

Small-cap, mid-cap, and large-cap investors are frequently also classified as value, growth, or market-oriented investors within their capitalization domain.

> **EXAMPLE 4**
>
> ## One Style or Two?
>
> Jeff Fujimori is responsible for the investment of a new ¥10 billion contribution to the Honshu Bank's pension fund. The mandate is to invest with active managers. The equity portion of the pension plan has a broad equity market benchmark. Discuss the advantages and disadvantages of hiring a single manager in either a growth or value style, one manager in each style, or one manager in a market-oriented style.
>
> ### Solution:
>
> **Value** or **growth manager (but not both).**
>
> *Advantage*: If the investor has a position on the desirability of these equity investment styles, this choice would lead to a portfolio expressing the clear conviction of the investor. Such a portfolio has the potential for strong gains if the investor's style is favored by the market.
>
> *Disadvantages*: The choice creates tracking risk relative to the equity benchmark. Substantial underperformance may occur if the manager's style is not in favor. Furthermore, Fujimori must confirm that Honshu Bank finds it acceptable to deviate from an overall broad market orientation of the benchmark before undertaking this alternative.
>
> **Value** and **growth manager.**
>
> *Advantage*: We would expect this choice to have lower tracking risk relative to the benchmark than investing in a single growth or value-oriented portfolio, because it does not make an overall style bet. It is a kind of barbell approach to achieving an overall market orientation, which may have the advantage of combining the expertise of two managers.
>
> *Disadvantage*: This choice may have higher overall management fees than investing in a single portfolio. The investor must rely on security selection alone to overcome the transaction costs and higher fees associated with active management.
>
> **One manager with a market-oriented style.**
>
> *Advantage*: This is the simplest way to invest consistently with the equity benchmark.
>
> *Disadvantage*: Fujimori needs to confirm that the market-oriented style reflects an appropriate and consistent process that promises to add value, as opposed to an unfocused process that has averaged to a market orientation. With that qualification, no obvious disadvantages to this approach exist.

5.1.4 Techniques for Identifying Investment Styles

Two major approaches to identifying style are returns-based style analysis, which relies on portfolio returns, and holdings-based style analysis (also called composition-based style analysis), which relies on an analysis of the characteristics of individual security

Active Equity Investing

holdings. The analyst can use the information from either technique to identify a manager's style for performance attribution purposes and/or to formulate expectations about the manager's future performance.

The first technique of style identification was Sharpe's (1988, 1992) **returns-based style analysis** (RBSA). This technique focuses on characteristics of the overall portfolio as revealed by a portfolio's realized returns. It involves regressing portfolio returns (generally monthly returns) on return series of a set of securities indices. In principle, these indices are:

- mutually exclusive;
- exhaustive with respect to the manager's investment universe; and
- distinct sources of risk (ideally they should not be highly correlated).[41]

Returns-based style analysis involves a constraint that the coefficients or betas on the indices are nonnegative and sum to 1.[42] That constraint permits us to interpret a beta as the portfolio's proportional exposure to the particular style (or asset class) represented by the index.[43] For example, if a portfolio had a beta of 0.75 on a large-cap value index, a beta of 0 on a large-cap growth index, a beta of 0.25 on a small-stock value index, and a beta of 0 on a small-stock growth index, we would infer that the portfolio was run as a value portfolio with some exposure to small stocks. The factor weights on large-cap value, large-cap growth, small-cap value, and small-cap growth indices are 75 percent, 0, 25 percent, and 0, respectively. (The factor weights are also known as style weights or Sharpe style weights.) We expect the portfolio to move 0.75 times whatever happens to large-cap value stocks (holding everything else constant) and 0.25 times whatever happens to small-cap value stocks (holding everything else constant).

The large-cap value index and the small-cap value index held in weights of 0.75 and 0.25, respectively, would constitute a natural benchmark for this portfolio, given that the overall fit of the model was excellent. Such a benchmark is sometimes referred to as the **normal portfolio** or normal benchmark for a manager. As defined in the reading on performance evaluation, a normal portfolio is a portfolio with exposures to sources of systematic risk that are typical for a manager, using the manager's past portfolios as a guide. A manager's normal portfolio or normal benchmark in effect represents the universe of securities from which a manager normally might select securities for his portfolio.

EXAMPLE 5

The Choice of Indices in Returns-Based Style Analysis

In the example just given in the text, the style analysis used four indices. Suppose that instead we used the following three indices:

- a large-cap value index

---

[41] Sharpe (1992), examining US mutual funds, used 12 indices representing US Treasury bills, intermediate-term government bonds, long-term government bonds, corporate bonds, mortgage-related securities, large-cap value stocks, large-cap growth stocks, mid-cap stocks, small-cap stocks, non-US bonds, European stocks, and Japanese stocks.
[42] With this constraint, the model must be solved using quadratic programming (e.g., Solver in Microsoft Excel). It is possible to do a returns-based style analysis constraining the coefficients to sum to 1 but not constraining the coefficients to be nonnegative; that approach could capture elements such as the use of leverage (a negative coefficient on T-bills, included as an index).
[43] Furthermore, Lobosco and DiBartolomeo (1997) have shown how to calculate approximate confidence intervals for the weights.

- a large-cap growth index
- a small stock index

We find a large weight on large-cap value, no weight on large-cap growth, and a small weight on small stocks and we conclude that the portfolio was run as a value portfolio with some exposure to small stocks. Critique the conclusion.

Solution:

The evidence does not contradict the conclusion, but does not completely validate the value characterization. In particular, the portfolio's weight on small stocks might be explained (at least in part) by a positive weight on small-cap growth. By breaking down small stocks into small-cap value and small-cap growth and running the style analysis with four indices (including large-cap value and large-cap growth), we can remove all ambiguity.

We can use a returns-based style analysis to calculate a coefficient of determination measuring style fit. The quantity 1 minus the style fit equals selection, the fraction of return variation unexplained by style. The error term in the style analysis equation—the difference between the portfolio's return and a passive asset mix with the same style as the portfolio—represents selection return (the return from active security selection ability).

Example 6 shows the use of returns-based style analysis to independently evaluate a portfolio manager's style. In this example, Exhibit 13 is a rolling style chart showing the evolution of a portfolio's style exposures through time.

EXAMPLE 6

Returns-Based Style Analysis (1)

Giles Hébert is chief pension officer of Compagnie Minière de l'Ouest SA (CMO). One of Hébert's outside managers for the US equity portion of his portfolio is Arizona Capital Partners (ACP). Hébert is conducting a review of ACP's performance as of mid-2011. CMO decided to pursue a large-cap growth strategy for its US equity investments and selected ACP's US large-cap growth strategy for the investment of part of its allocation to US large-cap growth stocks. When the relationship was established, Hébert and ACP agreed that the Russell 1000 Growth Index fairly represents the investment universe of this strategy. CMO uses returns-based style analysis in evaluating its investment managers.

Hébert knows from the portfolio's custodian that, following its mandate, the portfolio has remained fully invested in US equities. He thus selects the following four benchmarks as the independent variables for a returns-based style analysis:

- Russell 1000 Growth Index (R1000G)
- Russell 1000 Value Index (R1000V)
- Russell 2000 Growth Index (R2000G)
- Russell 2000 Value Index (R2000V)

Hébert includes the R1000G because it is the account's benchmark. He adds the R1000V to capture the degree to which the manager may not be adhering to a growth orientation. Finally, Hébert includes the R2000G and R2000V to capture the degree to which ACP may be failing to adhere to a large-cap orientation. Exhibit 12 gives the results of the returns-based style analysis. Hébert also notes the following facts:

- Exhibit 12 is based on the most recent three years of monthly data as of 31 March 2011.
- Exhibit 13 is based on rolling three-year monthly data ending 31 March 2011.
- For the data period shown in Exhibit 12, selection is 8.1 percent and the style fit is 91.9 percent.
- For the data period shown in Exhibit 12, the annualized active return is −0.38 percent and the annualized tracking risk is 6.58 percent.

Exhibit 12   Returns-Based Style Analysis: Effective Style as of 31 March 2011

Index	Weight
R2000V	0
R2000G	0.039587
R1000V	0.388712
R1000G	0.571701

Note: Based on 36 months of data ending 31 March 2011.

Exhibit 13 Style History: A Rolling Style Chart, 30 September 2000 to 31 March 2011

[Chart: Effective Style Allocation from 9/30/2000 to 3/31/2011, showing stacked areas for R1000G, R1000V, R2000G, R2000V]

Using the information given, address the following:

1. State and justify whether the ACP product in which CMO is invested is accurately described as a US large-cap growth active equity product.
2. Characterize the historical style of the ACP product and evaluate whether the historical analysis supports the answer to the previous question.
3. Calculate and interpret the information ratio of the ACP product.
4. Recommend a course of action to CMO.

Solution to 1:

The ACP product cannot accurately be described as a US large-cap growth active equity product. The product does indeed appear to be actively managed, because the fraction of return variation unexplained by style (selection) is 8.1 percent; the product is not merely replicating the returns on more-passive benchmarks. The very low weights on the R2000G and R2000V small-cap indices, at 4 percent and 0 respectively, also confirm that the product is essentially large-cap. Furthermore, the largest factor weight at 57.2 percent is on the manager's large-cap benchmark, the R1000G. However, the product has a substantial factor weight of 38.9 percent on large-cap value as represented by the R1000V. Considering all these facts, the portfolio appears to be an actively managed large-cap market-oriented portfolio with a growth bias.

Solution to 2:

As Exhibit 13 shows, the ACP product has generally had substantial exposure to both large-cap growth and large-cap value; the factor weight on large-cap value was greatest in the first third of the overall period, peaking in 30 September 2003 when it exceeded the weight on large-cap growth. In the middle period, the factor weight on large-cap growth increased at the expense of large-cap value; however, the weight on small-cap stocks, particularly small-cap value, increased to noticeable levels. Since the end of 2008, the style weights have been fairly close to the values shown in Exhibit 12. The ACP product appears to always have had

Active Equity Investing

a meaningful weight on value. For the most part, the ACP product has adhered to its specified large-cap orientation. Thus the historical analysis supports the conclusions reached in the previous question.

Solution to 3:

The information ratio is the mean historical active return divided by the tracking risk, or –0.38%/6.58% = –0.0578. For each percentage point of tracking risk, the ACP product earned approximately –0.06 percentage points of active return. Thus the portfolio's active risk has been unrewarded.

Solution to 4:

CMO wants to pursue a large-cap growth strategy for its US equity investments. The ACP US large-cap growth active equity product does not meet its needs because it is essentially a large-cap market-oriented fund with a growth bias. The product was not correctly represented by ACP, which indicated that the Russell 1000 Growth Index fairly represented the product's investment universe. An appropriate recommendation would be to move the funds invested in the ACP growth strategy to another investment manager.

Example 7 shows an error that can occur in returns-based style analysis.

EXAMPLE 7

Returns-Based Style Analysis (2)

Frank Harvey is analyzing a US equity mutual fund that states the investment objective of investing for growth and income, with an orientation to mid-cap stocks within the universe of US-domiciled companies. Harvey may select from the following indices for use in a returns-based style analysis:

- the S&P/Citigroup 500 Growth and Value indices, which have a large-cap orientation;
- the Russell 2000 Growth and Value indices, which have a small-cap orientation;
- the Russell 1000 Growth and Value indices, which include large-cap and mid-cap shares;
- the Russell Top 200 Growth and Value indices, which together represent the 200 largest market-cap securities in the Russell 1000 Index; and
- the Russell Midcap Growth and Value indices, which together represent the 800 smallest market-cap issues in the Russell 1000 Index (the Russell Top 200 Index and the Russell Midcap Index together constitute the Russell 1000 Index).

Harvey selects the S&P/Citigroup 500 Growth and Value indices and the Russell 2000 Growth and Value indices for the style analysis.

1. Critique Harvey's selection.
2. Recommend a more appropriate selection of indices.

Solution to 1:

Harvey's choice omits from coverage a substantial number of stocks: those with market caps too small for the S&P 500 but too large for the Russell 2000. Many of the excluded stocks could be characterized as mid-cap. This omission is significant because Harvey should seek to confirm whether the fund being analyzed is actually oriented to mid-cap stocks as it claims to be. The selection of indices should be mutually exclusive and at least approximately exhaustive with respect to the investment manager's universe. The results of an RBSA using a faulty set of indices can be misleading.

Solution to 2:

The following selection of indices would be best:

- Russell Top 200 Growth
- Russell Top 200 Value
- Russell Midcap Growth
- Russell Midcap Value
- Russell 2000 Growth
- Russell 2000 Value

This selection of indices is not only exhaustive, in contrast to the one critiqued in Part 1, but also adequate for determining a distinct style weight for mid-cap issues (because it breaks out mid-cap issues via the Russell Midcap indices).

A less satisfactory selection, but an improvement over Harvey's selection, is the Russell 1000 Growth and Value indices and the Russell 2000 Growth and Value indices. This selection is exhaustive, in contrast to Harvey's selection, but would be inferior to the one recommended: It does not suffice to give a specific weight for mid-cap because the Russell 1000–based indices include both large- and mid-cap stocks.

The second major broad approach to style identification is **holdings-based style analysis**, which categorizes individual securities by their characteristics and aggregates results to reach a conclusion about the overall style of the portfolio at a given point in time. For example, the analyst may examine the following variables:

- *Valuation levels*. A value-oriented portfolio has a very clear bias toward low P/Es, low P/Bs, and high dividend yields. A growth-oriented portfolio exhibits the opposite characteristics. A market-oriented portfolio has valuations close to the market average.

- *Forecast EPS growth rate*. A growth-oriented portfolio will tend to hold companies experiencing above-average and/or increasing earnings growth rates (positive earnings momentum). Typically, trailing and forecast EPS growth rates are higher for a growth-oriented portfolio than for a value-oriented portfolio. The companies in a growth portfolio typically have lower dividend payout ratios than those in a value portfolio, because growth companies typically want to retain most of their earnings to finance future growth and expansion.

- *Earnings variability*. A value-oriented portfolio will hold companies with greater earnings variability because of the willingness to hold companies with cyclical earnings.

- *Industry sector weightings*. Industry sector weightings can provide some information on the portfolio manager's favored types of businesses and security characteristics, thus furnishing some information on style. In many markets, value-oriented portfolios tend to have larger weights in the finance and utilities sectors than growth portfolios, because of these sectors' relatively high dividend yields and often moderate valuation levels. Growth portfolios often have relatively high weights in the information technology and health care sectors, because historically these sectors have often included numerous high-growth enterprises. Industry sector weightings must be interpreted with caution,

Active Equity Investing

however. Exceptions to the typical characteristics exist in most if not all sectors, and some sectors (e.g., consumer discretionary) are quite sensitive to the business cycle, possibly attracting different types of investors at different points in the cycle.

Example 8 illustrates the use of a holdings-based style analysis.

EXAMPLE 8

Do Portfolio Characteristics Match the Stated Investment Style?

Charles Simpson is a consultant analyzing a portfolio for consistency with the portfolio manager's stated value investment style. Exhibit 14 summarizes the characteristics of the portfolio and those of a representative market benchmark portfolio.

Exhibit 14 Simpson's Portfolio Analysis (1)

	Portfolio	Market Benchmark
Number of stocks	30	750
Weighted-average market cap	$37 billion	$45 billion
Dividend yield	3%	2.1%
P/E	15	20
P/B	1.2	2
EPS growth (5-year projected)	10%	12%
Sector		
Consumer Discretionary	18%	13%
Consumer Staples	5	10
Energy	11	9
Finance	25	20
Health Care	2	7
Industrials	10	9
Information Technology	2	7
Materials	10	8
Telecommunications	5	10
Utilities	12	7

What can Simpson infer about the firm's investment style?

Solution:

Simpson can be fairly confident that the manager is following a value style. The portfolio's P/E and P/B are below those of the benchmark, but the dividend yield is above that of the benchmark, consistent with a value bias. EPS growth expectations that are slightly below average support the inference that the portfolio is not growth oriented. The sector breakdown suggests value as well. Finance and utilities tend to have relatively high dividend yield and moderate P/Es. On the

> other hand, sectors with a greater growth orientation, in particular health care and information technology, are underweighted. Thus the portfolio appears to follow a value discipline.

In Example 8, Simpson included some of the types of variables previously mentioned in the text (market capitalization and valuation ratios, such as dividend yield, P/E, P/B, and industry sector weightings) but not others (e.g., earnings variability). Such variation is typical of holdings-based style analysis. Holdings-based analysis involves a number of modeling decisions. One decision is the set of characteristics that discriminate among different styles: Analysts use a variety of sets of discriminating characteristics. The number of discriminating characteristics may run from one (such as the value of the P/B) to a large set, as in the Barra fundamental multifactor risk models, commercial models that have been used in holdings-based analysis. Besides modeling characteristics, a decision must be made on aggregating security-level information. A security may be assigned:

- to value exclusively or to growth exclusively in all instances;
- to value exclusively or to growth exclusively but only if the value of some characteristic exceeds or is less than a specified threshold value; or
- in part to growth and in part to value.

Threshold values must be specified in order to make exclusive (also known as "0-1") assignments. For example, in the first-given assignment method, the market value–weighted average value of an attribute (or set of attributes) may determine the cutoff point for assigning a stock to growth or to value. To illustrate the second approach, assuming that the classification focuses on the P/E, if the P/E is below a specified value (e.g., 16.50) it would be assigned to value; if it is above a higher value (e.g., 24.50) it would be assigned to growth, and if it is in between (i.e., between 16.50 and 24.50), it would be viewed as neither value nor growth. In the description of the final assignment approach, "in part" means up to 100 percent so that the assignments to value and growth sum to 100 percent. To use the terminology of Lazzara (2004), in the first two approaches, style is viewed as a *category*; in the third approach, in which a stock can be "spread over" growth and value, style is viewed as a *quantity*.

Exhibit 15 contrasts the advantages and disadvantages of returns-based and holdings-based style analysis. Because of its less intense data needs, returns-based style analysis might often be performed first and suffice by itself; however, an analysis of holdings obviously can reveal important details of a manager's investment discipline. Both approaches have uses in practice.

Exhibit 15 Two Approaches to Style Analysis: Advantages and Disadvantages

	Advantages	Disadvantages
Returns-based style analysis	■ Characterizes entire portfolio ■ Facilitates comparisons of portfolios ■ Aggregates the effect of the investment process ■ Different models usually give broadly similar results and portfolio characterizations ■ Clear theoretical basis for portfolio categorization ■ Requires minimal information ■ Can be executed quickly ■ Cost effective	■ May be ineffective in characterizing current style ■ Error in specifying indices in the model may lead to inaccurate conclusions
Holdings-based style analysis	■ Characterizes each position ■ Facilitates comparisons of individual positions ■ In looking at present, may capture changes in style more quickly than returns-based analysis	■ Does not reflect the way many portfolio managers approach security selection ■ Requires specification of classification attributes for style; different specifications may give different results ■ More data intensive than returns-based analysis

The next section discusses the increasing variety of style indices available.

5.1.5 Equity Style Indices

Significant debate exists—and probably should—about how to divide the stock universe into growth and value components. Allocating stocks between growth and value indices can be as simple as ranking them by a single variable such as P/B, or it can involve multiple variables. The clear trend has been to construct style indices based on multiple variables.[44] Typical elements in many classification approaches include price, earnings, book value, dividends, and past and projected growth rates in these or other elements. Each element can be part of more than one factor in a multifactor growth/value stock allocation system, creating some (probably) benign redundancy. Attention to the details of style index construction has increased as index publishers compete to serve and capture licensing fees from ETFs and other investment products.

Exhibit 16 summarizes information on some major style indices. Characteristically, all the indices in this exhibit essentially feature holding-based style analysis, focusing on individual stock or company attributes. In the exhibit, "overlap" means that some securities may be assigned in part to both value and growth. **Buffering** refers to rules for maintaining the style assignment of a stock consistent with a previous assignment when the stock has not clearly moved to a new style. Buffering reduces turnover in style classification and serves to reduce the transaction expenses of funds that track the style index.

---

[44] With the replacement of the S&P/BARRA style indices (which were based only on P/B) by the S&P/Citigroup style indices in December 2005, all major commercial style indices employ multiple factors.

Exhibit 16 Select Style Index Families: Principal Growth/Value Allocation Criteria and Rebalancing Rules

Index Family	Criteria	Rebalancing	Comments
Dow Jones Wilshire	Projected P/E Projected earnings growth P/B Dividend yield Trailing P/E Trailing earnings growth	March, September (with buffering)	Two categories (value, growth), no overlap.
FTSE	*Value* P/B P/S Dividend yield Price/Cash flow *Growth* 3-year historical sales growth rate 3-year historical EPS growth rate 2-year forward sales growth estimate 2-year forward EPS growth estimate Internal growth rate (ROE × [1 − Payout ratio]) Long-term Past book value growth	June and December	Two categories (value, growth). Constituents are members of the FTSE All-World Index, and Value and Growth indices are calculated for the FTSE World Index, derivatives of the FTSE World Index, plus regional and country indices in the FTSE World index. Constituents showing high growth (value) characteristics are assigned to growth (value); an intermediate group is apportioned to both growth and value.
Morningstar	*Value* — Weight Price/Projected earnings — 50.0% P/B — 12.5 P/S — 12.5 Price/Cash flow — 12.5 Dividend yield — 12.5 *Growth* — Weight Long-term projected earnings growth — 50.0% Past earnings growth — 12.5 Past sales growth — 12.5 Past cash flow growth — 12.5 Past book value growth — 12.5	June, December (with buffering)	Three categories (value, core, growth), no overlap.
MSCI	*Value* P/B 12-month forward earnings/Price Dividend yield *Growth* Long-term forward EPS growth rate Short-term forward EPS growth rate Long-term historical EPS growth trend Long-term historical sales per share	May, November (with buffering)	Two categories (value, growth), no overlap.
Russell	P/B IBES growth estimates	Approximately June 30	Two categories (value, growth), with overlap.

Exhibit 16 (Continued)

Index Family	Criteria	Rebalancing	Comments
S&P/Citigroup World	*Value* Book/Price Sales/Price Cash flow/Price Dividend yield *Growth* 5-year average internal growth rate* 5-year historical EPS growth rate 5-year historical sales per share growth rate	July 1	Style Index series: two categories (value, growth), with overlap. Pure Style Index series: two categories (value, growth), no overlap.

*The internal growth rate is defined as Return on equity × Earnings retention rate.
Source: www.djindexes.com, www.ftse.com, http://indexes.morningstar.com, www.msci.com, www.russell.com/US/Indexes, www.globalindices.standardandpoors.com.

As Exhibit 16 illustrates (and consistent with our earlier discussion of holdings-based style analysis), style index publishers use growth and value either as categories (no overlap) or as quantities (with overlap).[45] If MSCI, a categorizer, assigns a stock to the growth or value category, the company will be labeled as either growth or value and is never divided between the two. In contrast, index providers that treat growth and value as quantities will often assign a stock partly to growth and partly to value. This split allocation recognizes that some stocks do not fit neatly into either growth or value. Among the style index families in Exhibit 16, Morningstar confronts this issue most directly by explicitly distinguishing three mutually exclusive categories (value, core, and growth). The two-category value/growth split of other index families reflects the consideration that most active equity mandates specifying style are an order for the portfolio manager to manage according to one of these two styles (value or growth).

EXAMPLE 9

Returns-Based and Holdings-Based Style Analyses

John Whitney is a consultant being asked to evaluate a portfolio managed by California Investment Management. He uses proprietary software to do both returns-based and holdings-based style analyses.

Returns-Based Style Analysis

- Effective Style for 36 monthly periods ending 30 June 2011
- 44.9 percent Growth
- 55.1 percent Value
- Style Fit: 99.5 percent; Selection: 0.5 percent

---

[45] See Lazzara (2004) for more information.

Holdings-Based Style Analysis (Based on 30 June 2011 Holdings)

Exhibit 17 Holdings-Based Analysis, 30 June 2011

	Portfolio	Market Benchmark	Difference
P/E	18.34	19.54	−1.20
P/B	2.87	2.96	−0.09
Dividend yield	1.53%	1.70%	−0.17%

	Size (Market-Cap) Analysis		
Largest quintile	25.40%	24.87%	0.53%
Quintile 2	22.34	26.00	−3.66
Quintile 3	23.75	24.37	−0.62
Quintile 4	22.03	21.74	0.29
Smallest quintile	6.48	3.02	3.46

How should Whitney interpret the style analysis results from the two approaches?

Solution:

The two methods offer complementary and essentially confirming views of the portfolio. The holdings-based analysis suggests a market-oriented portfolio with a very slight tilt to value (the portfolio's P/E and P/B both are slightly lower than those of market benchmark, suggesting a tilt toward value, although dividend yield is also lower, suggesting a tilt toward growth). The portfolio also seems to have a slight bias toward smaller-cap stocks relative to the market benchmark.

The returns-based analysis produces similar conclusions. The results also suggest a market orientation, with perhaps a slight leaning toward value. The style fit (R^2) is very high at 99.5 percent. Any performance difference between this portfolio and the market benchmark can likely be attributed to the slight tilts toward value and smaller stocks.

5.1.6 The Style Box

Today, the style box is probably the most popular way of, literally, looking at style. Although an early version of the style box with four component boxes appeared in Sharpe's 1992 paper (see Exhibit 11), his original style divisions were only between growth and value among large-cap funds and among large-cap, midcap, and small-cap funds on the market capitalization dimension. The most widely recognized version of the style box is probably Morningstar's because of that firm's high-profile use of the 3×3-style box to categorize mutual funds and, more recently, individual common stocks. The Morningstar style box, shown in Exhibit 18, divides a fund portfolio or stock universe by market capitalization (large-cap through mid-cap to small-cap, from top to bottom), and style (value through blend to growth, from left to right), creating a total of nine boxes. Morningstar uses holdings-based style analysis and classifies roughly one-third of its stock universe as growth, one-third as value, and another third as blend. We see from Exhibit 18 that most of the value of Vanguard Mid-Cap Growth Fund is indeed centered in mid-cap growth holdings as defined by Morningstar.

Exhibit 18 Morningstar Style Box for Vanguard Mid-Cap Growth Fund

	Value	Blend	Growth
Large-cap	0	2	5
Mid-cap	7	27	58
Small-cap	1	0	0

Source: www.morningstar.com, October 2011.

Different criteria may lead to noticeably different style box characterizations for the same portfolio. The techniques used to categorize a stock or the components of a portfolio by size are relatively standard, if the size division is based on market capitalization.[46] The specifics of the techniques used to distinguish among value, growth, and (sometimes) market-oriented stocks, however, are almost as diverse as the firms selling style-based indices and financial products/services can make them. Price relative to earnings or book value or some other measure(s) typically forms the basis of value categorization and measurement, whereas historical, forecast, or implied (by market valuation) growth in earnings, sales, or dividends typically forms the basis for growth categorization. The market-oriented category is characterized by a mix of growth and value characteristics in a portfolio. The market-oriented designation usually reflects an inability to clearly categorize a stock or a portfolio as definitively growth or value in nature. In rare cases (e.g., Morningstar's style box and the Morningstar equity style indices), a technique makes a deliberate attempt to define a group of stocks as being *neither* growth *nor* value. An alternative interpretation is that the group constitutes a *blend* of growth and value characteristics.

The numbers in each box represent the percentage of this fund's portfolio value consisting of stocks that fall in that style box (using Morningstar's own index classification). For example, in the Vanguard Mid-Cap Growth Fund, 58 percent of the portfolio by market value falls in the mid-cap growth box and 27 percent falls in the mid-cap blend box.

5.1.7 Style Drift

Professional investors view inconsistency in style, or **style drift**, as an obstacle to investment planning and risk control. Ordinarily a value manager holding what is perceived by the market to be a growth stock would have some trouble explaining that holding to his or her clients. One stock in isolation may not be much of an issue; but if a manager is hired as a value manager and over time begins to hold stocks that would be primarily characterized as growth stocks, that manager can be said to be experiencing style drift. Investors should be concerned about style drift because they hired the investment manager (bought the mutual fund or unit trust) to achieve a particular exposure to an equity market segment—be it large-cap, mid-cap, small-cap, value, growth or market-oriented. Managers are also hired for their expertise in a given style. Consequently, when a manager begins to stray from her stated style to the style currently in favor, the investor understandably should worry—the investor may no longer be getting exposure to the particular style desired, and the manager may now be operating outside her area of expertise.

---

[46] Most float-weighted indices rank companies by total capitalization before adjusting their index weightings for float.

EXAMPLE 10

Style Drift or Not?

Six months later, Charles Simpson is reexamining the portfolio that he analyzed in Example 8. In that example, we determined that the portfolio was managed according to a value style. Exhibit 19 provides the portfolio's current characteristics. What can Simpson infer about consistency of the firm's investment style?

Exhibit 19 Simpson's Portfolio Analysis (2)

	Portfolio	Market Benchmark
Number of stocks	45	750
Weighted-average market cap	$46 billion	$45 billion
Dividend yield	2.0%	2.1%
P/E	19	20
P/B	1.9	2
EPS growth (5-year projected)	13%	12%
Sector		
Consumer Discretionary	15%	13%
Consumer Staples	8%	10%
Energy	11%	9%
Finance	22%	20%
Health Care	5%	7%
Industrials	10%	9%
Information Technology	5%	7%
Materials	10%	8%
Telecommunications	5%	10%
Utilities	9%	7%

Solution:

The portfolio's style has definitely drifted from value (in Example 8) to become market oriented. Looking at the valuation measures, the portfolio does not deviate much from the market benchmark. Although the sector weights still lean very slightly toward value (see the weights on finance, utilities, and information technology, and health care), the magnitudes of these biases relative to the market benchmark have decreased significantly compared with the prior period.

5.2 Socially Responsible Investing

Socially responsible investing, also called ethical investing, integrates ethical values and societal concerns with investment decisions. With increasing demand for SRI coming from individual investors, public pension fund sponsors, religious-affiliated groups, and others in many of the world's major markets, an increasing number of equity portfolio managers are responsible for, or have contact with, SRI mandates.

SRI commonly involves the use of stock screens involving SRI-related criteria. SRI stock screens include negative screens and positive screens. Negative SRI screens apply a set of SRI criteria to reduce an investment universe to a smaller set of securities satisfying SRI criteria. SRI criteria may include:

- industry classification, reflecting concern for sources of revenue judged to be ethically questionable (tobacco, gaming, alcohol, and armaments are common focuses); and
- corporate practices (for example, practices relating to environmental pollution, human rights, labor standards, animal welfare, and integrity in corporate governance).

Positive SRI screens include criteria used to identify companies that have ethically desirable characteristics. Internationally, SRI portfolios most commonly employ negative screens only, a smaller number employ both negative and positive screens, and even fewer employ positive screens only.[47] The particulars of the SRI screening process should reflect the concerns and values communicated by the client.

Portfolio managers should be alert to an SRI discipline's effects on a portfolio's financial characteristics. In particular, managers should track any style biases induced by the SRI portfolio selection process. For example, applying a negative screen, the portfolio manager may exclude (because of environmental concerns) companies from basic industries and energy, which sometimes present a concentration of value stocks; as a result the portfolio could have a growth bias.[48] SRI mutual funds have been documented to have an average market-cap bias toward small-cap shares.[49] At least two benefits for the client can result from measuring and managing these style biases. First, the portfolio manager may be able to address the SRI mandate fully while neutralizing any style biases inconsistent with the client's financial objectives or risk tolerance. Second, the manager can choose an appropriate performance benchmark given an accurate picture of the SRI portfolio's style. Among the methods used to identify and measure progress toward addressing issues of style bias is returns-based style analysis.

5.3 Long–Short Investing

Whereas style investing is concerned with portfolio characteristics (low P/E, high earnings growth, etc.), long–short investing focuses on a constraint. Essentially, many investors face an investment policy and/or regulatory constraint against selling short stocks. Indeed, the constraint is so common and pervasive that many investors do not even recognize it as a constraint.

In a traditional long-only strategy, the value added by the portfolio manager is called **alpha**—the portfolio's return in excess of its required rate of return, given its risk. Equivalently, alpha is the portfolio's return in excess of that on a risk-matched benchmark. In a market-neutral long–short strategy, however, the value added can be equal to two alphas. This is because the portfolio manager can use a given amount of capital to purchase a long position and to support a short position. One alpha can come from the long position and another from the short position. In addition, a market-neutral strategy is constructed to have an overall zero beta and thus show

---

[47] See Derwall, Koedijk, and Ter Horst (2011) for a discussion of the performance of negatively and positively screened SRI investments.
[48] For example, see Guerard (1997) and Statman and Glushko (2009) who find a tilt towards growth for SRI investments, and Bauer, Koedijk, and Otten (2005), who found a growth bias tendency among German, US, and UK mutual funds.
[49] See Bauer, Koedijk, and Otten and references therein.

a pattern of returns expected to be uncorrelated with equity market returns. As discussed later, the alpha from such a strategy is **portable**—that is, it can be added to a variety of different systematic (beta) risk exposures.

In the basic long–short trade, known as a **pairs trade** or pairs arbitrage, an investor is long and short equal currency amounts of two common stocks in a single industry (long a perceived undervalued stock and short a perceived overvalued stock), and the risks are limited almost entirely to the specific company risks. Even such a simple convergence trade can go terribly wrong, however, if the value of the short position surges and the value of the long position collapses.

Probably the greatest risk associated with a long–short strategy involves leveraging. In order to magnify the difference in alphas between two stocks, long–short managers (in particular hedge fund managers) sometimes leverage their capital as much as two to three times using borrowed money. Although leverage magnifies the opportunity to earn alpha, it also magnifies the possibility that a negative short-term price move may force the manager to liquidate the positions prematurely in order to meet margin calls (requests for additional capital) or return borrowed securities.

5.3.1 Price Inefficiency on the Short Side

Some investors believe that more price inefficiency can be found on the short side of the market than the long side for several reasons.

First, many investors look only for undervalued stocks, but because of impediments to short selling, relatively few search for overvalued stocks. These impediments prevent investor pessimism from being fully expressed. For example, in order to short a stock, a short seller must borrow the shares from someone who already owns them.[50] When the original investor wants to sell, the securities loan is called and the short seller must return the stock. When many investors are willing to lend the stock, a replacement loan of stock is quickly arranged. When a stock is a popular short (e.g., many internet stocks during the late 1990s) and few shares are available to borrow, the short seller may have to cover the loan by buying back the stock at an inopportune time.

Second, opportunities to short a stock may arise because of management fraud, "window-dressing" of accounts, or negligence. Few parallel opportunities exist on the long side because of the underlying assumption that management is honest and that the accounts are accurate. Rarely do corporate managers deliberately understate profits.

Third, sell-side analysts issue many more reports with buy recommendations than with sell recommendations.[51] One explanation for this phenomenon is related to commissions that a recommendation may generate: Although most customers may be potential buyers of a stock, only those who already own shares or who are short sellers—usually a smaller group—can sell it. Moreover, those customers who already own a stock may become angry when an analyst issues a sell recommendation because it can cause them to lose money.[52]

Fourth, sell-side analysts may be reluctant to issue negative opinions on companies' stocks for reasons other than generic ones such as that a stock has become relatively expensive. Most companies' managements have a vested interest in seeing their share price rise because of personal shareholdings and stock options. After an analyst issues a sell recommendation, therefore, he can find himself suddenly cut

---

[50] Borrowing can be done in a number of ways. Institutional investors typically borrow/lend shares through securities lending programs run by custodian banks or prime brokers.
[51] See Womack (1996) and Dhiensiri, Mandelker, and Sayrak (2005) for evidence on the distribution of buy and sell recommendations.
[52] Irvine (2000) provides evidence that sell-side analysts' choice to cover a security is positively related to the security's potential to generate commission revenue for their firm. Groysberg, Healey, and Maber (2011) find that analyst compensation is related to the firm revenue generated.

off from communicating with management and threatened with libel suits.[53] His employer may also face the prospect of losing highly lucrative corporate finance business.[54] Although such retaliations have occurred, they are not consistent with the Best Practice Guidelines Governing Analyst/Corporate Issue Relations sponsored by the CFA Centre for Financial Market Integrity and the National Investor Relations Institute. Furthermore, despite any such pressures, CFA Institute members and candidates are bound by the Code of Ethics and Standards of Professional Conduct, including Standard I(B) requiring independence and objectivity.[55]

Long–short strategies can make better use of a portfolio manager's information because both rising and falling stocks offer profit potential. Rather than simply avoiding a stock with a bad outlook, a long–short manager can short it, thereby earning the full performance spread.

5.3.2 Equitizing a Market-Neutral Long–Short Portfolio

A market-neutral long–short portfolio can be **equitized** (given equity market systematic risk exposure) by holding a permanent stock index futures position (rolling over contracts), giving the total portfolio full stock market exposure at all times. In carrying out this strategy, the manager may establish a long futures position with a notional value approximately equal to the value of the cash position resulting from shorting securities. Equitizing a market-neutral long–short portfolio is appropriate when the investor wants to add an equity-beta to the skill-based active return the investor hopes to receive from the long–short investment manager. The rate of return on the total portfolio equals the sum of the gains or losses on the long and short securities positions, the gain or loss on the long futures position, and any interest earned by the investor on the cash position that results from shorting securities, all divided by the portfolio equity.

Depending on carrying costs and the ability to borrow ETF shares for short selling, ETFs may be a more attractive way than futures to equitize or de-equitize a long–short alpha over a longer period than the life of a single futures contract. The general ease of borrowing ETF shares for institutional-sized short-sale transactions, as well as the fact that the fund's expense ratio lowers the expected cost of shorting, can make shorting ETFs an attractive alternative to rolling short futures contracts.[56]

A long–short spread can be transported to various asset classes. An investment with no systematic risk should earn the risk-free rate. Therefore, a market-neutral portfolio's performance should be measured against a nominally risk-free rate such as a Treasury bill return, provided the portfolio is truly market neutral rather than simply leveraged equity. If the long–short portfolio has been equitized, then it should be treated as equity, with returns benchmarked against the index underlying the equitizing instrument.

5.3.3 The Long-Only Constraint

Long–short strategies have an inherent efficiency advantage over long-only portfolios. That inherent advantage is the ability to act on negative insights that the investor may have, which can never be fully exploited in a long-only context. First, consider

---

[53] Lim (2001) finds evidence consistent with this hypothesis.
[54] See Michaely and Womack (1999). Sette (2011) finds that the recommendations of analysts affiliated with the lead underwriter in an IPO are significantly more optimistic than those of analysts affiliated with the co-managers.
[55] See the *Standards of Practice Handbook* (2010). Furthermore, a variety of self-regulatory organizations (e.g., the New York Stock Exchange in the United States) have issued rules for their members concerning analyst conflicts of interest.
[56] Individual investors often find it difficult to borrow a small number of ETF shares or other securities to sell short. Small stock loan transactions are often uneconomic for a brokerage firm to arrange.

the example of the long-only investor whose benchmark is the FTSE 100 and whose portfolio holds 45 stocks. One way of thinking about that portfolio is to characterize each stock held relative to that stock's weight in the FTSE 100. A stock that is 4 percent of the portfolio but whose index weight is 3 percent can be said to have an active weight of 1 percent. A stock not included in the portfolio but whose index weight is 5 percent is said to have an active weight of –5 percent, and so on.

Looking at the portfolio this way, the investor can think of the portfolio as being long–short (positive active weights/negative active weights) around the FTSE 100 index. The problem with this portfolio, however, is that its maximum short position (negative active weight) in any given stock is limited by that stock's index weight. If the investor has a strong negative view on a company with a 5 percent index weight, the best she could do is not to hold it at all. On the other hand, if the investor has a very favorable view on a company with a 1 percent index weight, she can (at least theoretically) invest the entire portfolio in that company. The bottom line is that the investor's opportunity set is not symmetric.

A true long–short portfolio, built around a cash benchmark, solves this problem of symmetry. Subject to borrowing constraints and other risks outlined above, a long–short portfolio allows an investor to fully exploit both positive and negative views on a stock. One significant caveat exists, however. The investor needs to have both positive and negative insights about stocks in the investment universe. Stocks excluded from further research because they fail to pass some preliminary screen are not necessarily good candidates for shorting.

5.3.4 Short Extension Strategies

Short extension strategies (also known as partial long–short strategies) modify equity long-only strategies by specifying the use of a stated level of short selling. These strategies attempt to benefit from a partial relaxation of the long-only constraint while controlling risk by not relaxing it completely. In contrast to market-neutral long–short strategies which specify long and short positions of equal value and an overall market beta of zero, short extension strategies are generally designed to have a market beta of one with long positions of 100 percent + x percent and short positions of x percent of capital invested. For example, a common implementation of the short extension strategy is a 130/30 portfolio. In this type of portfolio, for every €100 received from the client, the portfolio manager shorts 0.30(€100) = €30 worth of securities and invests €100 + €30 = €130 long—the initial €100 plus €30 provided by short sales proceeds. The costs of a short extension strategy include trade execution costs and stock loan fees paid to brokers lending securities for short sale.

The idea behind short extension strategies is that the partial relaxation of the long-only constraint allows the portfolio manager to make more efficient use of his or her information. In a long-only portfolio, the manager's maximum response to negative information is to avoid holding the stock (selling an existing position or not adding it to the portfolio). With a short extension strategy, the manager can also go short the stock. This shorting activity has the follow-on effect of releasing money with which to take on larger long positions than would otherwise be possible (apart from using borrowed money). That is to say, every €1 of shorts allows a portfolio manager to invest €1 in long positions that he would not otherwise have been able to establish. That €1 in longs could be an addition to an equity already held or an entirely new equity. This is an important point because the long-only constraint not only limits the portfolio manager's ability to take advantage of negative information, but also limits his or her ability to exploit positive information.

A 130/30 short extension strategy is inherently different from a 100/0 long-only strategy plus a 30/30 strategy. The key difference is that in the 130/30 strategy, portfolio decisions on long and short positions are coordinated, whereas with a combination of 100/0 and 30/30 strategies they are generally not. In managing a 130/30 portfolio, the portfolio manager thinks in terms of a single portfolio rather than two separate portfolios. Separate 30/30 and 100/0 strategies, by contrast, may be uncoordinated to the extent of having offsetting positions in the two portfolios, particularly if the 100/0 strategy is an indexed portfolio. For example, the 100/0 strategy could have a 0.5 percent long position in an issue, matching the issue's benchmark weight, at the same time that the 30/30 strategy has a short position (e.g., −2 percent) in the issue.

A short extension strategy has several potential advantages. In contrast to a long–short market neutral portfolio that is equitized using futures or swaps, a short extension strategy can be established even in the absence of a liquid swap or futures market. Another advantage is that relaxing the long-only constraint even to the extent of 20 percent to 30 percent can result in an appreciable increase in the proportion of a manager's investment insight that is incorporated in the portfolio. The long-only constraint's effects on the portfolio manager's opportunity set are more serious in the case of negative information about small and mid-sized companies than they are in the case of such information about large-sized companies, given that the manager's benchmark is market capitalization weighted. Therefore, relaxing the long-only constraint helps the portfolio manager first in the place where the long-only constraint is most limiting, namely, stocks with small market capitalizations.

A disadvantage of short extension strategies is that they gain their market return and earn their alpha from the same source. By contrast, with an equitized long–short market neutral portfolio, it is possible to earn the market return from one source and the alpha from another. This is an appealing feature to investors because it gives them flexibility to pursue alpha wherever it may be found without having to adjust their strategic asset allocation.

Short extension strategies also differ from long–short market neutral strategies in how investors tend to perceive them. Because they are beta zero, long–short market neutral strategies are typically seen by investors as an alternative investment (even if the underlying investments are equities). Short extension strategies, however, are often seen as a substitute for long-only strategies in an investor's portfolio largely because of their inherent market exposure.

EXAMPLE 11

Long–Short and Market Structure

Jim Summers is being asked to investigate two alternatives for his company's pension plan. The first is a market-oriented active long-only portfolio benchmarked to the FTSE 100 index. Only moderate tracking risk with respect to the FTSE 100 is acceptable. The second alternative involves building a long–short portfolio using British stocks and then overlaying that portfolio with FTSE 100 futures. Summers is familiar with the FTSE 100 index and knows that the nine largest stocks account for slightly more than 50 percent of the index's weight. Explain a rationale for choosing a long–short strategy.

Solution:

Summers recognizes that a market-oriented active manager will have some difficulty outperforming the FTSE 100 index because relatively few stocks make up such a large portion of the index's weight. He reasons that if the portfolio is to be market oriented, the investment manager will have to produce a portfolio with an average market capitalization somewhat in line with the index. The fact that only nine stocks make up half the index weight means that roughly half of the portfolio value will also need to be concentrated in these largest companies. The availability of insights concerning these nine stocks (a relatively small number) would have an important effect on the portfolio's benchmark-relative

> results. Summers concludes that this concentration of market value in a small number of issues will hinder the market-oriented active manager's ability to outperform the benchmark.
>
> Summers then examines the long–short approach and quickly concludes that not only can the investment manager take equivalent long or short positions in all 100 stocks in the index, to increase the opportunity set the manager may also be able to use stocks not included in the index.

5.4 Sell Disciplines/Trading

Equity portfolios are not unchanging. Besides sales associated with rebalancing or a change in asset allocation, investors may sell stocks from their portfolios to raise needed cash or replace existing holdings with other stocks. Turnover may be related to the investment discipline. Several recognized categories of selling disciplines exist.

First, an investor can follow a strategy of substitution. In this situation, the investor is constantly looking at potential stocks to include in the portfolio and will replace an existing holding whenever a better opportunity presents itself. This strategy revolves around whether the new stock being added will have a higher risk-adjusted return than the stock it is replacing net of transaction costs and taking into account any tax consequences of the replacement. Such an approach may be called an opportunity cost sell discipline. Based on the portfolio manager's ongoing review of portfolio holdings, the manager may conclude that a company's business prospects will deteriorate, initiating a reduction or elimination of the position. This approach may be called a deteriorating fundamentals sell discipline.

Another group of sell disciplines is more rule driven. A value investor purchasing a stock based on its low P/E multiple may choose to sell if the multiple reaches its historical average. This approach may be called a valuation-level sell discipline. Also rule based are down-from-cost, up-from-cost, and target price sell disciplines. As an example of a down-from-cost sell discipline, the manager may decide at the time of purchase to sell any stock in the portfolio once it has declined 15 percent from its purchase price; this strategy is a kind of stop-loss measure. An up-from-cost may specify at purchase a percent or absolute gain that will trigger a sale. At the time of purchase, the manager may specify a target price, representing an estimate of intrinsic value, and the stock reaching that price triggers a sale.

The manager may use a combination of sell disciplines. Sales typically generate realized capital gains or losses. Thus, the implications of a sell discipline need to be evaluated on an after-tax basis for tax-sensitive investors such as private wealth investors and certain institutional investors such as insurance companies.

So how much trading in a portfolio is normal? To answer that question, we need to understand what drives the manager's stock selection. Ultimately, the nature of the ideas motivating the purchase should determine what level of turnover is reasonable. Value investors frequently have relatively low turnover; they buy cheap stocks hoping to reap a longer-term reward. Annual turnover levels for a value manager typically range from 20 percent to 80 percent.[57] Growth managers are trying to capitalize on earnings growth and stability. Company earnings are reported quarterly, semiannually, or annually, depending on the stock's country of domicile. In any case, it is easy to understand that a growth portfolio would generally tend to have higher turnover than value—a range of 60 percent to several hundred percent for more short-term oriented investors.

---

[57] This level of turnover translates to a holding period of between 1.25 and 5 years.

SEMIACTIVE EQUITY INVESTING

Semiactive strategies (also known as "enhanced index" or "risk-controlled active" strategies) are designed for investors who want to outperform their benchmark while carefully managing their portfolio's risk exposures. An enhanced index portfolio is designed to perform better than its benchmark index without incurring much additional risk. The portfolio manager creates such a portfolio by making use of his investment insights while neutralizing the portfolio's risk characteristics inconsistent with those insights. Although tracking risk (also called active risk) will increase, the enhanced indexer believes that the incremental returns more than compensate for the small increase in risk. Such a portfolio is expected to perform better than the benchmark on a risk-adjusted basis. As Exhibit 3 showed, enhanced indexing strategies with their strict control of tracking risk have tended to have the highest information ratios.

Semiactive equity strategies come in two basic forms: derivatives based (also called synthetic) and stock based. Derivatives-based semiactive equity strategies intend to provide exposure to the desired equity market through a derivative and the enhanced return through something other than equity investments. A common and straightforward derivatives-based semiactive equity strategy is to equitize a cash portfolio and then attempt to add value by altering the duration of the underlying cash.[58] For example, one simple approach could be to vary the duration between 90-day bills (cash) and 3-year notes based on yield curve slope. When this segment of the yield curve slopes steeply, the manager should invest in longer-duration fixed income, because the higher yield compensates the investor for the increased risk. When the slope is flat, the manager should stay short because no increased yield exists for investing in longer maturities. In this way, a portfolio manager can attempt to achieve some incremental return over cash from the short-term fixed-income portfolio while obtaining equity exposure through the futures market, thereby creating an enhanced index fund.

Enhanced indexing strategies based on stock selection attempt to generate alpha by identifying stocks that will either outperform or underperform the index. Risk control is imposed in order to limit the degree of individual stock underweighting or overweighting and the portfolio's exposure to factor risks and industry concentrations. The resulting portfolio is intended to look like the benchmark in all respects except in those areas on which the manager explicitly wishes to bet.

One way of thinking about an enhanced index stock-selection strategy versus traditional active management involves considering the investment manager's frame of reference. A traditional active manager begins with a pool of investment capital, tries to identify stocks that will appreciate the most, and includes those in the portfolio. Whatever that manager's benchmark, if the manager is uninformed about a particular stock, she will not hold it in the portfolio. In an enhanced index stock selection strategy, the neutral portfolio is the benchmark. If the manager has no opinion about a given stock, that manager holds the stock at its benchmark weight. Every portfolio position is evaluated relative to the benchmark weight.

How do semiactive equity managers try to generate alpha using stock selection? Mostly, they do it the same way traditional active managers do. They may look at broad themes relating to a company's valuation or growth. They may also build complex

---

[58] To equitize is to go long on sufficient futures contracts to provide equity exposure to the underlying cash investment. For example, to equitize cash using a $10 million cash portfolio with S&P 500 futures, divide $10 million by the notional value of each S&P 500 contract to determine how many long position contracts are required. (In practice, a small adjustment called "tailing" is made to this calculation to account for the time value of money on the daily futures marks received or paid. A discussion of tailing is outside the scope of this reading.)

models to process vast quantities of information in their quest for alpha. But the bottom line is that these portfolio managers are essentially active managers who build portfolios with a high degree of risk control.

In addition to a high degree of risk control, another reason for the popularity of enhanced index portfolios can be explained in terms of Grinold and Kahn's **Fundamental Law of Active Management**.[59] The law states that

$$IR \approx IC \sqrt{Breadth} \qquad (1)$$

Translated, this means that the information ratio (IR) is approximately equal to what you know about a given investment (the **information coefficient** or IC)[60] multiplied by the square root of the investment discipline's breadth, which is defined as the number of independent, active investment decisions made each year. Therefore, a lower-breadth strategy necessarily requires more accurate insight about a given investment to produce the same IR as a strategy with higher breadth. Well-executed enhanced indexed strategies may have a relatively high combination of insight and breadth, resulting from the disciplined use of information across a wide range of securities that differ in some important respects. (Note, however, that the number of *independent* decisions available per period does not *necessarily* increase with the size of the research universe.)

EXAMPLE 12

Illustration of the Fundamental Law of Active Management

Gerhardt Holz is evaluating two investment managers:

- Manager A follows 500 stocks with annual forecasts, and the IC for each of the forecasts is 0.03.
- Manager B follows 100 stocks with annual forecasts, and the IC for each of the forecasts is twice that of Manager A's security forecasts.

Based only on the above information, which manager should Holz select?

Solution:

Manager A's breadth of 500 and IC of 0.03 translates into an information ratio of approximately $0.03\sqrt{500} = 0.67$ (on an annual basis). Manager B's breadth of 100 and IC of 0.06 translates into an information ratio of approximately $0.06\sqrt{100} = 0.60$ (on an annual basis). Based only on the information given, Holz would select Manager A.

A semiactive stock-selection approach has several possible limitations. The first is that any technique that generates positive alpha may become obsolete as other investors try to exploit it. A successful enhanced indexer is always innovating. Also, quantitative and mathematical models derived from analysis of historical returns and prices may be invalid in the future. Markets undergo secular changes, lessening the effectiveness

---

[59] See Grinold and Kahn (2000) for a complete development.
[60] The information coefficient is more formally defined as the correlation between forecast return and actual return. In essence, it measures the effectiveness of investment insight.

Semiactive Equity Investing

of the past as a guide to the future. Markets also occasionally undergo shocks that, at least temporarily, render forecasting or risk models ineffective. Example 13 illustrates a comparison made in terms of alpha and tracking risk.[61]

EXAMPLE 13

Derivatives-Based versus Stock-Based Semiactive Strategies

Heidi Erikson is an investment officer with a large Swedish pension plan. Her supervisor is thinking about investing in an enhanced index product focused on Japanese equities benchmarked against the Index. He asks Erikson to investigate the various alternative approaches. Exhibit 20 presents her findings.

Exhibit 20 Semiactive Alternatives

	Expected Alpha	Tracking Risk
Stock-based semiactive	1.2%	2.7%
Derivative-based semiactive	1.0	2.1

Using the information given, address the following:

1. Contrast stock-based and derivative-based semiactive investment strategies.
2. State an appropriate quantitative criterion for evaluating alternative semiactive approaches.
3. Recommend and justify a semiactive approach for the pension plan.

Solution to 1:

A stock-based semiactive approach involves controlled under- and overweighting of securities relative to their index weights. This approach attempts to pick up active return through equity insights. By contrast, a derivative-based semiactive approach involves using derivatives to equitize cash and attempting to pick up active return by adjusting the duration of the fixed-income position.

Solution to 2:

The information ratio (IR), defined as mean active return divided by tracking risk, is the appropriate quantitative criterion for evaluating alternative active strategies because it permits comparison based on the mean active return gained for bearing a unit of active risk in each strategy.

Solution to 3:

The stock-based semiactive strategy has an IR of 1.2/2.7 = 0.44 versus 1/2.1 = 0.48 for the derivative-based strategy. Because it has the higher information ratio, based only on the information given, Erikson should recommend using a derivative-based strategy.

---

[61] In the example, the use of alpha rather than active return in calculating the information ratio means only that the portfolio's benchmark has been matched in terms of systematic risk.

7 MANAGING A PORTFOLIO OF MANAGERS

When investing a pool of assets, every investor must decide first on the overall asset allocation of the investments—which asset classes to use and how much to invest in each. The investor then needs to decide how to invest the assets within each class. Should the investor use index funds or have the money managed actively? What is the correct level of active risk? How many managers should be used?

When developing an asset allocation policy, the investor seeks an allocation to asset classes that maximizes expected total return subject to a given level of *total* risk. The framework of optimizing allocations to a group of managers (in this context, equity managers within the equity allocation) takes a parallel form, but with the investor now maximizing active return for a given level of active risk determined by his level of aversion to active risk:[62]

$$\text{Maximize by choice of managers} \quad U_A = r_A - \lambda_A \sigma_A^2 \tag{2}$$

Where

U_A = expected utility of the active return of the manager mix

r_A = expected active return of the manager mix

λ_A = the investor's trade-off between active risk and active return; measures risk aversion in active risk terms

σ_A^2 = variance of the active return

The efficient frontier specified by this objective function is drawn in active risk and active return space, because once active or semiactive managers are potentially in the mix, the investor's trade-off becomes one of active return versus active risk (the asset allocation decision determines the trade-off between total risk and return). How much active risk an investor wishes to assume determines the mix of specific managers. For example, an investor wishing to assume no active risk at all would hold an index fund. On the other hand, investors desiring a high level of active risk and active return may find their mix skewed toward some combination of higher active risk managers with little or no exposure to index funds.

Take the hypothetical case of Yasu Nakasone, an investment officer with the pension fund of RBG Electronics. Nakasone wants to invest ¥60 billion in Japanese equities benchmarked to TOPIX. He is considering the managers shown in Exhibit 21. The active managers and semiactive managers follow distinct investment styles.[63]

Exhibit 21 Portfolio Statistics

	Expected Active Return	Expected Tracking Risk
Index	0.0%	0%
Semiactive	1.5	2
Active A	2.0	3

---

[62] See Waring, Whitney, Pirone, and Castille (2000), on which this discussion is based. The objective function shown does not consider fees and other costs associated with the mix of managers. Investment management fees and custody costs also must be considered, and these will be higher for active and semiactive managers than for index funds. One way of incorporating costs into the optimization is simply to subtract them from each manager's expected returns.

[63] Because these investment managers have different investment styles, the assumption of uncorrelated alphas made subsequently is reasonable. The model also applies if alphas are correlated, although the details will be more complex.

Managing a Portfolio of Managers

Exhibit 21 (Continued)

	Expected Active Return	Expected Tracking Risk
Active B	3.0	5
Active C	4.0	8

For his analysis, Nakasone assumes that all five managers' active returns are uncorrelated; he generates the efficient frontier in Exhibit 22 using a mean–variance optimizer. The question Nakasone must ask himself is how much active risk he wishes to take in the aggregate equity portfolio. The answer will help him determine the required manager mix.

Exhibit 22 Efficient Frontier of Managers

Plot of Expected Alpha (y-axis, 0.00 to 4.00) versus Expected Active Risk (x-axis, 0.00 to 8.00). Points shown: Index (0, 0); Semi-Active (~2, 1.5); Active A (~3, 2.0); Active B (~5, 3.0); Active C (~8, 4.0). The efficient frontier curve passes through Index, Semi-Active, and Active C.

In addition to generating the efficient frontier, Nakasone has also put together a "waterfall" chart (Exhibit 23) that breaks down manager mix for each level of active risk.

Exhibit 23   Manager Allocation by Active Risk Level

[Area chart titled "Manager Allocation" showing stacked allocations across Active Risk from 0.00% to 7.63%, with categories: Active C, Active B, Active A, Semi-Active, Index]

Nakasone must now select the appropriate level of active risk. Generally, investors are far more risk averse in active risk terms than in total risk terms, for several reasons. For example, an investor can achieve the benchmark return by purchasing an index portfolio. To achieve an active return in his portfolio, however, Nakasone must believe both that successful active management is possible and that he has the necessary skill to select active managers who will outperform. Second, Nakasone is responsible for the whole equity portfolio, and his superiors will judge him based on how well the overall portfolio performs relative to the benchmark. Successful active management is difficult, and many who attempt it underperform.[64] This fact produces a sort of institutional conservatism on the part of many investors. Finally, Nakasone realizes that as one moves up on the efficient frontier assuming more active risk, less manager diversification exists. For institutional investors, an overall active risk budget (target) in the range of 1.5 percent to 2.5 percent is fairly typical.[65]

Nakasone decides that he is willing to assume only 1.51 percent active risk, leading him to select the portfolio shown in Exhibit 24:

Exhibit 24   RBG Pension Fund Manager Mix

	Allocation
Index	8%
Semiactive	44
Active A	26
Active B	14
Active C	8

---

64 The average actively managed dollar, yen, euro, etc. must necessarily underperform, per Sharpe (1991).
65 See Waring et al. (2000).

Despite its relatively modest level of active risk, this manager mix is expected to produce an active return of 1.92 percent, leading to a very strong IR of 1.27. The active return for the overall portfolio is a weighted average of the active returns for the individual managers.

$$\text{Portfolio active return} = \sum_{i=1}^{n} h_{Ai} r_{Ai}$$

where

h_{Ai} = weight assigned to the ith manager
r_{Ai} = active return of the ith manager

The active risk is a bit more complex. Recall that Nakasone assumes the active returns are uncorrelated. Therefore,

$$\text{Portfolio active risk} = \sqrt{\sum_{i=1}^{n} h_{Ai}^2 \sigma_{Ai}^2}$$

where

h_{Ai} = the weight assigned to the ith manager
σ_{Ai} = the active risk of the ith manager

The portfolio active risk in this case is the square root of the weighted sum of the individual managers' variances.[66]

7.1 Core-Satellite

The type of portfolio that Nakasone constructed in the previous section is referred to as a **core-satellite portfolio**.[67] Specifically, 52 percent of the overall portfolio—the index and semiactive managers—constitutes the core holding, and the three active managers represent a ring of satellites around this core. When we apply the optimization shown in Equation 2 to a group of equity managers that includes effective indexers and/or enhanced indexers and successful active managers (as judged by information ratios), a core-satellite portfolio is a likely result.

Core-satellite portfolios can be constructed using Nakasone's rigorous approach or much more simply, as demonstrated in Example 14 below. In either case, the objective is to anchor a strategy with either an index portfolio or an enhanced index portfolio and to use active managers opportunistically around that anchor to achieve an acceptable level of active return while mitigating some of the active risk associated with a portfolio consisting entirely of active managers. The index or enhanced index portfolios used in the core generally should resemble as closely as possible the investor's benchmark for the asset class. The satellite portfolios may also be benchmarked to the overall asset class benchmark, but there is greater latitude for them to have different benchmarks as well (e.g., having a growth or value focus rather than the more likely core benchmark for the asset class).

---

[66] Had the active returns been correlated, the portfolio active risk equation would also have included covariance terms under the square root sign.
[67] Core-satellite is sometimes discussed as an approach to overall asset allocation in which certain asset classes are held in a passively managed core while others (believed to be inefficiently priced) are held in actively managed satellites. See Singleton (2005). The text discusses the concept in terms of allocating assets within a single asset class, another frequent usage of the term.

EXAMPLE 14

A Pension Fund's Performance Objectives

Jim Smith manages the international equity portion of the pension portfolio of ACME Minerals, a large Australian mining company. Smith is responsible for a portfolio of A$700 million of non-Australian equities. Smith's annual compensation is related to the performance of this portfolio versus the MSCI World ex-Australia Index, the benchmark for the pension portfolio's international equity portion. He has hired the following managers with expected alphas and active risk shown.

Exhibit 25 Portfolio Managers' Characteristics

	AUM (Millions)	Expected Alpha	Expected Tracking Risk
Manager A	A$400	0%	0%
Manager B	100	2	4
Manager C	100	4	6
Manager D	100	4	6

All four managers' alphas are uncorrelated and are measured against the MSCI World ex-Australia benchmark.

The pension fund's trustees have stated objectives of achieving a ratio of alpha to tracking risk of 0.6 or greater, with tracking risk of no more than 2 percent a year. An optimization based on Equation 2 results in weights on Managers A, B, C, and D of 4/7, 1/7, 1/7, and 1/7, respectively. Based only on the information given, address the following:

1. Identify the investment approach of Manager A.
2. Characterize the structure of the optimal portfolio of managers.
3. Evaluate whether the optimal portfolio of managers is expected to meet the trustees' investment objectives.

Solution to 1:

Because Manager A has expected tracking risk of 0 percent, we can infer that this manager is an indexer.

Solution to 2:

The portfolio of managers represents a core-satellite portfolio. An indexed investment (Manager A) represents more than half the portfolio's value and functions as the core. Actively managed portfolios (Managers B, C, and D) represent the satellite portfolios surrounding the core.

Solution to 3:

We need to calculate the expected alpha and active tracking risk for the portfolio of managers to evaluate whether this portfolio meets the trustees' performance objectives. The portfolio's expected alpha is

$$(4/7)(0\%) + (1/7)(2\%) + (1/7)(4\%) + (1/7)(4\%) = 1.43\%$$

The portfolio's tracking risk is

$$\left[(4/7)^2(0)^2 + (1/7)^2(4\%)^2 + (1/7)^2(6\%)^2 + (1/7)^2(6\%)^2\right]^{1/2} = 1.34\%$$

Tracking risk of 1.34 percent satisfies the trustees' objective of tracking risk of no more than 2 percent annually. The ratio of 1.43%/1.34% = 1.07 exceeds the target of 0.6. Thus the portfolio of managers meets the performance requirements of the trustees. Note that the tracking risk calculation used the assumption that the managers' alphas are uncorrelated.

Example 14 assumed that the managers under consideration were all benchmarked to the benchmark for the overall international equity allocation—that is, all of the managers are essentially broad capitalization market-oriented managers. In reality, investors often wish to consider managers that are either value or growth and perhaps specialize within a given range of market capitalization. To evaluate such managers, it is useful to divide their total active return into two components:

1 Manager's return − Manager's normal benchmark = Manager's "true" active return

2 Manager's normal benchmark − Investor's benchmark = Manager's "misfit" active return

To review, the manager's normal benchmark (normal portfolio) represents the universe of securities from which a manager normally might select securities for her portfolio. The term **investor's benchmark** refers to the benchmark the investor uses to evaluate performance of a given portfolio or asset class.

The standard deviation of "true" active return is called manager's "true" active risk (or "true" active risk); the standard deviation of "misfit" active return is manager's "misfit" risk (or "misfit" risk). The manager's total active risk, reflecting both "true" and "misfit" risk, is

Manager's total active risk = [(Manager's "true" active risk)^2
+ (Manager's "misfit" active risk)^2]^{½}

The most accurate measure of the manager's risk-adjusted performance is the IR computed as (Manager's "true" active return)/(Manager's "true" active risk).

The "true"/"misfit" distinction has two chief uses: One relates to performance appraisal, and the other relates to optimizing a portfolio of managers. We can illustrate the technically less complex of these two uses, that related to performance appraisal, using the numbers given in Exhibit 25 in Example 14, and the following additional facts:

- Manager C is a value-oriented manager;
- the MSCI World ex-Australia Value Index well represents Manager C's investment universe;
- Manager C, the MSCI World ex-Australia Index, and the MSCI World ex-Australia Value Index respectively return 12 percent, 10 percent, and 15 percent per year, for a given time period; and
- Manager C's total active risk computed with respect to MSCI World ex-Australia Index is 5.5 percent annually. The manager's "misfit" risk is 4 percent annually.

Based on the second fact above, the MSCI World ex-Australia Value Index is appropriate as Manager C's normal benchmark. By contrast, the MSCI World ex-Australia Index is the investor's benchmark. Although Manager C appears to outperform the asset class benchmark (12 percent versus 10 percent), in reality the manager has not done such a great job:

- The manager's "true" active return is 12% − 15% = −3%.
- The manager's "misfit" active return is 15% − 10% = 5%.

Measuring the manager's results against the normal benchmark rather than the investor's benchmark far more accurately evaluates performance. The positive "misfit" active return indicates that the manager would be expected to outperform the asset class benchmark for the simple reason that value stocks outperformed the investor's benchmark. The manager's negative "true" active return, however, indicates that the manager actually underperformed a passive investment in the normal benchmark. The manager's performance relative to the investor's benchmark reflects the sum of "true" active return and "misfit" active return and misleadingly nets to a positive value: −3% + 5% = 2%. To complete the picture, we need to calculate the manager's IR based on "true" active risk and "true" active return. Using the expression for manager's total active risk and letting X represent "true" active risk, $5.5\% = [X^2 + (4\%)^2]^{1/2}$, $X = 3.775\%$ is "true" active risk. The manager's "true" IR was thus quite poor: −3%/3.775% = −0.7947.

The second use of the "true"/"misfit" distinction is in optimization. By disaggregating the active risk and return into two components, it is possible to create optimal solutions that maximize total active return at every level of total active risk and that also allow for the optimal level of "misfit" risk. Although it may seem that no "misfit" risk is desired, a nonzero amount may actually be optimal, because a high level of "true" active return may more than compensate for a given level of "misfit" risk.

7.2 Completeness Fund

The Nakasone and Smith examples illustrated a rigorous approach to constructing a portfolio of managers. Some investors will construct a portfolio of active managers using an equal-weighting approach or other heuristic. Whether the active manager's normal portfolio is the overall equity benchmark or some other benchmark (especially in this latter case), the aggregate portfolio of active managers may have any number of risk exposures or biases, such as sector underweighting or overweighting, relative to the investor's overall equity benchmark. The portfolios of bottom-up stock pickers often evidence industry concentrations as an outcome of their stock selection processes rather than intentional macro bets.

In such cases, the fund sponsor should consider establishing a completeness fund for the equity portfolio. A **completeness fund**, when added to active managers' positions, establishes an overall portfolio with approximately the same risk exposures as the investor's overall equity benchmark.[68] For example, the completeness fund may be constructed with the objective of making the overall portfolio sector and/or style neutral with respect to the benchmark while attempting to retain the value added from the active managers' stock-selection ability. The completeness portfolio may be managed passively or semiactively. This portfolio needs to be re-estimated periodically to reflect changes in the active portfolios.

---

[68] Completeness funds are sometimes referred to as dynamic completion funds or as bias control funds. Tierney and Winston (1990) offer an early presentation of the rationale for this technique.

One drawback of completeness portfolios is that they essentially seek to eliminate misfit risk. As stated above, a nonzero amount of misfit risk may be optimal. In seeking to eliminate misfit risk through a completeness fund, a fund sponsor may be giving up some of the value added from the stock selection of the active managers.

7.3 Other Approaches: Alpha and Beta Separation

Another method which may be used to build a portfolio of multiple managers involves what has become known as **alpha and beta separation**. A typical long active equity portfolio provides an investor with exposure to the market (beta) as well as to the active manager's stock selection ability (alpha). As previously discussed, a market-neutral long–short strategy is a pure alpha strategy with no beta exposure.

For example, an investor might choose to hire a comparatively inexpensive index fund manager to provide beta exposure and pay explicitly for alpha by hiring a market-neutral long–short manager. The second approach adds the advantage of allowing the investor to mix and match beta and alpha in a way that long-only active management cannot accomplish. For example, an investor may need beta exposure to a relatively efficient part of the equity market (e.g., the Russell Top 200, representing the 200 largest securities in the Russell 3000) but will also want to outperform that part of the market. This may be difficult to do with long-only active management. The investor, however, may choose to hire a Russell Top 200 index fund manager and a manager that seeks to add 4 percent annual alpha by managing a long–short portfolio of Japanese equities. Assuming that the long–short portfolio is also market neutral (i.e., beta of zero with respect to the Japanese equity market) and that the long–short manager delivers on the alpha target, the strategy becomes a Russell Top 200 + 4% strategy. This is an example of **portable alpha**—that is, alpha available to be added to a variety of systematic risk exposures.

One of this approach's big advantages is that an investor can obtain the beta exposure desired while broadening the opportunity set for alpha to cover styles and even asset classes outside the beta asset class. In the example above, the long–short manager could also have been a bond manager. Alpha and beta separation allows the investor to manage the market and active risks more effectively than if dealing solely with long-only managers. In doing so, the investor can also very clearly understand the fees being paid to capture market (inexpensive) and active (costly) returns. That said, certain markets may constrain the ability to manage long–short alpha-generating strategies. Short positions may be very costly to establish in smaller or emerging markets. Also, investors need to realize that not all long–short strategies that appear to be market neutral really are. Some may have a degree of market risk.

Some investors may be explicitly precluded from investing on a long–short basis. These investors may still be able to use portable alpha, although in a less efficient way than described above. For example, assume that an investor desires S&P 500 market exposure but has identified a capable active manager of Japanese equities benchmarked to the TOPIX index. The investor can port the manager's alpha by taking a short futures position in TOPIX and a corresponding long position in S&P 500 futures.[69] The resulting portfolio is S&P 500 plus an alpha associated with the Japanese equity portfolio.

---

69 The short exposure to TOPIX can be seen as a hedge of sorts and might not violate specific pension plan restrictions in the way that an explicit net short position in an equity issue would.

8 IDENTIFYING, SELECTING, AND CONTRACTING WITH EQUITY PORTFOLIO MANAGERS

Institutional and private wealth investors face critical decisions when deciding what funds (if any) to manage themselves and, second, what investment managers to engage for the funds they delegate to outside management. Frequently, investors will work with a consultant in an investment manager search. The following sections address some of the issues that investors will face in identifying, selecting, and contracting with equity managers.

8.1 Developing a Universe of Suitable Manager Candidates

The process of developing a universe of suitable manager candidates starts with a general evaluation of the large number of investment managers, and then researching and monitoring those that are worthy of further consideration. Investment consultants typically have a research staff whose job is to collect information on investment managers and to meet with them to understand the managers' investment approach and organization. Consultants employ various tools to determine which managers have talented individuals and truly add value in their investment style.

Consultants use both qualitative and quantitative factors in evaluating investment managers. The qualitative factors include the people and organizational structure, the firm's investment philosophy, the decision-making process, and the strength of its equity research. The quantitative factors include performance comparisons with benchmarks and peer groups, as well as the measured style orientation and valuation characteristics of the firm's portfolios. At all times, the investment consultant seeks consistency between a firm's *stated* philosophy and process and its *actual* practices.

8.2 The Predictive Power of Past Performance

Anyone who invests in the stock market is well aware that the best performing stock or sector in any given year is rarely the best performer in the next. In fact, one reasonable approach to investing could be simply to sell the winners and buy the losers (although many investors tend to do the opposite). The same holds true of investment performance, which is one reason why fund managers are legally required to state in their advertisements that "past performance is no guarantee of future results."

The evidence generally supports this caution. For example, the Frank Russell Company, a multimanager investment strategies firm, found that of the 81 managers who were in the top quartile of their 293 US equity manager database in 1997, only 16 remained in the top quartile in 1998, and only 7 remained in 1999. None of these original top performers in 1997 was still in the top quartile in 2000, 2001, or 2002. Busse, Goyal, and Wahal (2010) examined the performance of over 1,400 investment management firms and found little to no persistence in their risk-adjusted excess returns. These results do not mean that past performance goes unexamined, however. A portfolio manager who has consistently underperformed his benchmark is unlikely to be considered for an active manager role, because an active manager is expected to generate positive alpha.

Investors and their consultants place considerable weight on an equity manager's investment process and the strength of the manager's organization. A good investment record achieved by the same set of managers over a long period, following consistent investment disciplines, is more likely to indicate future satisfactory results for the client than a record with comparable statistics but an underlying history of manager turnover and shifts in investment orientation.

8.3 Fee Structures

Investors must pay attention to the management fees of the investment managers that they hire. Absent such fees, the investor would realize exactly the same alpha that the manager achieves (after transactions costs). With management fees, the investor earns a net-of-fee alpha that is smaller and possibly negative even when the manager's alpha (gross of fees) is positive. In short, the investment management fee represents a wedge between managerial skill and investor results.[70]

Fees are typically set in one of two basic ways: ad valorem and performance based. **Ad valorem fees** are calculated by multiplying a percentage by the value of assets managed (e.g., 0.60 percent on the first £50 million, and 0.45 percent on assets above £50 million). Ad valorem fees are also called assets under management (AUM) fees.

A simple **performance-based fee** is usually specified by a combination of a base fee plus sharing percentage (e.g., 0.20 percent on all assets managed plus 20 percent of any performance in excess of the benchmark return). Performance-based fees can also include other features such as fee caps and "high-water marks." A **fee cap** limits the total fee paid regardless of performance and is frequently put in place to limit the portfolio manager's incentive to aim for very high returns by taking a high level of risk. A **high-water mark** is a provision requiring the portfolio manager to have cumulatively generated outperformance since the last performance-based fee was paid. As an example, ABC Investments charged a performance-based fee based on its performance in 2011. In 2012, however, the firm underperformed its benchmark and could collect only the base fee. If ABC is subject to a high-water mark provision, in 2013 it will need to outperform its benchmark by an amount greater than the 2012 underperformance in order to collect a performance-based fee.

Ad valorem fees have the advantage of simplicity and predictability. If a plan sponsor must budget fees in advance, an ad valorem approach makes estimation much simpler. In contrast, performance-based fees are typically quite involved, as every term of the performance-based fee must be precisely defined. But performance-based fees—particularly symmetric incentive fees that reduce as well as increase compensation—may align the plan sponsor's interests with those of the portfolio manager by spurring the manager to greater effort. The better the manager's performance, the greater the reward for both sides. For the client, the impact of poor performance is reduced by the smaller fees paid to the investment manager. On the other hand, reliance on such arrangements can create revenue volatility for the investment manager, which might present practical issues (e.g., staff retention) when the manager performs relatively poorly in a year in which its competitors have done better.[71] A one-sided performance-based fee, by contrast, conveys a call option to the investment manager whose value can be determined by option pricing methodology and whose expected net cost to the fund sponsor may be judged relative to expected fee if a strictly ad valorem compensation contract were in place.

8.4 The Equity Manager Questionnaire

A typical equity manager questionnaire examines five key areas: organization/people, philosophy/process, resources, performance, and fees. The questionnaire creates a formal basis for directly comparing different investment firms.

---

[70] Ennis (2005) quantifies the extent of this wedge for various fee levels and levels of managerial skill. Fabozzi, Focardi, and Jonas (2010) report that the weighted average expense ratio for mutual funds has declined as assets are increasingly shifted to lower cost investments.
[71] See Arnott (2005) for a further discussion.

In the questionnaire's first section, Organization/People, the investment firm must describe the firm's organization and who will be managing the portfolio. Equity portfolio management is a people business; nothing is more important than having the right people in place. Typical questions cover such areas as the vision of the firm, its competitive advantages, and how it defines success; the organization of the group and the role of portfolio managers, traders, and analysts; the delegation of responsibility for decisions on asset allocation, portfolio construction, research, and security selection; the structure of the compensation program, with an emphasis on the manner in which talented individuals are rewarded; the background of the professionals directly involved in managing the assets, such as prior experience, education, and professional qualifications such as the CFA designation; and finally, the length of time the team has been together and the reasons for any turnover.

The second section, Philosophy/Process, asks questions about how the equity portfolio will be managed. Typical questions concern:

- the firm's investment philosophy and the market inefficiency that it is trying to capture, along with any supporting evidence for this inefficiency;
- the research process, including whether or not a top-down analysis is applied (**top-down** analysis is analysis that proceeds from the macroeconomy to the economic sector level to the industry level to the firm level);
- the risk management function, including management and monitoring of risk and risk models;
- how the firm monitors the portfolio's adherence to its stated investment style, philosophy, and process;
- the stock selection process, including unique sources of information, and how the buy or sell decision is made; and
- the portfolio construction process.

The third section, Resources, looks at the allocation of resources within the organization. In particular, the focus is on the research process: how and by whom research is conducted, the outputs of this research, how the research outputs are communicated, and how the research is incorporated into the portfolio construction process. In addition, there are questions addressing any quantitative models used in research and portfolio construction, and the investments that have been made in technology. Finally, the trading function is examined in terms of turnover, traders, trading strategies, and the measurement of costs.

The fourth section, Performance, asks questions about what the equity manager considers to be an appropriate benchmark (and why) and what level of excess return is appropriate. There are also questions about how performance is evaluated within the firm, including causes of dispersion in the returns of similarly managed portfolios. The firm must then normally submit monthly or quarterly returns as well as holdings, so that the evaluator can calculate performance for all candidates in the same way.

The final section deals with fees. Questions are typically about what is included in the fee, the type of fee (ad valorem or performance based), and any specific terms and conditions relating to the fees quoted.

The equity manager questionnaire is used to identify a short list of the fund managers most suitable for the sponsor's needs. This process is followed up with face-to-face interviews (and sometimes on-site visits) to better understand the fund manager and to ask additional questions raised by any responses to the questionnaire before the final selection decision.

> **EXAMPLE 15**
>
> ## Equity Manager Questionnaire (Excerpt)
>
> ### A. Organization, Structure, and Personnel
>
> 1. Provide a brief history of the firm, including:
>   - **a** the month and year of SEC 1940 Act registration;
>   - **b** the month and year the subject product was introduced; and
>   - **c** ownership structure.
> 2. Form of ownership (if an affiliate, designate percent of parent firm's total revenue generated by your organization).
> 3. If the firm is a joint venture partner, identify the percentage of ownership and revenues recognized by each partner to the combined association.
> 4. Provide an organizational chart diagramming the relationships between the professional staff as well as the parent–subsidiary, affiliate, or joint venture entities.
> 5. Describe the levels (US dollar amounts) of coverage for SEC-required (17g-1) fidelity bonds, errors and omissions coverage, and any other fiduciary coverage which your firm carries. List the insurance carriers supplying the coverage.
> 6. During the past five years, has your organization or any of its affiliates or parent, or any officer or principal been involved in any business litigation, regulatory, or legal proceedings? If so, provide a detailed explanation and indicate the current status. Also provide complete Form ADV (Parts I and II) or explain the nature of the exemption.
> 7. Has your firm been the subject of an audit, censure (fine), inquiry, or administrative action by the SEC, IRS, State Attorney General, or Department of Labor in the past seven years? If so, explain findings and provide a copy, as well as evidence of any changes in procedures implemented as a result of such audit.
> 8. Describe in detail the material developments in your organization (changes in ownership, restructuring, personnel, business, etc.) during the past three years.
> 9. Provide the location and function of each of your firm's offices.
> 10. Provide details on the financial condition of the firm (i.e., most recent annual report filed with the SEC).
> 11. Investment Professionals
>   - **a** List all senior investment professionals and portfolio managers involved with the subject product. Please also separately provide appropriate biographical information. Highlight the person(s) who would be responsible for this account.
>   - **b** Indicate when and why any investment professionals left or joined the firm in the last three years. In which products were they involved? For personnel who have left, indicate job titles and years with the firm. Please include all additions and departures, regardless of seniority.

- **c** Discuss your organization's compensation and incentive program. How are professionals evaluated and rewarded? What incentives are provided to attract and retain superior individuals? If equity ownership is possible, on what basis is it determined and distributed? How is the departure of a shareholder treated?
- **d** Describe your firm's backup procedures in the event the key investment professional assigned to this account should leave the firm.

For Items 12 through 14, please provide the following information for the years ending on 30 June from 2007 through 2012 (all in $ millions and number of accounts, counting funds as one account):

12 Total assets under management—all products.

13 Total discretionary US equity assets—all products.

14 Total assets in subject product—distinguish between retail and institutional.

15 Provide the names and the size of the mandate for your top five clients.

16 Provide the names and the size of your top five clients in the strategy under review.

17 List all clients (or the number and type) and asset amounts gained in the subject product during the past five years as of June 30, 2012.

18 List all clients (or the number and type) and asset amounts lost in the subject product during the past five years as of June 30, 2012.

19 Identify three clients that have terminated accounts in the subject product during the past three years that can be contacted as references. Provide the firm name, contact person and title, phone number, product name, and reason for termination.

20 Provide the client name, address, phone number, contact name, title, and account type (e.g., defined benefit, defined contribution, endowment) of three accounts, who are invested in the subject product that can be contacted as references. Also indicate the length of your relationship and AUM for each reference.

B. Investment Philosophy, Policy, and Process

1 Describe your investment philosophy for the product.
- **a** What market anomaly or inefficiency are you trying to capture?
- **b** Why do you believe this philosophy will be successful in the future?
- **c** Provide any evidence or research that supports this belief.
- **d** How has this philosophy changed over time?
- **e** What are the product's shortcomings or limitations?
- **f** In what market environment(s) will your product have difficulty outperforming?

2 Describe your investment decision process and valuation approaches used in regard to the following:
- **a** security selection;
- **b** sector selection; and
- **c** portfolio construction.

3 Indicate what fundamental/quantitative factors are used to analyze a stock and indicate their relative importance in the decision-making process. If applicable, who developed and maintains your quantitative models?

4 Describe the techniques used to identify and control overall portfolio risk. What limits/constraints do you establish, if any?

   a What is the market liquidity criteria applied by your firm for the companies in which it invests?

   b Provide the typical number of securities in a portfolio of $50 million, $100 million, $1 billion, and $2 billion.

   c Describe the use of futures, options, or other derivatives (when and how much?).

5 Describe the decision process used to make sell decisions. When would your firm deviate from its sell disciplines?

6 Over what time horizon could your strategy be expected to meet performance objectives?

7 Provide the average annual portfolio turnover for the past three years and the source of this turnover.

8 Describe your firm's policy regarding cash and cash equivalents. Would your firm accept a "fully invested" mandate?

9 Describe your firm's process for executing trades. Include answers to the following:

   a Does your firm use electronic trading systems?

   b What guidelines do you have pertaining to dealing/trading execution parameters/costs?

   c How are trading costs monitored? How are these costs minimized?

   d Describe how your firm evaluates trading execution.

   e What is the firm's average commission (cents/share) for the product in question?

   f Does your firm trade with an affiliate broker/dealer?

10 Submit a sample portfolio (an actual portfolio) as of June 30, 2012, that reflects the investments of the product proposed for this account.

11 Provide the following characteristics as of June 30, 2012 and for the years ending 2007 through 2011:

- typical number of holdings
- typical turnover rate
- average market capitalization
- median market capitalization
- P/E
- P/B
- beta
- sector limitations
- highest sector weightings
- tracking error
- since-inception information ratio

C. Research Capabilities and Resources

1 Explain your firm's research process as it pertains to the product.
2 Rate your firm's reliance on the following sources of research; average rating should approximate 3 (*1 = very important, 5 = unimportant*).
   a Internal
   b Broker/dealer
   c Third-party fundamental research
   d External economists
   e Company visits
   f Other (explain)
3 Describe the software packages used to manage portfolios. If owned, were they internally developed and by whom? Are they internally maintained? How long have the current systems been in place?

D. Historical Performance/Risk Factors

1 Provide your monthly gross and net-of-fees composite performance in the subject product, since the inception of the product, in an attached Microsoft Excel spreadsheet file in the following format:

	A	B	C
1	Date	Gross Returns	Net Returns
2	12/2010	1.01	0.81
3	1/2011	−3.04	−3.24
4	2/2011	5.02	4.82
5	3/2011	12.10	11.90

2 Provide a description of composite:
   a Number of accounts and market value of assets represented in composite as of each annual period shown.
   b Include low/high and median return for each annual period.
   c Is composite in compliance with the Global Investment Performance Standards?
   d Has composite been verified for compliance? If not, why not?
   e Is there a period for which composite is not in compliance?
3 What benchmark is most appropriate for evaluating the performance results of your process?

E. Fee Structure

1 Provide a proposed fee schedule for the proposed strategy, including any breakpoints. In addition, please provide a proposed fee schedule for the various portfolio sizes of: $50 million, $100 million, and $500 million.

Identifying, Selecting, and Contracting with Equity Portfolio Managers

2. Will you certify that the fee schedule provided above is the most favorable fee schedule that the firm offers for accounts of similar size? If not, please explain why.
3. Do you offer clients performance-based fees?

Note: Exhibits and other sections omitted.

Example 16 shows a highly simplified fee proposal. In practice, fees stated as an annual rate are usually paid at regular intervals during the year, and asset valuations within a given payment interval are important. For instance, in practice an ad valorem fee of 0.50 percent a year of assets under management might be billed at the end of each quarter at a rate of 0.50%/4 = 0.125%, based on the average AUM during the quarter. Nevertheless, the principles involved would be the same as those illustrated.

EXAMPLE 16

A Fee Proposal

Helen Warburton is evaluating a fee proposal from Buckingham Equity Investors. She has been quoted both ad valorem and performance-based fees.

Ad Valorem
First £25 million @ 0.80%
Next £25 million @ 0.60%
Balance @ 0.40%
The above fees are payable in advance.

Performance Based
Base fee of 0.20% of beginning AUM plus 20% of outperformance versus the FTSE All-Share Index, to be paid annually at the end of each 12-month period.

Warburton expects to invest a £100 million lump sum, and based on Buckingham's questionnaire response, she expects the firm to outperform the FTSE All-Share by 2.50 percent gross of fees. If Warburton assumes that the FTSE All-Share returns 0 percent, what fee approach should she choose? What other considerations might she make in deciding which fee structure makes more sense?

Solution:

The fees for a £100 million account given Buckingham's expected performance are:

Ad Valorem
£550,000 = (£25 million)(0.80%) + (£25 million)(0.60%) + (£50 million)(0.40%)

Performance Based
£700,000 = (£100 million)(0.20%) + (£100 million)(20%)(2.50%)

The ad valorem fee is lower assuming that Buckingham delivers its expected outperformance. Investors should consider a firm's performance history when determining which approach to choose. If Buckingham's FTSE All-Share strategy has a very high information ratio, implying a high degree of consistency in annual outperformance, Warburton might prefer using an ad valorem fee because Warburton might expect to pay higher fees over time under a performance-based fee arrangement. The reverse is true if Buckingham's history of outperformance

> was less consistent. (Note that in setting its fee structure, Buckingham could factor in the volatility of its outperformance. This element would make both Buckingham and Warburton indifferent to the fee structure.)

9. STRUCTURING EQUITY RESEARCH AND SECURITY SELECTION

Equity research is a necessary component of both active and semiactive investing. The security selection process varies from firm to firm, but some generalities apply.

9.1 Top-Down versus Bottom-Up Approaches

Investors focusing their research primarily on macroeconomic factors or investment themes are said to use a top-down approach. For example, an investor focused on a single country might favor certain defensive industries like consumer staples and utilities if she believes the economy may be heading into a recession. Although top-down investors build portfolios from individual stocks, they want those stocks to reflect their macro insights.

A more complex top-down example might involve a global portfolio. The investor might wish to identify:

1. themes affecting the global economy;
2. the effect of those themes on various economic sectors and industries;
3. any special country or currency considerations; and
4. individual stocks within the industries or economic sectors that are likely to benefit most from the global themes.

On the other hand, an investor focusing on company-specific fundamentals or factors such as revenues, earnings, cash flow, or new product development is said to follow a **bottom-up** approach. This investor pays attention to company specifics when doing research and building a portfolio. For example, a value investor might screen stocks based on P/E or dividend yield. His focus is on the individual company. Bottom-up investors have little interest in the state of the economy or other macro factors but rather try to put together the best portfolio of stocks based on company-specific information.

A more complex bottom-up example might also involve a global portfolio. The investor might approach the problem by:

1. identifying factors with which to screen the investment universe (e.g., stocks in the lowest P/E quartile that also have expected above-median earnings growth);
2. collecting further financial information on companies passing the screen; and
3. identifying companies from this subset that may be potential investments based on other company-specific criteria.

That said, many investors use some combination of the two approaches. An investor managing a global portfolio can, for example, decide which countries to favor based on a top-down analysis but build the portfolio of stocks within each country based on a bottom-up analysis. Furthermore, some analysts use technical analysis, which attempts to predict future stock prices from the time series of their past values.

9.2 Buy-Side versus Sell-Side Research

The terms "buy side" and "sell side" refer to the source of the equity research. **Buy side** refers to those who do research with the intent of assembling a portfolio, such as investment management firms. **Sell side** refers either to independent researchers who sell their work, or to investment banks/brokerage firms that use research as a means to generate business for themselves. Sell-side research is also what most people hear on TV or read about in the newspaper. Buy-side research by its very nature is generally inaccessible to those outside of the investment firm generating the research.

Sell-side and buy-side research frequently are developed in a different manner. Sell-side research is generally organized by sector/industry with a regional delineation (e.g., US autos, European telecommunications, Japanese banks, etc.). Analysts work either in teams or by themselves and produce reports on individual companies and also on the industries they cover. In addition to providing information such as earnings forecasts, sell-side analysts also rate companies as buy, hold, or sell (the nomenclature varies from firm to firm).

Because buy-side research is concerned with assembling a portfolio rather than just rating a company, decisions on buy-side research are usually made through a committee structure. An analyst may investigate a particular theme or individual company, but usually an investment committee makes the decisions. The analyst prepares a report to substantiate the idea and why it should be included in the portfolio or sold; she then uses the research to persuade the investment committee.

> **EXAMPLE 17**
>
> ### Top Down or Bottom Up?
>
> Maria Ramirez is watching a financial program on television in which a unit trust portfolio manager is explaining the investment approach he uses in managing the global equity unit trust. He says, "Right now, I really like Japan. The economic growth we see there looks to us like it is solid and driven as much by consumer demand as it is by capital investment. One market that we really don't like very much is the United Kingdom, which we are avoiding because we fear further interest rate hikes by the Bank of England." From this brief statement what can Maria conclude about the portfolio manager's research approach?
>
> **Solution:**
>
> The portfolio manager is employing a top-down approach, because his comments are focused exclusively on macro factors driving the British and Japanese markets. A bottom-up investor might also have favored Japan over the United Kingdom but would have emphasized that he finds more stocks that are attractive investments in one market rather than another.

9.3 Industry Classification

Many equity research departments are organized along industry or sector lines. Given the need to do sector/industry research across many countries, it is important to have a system for like companies to be classified in the same categories. Developed by Standard & Poor's and MSCI, the Global Industry Classification Standard is one representative industry classification method that does exactly this. GICS divides stocks into:

- 10 Sectors (Consumer Discretionary, Consumer Staples, Energy, Financials, Health Care, Industrials, Information Technology, Materials, Telecommunication, and Utilities);
- 24 Industry Groups;
- 68 Industries;
- 154 Sub-Industries.

GICS assigns a company to a particular category based on the percentage of revenue derived from each of that company's businesses. The company is then categorized into one and only one sector, industry group, industry, and sub-industry. For example, Michelin is included in the Consumer Discretionary Sector, the Automobiles & Components Industry Group, the Auto Components Industry, and the Tires & Rubber Sub-Industry. Other classification systems include:

- the Industry Classification Benchmark, proprietary to FTSE International Ltd and Dow Jones & Co., consisting of 10 industries (Oil & Gas, Basic Materials, Industrials, Consumer Goods, Health Care, Consumer Services, Telecommunications, Utilities, Financials, and Technology), 19 supersectors, 41 sectors and 114 subsectors; and
- the highly detailed North American Industry Classification System (NAICS—pronounced "nakes"), sponsored by the US, Canadian, and Mexican governments.

SUMMARY

Equity portfolio management is not only challenging; for many investors, the skill applied to it can determine their long-term investment success. This reading has provided a detailed introduction to the major concepts and tools that professional equity investors use.

- Equities play a growth role in investment portfolios.
- The major investment approaches are passive, active, and semiactive. The major passive approach is indexing, which is based on the rationale that after costs, the return on the average actively managed dollar should be less than the return on the average passively managed dollar. Active management is historically the dominant approach to investment and is based on the rationale that markets offer opportunities to beat a given equity benchmark. Semiactive or enhanced indexing is a growing discipline based on the rationale that markets offer opportunities to achieve a positive information ratio with limited risk relative to a benchmark.
- A successful active equity manager will have an expected active return of 2 percent or higher, but his tracking error is likely to be more than 4 percent. Hence, his information ratio will be 0.5 or lower. At the opposite end of the spectrum, an index fund will have minimal tracking risk and an expected active return of 0 percent, implying an information ratio of zero. Enhanced indexing strategies tend to have the highest information ratios, often in the range of 0.5 to 2.0.

Summary

- An indexer must choose the index that the portfolio will track and understand the details of the index's construction. The major types of indices are:
  - *Price weighted.* In a price-weighted index, each stock in the index is weighted according to its absolute share price.
  - *Value weighted* (or *market-capitalization weighted*). In a value-weighted index, each stock in the index is weighted according to its market capitalization (share price multiplied by the number of shares outstanding). A subset of the value-weighted method is the float-weighted method, which adjusts value weights for the floating supply of shares (the fraction of shares outstanding that is actually available to investors).
  - *Equal weighted.* In an equal-weighted index, each stock in the index is weighted equally.

  A price-weighted index is biased toward shares with the highest price, and a value- or float-weighted index is biased toward the largest market cap companies, which may reflect positive valuation errors. An equal-weighted index is biased toward smaller-cap companies.

- Indexed separate or pooled accounts, index mutual funds, exchange traded funds, equity index futures, and equity total return swaps are the major methods for implementing an indexing strategy. Indexed separate or pooled accounts are typically very low cost. Index mutual funds are a widely accessible alternative with a considerable range of cost structures. Exchange traded funds may have structural advantages compared with mutual funds and also permit short positions. Equity index futures are relatively low-cost vehicles for obtaining equity market exposure that require a rollover to maintain longer term. Equity total return swaps are a relatively low-cost way to obtain long-term exposure to an equity market that may offer tax advantages.

- Three methods of indexation include full replication (in which every index security is held in approximately the same weight in the fund as in the index), stratified sampling (which samples from the index's securities organized into representative cells), and optimization (which chooses a portfolio of securities that minimizes expected tracking risk relative to the index based on a multifactor model of index risk exposures). Full replication is the most common procedure for indices composed of highly liquid securities. Stratified sampling and optimization are applicable when full replication is not feasible or cost-effective.

- All else being equal, value investors are more concerned about buying a stock that is deemed relatively cheap in terms of the purchase price of earnings or assets than about the company's future growth prospects. In contrast to value investors' focus on price, growth investors are more concerned with earnings growth. Value has substyles of low P/E, contrarian, and high yield. Growth has substyles of consistent growth and earnings momentum.

- The main risk for a value investor is the potential for misinterpreting a stock's cheapness; it may be cheap for a very good economic reason that the investor does not fully appreciate. The major risk for growth investors is that the forecasted EPS growth fails to materialize as expected. In that event, P/E multiples may contract at the same time as EPS, amplifying the investor's losses.

- Two major approaches to identifying style are returns-based style analysis, based on portfolio returns, and holdings-based style analysis based on analysis of security holdings. Returns-based style analysis is quickly executed, cost-effective, and requires minimal information. Holdings-based style analysis requires detailed information on security holdings and can give an up-to-date and detailed picture of a manager's style. Most current style indices are constructed using a holdings-based approach.

- The style box is a means of visualizing a manager's style exposures, which is typically based on a holdings-based analysis. It may contain as many as nine cells representing a portfolio on value–market-oriented–growth and small–mid–large spectrums.

- Inconsistency in style, or style drift, is of concern to investors because 1) the investor may no longer have exposure to the particular style desired and 2) the manager may be operating outside her area of expertise.

- A long-only strategy can capture one overall alpha. With a long–short strategy, however, the value added can be equal to two alphas, one from the long position and one from the short position. A market-neutral strategy is constructed to have an overall zero beta. Long–short strategies may benefit from pricing inefficiencies on the short side (a greater supply of overvalued than undervalued securities).

- The Fundamental Law of Active Management states that $IR \approx IC \sqrt{Breadth}$, which implies that the information ratio approximately equals what the investor knows about the company multiplied by the square root of the number of independent active investment decisions made each year.

- The framework for optimizing allocations to a group of managers (in this context, equity managers within the equity allocation) involves maximizing active return for a given level of active risk determined by the investor's aversion to active risk.

- A core-satellite portfolio involves an indexed and/or enhanced indexed core portfolio and actively managed satellite portfolios.

- A completion fund may be used to neutralize unintended bets against the overall equity benchmark.

- Investment management contracts may involve an ad valorem fee schedule and/or an incentive fee schedule.

- Selecting and monitoring good managers is as complex a process as selecting and managing good investments.

PRACTICE PROBLEMS

1 Katrina Lowry works for the pension department of National Software. Her supervisor has asked her to evaluate the different style alternatives for a large-cap mandate and to highlight their differences.

   A State the three main large-cap styles.

   B Describe the basic premise and risks of each style identified in Part A.

2 Juan Varga is concerned about the performance and investment positions of an investment firm he hired five years ago. The firm, Galicia Investment Management, has been tasked with managing an active portfolio with a developed market mandate (MSCI World countries). Galicia is a well-known value manager. Varga performs some returns-based style analysis and finds the following results for the last two years (each quarterly snapshot is the result of a regression using the prior 36 months return data).

	MSCI World Value (%)	MSCI World Growth (%)	Other (%)
1Q 2011	83	16	1
2Q 2011	77	20	3
3Q 2011	79	19	2
4Q 2011	68	29	3
1Q 2012	55	40	5
2Q 2012	48	45	7
3Q 2012	52	45	3
4Q 2012	55	43	2

What reasonable conclusions can Varga reach regarding the Galicia investment process?

3 David Burke is considering investing in a mutual fund that is classified generically under the term "growth and income." In preparation for his CFA exams, Burke studied style investing. Using publicly available data sources, he gathered the following information about the mutual fund in question. How should he characterize the fund based on what he has learned in his CFA exam preparation?

	Fund	Market Benchmark
Number of stocks	80	600
Weighted-average market cap	$37 billion	$40 billion
Dividend yield	2.5%	2.1%
P/E	16	19
P/B	1.6	1.9
EPS growth (5-year projected)	11%	12%

Sector

| Consumer Discretionary | 16% | 10% |

(continued)

Practice Problems and Solutions: 1–11 taken from *Managing Investment Portfolios: A Dynamic Process*, Third Edition, John L. Maginn, CFA, Donald L. Tuttle, CFA, Jerald E. Pinto, CFA, and Dennis W. McLeavey, CFA, editors. Copyright © 2007 by CFA Institute. All other problems and solutions copyright © CFA Institute.

	Fund	Market Benchmark
Consumer Staples	9	12
Energy	9	9
Finance	15	20
Health Care	9	7
Industrials	12	9
Information Technology	8	7
Materials	5	8
Telecommunications	7	10
Utilities	10	7

4 Phillipa Jenkins has been asked to manage internally a FTSE 100 index fund. Because the index's 10 largest stocks make up more than 50 percent of its weight, Jenkins is considering using optimization to build the portfolio using many fewer than 100 stocks. All 100 stocks in the index are considered liquid. Is optimizing the best approach?

5 Shawn Miller plans to use returns-based style analysis to analyze his global portfolio. He will use style indices as a proxy for style in the analysis and is debating whether to use indices like Dow Jones (which categorizes stocks as value, growth, or neutral) or like MSCI (which categorize stocks only as value or growth).

   A What are the benefits and drawbacks of each method?

   B Does it matter which type Miller chooses for a returns-based style analysis?

6 Explain the principal benefit of a market-neutral long–short portfolio. What risks are inherent in such a portfolio that a long-only equity portfolio lacks?

7 Simon Hayes is a long–short portfolio manager with Victoria Investment Management in London. His expertise lies in building market-neutral long–short strategies using UK equities. After meeting with his most important client, Hayes learns that the client is planning to hire an investment firm to manage a Japanese equity portfolio. How can Hayes satisfy this mandate using UK equities and no Japanese equities?

8 Yoko Suzuki manages an enhanced index portfolio benchmarked to the index for Kyushu Motors' pension fund. The strategy has a target alpha of 1.5 percent annually with an annualized active risk of 2 percent. Her client is quite pleased that the portfolio has met its stated objective for the last five years. Kyushu's other investment managers have not done so well against their objectives, however, and the pension fund now suffers from a large shortfall between its assets and liabilities. To make up this shortfall, Kyushu asks her to double the portfolio's active risk with the intention of doubling the alpha as well. How should Suzuki respond to this suggestion?

9 Mike Smith is a consultant evaluating a market neutral long–short strategy for his client. Based on the holdings data he receives from the client, Smith notices a small but persistent difference between the alphas generated on the long side and those generated on the short side. State which of the two alphas is more likely the larger one, and provide three reasons why that might be the case.

10 Karen Johnson is responsible for the US equity portion of her company's pension plan. She is thinking about trying to boost the overall alpha in US equities by using an enhanced index fund to replace her core index fund holding.

Practice Problems

   A The US equity portion of the pension plan currently consists of three managers (one index, one value, and one growth) and is expected to produce a target annual alpha of 2.4 percent with a tracking risk of 2.75 percent. By replacing the index manager with an enhanced indexer the target alpha changes to 2.8 percent with a tracking risk of 2.9 percent. Does this change represent an improvement? Why?

   B Johnson also needs to decide whether she prefers a stock-based or a synthetic enhanced index manager. What are the advantages and disadvantages of each?

11 Stephanie Whitmore is evaluating several alternatives for the US equity portfolio of her company's pension plan, involving the following managers:

	Active Return	Active Risk (with Respect to Normal Benchmark)	Normal Benchmark
Index	0%	0%	Russell 3000
Semiactive	1	1.5	Russell 3000
Active A (Value)	3	5	Russell 1000 Value
Active B (Growth)	4	6	Russell 1000 Growth
Long–Short	6	6	Cash with Russell 1000 overlay

Active A's misfit risk is 7.13 percent. In all of the questions below, assume that the active returns are uncorrelated. The overall equity portfolio benchmark is the Russell 3000.

   A Whitmore has taken the information in the table above and used a mean variance optimizer to create an implementation efficient frontier. The highest risk point on the efficient frontier is a 100 percent allocation to the long–short manager with a 100 percent Russell 1000 overlay. The active risk of this portfolio is 6.1 percent. Why is the risk greater than 6 percent?

   B Calculate the total active risk for Active A.

   C Whitmore's current equity manager allocation is 30 percent Index and 70 percent Semiactive. Calculate this portfolio's current expected active return, active risk, and information ratio.

   D After determining the desired level of active risk, Whitmore selected the appropriate portfolio from the efficient frontier. The portfolio allocates 39 percent to the Index manager, 34 percent to the Semiactive manager, 7 percent to Active Manager A, 8 percent to Active Manager B, and 12 percent to the Long–Short manager. This portfolio has an expected active return of 1.59 percent and an expected active risk of 1.10 percent. Does this portfolio represent an improvement over the current allocation? If so, by how much?

   E Upon further investigation of the long–short manager, Whitmore learns that approximately 20 percent of the active return generated comes from equity positions in non-US companies. Is this a concern? Why or why not?

The following information relates to Questions 12–17

Carl Tyner is a portfolio manager for the Gibson State University (GSU) Endowment Fund. The GSU Endowment's Investment Policy Statement mandates a core-satellite portfolio for the equity portion of the Endowment's assets. The portfolio assets are managed with institutional commingled (or pooled) investment funds. The details for the managers of each of the commingled funds are presented in Exhibit 1.

Exhibit 1 Investment Manager Data

	Manager A	Manager B	Manager C
Assets under management ($ millions)	$678	$4,200	$1,600
Weighted-average market cap (billions)	$50.60	$52.30	$54.10
P/E	12.20	15.55	19.61
EPS growth (long-term projected)	8.50%	11.00%	14.00%
Dividend yield	2.90%	1.65%	1.00%
Portfolio active return	2.50%	0.00%	2.50%
Portfolio active risk	4.00%	0.00%	4.00%
Management fees & expenses (% of portfolio)	0.40%	0.18%	0.41%
Allocation to GSU Endowment Equity Portfolio	20%	45%	35%

The investment committee would like Tyner to invest a small portion, $2.0 million, in international equities. The committee suggests that the MSCI ACWI Index would be an appropriate benchmark for the international equity exposure. Tyner responded that there are several index strategies that GSU could use to gain exposure to the MSCI ACWI index. The committee wants Tyner to use a strategy that will minimize tracking error.

12 Which of the managers *most likely* is following a passive investment strategy?
   A Manager A.
   B Manager B.
   C Manager C.

13 Which of the managers is *most likely* following a growth investment style?
   A Manager A.
   B Manager B.
   C Manager C.

14 Which of the following substyles is *least consistent* with Manager A's investment style?
   A Contrarian.
   B High Yield.
   C Momentum.

15 The portfolio active return and portfolio active risk for GSU Endowment's equity portfolio are *closest* to:

Practice Problems

	Portfolio Active Return	Portfolio Active Risk
A	1.38%	1.61%
B	1.38%	3.27%
C	1.67%	3.27%

16 Which of the following index strategies for the international equity exposure is *most* appropriate given the investment committee's goal related to tracking error?

　A Optimization.

　B Style Indexing.

　C Full replication.

17 Which of the following is *most likely* to have the highest investment cost associated with meeting the investment committee's tracking error goal?

　A MSCI ACWI ETF.

　B MSCI ACWI mutual fund.

　C Full replication of the index.

The following information relates to Questions 18–23

Roy Bernard is a portfolio manager with an institutional investment management firm. He has several US-based clients seeking domestic and international equity exposure. Three of these clients are discussed below.

Satellite Fund

Satellite Fund is a new client seeking international equity management services. Simon Day, President of Satellite Fund, tells Bernard that the fund's objectives are to exploit information not reflected in current stock prices, maximize the information ratio, and maintain a low tracking error. The portfolio's constraints include substantial unpredictable cash inflows and outflows.

　Day asks Bernard for assistance in selecting a suitable international benchmark. Bernard advises him of the various trade-offs to consider when choosing an international index benchmark.

Eastern Reserve College

A second client, Eastern Reserve College, has chosen to index a portion of its large endowment fund to the S&P 500 Index. The college's finance director wants to minimize ongoing rebalancing costs and tracking error. Bernard recommends stratified sampling as the indexing strategy that best meets the college's objectives and constraints.

　The college wants another portion of its endowment fund managed to maximize alpha by fully exploiting available investment opportunities in international equity markets. Bernard suggests a market-neutral, long–short portfolio using UK equities. He makes the following statements comparing the market-neutral, long–short portfolio strategy to a long-only portfolio strategy:

　　Statement 1　A market-neutral, long–short portfolio can generate two alphas, one from the long position and one from the short position.

Statement 2 In a long-only portfolio, alpha can be doubled by doubling the active risk.

Statement 3 The opportunity set for a long-only portfolio strategy is asymmetrical.

Gardelli

Bernard has another client, Gardelli Fund, that has inquired about semiactive portfolio management. Paolo Caruso, the manager of the fund, says he wants to avoid benchmarks biased toward small-capitalization stocks.

Bernard evaluates two forms of semiactive equity styles for Gardelli's fund, stock based and derivatives based.

Bernard prepares Exhibit 1 comparing the two:

Exhibit 1 Semiactive Equity Styles

	Expected Alpha	Tracking Risk
Stock-based semiactive	1.5%	2.9%
Derivatives-based semiactive	1.2%	2.1%

18 The investment approach *most* consistent with Satellite Fund's objectives is:
  A enhanced indexing.
  B active management.
  C indexing using optimization.

19 Given Satellite Fund's constraints, the *most* appropriate international benchmark will favor:
  A investability over breadth.
  B float bands over judgment-based construction.
  C fewer reconstitution effects over fewer crossing opportunities.

20 Is stratified sampling the *most* appropriate construction method for the indexed portion of the Eastern Reserve endowment fund?
  A Yes.
  B No, optimization is more appropriate.
  C No, full replication is more appropriate.

21 Which of Bernard's statements comparing the market-neutral, long–short strategy to the long-only strategy is incorrect?
  A Statement 1.
  B Statement 2.
  C Statement 3.

22 The type of index that would *least likely* address Caruso's concern about bias is:
  A a price-weighted index.
  B a value-weighted index.
  C an equal-weighted index.

23 Which is the *most* appropriate strategy for Bernard to recommend for Gardelli's fund?
  A The derivatives-based strategy, because it has lower tracking risk.

B The stock-based strategy, because it has a higher information ratio.

C The derivatives-based strategy, because it has a higher information ratio.

SOLUTIONS

1 A The three main large-cap styles are value, growth, and market oriented.

B Value managers seek to buy stocks below their intrinsic value. That said, the stocks may be cheap for good reason. Also, it may take a long time for stocks to reach their intrinsic value. Growth managers buy stocks of companies with either steadily growing earnings or companies whose earnings they expect to sharply appreciate. On the other hand, they may overpay for these earnings or the expected earnings may not materialize. Managers following the third style, market oriented, may forecast stock returns using a combination of growth or value considerations but endeavor to build portfolios that more closely resemble the market than either value or growth managers. If their fees are relatively high for achieving market-like returns, indexing or enhanced indexing may be a more cost-effective alternative.

2 The portfolio managed by Galicia is experiencing style drift. The threefold increase in the weighting of growth stocks suggests that Galicia has decided to shift to more of a market orientation, although some or all of the drift may have occurred because the stocks in the portfolio have become less value-like during the two-year period. The relatively low percentages given to "Other" suggest that Galicia's style bets explain the overwhelming majority of the portfolio's performance.

3 The fund has a modest value orientation. P/E, P/B, and EPS growth are all slightly lower than the market benchmark, and dividend yield is slightly higher. The sector weights are a bit more mixed. Some sectors that typically contain stocks with value characteristics (consumer discretionary and utilities) are overweight, while others (finance and energy) are underweight or equal weight to the benchmark. Also, traditionally growth-oriented sectors like health care and information technology are modestly overweight—unlikely in a deep value portfolio.

4 A better approach would be full replication. The main justification for using full replication is that all the components of the FTSE 100 are very liquid, so full replication can be accomplished readily and inexpensively. Because full replication minimizes tracking risk, it is the preferred method when the index consists of liquid securities. Another point is that full replication allows for the creation of a self-rebalancing portfolio in the case of a value-weighted (or float-weighted index): Trading is required only to reinvest dividends and to reflect changes in index composition. A self-rebalancing portfolio is one in which the portfolio moves in line with the index without any need for trading activity. An optimized portfolio may indeed hold fewer than 100 stocks. Because it does not contain every stock in the index in the proper capitalization weight, however, periodic trading will be required (even in the absence of index changes and dividend flows) simply to realign the portfolio's characteristics with those of the index. Over time, the trading-related costs will drag down performance. In general, optimization should be used only in situations in which full replication would result in substantial transaction costs.

5 A The principal benefit of all stocks being categorized as either growth or value (MSCI approach) is that it is collectively exhaustive. That said, many stocks are "border" stocks (i.e., have characteristics that place them near the value/growth border) that don't really exhibit significant value or growth characteristics but are categorized in one of these styles anyway. The Dow

Jones method's neutral/core category eliminates this problem, but the value and growth indices by definition do not contain all of the stocks in the broad index.

B Either set of indices can be used for returns-based style analysis. That said, Miller is likely to obtain a higher R^2 in a regression of the portfolio returns on the style index returns if he uses the more "granular" set of style indices—those by Dow Jones. For example, if the portfolio is a deep value portfolio or a strong growth portfolio, the Dow Jones indices are more likely to better explain the portfolio's style than a set of style indices in which every stock is forced into either value or growth. Specifically, the deep value portfolio will be better represented by the Dow Jones Value Index because that index focuses more on deep value stocks. That same portfolio's returns regressed versus the MSCI Value Index is likely to show a lower R^2.

6 The principal benefit of a market-neutral long–short portfolio is absence of a long-only constraint. A long-only constraint penalizes portfolios in two ways. First, it prevents the portfolio manager from fully exploiting a negative forecast on a given stock. Second, in a long-only portfolio, being unable to fully exploit a negative forecast also limits the ability of the portfolio manager to maximize positive forecasts. The main risk with long–short portfolios is the unlimited liability on the short trades. If a stock in which an investor has a long position loses all of its value, the most that could happen is that the investor loses his entire investment. With a short position, however, the investor's upside is limited (stock goes to zero) but the liability is unlimited (theoretically, a stock can appreciate infinitely).

7 Hayes can produce such a portfolio through the use of a portable alpha. He submits a proposal to manage a market-neutral long–short portfolio of UK stocks. This strategy generates alpha (α). To produce beta (β), the Japanese equity exposure, Hayes takes a long position in a notional value of futures equal to the size of the portfolio.

8 Suzuki tells her client that although she can certainly double the portfolio's tracking risk to 4 percent, the portfolio's alpha will increase but not double. The problem is that as an investor increases a portfolio's tracking risk, the long-only constraint increasingly limits the portfolio manager from taking full advantage of her investment insights. Remember, $IR \approx IC \sqrt{Breadth}$. If the breadth is constant but the IC falls because a smaller portion of the manager's insight is translated into the portfolio, then the IR must also fall.

9 The short side alpha is likely the larger of the two. Many investors look for cheap stocks in which to take long positions, but comparatively few look for expensive stocks to short. Shorting is operationally more cumbersome than taking a long position, which contributes to the limited use of shorting by most investors. Also, sell recommendations from the analyst community are relatively uncommon. Analysts are more likely to simply not cover a stock on which they have an unfavorable opinion. Also, analysts working for investment banking firms have a strong incentive not to issue negative reports on companies with which the bank may wish to do business.

10 A The change is in fact positive (assuming that Johnson is willing to accept a slightly higher level of tracking risk) because the information ratio improves. Her current portfolio has an information ratio of 0.87 (2.4%/2.75%). The portfolio with the enhanced indexer has an information ratio of 0.97 (2.8%/2.9%).

B Stock-based enhanced indexing begins with an index portfolio and then over- or underweights individual stocks based on the portfolio manager's return expectations for those stocks. The portfolio is built to look like its target benchmark but to add some level of outperformance on a fairly consistent basis. The advantage of this approach is greater breadth than the synthetic approach. That said, as with all active strategies, obtaining a satisfactory IC or level of investment insight is the challenge. Synthetic enhanced index strategies involve gaining exposure to the benchmark with futures (or a swap) while generating an alpha, typically using fixed income. This strategy has the advantage of being straightforward. It generally has narrower breadth (usually a duration or credit bet) and so requires a high IC to produce the same level of IR as the stock-based approach.

11 A The total active risk is greater than 6 percent because in the calculation, the long–short manager would be benchmarked to the Russell 1000 rather than the manager's normal benchmark, which most closely captures the manager's orientation. We can see this by noting the positive level of misfit risk. The misfit risk is calculated with the equation

$$\sqrt{6.0\%^2 + (\text{Misfit risk})^2} = 6.1\%, \text{ which equals 1.1 percent.}$$

B The total active risk is $\sqrt{5\%^2 + 7.13\%^2} = 8.71\%$.

C The expected total active return is $(0.3 \times 0\%) + (0.7 \times 1\%) = 0.7\%$. The expected total active risk for the portfolio is

$$\sqrt{(0.3^2 \times 0\%^2) + (0.7^2 \times 1.5\%^2)} = 1.05\%.$$

The expected IR is $0.7\%/1.05\% = 0.67$.

D The efficient combination of managers leads to a portfolio with an IR of $1.59\%/1.10\% = 1.45$. Hence, despite the slightly greater active risk exposure, the overall portfolio IR increases by a factor of 2.17 versus the current mix.

E In general, the exposures to non-US equities in the long–short portfolio should not concern Whitmore as long as she believes that the manager has skill in managing non-US equities. As shown in Part A of this problem, the misfit risk for the strategy is relatively small because the manager overlays the long–short portfolio with Russell 1000 futures and thus has a high correlation with the Russell 3000 benchmark. The large majority of the strategy's total active risk is driven by the manager's active return volatility.

12 B is correct. Both the active return and active risk are expected to be 0.00%, which would indicate a passive or index investment style.

13 C is correct. Relative to the other managers' portfolio characteristics, Portfolio C has characteristics most like a growth portfolio, such as a higher average P/E, higher average earnings growth rate, and lower average dividend-yield.

14 C is correct. Manager A most likely is pursuing a value investment style, not a growth investment style. This is evidenced by the relatively low long-term projected EPS growth. Contrarian and high yield, along with low P/E, are examples of value investment substyles. Momentum is an investment substyle consistent with a growth investment style.

Solutions

15 A is correct. Portfolio active return and portfolio active risk are calculated as follows:

$$\text{Portfolio active return} = (0.20 \times 0.025) + (0.45 \times 0.0) + (0.35 \times 0.025)$$
$$= 0.01375 = 1.38\%$$

$$\text{Portfolio active risk} = \left[(0.20^2 \times 0.04^2) + (0.45^2 \times 0.0^2) + (0.35^2 \times 0.04^2)\right]^{0.5}$$
$$= (0.000260)^{0.5} = 0.0161 = 1.61\%$$

16 C is correct. Full replication of an index is the indexing methodology that is most likely to have the least tracking error because every issue in the index is represented in the portfolio in approximately the same weight as in the index.

17 C is correct. Full replication is likely to have the highest investment cost. The other choices are low-cost index options of large pooled investments. While full replication of an index will generally have the least tracking error, a portfolio of just $2.0 million on an index as large as the MSCI ACWI would be very inefficient and cost-ineffective due to the inherent costs of managing and administering the portfolio, transaction costs of portfolio adjustments, transaction costs of investing and disinvesting cash flows, and a drag on performance from cash positions in an upward-trending equity market.

18 A is correct. Enhanced indexing seeks to outperform a given index (exploit information not yet reflected in stock prices) and limit tracking risk: "... enhanced indexing strategies with their strict control of tracking risk have tended to have the highest information ratios."

19 A is correct. A client with unpredictable cash inflows and outflows needs greater liquidity and furthermore would not want an index with a large number of stocks.

20 C is correct. Full replication has self-rebalancing properties when used for a float-weighted index, which would translate into lower costs from lower transaction fees and also should result in minimal tracking risk. In addition, full replication is generally the preferred index construction method for indices such as the S&P 500 that are composed of highly liquid securities. It is usually used for indices with fewer than 1,000 stocks.

21 B is correct. You cannot double a long-only portfolio's alpha by doubling its risk. As tracking risk increases, the long-only constraint limits the investor's investment opportunity set. Because IR (active return/active risk) = IC (effectiveness of investment insight, or correlation between forecast return and actual return) * $\sqrt{\text{breadth}}$ (number of independent active decisions made), if the breadth is constant but the IC falls because a smaller portion of the manager's insight is translated into the portfolio, then the IR must also fall.

22 C is correct. An equal-weighted index is biased toward small-cap companies.

23 C is correct. An enhanced indexed portfolio is designed to perform better than its benchmark index without incurring much additional risk. The derivatives-based strategy has the higher information ratio of the two, meaning it generates a higher mean active return for each unit of active risk:

Stock based	1.5/2.9 = .52
Derivatives based	1.2/2.1 = .57

Glossary

Absolute return benchmark A minimum target return that an investment manager is expected to beat.

Absolute-return vehicles Investments that have no direct benchmark portfolios.

Accounting risk The risk associated with accounting standards that vary from country to country or with any uncertainty about how certain transactions should be recorded.

Accumulated benefit obligation (ABO) The present value of pension benefits, assuming the pension plan terminated immediately such that it had to provide retirement income to all beneficiaries for their years of service up to that date.

Accumulated service Years of service of a pension plan participant as of a specified date.

Active/immunization combination A portfolio with two component portfolios: an immunized portfolio which provides an assured return over the planning horizon and a second portfolio that uses an active high-return/high-risk strategy.

Active investment strategies An approach to investing in which the portfolio manager seeks to outperform a given benchmark portfolio.

Active-lives The portion of a pension fund's liabilities associated with active workers.

Active management An approach to investing in which the portfolio manager seeks to outperform a given benchmark portfolio.

Active/passive combination Allocation of the core component of a portfolio to a passive strategy and the balance to an active component.

Active return The portfolio's return in excess of the return on the portfolio's benchmark.

Active risk A synonym for tracking risk.

Actual extreme events A type of scenario analysis used in stress testing. It involves evaluating how a portfolio would have performed given movements in interest rates, exchange rates, stock prices, or commodity prices at magnitudes such as occurred during past extreme market events (e.g., the stock market crash of October 1987).

Ad valorem fees Fees that are calculated by multiplying a percentage by the value of assets managed; also called assets under management (AUM) fees.

Adaptive markets hypothesis (AMH) A hypothesis that applies principles of evolution—such as competition, adaptation, and natural selection—to financial markets in an attempt to reconcile efficient market theories with behavioral alternatives.

Adverse selection risk The risk associated with information asymmetry; in the context of trading, the risk of trading with a more informed trader.

Algorithmic trading Automated electronic trading subject to quantitative rules and user-specified benchmarks and constraints.

Allocation/selection interaction return A measure of the joint effect of weights assigned to both sectors and individual securities; the difference between the weight of the portfolio in a given sector and the portfolio's benchmark for that sector, times the difference between the portfolio's and the benchmark's returns in that sector, summed across all sectors.

Alpha Excess risk-adjusted return.

Alpha and beta separation An approach to portfolio construction that views investing to earn alpha and investing to establish systematic risk exposures as tasks that can and should be pursued separately.

Alpha research Research related to capturing excess risk-adjusted returns by a particular strategy; a way investment research is organized in some investment management firms.

Alternative investments Groups of investments with risk and return characteristics that differ markedly from those of traditional stock and bond investments.

Anchoring and adjustment An information-processing bias in which the use of a psychological heuristic influences the way people estimate probabilities.

Anchoring and adjustment bias An information-processing bias in which the use of a psychological heuristic influences the way people estimate probabilities.

Anchoring trap The tendency of the mind to give disproportionate weight to the first information it receives on a topic.

Angel investor An accredited individual investing chiefly in seed and early-stage companies.

Anomalies Apparent deviations from market efficiency.

Ask price The price at which a dealer will sell a specified quantity of a security. Also called *ask*, *offer price*, or *offer*.

Ask size The quantity associated with the ask price.

Aspirational risk bucket In goal-based portfolio planning, that part of wealth allocated to investments that have the potential to increase a client's wealth substantially.

Asset allocation reviews A periodic review of the appropriateness of a portfolio's asset allocation.

Asset covariance matrix The covariance matrix for the asset classes or markets under consideration.

Asset/liability management The management of financial risks created by the interaction of assets and liabilities.

Asset/liability management (ALM) approach In the context of determining a strategic asset allocation, an asset/liability management approach involves explicitly modeling liabilities and adopting the allocation of assets that is optimal in relationship to funding liabilities.

Asset location The type of account an asset is held within, e.g., taxable or tax deferred.

Asset-only (AO) approach In the context of determining a strategic asset allocation, an approach that focuses on the characteristics of the assets without explicitly modeling the liabilities.

Assurity of completion In the context of trading, confidence that trades will settle without problems under all market conditions.

Assurity of the contract In the context of trading, confidence that the parties to trades will be held to fulfilling their obligations.

Asynchronism A discrepancy in the dating of observations that occurs because stale (out-of-date) data may be used in the absence of current data.

AUM fee A fee based on assets under management; an ad valorem fee.

Automated trading Any form of trading that is not manual, including trading based on algorithms.

Availability bias An information-processing bias in which people take a heuristic approach to estimating the probability of an outcome based on how easily the outcome comes to mind.

Average effective spread A measure of the liquidity of a security's market. The mean effective spread (sometimes dollar weighted) over all transactions in the stock in the period under study.

Back office Administrative functions at an investment firm such as those pertaining to transaction processing, record keeping, and regulatory compliance.

Backtesting A method for gaining information about a model using past data. As used in reference to VaR, it is the process of comparing the number of violations of VaR thresholds over a time period with the figure implied by the user-selected probability level.

Backwardation A condition in the futures markets in which the benefits of holding an asset exceed the costs, leaving the futures price less than the spot price.

Balance of payments An accounting of all cash flows between residents and nonresidents of a country.

Bancassurance The sale of insurance by banks.

Barbell portfolio A portfolio made up of short and long maturities relative to the investment horizon date and interim coupon payments.

Base With respect to a foreign exchange quotation of the price of one unit of a currency, the currency referred to in "one unit of a currency."

Base-rate neglect A type of representativeness bias in which the base rate or probability of the categorization is not adequately considered.

Basis The difference between the cash price and the futures price.

Basis point value (BPV) The change in the bond price for a 1 basis point change in yield. Also called *present value of a basis point* or *price value of a basis point (PVBP)*.

Basis risk The risk resulting from using a hedging instrument that is imperfectly matched to the investment being hedged; in general, the risk that the basis will change in an unpredictable way.

Batch auction markets Auction markets where multilateral trading occurs at a single price at a prespecified point in time.

Bayes' formula A mathematical rule explaining how existing probability beliefs should be changed given new information; it is essentially an application of conditional probabilities.

Bear spread An option strategy that involves selling a put with a lower exercise price and buying a put with a higher exercise price. It can also be executed with calls.

Behavioral finance An approach to finance based on the observation that psychological variables affect and often distort individuals' investment decision making.

Behavioral finance macro A focus on market level behavior that considers market anomalies that distinguish markets from the efficient markets of traditional finance.

Behavioral finance micro A focus on individual level behavior that examines the behavioral biases that distinguish individual investors from the rational decision makers of traditional finance.

Benchmark In an investments context, a standard or point of reference for evaluating the performance of an investment portfolio.

Best efforts order A type of order that gives the trader's agent discretion to execute the order only when the agent judges market conditions to be favorable.

Beta A measure of the sensitivity of a given investment or portfolio to movements in the overall market.

Beta research Research related to systematic (market) risk and return; a way investment research is organized in some investment management firms.

Bid The price at which a dealer will buy a specified quantity of a security. Also called *bid price*.

Bid–ask spread The difference between the current bid price and the current ask price of a security.

Bid price In a price quotation, the price at which the party making the quotation is willing to buy a specified quantity of an asset or security.

Bid size The quantity associated with the bid price.

Binary credit options Options that provide payoffs contingent on the occurrence of a specified negative credit event.

Block order An order to sell or buy in a quantity that is large relative to the liquidity ordinarily available from dealers in the security or in other markets.

Bond-yield-plus-risk-premium method An approach to estimating the required return on equity which specifies that required return as a bond yield plus a risk premium.

Bottom-up Focusing on company-specific fundamentals or factors such as revenues, earnings, cash flow, or new product development.

Bounded rationality The notion that people have informational and cognitive limitations when making decisions and do not necessarily optimize when arriving at their decisions.

Box spread An option strategy that combines a bull spread and a bear spread having two different exercise prices, which produces a risk-free payoff of the difference in the exercise prices.

Broad market indexes An index that is intended to measure the performance of an entire asset class. For example, the S&P 500 Index, Wilshire 5000, and Russell 3000 indexes for US common stocks.

Broker An agent of a trader in executing trades.

Brokered markets Markets in which transactions are largely effected through a search-brokerage mechanism away from public markets.

Bubbles Episodes in which asset market prices move to extremely high levels in relation to estimated intrinsic value.

Buffering With respect to style index construction, rules for maintaining the style assignment of a stock consistent with a previous assignment when the stock has not clearly moved to a new style.

Build-up approach Synonym for the risk premium approach.

Bull spread An option strategy that involves buying a call with a lower exercise price and selling a call with a higher exercise price. It can also be executed with puts.

Bullet portfolio A portfolio made up of maturities that are very close to the investment horizon.

Business cycle Fluctuations in GDP in relation to long-term trend growth, usually lasting 9–11 years.

Business risk The equity risk that comes from the nature of the firm's operating activities.

Butterfly spread An option strategy that combines two bull or bear spreads and has three exercise prices.

Buy side Investment management companies and other investors that use the services of brokerages.

Buy-side traders Professional traders that are employed by investment managers and institutional investors.

Calendar-and-percentage-of-portfolio rebalancing Monitoring a portfolio at regular frequencies, such as quarterly. Rebalancing decisions are then made based upon percentage-of-portfolio principles.

Calendar rebalancing Rebalancing a portfolio to target weights on a periodic basis; for example, monthly, quarterly, semiannually, or annually.

Calmar ratio The compound annualized rate of return over a specified time period divided by the absolute value of maximum drawdown over the same time period.

Cap A combination of interest rate call options designed to hedge a borrower against rate increases on a floating-rate loan.

Cap rate With respect to options, the exercise interest rate for a cap.

Cap weighting See *capitalization weighting*.

Capital adequacy ratio A measure of the adequacy of capital in relation to assets.

Capital allocation line A graph line that describes the combinations of expected return and standard deviation of return available to an investor from combining an optimal portfolio of risky assets with a risk-free asset.

Capital flows forecasting approach An exchange rate forecasting approach that focuses on expected capital flows, particularly long-term flows such as equity investment and foreign direct investment.

Capital market expectations (CME) Expectations concerning the risk and return prospects of asset classes.

Capitalization weighting The most common security weighting scheme in which constituents are held in proportion to their market capitalizations, calculated as price times available shares. Also known as *market value*, *market cap*, or *cap weighting*.

Caplet Each component call option in a cap.

Carried interest A private equity fund manager's incentive fee; the share of the private equity fund's profits that the fund manager is due once the fund has returned the outside investors' capital.

Carry trade A trading strategy of borrowing in low-yield currencies and investing the borrowed amount in high-yield currencies.

Cash balance plan A defined-benefit plan whose benefits are displayed in individual recordkeeping accounts.

Cash flow at risk A variation of VaR that measures the risk to a company's cash flow, instead of its market value; the minimum cash flow loss expected to be exceeded with a given probability over a specified time period.

Cash flow matching An asset/liability management approach that provides the future funding of a liability stream from the coupon and matured principal payments of the portfolio. A type of dedication strategy.

Cell-matching technique (stratified sampling) A portfolio construction technique used in indexing that divides the benchmark index into cells related to the risk factors affecting the index and samples from index securities belonging to those cells.

Certainty equivalent The maximum sum of money a person would pay to participate or the minimum sum of money a person would accept to not participate in an opportunity.

Chain-linking A process for combining periodic returns to produce an overall time-weighted rate of return.

Cheapest-to-deliver A bond in which the amount received for delivering the bond is largest compared with the amount paid in the market for the bond.

Civil law A legal system derived from Roman law, in which judges apply general, abstract rules or concepts to particular cases. In civil systems, law is developed primarily through legislative statutes or executive action.

Claw-back provision With respect to the compensation of private equity fund managers, a provision that specifies that money from the fund manager be returned to investors if, at the end of a fund's life, investors have not received back their capital contributions and contractual share of profits.

Closed-book markets Markets in which a trader does not have real-time access to all quotes in a security.

Closeout netting In a bankruptcy, a process by which multiple obligations between two counterparties are consolidated into a single overall value owed by one of the counterparties to the other.

Cobb-Douglas model A production function (model for economic output) based on factors of labor and capital that exhibits constant returns to scale.

Cobb-Douglas production function A production function (model for economic output) based on factors of labor and capital that exhibits constant returns to scale.

Cognitive dissonance The mental discomfort that occurs when new information conflicts with previously held beliefs or cognitions.

Cognitive errors Behavioral biases resulting from faulty reasoning; cognitive errors stem from basic statistical, information processing, or memory errors.

Collar An option strategy involving the purchase of a put and sale of a call in which the holder of an asset gains protection below a certain level, the exercise price of the put, and pays for it by giving up gains above a certain level, the exercise price of the call. Collars also can be used to provide protection against rising interest rates on a floating-rate loan by giving up gains from lower interest rates.

Collateral return The component of the return on a commodity futures contract that comes from the assumption that the full value of the underlying futures contract is invested to earn the risk-free interest rate. Also called *collateral yield*.

Collateralized debt obligation A securitized pool of fixed-income assets.

Combination matching A cash flow matching technique; a portfolio is duration-matched with a set of liabilities with the added constraint that it also be cash-flow matched in the first few years, usually the first five years. Also called *horizon matching*.

Commingled real estate funds (CREFs) Professionally managed vehicles for substantial commingled (i.e., pooled) investment in real estate properties.

Commitment period The period of time over which committed funds are advanced to a private equity fund.

Commodities Articles of commerce such as agricultural goods, metals, and petroleum; tangible assets that are typically relatively homogeneous in nature.

Commodity trading advisors Registered advisors who manage futures funds.

Common law A legal system which draws abstract rules from specific cases. In common law systems, law is developed primarily through decisions of the courts.

Community property regime A marital property regime under which each spouse has an indivisible one-half interest in property received during marriage.

Company-specific risk The non-systematic or idiosyncratic risk specific to a particular company's operations, reputation, and business environment.

Completeness fund A portfolio that, when added to active managers' positions, establishes an overall portfolio with approximately the same risk exposures as the investor's overall equity benchmark.

Confidence band With reference to a quality control chart for performance evaluation, a range in which the manager's value-added returns are anticipated to fall a specified percentage of the time.

Confidence interval An interval that has a given probability of containing the parameter it is intended to estimate.

Confirmation bias A belief perseverance bias in which people tend to look for and notice what confirms their beliefs, to ignore or undervalue what contradicts their beliefs, and to misinterpret information as support for their beliefs.

Confirming evidence trap The bias that leads individuals to give greater weight to information that supports an existing or preferred point of view than to evidence that contradicts it.

Conjunction fallacy An inappropriate combining of probabilities of independent events to support a belief. In fact, the probability of two independent events occurring in conjunction is never greater than the probability of either event occurring alone; the probability of two independent events occurring together is equal to the multiplication of the probabilities of the independent events.

Conservatism bias A belief perseverance bias in which people maintain their prior views or forecasts by inadequately incorporating new information.

Consistent growth A growth investment substyle that focuses on companies with consistent growth having a long history of unit-sales growth, superior profitability, and predictable earnings.

Constant returns to scale A characteristic of a production function such that a given percentage increase in capital stock and labor input results in an equal percentage increase in output.

Contango A condition in the futures markets in which the costs of holding an asset exceed the benefits, leaving the futures price more than the spot price.

Contingent immunization A fixed-income strategy in which immunization serves as a fall-back strategy if the actively managed portfolio does not grow at a certain rate.

Continuous auction markets Auction markets where orders can be executed at any time during the trading day.

Contrarian A value investment substyle focusing on stocks that have been beset by problems.

Controlled foreign corporation A company located outside a taxpayer's home country and in which the taxpayer has a controlling interest as defined under the home country law.

Conversion factor An adjustment used to facilitate delivery on bond futures contracts in which any of a number of bonds with different characteristics are eligible for delivery.

Convexity A measure of how interest rate sensitivity changes with a change in interest rates.

Convexity adjustment An estimate of the change in price that is not explained by duration.

Core capital The amount of capital required to fund spending to maintain a given lifestyle, fund goals, and provide adequate reserves for unexpected commitments.

Core-plus A fixed-income mandate that permits the portfolio manager to add instruments with relatively high return potential to core holdings of investment-grade debt.

Core–satellite A way of thinking about allocating money that seeks to define each investment's place in the portfolio in relation to specific investment goals or roles.

Core-satellite portfolio A portfolio in which certain investments (often indexed or semiactive) are viewed as the core and the balance are viewed as satellite investments fulfilling specific roles.

Corner portfolio Adjacent corner portfolios define a segment of the minimum-variance frontier within which portfolios hold identical assets and the rate of change of asset weights in moving from one portfolio to another is constant.

Corner portfolio theorem In a sign-constrained mean–variance optimization, the result that the asset weights of any minimum-variance portfolio are a positive linear combination of the corresponding weights in the two adjacent corner portfolios that bracket it in terms of expected return (or standard deviation of return).

Corporate governance The system of internal controls and procedures used to define and protect the rights and responsibilities of various stakeholders.

Corporate venturing Investments by companies in promising young companies in the same or a related industry.

Country beta A measure of the sensitivity of a specified variable (e.g., yield) to a change in the comparable variable in another country.

Covered call An option strategy involving the holding of an asset and sale of a call on the asset.

Credit default swap A swap used to transfer credit risk to another party. A protection buyer pays the protection seller in return for the right to receive a payment from the seller in the event of a specified credit event.

Credit derivative A contract in which one party has the right to claim a payment from another party in the event that a specific credit event occurs over the life of the contract.

Credit event An event affecting the credit risk of a security or counterparty.

Credit forwards A type of credit derivative with payoffs based on bond values or credit spreads.

Credit method When the residence country reduces its taxpayers' domestic tax liability by the amount of taxes paid to a foreign country that exercises source jurisdiction.

Credit protection seller With respect to a credit derivative, the party that accepts the credit risk of the underlying financial asset.

Credit risk The risk of loss caused by a counterparty's or debtor's failure to make a timely payment or by the change in value of a financial instrument based on changes in default risk. Also called *default risk*.

Credit spread forward A forward contract used to transfer credit risk to another party; a forward contract on a yield spread.

Credit spread option   An option based on the yield spread between two securities that is used to transfer credit risk.

Credit spread risk   The risk that the spread between the rate for a risky bond and the rate for a default risk-free bond may vary after the purchase of the risky bond.

Credit VaR   A variation of VaR related to credit risk; it reflects the minimum loss due to credit exposure with a given probability during a period of time.

Credited rates   Rates of interest credited to a policyholder's reserve account.

Cross-default provision   A provision stipulating that if a borrower defaults on any outstanding credit obligations, the borrower is considered to be in default on all obligations.

Cross hedge   A hedge involving a hedging instrument that is imperfectly correlated with the asset being hedged; an example is hedging a bond investment with futures on a non-identical bond.

Currency-hedged instruments   Investment in nondomestic assets in which currency exposures are neutralized.

Currency overlay programs   A currency overlay program is a program to manage a portfolio's currency exposures for the case in which those exposures are managed separately from the management of the portfolio itself.

Currency return   The percentage change in the spot exchange rate stated in terms of home currency per unit of foreign currency.

Currency risk   The risk associated with the uncertainty about the exchange rate at which proceeds in the foreign currency can be converted into the investor's home currency.

Currency swap   A swap in which the parties make payments based on the difference in debt payments in different currencies.

Current credit risk   The risk of credit-related events happening in the immediate future; it relates to the risk that a payment currently due will not be paid. Also called *jump-to-default risk*.

Cushion spread   The difference between the minimum acceptable return and the higher possible immunized rate.

Custom security-based benchmark   Benchmarks that are custom built to accurately reflect the investment discipline of a particular investment manager. Also called *strategy benchmarks* because they reflect a manager's particular strategy.

Custom security-based benchmarks   Benchmarks that are custom built to accurately reflect the investment discipline of a particular investment manager. Also called *strategy benchmarks* because they reflect a manager's particular strategy.

Cyclical stocks   The shares of companies whose earnings have above-average sensitivity to the business cycle.

Cyclically Adjusted P/E Ratio (CAPE)   A price-to-earnings ratio in which the numerator (in a US context) is defined as the real S&P 500 price index and the denominator as the moving average of the preceding 10 years of real reported earnings on the S&P 500.

Day traders   Traders that rapidly buy and sell stocks in the hope that the stocks will continue to rise or fall in value for the seconds or minutes they are prepared to hold a position. Day traders hold a position open somewhat longer than a scalper but closing all positions at the end of the day.

Dealer   A business entity that is ready to buy an asset for inventory or sell an asset from inventory to provide the other side of an order. Also called *market maker*.

Decision price   The prevailing price when the decision to trade is made. Also called *arrival price* or *strike price*.

Decision risk   The risk of changing strategies at the point of maximum loss.

Deduction method   When the residence country allows taxpayers to reduce their taxable income by the amount of taxes paid to foreign governments in respect of foreign-source income.

Deemed dispositions   Tax treatment that assumes property is sold. It is sometimes seen as an alternative to estate or inheritance tax.

Deemed distribution   When shareholders of a controlled foreign corporation are taxed as if the earnings were distributed to shareholders, even though no distribution has been made.

Default risk   The risk of loss if an issuer or counterparty does not fulfill its contractual obligations.

Default risk premium   Compensation for the possibility that the issue of a debt instrument will fail to make a promised payment at the contracted time and in the contracted amount.

Defaultable debt   Debt with some meaningful amount of credit risk.

Defined-benefit plan   A pension plan that specifies the plan sponsor's obligations in terms of the benefit to plan participants.

Defined-contribution plan   A pension plan that specifies the sponsor's obligations in terms of contributions to the pension fund rather than benefits to plan participants.

Deflation   A decrease in the general level of prices; an increase in the purchasing power of a unit of currency.

Delay costs   Implicit trading costs that arise from the inability to complete desired trades immediately due to order size or market liquidity. Also called *slippage*.

Delivery option   The feature of a futures contract giving the short the right to make decisions about what, when, and where to deliver.

Delta   The relationship between the option price and the underlying price, which reflects the sensitivity of the price of the option to changes in the price of the underlying.

Delta hedge   An option strategy in which a position in an asset is converted to a risk-free position with a position in a specific number of options. The number of options per unit of the underlying changes through time, and the position must be revised to maintain the hedge.

Delta hedging   Hedging that involves matching the price response of the position being hedged over a narrow range of prices.

Delta-normal method   A measure of VaR equivalent to the analytical method but that refers to the use of delta to estimate the option's price sensitivity.

Demand deposit   A deposit that can be drawn upon without prior notice, such as a checking account.

Demutualizing   The process of converting an insurance company from mutual form to stock.

Descriptive statistics   Methods for effectively summarizing data to describe important aspects of a dataset.

Differential returns   Returns that deviate from a manager's benchmark.

Diffusion index   An index that measures how many indicators are pointing up and how many are pointing down.

Direct commodity investment Commodity investment that involves cash market purchase of physical commodities or exposure to changes in spot market values via derivatives, such as futures.

Direct market access Platforms sponsored by brokers that permit buy-side traders to directly access equities, fixed income, futures, and foreign exchange markets, clearing via the broker.

Direct quotation Quotation in terms of domestic currency/foreign currency.

Discounted cash flow models (DCF models) Valuation models that express the idea that an asset's value is the present value of its (expected) cash flows.

Discretionary trust A trust structure in which the trustee determines whether and how much to distribute in the sole discretion of the trustee.

Disintermediation To withdraw funds from financial intermediaries for placement with other financial intermediaries offering a higher return or yield. Or, to withdraw funds from a financial intermediary for the purposes of direct investment, such as withdrawing from a mutual fund to make direct stock investments.

Disposition effect As a result of loss aversion, an emotional bias whereby investors are reluctant to dispose of losers. This results in an inefficient and gradual adjustment to deterioration in fundamental value.

Distressed debt arbitrage A distressed securities investment discipline that involves purchasing the traded bonds of bankrupt companies and selling the common equity short.

Distressed securities Securities of companies that are in financial distress or near bankruptcy; the name given to various investment disciplines employing securities of companies in distress.

Diversification effect In reference to VaR across several portfolios (for example, across an entire firm), this effect equals the difference between the sum of the individual VaRs and total VaR.

Dividend recapitalization A method by which a buyout fund can realize the value of a holding; involves the issuance of debt by the holding to finance a special dividend to owners.

Dollar duration A measure of the change in portfolio value for a 100 bps change in market yields.

Domestic asset An asset that trades in the investor's domestic currency (or home currency).

Domestic currency The currency of the investor, i.e., the currency in which he or she typically makes consumption purchases, e.g., the Swiss franc for an investor domiciled in Switzerland.

Domestic-currency return A rate of return stated in domestic currency terms from the perspective of the investor; reflects both the foreign-currency return on an asset as well as percentage movement in the spot exchange rate between the domestic and foreign currencies.

Donor-advised fund A fund administered by a tax-exempt entity in which the donor advises on where to grant the money that he or she has donated.

Double inflection utility function A utility function that changes based on levels of wealth.

Downgrade risk The risk that one of the major rating agencies will lower its rating for an issuer, based on its specified rating criteria.

Downside deviation A measure of volatility using only rate of return data points below the investor's minimum acceptable return.

Downside risk Risk of loss or negative return.

Due diligence Investigation and analysis in support of an investment action or recommendation, such as the scrutiny of operations and management and the verification of material facts.

Duration A measure of the approximate sensitivity of a security to a change in interest rates (i.e., a measure of interest rate risk).

Dynamic approach With respect to strategic asset allocation, an approach that accounts for links between optimal decisions at different points in time.

Dynamic hedge A hedge requiring adjustment as the price of the hedged asset changes.

Earnings at risk (EAR) A variation of VaR that reflects the risk of a company's earnings instead of its market value.

Earnings momentum A growth investment substyle that focuses on companies with earnings momentum (high quarterly year-over-year earnings growth).

Econometrics The application of quantitative modeling and analysis grounded in economic theory to the analysis of economic data.

Economic exposure The risk associated with changes in the relative attractiveness of products and services offered for sale, arising out of the competitive effects of changes in exchange rates.

Economic indicators Economic statistics provided by government and established private organizations that contain information on an economy's recent past activity or its current or future position in the business cycle.

Economic surplus The market value of assets minus the present value of liabilities.

Effective duration Duration adjusted to account for embedded options.

Effective spread Two times the distance between the actual execution price and the midpoint of the market quote at the time an order is entered; a measure of execution costs that captures the effects of price improvement and market impact.

Efficient frontier The graph of the set of portfolios that maximize expected return for their level of risk (standard deviation of return); the part of the minimum-variance frontier beginning with the global minimum-variance portfolio and continuing above it.

Electronic communications networks (ECNs) Computer-based auctions that operate continuously within the day using a specified set of rules to execute orders.

Emerging market debt The sovereign debt of nondeveloped countries.

Emotional biases Behavioral biases resulting from reasoning influenced by feelings; emotional biases stem from impulse or intuition.

Endogenous variable A variable whose values are determined within the system.

Endowment bias An emotional bias in which people value an asset more when they hold rights to it than when they do not.

Endowments Long-term funds generally owned by operating nonprofit institutions such as universities and colleges, museums, hospitals, and other organizations involved in charitable activities.

Enhanced derivatives products companies A type of subsidiary separate from an entity's other activities and not liable for the parent's debts. They are often used by derivatives dealers to control exposure to ratings downgrades. Also called *special purpose vehicles*.

Enterprise risk management An overall assessment of a company's risk position. A centralized approach to risk management sometimes called firmwide risk management.

Equal probability rebalancing Rebalancing in which the manager specifies a corridor for each asset class as a common multiple of the standard deviation of the asset class's returns. Rebalancing to the target proportions occurs when any asset class weight moves outside its corridor.

Equal weighted In an equal-weighted index, each stock in the index is weighted equally.

Equal weighting Security weighting scheme in which all constituents are held at equal weights at specified rebalancing times.

Equitized Given equity market systematic risk exposure.

Equity forward sale contract A private contract for the forward sale of an equity position.

Equity-indexed annuity A type of life annuity that provides a guarantee of a minimum fixed payment plus some participation in stock market gains, if any.

Equity monetization The realization of cash for an equity position through a manner other than an outright sale.

Equity q The ratio of a company's equity market capitalization divided by net worth measured at replacement cost.

Equity risk premium Compensation for the additional risk of equity compared with debt.

ESG risk The risk to a company's market valuation resulting from environmental, social, and governance factors.

Estate All of the property a person owns or controls; may consist of financial assets, tangible personal assets, immovable property, or intellectual property.

Estate planning The process of preparing for the disposition of one's estate (e.g., the transfer of property) upon death and during one's lifetime.

Estate tax freeze A plan usually involving a corporation, partnership, or limited liability company with the goal to transfer *future* appreciation to the next generation at little or no gift or estate tax cost.

Eurozone The region of countries using the euro as a currency.

***Ex post* alpha** (or Jensen's alpha) The average return achieved in a portfolio in excess of what would have been predicted by CAPM given the portfolio's risk level; an after-the-fact measure of excess risk-adjusted return.

Excess capital An investor's capital over and above that which is necessary to fund their lifestyle and reserves.

Excess currency return The expected currency return in excess of the forward premium or discount.

Excess return The difference between the benchmark return and the portfolio return, which may be either positive or negative.

Exchange A regulated venue for the trading of investment instruments.

Exchange fund A fund into which several investors place their different share holdings in exchange for shares in the diversified fund itself.

Execution uncertainty Uncertainty pertaining to the timing of execution, or if execution will even occur at all.

Exemption method When the residence country imposes no tax on foreign-source income by providing taxpayers with an exemption, in effect having only one jurisdiction impose tax.

Exogenous shocks Events from outside the economic system that affect its course. These could be short-lived political events, changes in government policy, or natural disasters, for example.

Exogenous variable A variable whose values are determined outside the system.

Externality Those consequences of a transaction (or process) that do not fall on the parties to the transaction (or process).

Factor covariance matrix The covariance matrix of factors.

Factor-model-based benchmark Benchmarks constructed by examining a portfolio's sensitivity to a set of factors, such as the return for a broad market index, company earnings growth, industry, or financial leverage.

Factor-model-based benchmarks Benchmarks constructed by examining a portfolio's sensitivity to a set of factors, such as the return for a broad market index, company earnings growth, industry, or financial leverage.

Factor push A simple stress test that involves pushing prices and risk factors of an underlying model in the most disadvantageous way to estimate the impact of factor extremes on the portfolio's value.

Factor sensitivities In a multifactor model, the responsiveness of the dependent variable to factor movements. Also called *factor betas* or *factor loadings*.

Fallen angels Debt that has crossed the threshold from investment grade to high yield.

Fed model An equity valuation model that relates the earnings yield on the S&P 500 to the yield to maturity on 10-year US Treasury bonds.

Federal funds rate The interest rate on overnight loans of reserves (deposits) between US Federal Reserve System member banks.

Fee cap A limit on the total fee paid regardless of performance.

Fiduciary A person or entity standing in a special relation of trust and responsibility with respect to other parties.

Financial buyers Buyers who lack a strategic motive.

Financial capital As used in the text, an individual investor's investable wealth; total wealth minus human capital. Consists of assets that can be traded such as cash, stocks, bonds, and real estate.

Financial equilibrium models Models describing relationships between expected return and risk in which supply and demand are in balance.

Financial risk Risks derived from events in the external financial markets, such as changes in equity prices, interest rates, or currency exchange rates.

Fiscal policy Government activity concerning taxation and governmental spending.

Fixed annuity A type of life annuity in which periodic payments are fixed in amount.

Fixed-rate payer The party to an interest rate swap that is obligated to make periodic payments at a fixed rate.

Fixed trust A trust structure in which distributions to beneficiaries are prescribed in the trust document to occur at certain times or in certain amounts.

Flexible-premium variable life A type of life insurance policy that combines the flexibility of universal life with the investment choice flexibility of variable life. Also called *variable universal life*.

Floating-rate payer The party to an interest rate swap that is obligated to make periodic payments based on a benchmark floating rate.

Floating supply of shares The number of shares outstanding that are actually available to investors. Also called *free float*.

Floor A combination of interest rate options designed to provide protection against interest rate decreases.

Floor broker An agent of the broker who, for certain exchanges, physically represents the trade on the exchange floor.

Floorlet Each component put option in a floor.

Forced heirship rules Legal ownership principles whereby children have the right to a fixed share of a parent's estate.

Foreign assets Assets denominated in currencies other than the investor's home currency.

Foreign currency Currency that is not the currency in which an investor makes consumption purchases, e.g., the US dollar from the perspective of a Swiss investor.

Foreign-currency return The return of the foreign asset measured in foreign-currency terms.

Formal tools Established research methods amenable to precise definition and independent replication of results.

Forward conversion with options The construction of a synthetic short forward position against the asset held long.

Forward discount The forward rate less the spot rate, divided by the spot rate; called the forward discount if negative, and forward premium if positive. Also called *forward premium*.

Forward hedging Hedging that involves the use of a forward contract between the foreign asset's currency and the home currency.

Forward rate bias Persistent violation of uncovered interest rate parity that is exploited by the carry trade.

Foundations Typically, grant-making institutions funded by gifts and investment assets.

Fourth market A term occasionally used for direct trading of securities between institutional investors; the fourth market would include trading on electronic crossing networks.

Framing An information-processing bias in which a person answers a question differently based on the way in which it is asked (framed).

Framing bias An information-processing bias in which a person answers a question differently based on the way in which it is asked (framed).

Front office The revenue generating functions at an investment firm such as those pertaining to trading and sales.

Front-run To trade ahead of the initiator, exploiting privileged information about the initiator's trading intentions.

Full replication When every issue in an index is represented in the portfolio, and each portfolio position has approximately the same weight in the fund as in the index.

Fully funded plan A pension plan in which the ratio of the value of plan assets to the present value of plan liabilities is 100 percent or greater.

Functional duration The key rate duration. Also called *multifunctional duration*.

Fund manager The professional manager of separate accounts or pooled assets structured in a variety of ways.

Fund of funds A fund that invests in a number of underlying funds.

Fundamental law of active management The relation that the information ratio of a portfolio manager is approximately equal to the information coefficient multiplied by the square root of the investment discipline's breadth (the number of independent, active investment decisions made each year).

Fundamental weighting Patented by Research Affiliates LLC, this scheme uses company characteristics such as sales, cash flow, book value, and dividends to weight securities.

Funded status The relationship between the value of a plan's assets and the present value of its liabilities.

Funding currencies The low-yield currencies in which borrowing occurs in a carry trade.

Funding ratio A measure of the relative size of pension assets compared to the present value of pension liabilities. Calculated by dividing the value of pension assets by the present value of pension liabilities. Also referred to as the *funded ratio* or *funded status*.

Funding risk The risk that liabilities funding long asset positions cannot be rolled over at reasonable cost.

Futures contract An enforceable contract between a buyer (seller) and an established exchange or its clearinghouse in which the buyer (seller) agrees to take (make) delivery of something at a specified price at the end of a designated period of time.

Futures price The price at which the parties to a futures contract agree to exchange the underlying.

Gain-to-loss ratio The ratio of positive returns to negative returns over a specified period of time.

Gamblers' fallacy A misunderstanding of probabilities in which people wrongly project reversal to a long-term mean.

Gamma A numerical measure of the sensitivity of delta to a change in the underlying's value.

Global custodian An entity that effects trade settlement, safekeeping of assets, and the allocation of trades to individual custody accounts.

Global investable market A practical proxy for the world market portfolio consisting of traditional and alternative asset classes with sufficient capacity to absorb meaningful investment.

Global minimum-variance (GMV) portfolio The portfolio on the minimum-variance frontier with smallest variance of return.

Gold standard currency system A currency regime under which currency could be freely converted into gold at established rates.

Gordon (constant) growth model A version of the dividend discount model for common share value that assumes a constant growth rate in dividends.

Government structural policies Government policies that affect the limits of economic growth and incentives within the private sector.

Grinold–Kroner model An expression for the expected return on a share as the sum of an expected income return, an expected nominal earnings growth return, and an expected repricing return.

Growth in total factor productivity A component of trend growth in GDP that results from increased efficiency in using capital inputs; also known as technical progress.

Guaranteed investment contract A debt instrument issued by insurers, usually in large denominations, that pays a guaranteed, generally fixed interest rate for a specified time period.

H-model A variant of the two-stage dividend discount model in which growth begins at a high rate and declines linearly throughout the supernormal growth period until it reaches a normal growth rate that holds in perpetuity.

Hague Conference on Private International Law An intergovernmental organization working toward the convergence of private international law. Its 69 members consist of countries and regional economic integration organizations.

Halo effect An emotional bias that extends a favorable evaluation of some characteristics to other characteristics.

Hedge funds A historically loosely regulated, pooled investment vehicle that may implement various investment strategies.

Hedge ratio The relationship of the quantity of an asset being hedged to the quantity of the derivative used for hedging.

Hedged return The foreign asset return in local currency terms plus the forward discount (premium).

Hedging A general strategy usually thought of as reducing, if not eliminating, risk.

Herding When a group of investors trade on the same side of the market in the same securities, or when investors ignore their own private information and act as other investors do.

High-water mark A specified net asset value level that a fund must exceed before performance fees are paid to the hedge fund manager.

High yield A value investment substyle that focuses on stocks offering high dividend yield with prospects of maintaining or increasing the dividend.

High-yield investing A distressed securities investment discipline that involves investment in high-yield bonds perceived to be undervalued.

Hindsight bias A bias with selective perception and retention aspects in which people may see past events as having been predictable and reasonable to expect.

Historical simulation method The application of historical price changes to the current portfolio.

Holdings-based style analysis An approach to style analysis that categorizes individual securities by their characteristics and aggregates results to reach a conclusion about the overall style of the portfolio at a given point in time.

Home bias An anomaly by which portfolios exhibit a strong bias in favor of domestic securities in the context of global portfolios.

Home currency See *domestic currency*.

Human capital An implied asset; the present value of expected future labor income. Also called *net employment capital*.

Hybrid markets Combinations of market types, which offer elements of batch auction markets and continuous auction markets, as well as quote-driven markets.

Hypothetical events A type of scenario analysis used in stress testing that involves the evaluation of performance given events that have never happened in the markets or market outcomes to which we attach a small probability.

Illiquidity premium Compensation for the risk of loss relative to an investment's fair value if an investment needs to be converted to cash quickly.

Illusion of control A bias in which people tend to believe that they can control or influence outcomes when, in fact, they cannot. Illusion of knowledge and self-attribution biases contribute to the overconfidence bias.

Illusion of control bias A bias in which people tend to believe that they can control or influence outcomes when, in fact, they cannot. Illusion of knowledge and self-attribution biases contribute to the overconfidence bias.

Immunization An asset/liability management approach that structures investments in bonds to match (offset) liabilities' weighted-average duration; a type of dedication strategy.

Immunized time horizon The time horizon over which a portfolio's value is immunized; equal to the portfolio duration.

Implementation shortfall The difference between the money return on a notional or paper portfolio and the actual portfolio return.

Implementation shortfall strategy A strategy that attempts to minimize trading costs as measured by the implementation shortfall method. Also called *arrival price strategy*.

Implied yield A measure of the yield on the underlying bond of a futures contract implied by pricing it as though the underlying will be delivered at the futures expiration.

Incremental VaR A measure of the incremental effect of an asset on the VaR of a portfolio by measuring the difference between the portfolio's VaR while including a specified asset and the portfolio's VaR with that asset eliminated.

Indexing A common passive approach to investing that involves holding a portfolio of securities designed to replicate the returns on a specified index of securities.

Indifference curve analysis A decision-making approach whereby curves of consumption bundles, among which the decision-maker is indifferent, are constructed to identify and choose the curve within budget constraints that generates the highest utility.

Indirect commodity investment Commodity investment that involves the acquisition of indirect claims on commodities, such as equity in companies specializing in commodity production.

Inferential statistics Methods for making estimates or forecasts about a larger group from a smaller group actually observed.

Inflation An increase in the general level of prices; a decrease in the purchasing power of a unit of currency.

Inflation hedge An asset whose returns are sufficient on average to preserve purchasing power during periods of inflation.

Inflation premium Compensation for expected inflation.

Information coefficient The correlation between forecast and actual returns.

Information-motivated traders Traders that seek to trade on information that has limited value if not quickly acted upon.

Information ratio The mean excess return of the account over the benchmark (i.e., mean active return) relative to the variability of that excess return (i.e., tracking risk); a measure of risk-adjusted performance.

Infrastructure funds Funds that make private investment in public infrastructure projects in return for rights to specified revenue streams over a contracted period.

Initial public offering The initial issuance of common stock registered for public trading by a formerly private corporation.

Input uncertainty Uncertainty concerning whether the inputs are correct.

Inside ask The lowest available ask price. Also called *market ask*.

Inside bid The highest available bid price. Also called *market bid*.

Inside bid–ask spread Market ask price minus market bid price. Also called *market bid–ask spread, inside spread*, or *market spread*.

Inside quote Combination of the highest available bid price with the lowest available ask price. Also called *market quote*.

Inside spread Market ask price minus market bid price. Also called *market bid–ask spread, inside bid–ask spread,* or *market spread.*

Institutional investors Corporations or other legal entities that ultimately serve as financial intermediaries between individuals and investment markets.

Interest rate management effect With respect to fixed-income attribution analysis, a return component reflecting how well a manager predicts interest rate changes.

Interest rate parity A formula that expresses the equivalence or parity of spot and forward rates, after adjusting for differences in the interest rates.

Interest rate risk Risk related to changes in the level of interest rates.

Interest rate swap A contract between two parties (counterparties) to exchange periodic interest payments based on a specified notional amount of principal.

Interest spread With respect to banks, the average yield on earning assets minus the average percent cost of interest-bearing liabilities.

Internal rate of return The growth rate that will link the ending value of the account to its beginning value plus all intermediate cash flows; money-weighted rate of return is a synonym.

Intestate Having made no valid will; a decedent without a valid will or with a will that does not dispose of their property is considered to have died intestate.

Intrinsic value The difference between the spot exchange rate and the strike price of a currency option.

Inventory cycle A cycle measured in terms of fluctuations in inventories, typically lasting 2–4 years.

Inverse floater A floating-rate note or bond in which the coupon is adjusted to move opposite to a benchmark interest rate.

Investment currencies The high-yielding currencies in a carry trade.

Investment skill The ability to outperform an appropriate benchmark consistently over time.

Investment style A natural grouping of investment disciplines that has some predictive power in explaining the future dispersion of returns across portfolios.

Investment style indexes Indices that represent specific portions of an asset category. For example, subgroups within the US common stock asset category such as large-capitalization growth stocks.

Investment universe The set of assets that may be considered for investment.

Investor's benchmark The benchmark an investor uses to evaluate performance of a given portfolio or asset class.

Irrevocable trust A trust arrangement wherein the settlor has no ability to revoke the trust relationship.

J factor risk The risk associated with a judge's track record in adjudicating bankruptcies and restructuring.

Joint ownership with right of survivorship Jointly owned; assets held in joint ownership with right of survivorship automatically transfer to the surviving joint owner or owners outside the probate process.

Justified P/E The price-to-earnings ratio that is fair, warranted, or justified on the basis of forecasted fundamentals.

Key rate duration A method of measuring the interest rate sensitivities of a fixed-income instrument or portfolio to shifts in key points along the yield curve.

Knock-in/knock-out Features of a vanilla option that is created (or ceases to exist) when the spot exchange rate touches a pre-specified level.

Lagging economic indicators A set of economic variables whose values correlate with recent past economic activity.

Leading economic indicators A set of economic variables whose values vary with the business cycle but at a fairly consistent time interval before a turn in the business cycle.

Legal/contract risk The possibility of loss arising from the legal system's failure to enforce a contract in which an enterprise has a financial stake; for example, if a contract is voided through litigation.

Leverage-adjusted duration gap A leverage-adjusted measure of the difference between the durations of assets and liabilities which measures a bank's overall interest rate exposure.

Leveraged floating-rate note (leveraged floater) A floating-rate note or bond in which the coupon is adjusted at a multiple of a benchmark interest rate.

Leveraged recapitalization A leveraging of a company's balance sheet, usually accomplished by working with a private equity firm.

Liability As used in the text, a financial obligation.

Liability-based benchmark A benchmark structured to accurately reflect the return required to meet the future obligations of an investor and to mimic the volatility of the liabilities.

Life annuity An annuity that guarantees a monthly income to the annuitant for life.

Lifetime gratuitous transfer A lifetime gift made during the lifetime of the donor; also known as *inter vivos* transfers.

Limit order An instruction to execute an order when the best price available is at least as good as the limit price specified in the order.

Linear programming Optimization in which the objective function and constraints are linear.

Liquidity The ability to trade without delay at relatively low cost and in relatively large quantities.

Liquidity-motivated traders Traders that are motivated to trade based upon reasons other than an information advantage. For example, to release cash proceeds to facilitate the purchase of another security, adjust market exposure, or fund cash needs.

Liquidity risk Any risk of economic loss because of the need to sell relatively less liquid assets to meet liquidity requirements; the risk that a financial instrument cannot be purchased or sold without a significant concession in price because of the market's potential inability to efficiently accommodate the desired trading size.

Lock-up period A minimum initial holding period for investments during which no part of the investment can be withdrawn.

Locked up Said of investments that cannot be traded at all for some time.

Logical participation strategies Protocols for breaking up an order for execution over time. Typically used by institutional traders to participate in overall market volumes without being unduly visible.

Longevity risk The risk of outliving one's financial resources.

Loss-aversion bias A bias in which people tend to strongly prefer avoiding losses as opposed to achieving gains.

Low P/E A value investment substyle that focuses on shares selling at low prices relative to current or normal earnings.

M^2   A measure of what a portfolio would have returned if it had taken on the same total risk as the market index.

Macaulay duration   The percentage change in price for a percentage change in yield. The term, named for one of the economists who first derived it, is used to distinguish the calculation from modified duration. (See also *modified duration*).

Macro attribution   Performance attribution analysis conducted on the fund sponsor level.

Macro expectations   Expectations concerning classes of assets.

Managed futures   Pooled investment vehicles, frequently structured as limited partnerships, that invest in futures and options on futures and other instruments.

Managed futures funds   Pools of private capital managed by commodity trading advisors.

Manager continuation policies   Policies adopted to guide the manager evaluations conducted by fund sponsors. The goal of manager continuation policies is to reduce the costs of manager turnover while systematically acting on indications of future poor performance.

Manager monitoring   A formal, documented procedure that assists fund sponsors in consistently collecting information relevant to evaluating the state of their managers' operations; used to identify warning signs of adverse changes in existing managers' organizations.

Manager peer group   See *manager universe*.

Manager review   A detailed examination of a manager that currently exists within a plan sponsor's program. The manager review closely resembles the manager selection process, in both the information considered and the comprehensiveness of the analysis. The staff should review all phases of the manager's operations, just as if the manager were being initially hired.

Manager universe   A broad group of managers with similar investment disciplines. Also called *manager peer group*.

Market-adjusted implementation shortfall   The difference between the money return on a notional or paper portfolio and the actual portfolio return, adjusted using beta to remove the effect of the return on the market.

Market ask   The lowest available ask price.

Market bid   The best available bid; highest price any buyer is currently willing to pay.

Market bid–ask spread   Market ask price minus market bid price. Also called *inside bid–ask spread*, *inside spread*, or *market spread*.

Market cap weighting   See *capitalization weighting*.

Market fragmentation   A condition whereby a market contains no dominant group of sellers (or buyers) that are large enough to unduly influence the market.

Market impact   The effect of the trade on transaction prices. Also called *price impact*.

Market index   Represents the performance of a specified security market, market segment, or asset class.

Market integration   The degree to which there are no impediments or barriers to capital mobility across markets.

Market microstructure   The market structures and processes that affect how the manager's interest in buying or selling an asset is translated into executed trades (represented by trade prices and volumes).

Market model   A regression equation that specifies a linear relationship between the return on a security (or portfolio) and the return on a broad market index.

Market-not-held order   A variation of the market order designed to give the agent greater discretion than a simple market order would allow. "Not held" means that the floor broker is not required to trade at any specific price or in any specific time interval.

Market on close order   A market order to be executed at the closing of the market.

Market on open order   A market order to be executed at the opening of the market.

Market order   An instruction to execute an order as soon as possible in the public markets at the best price available.

Market oriented   With reference to equity investing, an intermediate grouping for investment disciplines that cannot be clearly categorized as value or growth.

Market quote   Combination of the highest available bid price with the lowest available ask price. Also called *inside quote*.

Market risk   The risk associated with interest rates, exchange rates, and equity prices.

Market risk bucket   In goal-based portfolio planning, that part of wealth allocated to investments intended to maintain the client's current standard of living.

Market segmentation   The degree to which there are some meaningful impediments to capital movement across markets.

Market spread   Market ask price minus market bid price. Also called *market bid–ask spread*, *inside spread*, or *inside bid–ask spread*.

Market value weighting   See *capitalization weighting*.

Marking to market   A procedure used primarily in futures markets in which the parties to a contract settle the amount owed daily. Also known as the *daily settlement*.

Mass affluent   An industry term for a segment of the private wealth marketplace that is not sufficiently wealthy to command certain individualized services.

Matrix prices   Prices determined by comparisons to other securities of similar credit risk and maturity; the result of matrix pricing.

Matrix pricing   An approach for estimating the prices of thinly traded securities based on the prices of securities with similar attributions, such as similar credit rating, maturity, or economic sector.

Maturity premium   Compensation for the increased sensitivity of the market value of debt to a change in market interest rates as maturity is extended.

Maturity variance   A measure of how much a given immunized portfolio differs from the ideal immunized portfolio consisting of a single pure discount instrument with maturity equal to the time horizon.

Maximum loss optimization   A stress test in which we would try to optimize mathematically the risk variable that would produce the maximum loss.

Mega-cap buy-out funds   A class of buyout funds that take public companies private.

Mental accounting bias   An information-processing bias in which people treat one sum of money differently from another equal-sized sum based on which mental account the money is assigned to.

Micro attribution   Performance attribution analysis carried out on the investment manager level.

Micro expectations   Expectations concerning individual assets.

Middle-market buy-out funds   A class of buyout funds that purchase private companies whose revenues and profits are too small to access capital from the public equity markets.

Midquote The halfway point between the market bid and ask prices.

Minimum-variance frontier The graph of the set of portfolios with smallest variances of return for their levels of expected return.

Minimum-variance hedge ratio A mathematical approach to determining the optimal cross hedging ratio.

Mismatch in character The potential tax inefficiency that can result if the instrument being hedged, and the tool that is being used to hedge it, produce income and loss of a different character.

Missed trade opportunity costs Unrealized profit/loss arising from the failure to execute a trade in a timely manner.

Model risk The risk that a model is incorrect or misapplied; in investments, it often refers to valuation models.

Model uncertainty Uncertainty concerning whether a selected model is correct.

Modified duration An adjustment of the duration for the level of the yield. Contrast with *Macaulay duration*.

Monetary policy Government activity concerning interest rates and the money supply.

Monetize To access an item's cash value without transferring ownership of it.

Money markets Markets for fixed-income securities with maturities of one year or less.

Money-weighted rate of return Same as the internal rate of return; the growth rate that will link the ending value of the account to its beginning value plus all intermediate cash flows.

Mortality risk The risk of loss of human capital in the event of premature death.

Multifactor model A model that explains a variable in terms of the values of a set of factors.

Multifactor model technique With respect to construction of an indexed portfolio, a technique that attempts to match the primary risk exposures of the indexed portfolio to those of the index.

Multiperiod Sharpe ratio A Sharpe ratio based on the investment's multiperiod wealth in excess of the wealth generated by the risk-free investment.

Mutuals With respect to insurance companies, companies that are owned by their policyholders, who share in the company's surplus earnings.

Natural liquidity An extensive pool of investors who are aware of and have a potential interest in buying and/or selling a security.

Net employment capital See *human capital*.

Net interest margin With respect to banks, net interest income (interest income minus interest expense) divided by average earning assets.

Net interest spread With respect to the operations of insurers, the difference between interest earned and interest credited to policyholders.

Net worth The difference between the market value of assets and liabilities.

Net worth tax or net wealth tax A tax based on a person's assets, less liabilities.

Nominal default-free bonds Conventional bonds that have no (or minimal) default risk.

Nominal gross domestic product A money measure of the goods and services produced within a country's borders. Also called *nominal GDP*.

Nominal risk-free interest rate The sum of the real risk-free interest rate and the inflation premium.

Nominal spread The spread of a bond or portfolio above the yield of a Treasury of equal maturity.

Non-deliverable forwards Forward contracts that are cash settled (in the non-controlled currency of the currency pair) rather than physically settled (the controlled currency is neither delivered nor received).

Nonfinancial risk Risks that arise from sources other than the external financial markets, such as changes in accounting rules, legal environment, or tax rates.

Nonparametric Involving minimal probability-distribution assumptions.

Nonstationarity A property of a data series that reflects more than one set of underlying statistical properties.

Normal portfolio A portfolio with exposure to sources of systematic risk that are typical for a manager, using the manager's past portfolios as a guide.

Notional principal amount The amount specified in a swap that forms the basis for calculating payment streams.

Objective function A quantitative expression of the objective or goal of a process.

Offer price The price at which a counterparty is willing to sell one unit of the base currency.

Open market operations The purchase or sale by a central bank of government securities, which are settled using reserves, to influence interest rates and the supply of credit by banks.

Open outcry auction market Public auction where representatives of buyers and sellers meet at a specified location and place verbal bids and offers.

Operational risk The risk of loss from failures in a company's systems and procedures (for example, due to computer failures or human failures) or events completely outside of the control of organizations (which would include "acts of God" and terrorist actions).

Opportunistic participation strategies Passive trading combined with the opportunistic seizing of liquidity.

Optimization With respect to portfolio construction, a procedure for determining the best portfolios according to some criterion.

Optimizer A heuristic, formula, algorithm, or program that uses risk, return, correlation, or other variables to determine the most appropriate asset allocation or asset mix for a portfolio.

Option-adjusted spread (OAS) The current spread over the benchmark yield minus that component of the spread that is attributable to any embedded optionality in the instrument.

Options on futures Options on a designated futures contract. Also called *futures options*.

Options on physicals With respect to options, exchange-traded option contracts that have cash instruments rather than futures contracts on cash instruments as the underlying.

Order-driven markets Markets in which transaction prices are established by public limit orders to buy or sell a security at specified prices.

Ordinary life insurance A type of life insurance policy that involves coverage for the whole of the insured's life. Also called *whole life insurance*.

Orphan equities investing A distressed securities investment discipline that involves investment in orphan equities that are perceived to be undervalued.

Orphan equity Investment in the newly issued equity of a company emerging from reorganization.

Output gap The difference between the value of GDP estimated as if the economy were on its trend growth path (potential output) and the actual value of GDP.

Overall trade balance The sum of the current account (reflecting exports and imports) and the financial account (consisting of portfolio flows).

Overbought When a market has trended too far in one direction and is vulnerable to a trend reversal, or correction.

Overconfidence bias A bias in which people demonstrate unwarranted faith in their own intuitive reasoning, judgments, and/or cognitive abilities.

Overconfidence trap The tendency of individuals to overestimate the accuracy of their forecasts.

Oversold The opposite of overbought; see *overbought*.

Pairs trade A basic long–short trade in which an investor is long and short equal currency amounts of two common stocks in a single industry. Also called *pairs arbitrage*.

Panel method A method of capital market expectations setting that involves using the viewpoints of a panel of experts.

Partial correlation In multivariate problems, the correlation between two variables after controlling for the effects of the other variables in the system.

Partial fill Execution of a purchase or sale for fewer shares than was stipulated in the order.

Participate (do not initiate) order A variant of the market-not-held order. The broker is deliberately low-key and waits for and responds to the initiatives of more active traders.

Passive investment strategies A buy-and-hold strategy to investing in which an investor does not make portfolio changes based upon short-term expectations of changing market or security performance.

Passive management A buy-and-hold approach to investing in which an investor does not make portfolio changes based upon short-term expectations of changing market or security performance.

Passive traders Traders that seek liquidity in their rebalancing transactions, but are much more concerned with the cost of trading.

Payment netting A means of settling payments in which the amount owed by the first party to the second is netted with the amount owed by the second party to the first; only the net difference is paid.

Pension funds Funds consisting of assets set aside to support a promise of retirement income.

Pension surplus Pension assets at market value minus the present value of pension liabilities.

Percentage-of-portfolio rebalancing Rebalancing is triggered based on set thresholds stated as a percentage of the portfolio's value.

Percentage-of-volume strategy A logical participation strategy in which trading takes place in proportion to overall market volume (typically at a rate of 5–20 percent) until the order is completed.

Perfect markets Markets without any frictional costs.

Performance appraisal The evaluation of portfolio performance; a quantitative assessment of a manager's investment skill.

Performance attribution A comparison of an account's performance with that of a designated benchmark and the identification and quantification of sources of differential returns.

Performance-based fee Fees specified by a combination of a base fee plus an incentive fee for performance in excess of a benchmark's.

Performance evaluation The measurement and assessment of the outcomes of investment management decisions.

Performance measurement A component of performance evaluation; the relatively simple procedure of calculating an asset's or portfolio's rate of return.

Performance netting risk For entities that fund more than one strategy and have asymmetric incentive fee arrangements with the portfolio managers, the potential for loss in cases where the net performance of the group of managers generates insufficient fee revenue to fully cover contractual payout obligations to all portfolio managers with positive performance.

Periodic auction markets Auction markets where multilateral trading occurs at a single price at a prespecified point in time.

Permanent income hypothesis The hypothesis that consumers' spending behavior is largely determined by their long-run income expectations.

Personal risk bucket In goal-based portfolio planning, that part of wealth allocated to investments intended to protect the client from a drastic decrease in lifestyle.

Plan sponsor The trustee, company, or employer responsible for a public or private institutional investment plan.

Pledging requirement With respect to banks, a required collateral use of assets.

Point estimate A single-valued estimate of a quantity, as opposed to an estimate in terms of a range of values.

Policy portfolio A synonym of strategic asset allocation; the portfolio resulting from strategic asset allocation considered as a process.

Policyholder reserves With respect to an insurance company, an amount representing the estimated payments to policyholders, as determined by actuaries, based on the types and terms of the various insurance policies issued by the company.

Political risk The risk of war, government collapse, political instability, expropriation, confiscation, or adverse changes in taxation. Also called *geopolitical risk*.

Portable Moveable. With reference to a pension plan, one in which a plan participant can move his or her share of plan assets to a new plan, subject to certain rules, vesting schedules, and possible tax penalties and payments.

Portable alpha A strategy involving the combining of multiple positions (e.g., long and short positions) so as to separate the alpha (unsystematic risk) from beta (systematic risk) in an investment.

Portfolio segmentation The creation of subportfolios according to the product mix for individual segments or lines of business.

Portfolio trade A trade in which a number of securities are traded as a single unit. Also called *program trade* or *basket trade*.

Position a trade To take the other side of a trade, acting as a principal with capital at risk.

Post-trade transparency Degree to which completed trades are quickly and accurately reported to the public.

Potential output The value of GDP if the economy were on its trend growth path.

Preferred return With respect to the compensation of private equity fund managers, a hurdle rate.

Premium Regarding life insurance, the asset paid by the policy holder to an insurer who, in turn, has a contractual obligation to pay death benefit proceeds to the beneficiary named in the policy.

Prepackaged bankruptcy A bankruptcy in which the debtor seeks agreement from creditors on the terms of a reorganization before the reorganization filing.

Prepaid variable forward A collar and loan combined within a single instrument.

Present value distribution of cash flows A list showing what proportion of a portfolio's duration is attributable to each future cash flow.

Present value of a basis point (PVBP) The change in the bond price for a 1 basis point change in yield. Also called *basis point value* (BPV).

Pretrade transparency Ability of individuals to quickly, easily, and inexpensively obtain accurate information about quotes and trades.

Price discovery Adjustment of transaction prices to balance supply and demand.

Price improvement Execution at a price that is better than the price quoted at the time of order placement.

Price risk The risk of fluctuations in market price.

Price uncertainty Uncertainty about the price at which an order will execute.

Price value of a basis point (PVBP) The change in the bond price for a 1 basis point change in yield. Also called *basis point value* (BPV).

Price weighted With respect to index construction, an index in which each security in the index is weighted according to its absolute share price.

Price weighting Security weighting scheme in which constituents are weighted in proportion to their prices.

Priced risk Risk for which investors demand compensation.

Primary capital Assets held outside a concentrated position that are at least sufficient to provide for the owner's lifetime spending needs.

Primary risk factors With respect to valuation, the major influences on pricing.

Prime brokerage A suite of services that is often specified to include support in accounting and reporting, leveraged trade execution, financing, securities lending (related to short-selling activities), and start-up advice (for new entities).

Principal trade A trade with a broker in which the broker commits capital to facilitate the prompt execution of the trader's order to buy or sell.

Private equity Ownership interests in non-publicly-traded companies.

Private equity funds Pooled investment vehicles investing in generally highly illiquid assets; includes venture capital funds and buyout funds.

Private exchange A method for handling undiversified positions with built-in capital gains in which shares that are a component of an index are exchanged for shares of an index mutual fund in a privately arranged transaction with the fund.

Private placement memorandum A document used to raise venture capital financing when funds are raised through an agent.

Probate The legal process to confirm the validity of a will so that executors, heirs, and other interested parties can rely on its authenticity.

Profit-sharing plans A defined-contribution plan in which contributions are based, at least in part, on the plan sponsor's profits.

Projected benefit obligation (PBO) A measure of a pension plan's liability that reflects accumulated service in the same manner as the ABO but also projects future variables, such as compensation increases.

Prospect theory An alternative to expected utility theory, it assigns value to gains and losses (changes in wealth) rather than to final wealth, and probabilities are replaced by decision weights. In prospect theory, the shape of a decision maker's value function is assumed to differ between the domain of gains and the domain of losses.

Protective put An option strategy in which a long position in an asset is combined with a long position in a put.

Proxy hedge See *cross hedge*.

Proxy hedging Hedging that involves the use of a forward contract between the home currency and a currency that is highly correlated with the foreign asset's currency.

Prudence trap The tendency to temper forecasts so that they do not appear extreme; the tendency to be overly cautious in forecasting.

Public good A good that is not divisible and not excludable (a consumer cannot be denied it).

Purchasing power parity The theory that movements in an exchange rate should offset any difference in the inflation rates between two countries.

Pure sector allocation return A component of attribution analysis that relates relative returns to the manager's sector-weighting decisions. Calculated as the difference between the allocation (weight) of the portfolio to a given sector and the portfolio's benchmark weight for that sector, multiplied by the difference between the sector benchmark's return and the overall portfolio's benchmark return, summed across all sectors.

Put spread A strategy used to reduce the upfront cost of buying a protective put, it involves buying a put option and writing another put option.

Quality control charts A graphical means of presenting performance appraisal data; charts illustrating the performance of an actively managed account versus a selected benchmark.

Quality option With respect to Treasury futures, the option of which acceptable Treasury issue to deliver. Also called *swap option*.

Quantitative easing A policy measure in which a central bank buys financial assets to inject a predetermined quantity of money in the financial system.

Quote-driven markets Markets that rely on dealers to establish firm prices at which securities can be bought and sold. Also called *dealer markets*.

Quoted depth The number of shares available for purchase or sale at the quoted bid and ask prices.

Rate duration A fixed-income instrument's or portfolio's sensitivity to a change in key maturity, holding constant all other points along the yield curve.

Ratio spread An option strategy in which a long position in a certain number of options is offset by a short position in a certain number of other options on the same underlying, resulting in a risk-free position.

Rational economic man A self-interested, risk-averse individual who has the ability to make judgments using all available information in order to maximize his/her expected utility.

Re-base With reference to index construction, to change the time period used as the base of the index.

Real estate Interests in land or structures attached to land.

Glossary

Real estate investment trusts (REITs) Publicly traded equities representing pools of money invested in real estate properties and/or real estate debt.

Real option An option involving decisions related to tangible assets or processes.

Real risk-free interest rate The single-period interest rate for a completely risk-free security if no inflation were expected.

Rebalancing ratio A quantity involved in reestablishing the dollar duration of a portfolio to a desired level, equal to the original dollar duration divided by the new dollar duration.

Recallability trap The tendency of forecasts to be overly influenced by events that have left a strong impression on a person's memory.

Recession A broad-based economic downturn, conventionally defined as two successive quarterly declines in GDP.

Reference entity An entity, such as a bond issuer, specified in a derivatives contract.

Regime A distinct governing set of relationships.

Regret The feeling that an opportunity has been missed; typically an expression of *hindsight bias*.

Regret-aversion bias An emotional bias in which people tend to avoid making decisions that will result in action out of fear that the decision will turn out poorly.

Regulatory risk The risk associated with the uncertainty of how a transaction will be regulated or with the potential for regulations to change.

Reinvestment risk The risk of reinvesting coupon income or principal at a rate less than the original coupon or purchase rate.

Relative economic strength forecasting approach An exchange rate forecasting approach that suggests that a strong pace of economic growth in a country creates attractive investment opportunities, increasing the demand for the country's currency and causing it to appreciate.

Relative strength indicators A price momentum indicator that involves comparing a stock's performance during a specific period either to its own past performance or to the performance of some group of stocks.

Remaindermen Beneficiaries of a trust; having a claim on the residue.

Representativeness bias A belief perseverance bias in which people tend to classify new information based on past experiences and classifications.

Repurchase agreement A contract involving the sale of securities such as Treasury instruments coupled with an agreement to repurchase the same securities at a later date.

Repurchase yield The negative of the expected percent change in number of shares outstanding, in the Grinold–Kroner model.

Resampled efficient frontier The set of resampled efficient portfolios.

Resampled efficient portfolio An efficient portfolio based on simulation.

Residence jurisdiction A framework used by a country to determine the basis for taxing income, based on residency.

Residence–residence conflict When two countries claim residence of the same individual, subjecting the individual's income to taxation by both countries.

Residence–source conflict When tax jurisdiction is claimed by an individual's country of residence and the country where some of their assets are sourced; the most common source of double taxation.

Residue With respect to trusts, the funds remaining in a trust when the last income beneficiary dies.

Resistance levels Price points on dealers' order boards where one would expect to see a clustering of offers.

Retired-lives The portion of a pension fund's liabilities associated with retired workers.

Returns-based benchmarks Benchmarks constructed by examining a portfolio's sensitivity to a set of factors, such as the returns for various style indexes (e.g., small-cap value, small-cap growth, large-cap value, and large-cap growth).

Returns-based style analysis An approach to style analysis that focuses on characteristics of the overall portfolio as revealed by a portfolio's realized returns.

Reverse optimization A technique for reverse engineering the expected returns implicit in a diversified market portfolio.

Revocable trust A trust arrangement wherein the settlor (who originally transfers assets to fund the trust) retains the right to rescind the trust relationship and regain title to the trust assets.

Risk budgeting The establishment of objectives for individuals, groups, or divisions of an organization that takes into account the allocation of an acceptable level of risk.

Risk exposure A source of risk. Also, the state of being exposed or vulnerable to a risk.

Risk premium approach An approach to forecasting the return of a risky asset that views its expected return as the sum of the risk-free rate of interest and one or more risk premiums.

Risk profile A detailed tabulation of the index's risk exposures.

Risk reversal With respect to foreign exchange option strategies, one involving a long position in a call option and a short position in a put option.

Risk tolerance The capacity to accept risk; the level of risk an investor (or organization) is willing and able to bear.

Risk tolerance function An assessment of an investor's tolerance to risk over various levels of portfolio outcomes.

Roll return The component of the return on a commodity futures contract that comes from rolling long futures positions forward through time. Also called *roll yield*.

Rolling return The moving average of the holding-period returns for a specified period (e.g., a calendar year) that matches the investor's time horizon.

Sale and leaseback A transaction wherein the owner of a property sells that property and then immediately leases it back from the buyer at a rate and term acceptable to the new owner and on financial terms consistent with the marketplace.

Sample estimator A formula for assigning a unique value (a point estimate) to a population parameter.

Sample-size neglect A type of representativeness bias in which financial market participants incorrectly assume that small sample sizes are representative of populations (or "real" data).

Sandwich spread An option strategy that is equivalent to a short butterfly spread.

Satisfice A combination of "satisfy" and "suffice" describing decisions, actions, and outcomes that may not be optimal, but are adequate.

Savings–investment imbalances forecasting approach An exchange rate forecasting approach that explains currency movements in terms of the effects of domestic savings–investment imbalances on the exchange rate.

Scenario analysis A risk management technique involving the examination of the performance of a portfolio under specified situations. Closely related to *stress testing*.

Seagull spread   An extension of the risk reversal foreign exchange option strategy that limits downside risk.

Secondary offering   An offering after the initial public offering of securities.

Sector/quality effect   In a fixed-income attribution analysis, a measure of a manager's ability to select the "right" issuing sector and quality group.

Security selection effect   In a fixed-income attribution analysis, the residual of the security's total return after other effects are accounted for; a measure of the return due to ability in security selection.

Segmentation   With respect to the management of insurance company portfolios, the notional subdivision of the overall portfolio into sub-portfolios each of which is associated with a specified group of insurance contracts.

Self-attribution bias   A bias in which people take personal credit for successes and attribute failures to external factors outside the individual's control.

Self-control bias   A bias in which people fail to act in pursuit of their long-term, overarching goals because of a lack of self-discipline.

Sell side   Broker/dealers that sell securities and make recommendations for various customers, such as investment managers and institutional investors.

Semiactive management   A variant of active management. In a semiactive portfolio, the manager seeks to outperform a given benchmark with tightly controlled risk relative to the benchmark. Also called *enhanced indexing* or *risk-controlled active management*.

Semivariance   A measure of downside risk. The average of squared deviations that fall below the mean.

Separate property regime   A marital property regime under which each spouse is able to own and control property as an individual.

Settlement date   The designated date at which the parties to a trade must transact. Also called *payment date*.

Settlement netting risk   The risk that a liquidator of a counterparty in default could challenge a netting arrangement so that profitable transactions are realized for the benefit of creditors.

Settlement risk   When settling a contract, the risk that one party could be in the process of paying the counterparty while the counterparty is declaring bankruptcy.

Settlor (or grantor)   An entity that transfers assets to a trustee, to be held and managed for the benefit of the trust beneficiaries.

Shari'a   The law of Islam. In addition to the law of the land, some follow guidance provided by Shari'a or Islamic law.

Sharpe ratio   A measure of risk-adjusted performance that compares excess returns to the total risk of the account, where total risk is measured by the account's standard deviation of returns. Also called *reward-to-variability*.

Short sale against the box   Shorting a security that is held long.

Shortfall risk   The risk that portfolio value will fall below some minimum acceptable level during a stated time horizon; the risk of not achieving a specified return target.

Shrinkage estimation   Estimation that involves taking a weighted average of a historical estimate of a parameter and some other parameter estimate, where the weights reflect the analyst's relative belief in the estimates.

Shrinkage estimator   The formula used in shrinkage estimation of a parameter.

Sign-constrained optimization   An optimization that constrains asset class weights to be nonnegative and to sum to 1.

Smart routing   The use of algorithms to intelligently route an order to the most liquid venue.

Smoothing rule   With respect to spending rates, a rule that averages asset values over a period of time in order to dampen the spending rate's response to asset value fluctuation.

Social proof   A bias in which individuals tend to follow the beliefs of a group.

Socially responsible investing   An approach to investing that integrates ethical values and societal concerns with investment decisions. Also called *ethical investing*.

Soft dollars   The use of commissions to buy services other than execution services. Also called *soft dollar arrangements* or *soft commissions*.

Sole ownership   Owned by one person; assets held in sole ownership are typically considered part of a decedent's estate. The transfer of their ownership is dictated by the decedent's will through the probate process.

Solow residual   A measure of the growth in total factor productivity that is based on an economic growth model developed by economist Robert M. Solow.

Sortino ratio   A performance appraisal ratio that replaces standard deviation in the Sharpe ratio with downside deviation.

Source jurisdiction   A framework used by a country to determine the basis for taxing income or transfers. A country that taxes income as a source within its borders imposes source jurisdiction.

Source–source conflict   When two countries claim source jurisdiction of the same asset; both countries may claim that the income is derived from their jurisdiction.

Sovereign risk   A form of credit risk in which the borrower is the government of a sovereign nation.

Spot return   The component of the return on a commodity futures contract that comes from changes in the underlying spot prices via the cost-of-carry model. Also called *price return*.

Spread duration   The sensitivity of a non-Treasury security's price to a widening or narrowing of the spread over Treasuries.

Spread risk   Risk related to changes in the spread between Treasuries and non-Treasuries.

Stale price bias   Bias that arises from using prices that are stale because of infrequent trading.

Static approach   With respect to strategic asset allocation, an approach that does not account for links between optimal decisions in future time periods.

Static hedge   A hedge that is not sensitive to changes in the price of the asset hedged.

Static spread   The constant spread above the Treasury spot curve that equates the calculated price of the security to the market price. Also called *zero-volatility spread*.

Stationary   A series of data for which the parameters that describe a return-generating process are stable.

Status quo bias   An emotional bias in which people do nothing (i.e., maintain the "status quo") instead of making a change.

Status quo trap   The tendency for forecasts to perpetuate recent observations—that is, to predict no change from the recent past.

Sterling ratio The compound annualized rate of return over a specified time period divided by the average yearly maximum drawdown over the same time period less an arbitrary 10 percent.

Stock companies With respect to insurance companies, companies that have issued common equity shares.

Stock index futures Futures contracts on a specified stock index.

Stops Stop-loss orders involve leaving bids or offers away from the current market price to be filled if the market reaches those levels.

Straddle An option strategy involving the purchase of a put and a call on the same underlying with the same exercise price and expiration date. If the put and call are held long, it is a long straddle; if they are held short, it is a short straddle.

Straight-through processing Systems that simplify transaction processing through the minimization of manual and/or duplicative intervention in the process from trade placement to settlement.

Strangle A variation on a straddle in which the put and call have different exercise prices; if the put and call are held long, it is a long strangle; if they are held short, it is a short strangle.

Strap An option strategy involving the purchase of two calls and one put.

Strategic asset allocation 1) The process of allocating money to IPS-permissible asset classes that integrates the investor's return objectives, risk tolerance, and investment constraints with long-run capital market expectations. 2) The result of the above process, also known as the policy portfolio.

Strategic buyers Buyers who have a strategic motive (e.g., realization of synergies) for seeking to buy a company.

Strategy benchmarks See custom security-based benchmarks.

Stratified sampling A sampling method that guarantees that subpopulations of interest are represented in the sample. Also called *representative sampling*.

Strike spread A spread used to determine the strike price for the payoff of a credit option.

Strip An option strategy involving the purchase of two puts and one call.

Structural level of unemployment The level of unemployment resulting from scarcity of a factor of production.

Structured note A variation of a floating-rate note that has some type of unusual characteristic such as a leverage factor or in which the rate moves opposite to interest rates.

Style drift Inconsistency in style.

Style index A securities index intended to reflect the average returns to a given style.

Stylized scenario A type of analysis often used in stress testing. It involves simulating the movement in at least one interest rate, exchange rate, stock price, or commodity price relevant to the portfolio.

Sunshine trades Public display of a transaction (usually high-volume) in advance of the actual order.

Support levels Price points on dealers' order boards where one would expect to see a clustering of bids.

Surplus The difference between the value of assets and the present value of liabilities. With respect to an insurance company, the net difference between the total assets and total liabilities (equivalent to policyholders' surplus for a mutual insurance company and stockholders' equity for a stock company).

Surplus capital Capital that is in excess of primary capital.

Surplus efficient frontier The graph of the set of portfolios that maximize expected surplus for given levels of standard deviation of surplus.

Survey method A method of capital market expectations setting that involves surveying experts.

Survival probability The probability an individual survives in a given year; used to determine expected cash flow required in retirement.

Survivorship bias Bias that arises in a data series when managers with poor track records exit the business and are dropped from the database whereas managers with good records remain; when a data series as of a given date reflects only entities that have survived to that date.

Swap rate The interest rate applicable to the pay-fixed-rate side of an interest rate swap.

Symmetric cash flow matching A cash flow matching technique that allows cash flows occurring both before and after the liability date to be used to meet a liability; allows for the short-term borrowing of funds to satisfy a liability prior to the liability due date.

Tactical asset allocation Asset allocation that involves making short-term adjustments to asset class weights based on short-term predictions of relative performance among asset classes.

Tactical rebalancing A variation of calendar rebalancing that specifies less frequent rebalancing when markets appear to be trending and more frequent rebalancing when they are characterized by reversals.

Tail value at risk (or conditional tail expectation) The VaR plus the expected loss in excess of VaR, when such excess loss occurs.

Target covariance matrix A component of shrinkage estimation; allows the analyst to model factors that are believed to influence the data over periods longer than observed in the historical sample.

Target semivariance The average squared deviation below a target value.

Target value The value that the portfolio manager seeks to ensure; the value that the life insurance company has guaranteed the policyholder.

Tax avoidance Developing strategies that minimize tax, while conforming to both the spirit and the letter of the tax codes of jurisdictions with taxing authority.

Tax efficiency The proportion of the expected pretax total return that will be retained after taxes.

Tax evasion The practice of circumventing tax obligations by illegal means such as misreporting or not reporting relevant information to tax authorities.

Tax-exempt bonds Bonds whose interest payments are in whole or in part exempt from taxation; they are typically issued by governmental or certain government-sponsored entities.

Tax premium Compensation for the effect of taxes on the after-tax return of an asset.

Tax risk The uncertainty associated with tax laws.

Taylor rule A rule linking a central bank's target short-term interest rate to the rate of growth of the economy and inflation.

Term life insurance A type of life insurance policy that provides coverage for a specified length of time and accumulates little or no cash values.

Territorial tax system A framework used by a country to determine the basis for taxing income or transfers. A country that taxes income as a source within its borders imposes source jurisdiction.

Testamentary gratuitous transfer The bequeathing or transfer of assets upon one's death. From a recipient's perspective, it is called an inheritance.

Testator A person who makes a will.

Theta The change in price of an option associated with a one-day reduction in its time to expiration; the rate at which an option's time value decays.

Tick The smallest possible price movement of a security.

Time deposit A deposit requiring advance notice prior to a withdrawal.

Time-series estimators Estimators that are based on lagged values of the variable being forecast; often consist of lagged values of other selected variables.

Time to expiration The time remaining in the life of a derivative, typically expressed in years.

Time value The difference between the market price of an option and its intrinsic value, determined by the uncertainty of the underlying over the remaining life of the option.

Time-weighted average price (TWAP) strategy A logical participation strategy that assumes a flat volume profile and trades in proportion to time.

Time-weighted rate of return The compound rate of growth over a stated evaluation period of one unit of money initially invested in the account.

Timing option With respect to certain futures contracts, the option that results from the ability of the short position to decide when in the delivery month actual delivery will take place.

Tobin's q An asset-based valuation measure that is equal to the ratio of the market value of debt and equity to the replacement cost of total assets.

Top-down Proceeding from the macroeconomy, to the economic sector level, to the industry level, to the firm level.

Total factor productivity (TFP) A variable which accounts for that part of Y not directly accounted for by the levels of the production factors (K and L).

Total future liability With respect to defined-benefit pension plans, the present value of accumulated and projected future service benefits, including the effects of projected future compensation increases.

Total rate of return A measure of the increase in the investor's wealth due to both investment income (for example, dividends and interest) and capital gains (both realized and unrealized).

Total return The rate of return taking into account capital appreciation/depreciation and income. Often qualified as follows: **Nominal** returns are unadjusted for inflation; **real** returns are adjusted for inflation; **pretax** returns are returns before taxes; **post-tax** returns are returns after taxes are paid on investment income and realized capital gains.

Total return analysis Analysis of the expected effect of a trade on the portfolio's total return, given an interest rate forecast.

Total return equity swap A swap contract that involves a series of exchanges of the total return on a specified asset or equity index in return for specified fixed or floating rate payments.

Total return swap A swap in which one party agrees to pay the total return on a security. Often used as a credit derivative, in which the underlying is a bond.

Tracking risk The condition in which the performance of a portfolio does not match the performance of an index that serves as the portfolio's benchmark. Also called *tracking error, tracking error volatility,* or *active risk.*

Trade blotter A device for entering and tracking trade executions and orders to trade.

Trade settlement Completion of a trade wherein purchased financial instruments are transferred to the buyer and the buyer transfers money to the seller.

Trading activity In fixed-income attribution analysis, the effect of sales and purchases of bonds over a given period; the total portfolio return minus the other components determining the management effect in an attribution analysis.

Transaction exposure The risk associated with a foreign exchange rate on a specific business transaction such as a purchase or sale.

Translation exposure The risk associated with the conversion of foreign financial statements into domestic currency.

Transparency Availability of timely and accurate market and trade information.

Treasury spot curve The term structure of Treasury zero coupon bonds.

Twist With respect to the yield curve, a movement in contrary directions of interest rates at two maturities; a nonparallel movement in the yield curve.

Type I error With respect to manager selection, keeping (or hiring) managers with zero value-added. (Rejecting the null hypothesis when it is correct).

Type II error With respect to manager selection, firing (or not hiring) managers with positive value-added. (Not rejecting the null hypothesis when it is incorrect).

Unconstrained optimization Optimization that places no constraints on asset class weights except that they sum to 1. May produce negative asset weights, which implies borrowing or shorting of assets.

Underfunded plan A pension plan in which the ratio of the value of plan assets to the present value of plan liabilities is less than 100 percent.

Underlying An asset that trades in a market in which buyers and sellers meet, decide on a price, and the seller then delivers the asset to the buyer and receives payment. The underlying is the asset or other derivative on which a particular derivative is based. The market for the underlying is also referred to as the spot market.

Underwriting (profitability) cycle A cycle affecting the profitability of insurance companies' underwriting operations.

Unhedged return A foreign asset return stated in terms of the investor's home currency.

Unit-linked life insurance A type of ordinary life insurance in which death benefits and cash values are linked to the investment performance of a policyholder-selected pool of investments held in a so-called separate account. Also called *variable life insurance.*

Universal life insurance A type of life insurance policy that provides for premium flexibility, an adjustable face amount of death benefits, and current market interest rates on the savings element.

Unrelated business income With respect to the US tax code, income that is not substantially related to a foundation's charitable purposes.

Unstructured modeling Modeling without a theory on the underlying structure.

Uptick rules Trading rules that specify that a short sale must not be on a downtick relative to the last trade at a different price.

Urgency of the trade The importance of certainty of execution.

Utility The level of relative satisfaction received from the consumption of goods and services.

Utility theory Theory whereby people maximize the present value of utility subject to a present value budget constraint.

Valuation reserve With respect to insurance companies, an allowance, created by a charge against earnings, to provide for losses in the value of the assets.

Value The amount for which one can sell something, or the amount one must pay to acquire something.

Value at risk (VaR) A probability-based measure of loss potential for a company, a fund, a portfolio, a transaction, or a strategy over a specified period of time.

Value-motivated traders Traders that act on value judgments based on careful, sometimes painstaking research. They trade only when the price moves into their value range.

Value weighted With respect to index construction, an index in which each security in the index is weighted according to its market capitalization. Also called *market-capitalization weighted*.

Variable annuity A life annuity in which the periodic payment varies depending on stock prices.

Variable life insurance A type of ordinary life insurance in which death benefits and cash values are linked to the investment performance of a policyholder-selected pool of investments held in a so-called separate account. Also called *unit-linked life insurance*.

Variable prepaid forward A monetization strategy that involves the combination of a collar with a loan against the value of the underlying shares. When the loan comes due, shares are sold to pay off the loan and part of any appreciation is shared with the lender.

Variable universal life A type of life insurance policy that combines the flexibility of universal life with the investment choice flexibility of variable life. Also called *flexible-premium variable life*.

Vega A measure of the sensitivity of an option's price to changes in the underlying's volatility.

Venture capital The equity financing of new or growing private companies.

Venture capital firms Firms representing dedicated pools of capital for providing equity or equity-linked financing to privately held companies.

Venture capital fund A pooled investment vehicle for venture capital investing.

Venture capital trusts An exchange-traded, closed-end vehicle for venture capital investing.

Venture capitalists Specialists who seek to identify companies that have good business opportunities but need financial, managerial, and strategic support.

Vested With respect to pension benefits or assets, said of an unconditional ownership interest.

Vintage year With reference to a private equity fund, the year it closed.

Vintage year effects The effects on returns shared by private equity funds closed in the same year.

Volatility Represented by the Greek letter sigma (σ), the standard deviation of price outcomes associated with an underlying asset.

Volatility clustering The tendency for large (small) swings in prices to be followed by large (small) swings of random direction.

Volume-weighted average price (VWAP) The average price at which a security is traded during the day, where each trade price is weighted by the fraction of the day's volume associated with the trade.

Volume-weighted average price (VWAP) strategy A logical participation strategy that involves breaking up an order over time according to a prespecified volume profile.

Wealth relative The ending value of one unit of money invested at specified rates of return.

Whole life insurance A type of life insurance policy that involves coverage for the whole of the insured's life. Also called *ordinary life insurance*.

Wild card option A provision allowing a short futures contract holder to delay delivery of the underlying.

Will A document associated with estate planning that outlines the rights others will have over one's property after death. Also called *testament*.

Within-sector selection return In attribution analysis, a measure of the impact of a manager's security selection decisions relative to the holdings of the sector benchmark.

Worst-case scenario analysis A stress test in which we examine the worst case that we actually expect to occur.

Yardeni model An equity valuation model, more complex than the Fed model, that incorporates the expected growth rate in earnings.

Yield beta A measure of the sensitivity of a bond's yield to a general measure of bond yields in the market that is used to refine the hedge ratio.

Yield curve The relationship between yield and time to maturity.

Yield curve risk Risk related to changes in the shape of the yield curve.

Yield to worst The yield on a callable bond that assumes a bond is called at the earliest opportunity.

Zero-cost collar A transaction in which a position in the underlying is protected by buying a put and selling a call with the premium from the sale of the call offsetting the premium from the purchase of the put. It can also be used to protect a floating-rate borrower against interest rate increases with the premium on a long cap offsetting the premium on a short floor.

Zero-premium collar A hedging strategy involving the simultaneous purchase of puts and sale of call options on a stock. The puts are struck below and the calls are struck above the underlying's market price.

Index

A

accountable benchmarks, 15n.12
accumulated value, of immunized portfolios, 31–33
active/immunization combination of portfolios, 106
active investing
  with benchmark bond indexes, 27–29
    activities of active managers, 27–28
    total return and scenario analysis, 28–29
  in equities, 166–167, 184–210
    and equity styles, 184–204
    long–short investing, 205–210
    sell disciplines, 210
    socially responsible investing, 204–205
    trading frequency, 210
  semiactive equity investing, 165–166, 211–213
    derivatives- vs. stock-based, 211, 213
    and Fundamental Law of Active Management, 212
active management
  of benchmark bond indexes, 9, 27–28
  defined, 165
  of equity investments, 165–166
  full-blown, 10
  Fundamental Law of Active Management, 212
  of international bond investments, 129–131
  by larger risk factor mismatches, 10
  semiactive, 165–166
active/passive combination of portfolios, 106
active returns, 166
active risk
  and portfolio manager allocation, 215–216
  and tracking risk, 166
  true, 219–220
ad valorem fees, 223, 229–230
allocation
  asset
    equity total return swaps in, 183–184
    for global credit bond portfolio management, 87–88
    tactical, 184
  equities
    for indexes, 200–201
    for pension funds, 163
alpha
  alpha and beta separation, 221
  defined, 205
  in fixed-income manager selection, 141
  in long–short investing, 205–206
  portable, 206, 221
  in semiactive equity investing, 211–213
Apple Corporation, 186
Argentina, 88
Asia, 80. *see also specific countries*

Asian financial crisis (1997-1998), 76
  and "buy-and-hold" investors, 79
  emerging market debt, 137
  and sector rotation, 87, 88
  and "story" disagreement, 78–79
  ultra-long maturities in, 84
asset allocation
  equity total return swaps in, 183–184
  for global credit bond portfolio management, 87–88
  tactical, 184
asset/liability management, 121
assets
  convexity of, 41–42
  as inflation hedges, 163–164
assets under management (AUM) fees, 223
asset swaps, 84
assumptions, of classical single-period immunization theory, 37
AUM fees. *see* assets under management fees
Australia
  equity real rates of return, 164
  pension fund equity allocations, 163
  total returns between government bond indexes, 128
Australian dollar, 132–133

B

Bailey, Jeffery V., 15
bankers' acceptances, as interest rate swap benchmarks, 120
barbell portfolios, 43, 84
barbell strategy, credit, 86
Barclays, 66n.1
Barclays Capital Corporate Bond Index, 14
Barclays Capital Corporate High-Yield Bond Index, 12, 13
Barclays Capital Corporate Intermediate Bond Index, 12, 13
Barclays Capital Emerging Markets USD Aggregate Bond Index, 16–17
Barclays Capital Global Aggregate Bond Index, 24
Barclays Capital US Aggregate Bond Index, 14
Barclays Capital US Aggregate Index, 56
basis (term), 118
basis risk, 118
basket trades, 182
Becton Dickinson & Co., 188
Belgium, 164
benchmark bond indexes, 7–29
  active strategies, 27–29
  classification of strategies, 9–10
  indexing strategies, 11–27
    benchmarks for, 11–13
    bond index investability, 13–17
    enhanced, 25–27
    reasons for using, 10–11

risk exposures with, 17–21
and tracking risk, 22–25
monitoring/adjusting portfolio with, 29
benchmarks
  indexes as, 11–13, 171–174
  Industry Classification Benchmark, 232
  investor's, 219
  valid, 15–16
Best Practice Guidelines Governing Analyst/Corporate Issue Relations, 207
beta
  alpha and beta separation, 221
  country, 131
  yield, 120
biases, in market-oriented investment styles, 189
binary credit options
  and credit spread options/forwards, 126–127
  defined, 123
blend investment style, 188–189
BofA Merrill Lynch 1–3 Year Corporate Bond Index, 12, 13
BofA Merrill Lynch Long-Term Corporate Bond Index, 12, 13
Bogle, John, 167
bond duration
  and bond options, 121–122
  of foreign bonds, 131
  and variance, 114
bond options, 121–122
bonds. *see also* international bond investing
  Brady, 137
  corporate, 21, 76
  Eurobonds, 73, 83
  foreign, 131
  inflation's effects on, 164
  investment-grade credit
    credit spread, 86–87
    market for, 82–83
    returns, 67
    Sharpe ratio, 68
  management of bond portfolios (*see* fixed-income portfolio management)
  primary risk factors for, 9
bottom-up research approaches, 70, 230, 231
Brady bonds, 137
Brady plan, 137
Brazil, 87
breakeven spread analysis, 136–137
British Gas, 87
buffering, 199
bullet structures, 83–84
  and corporate bond market, 83
  front-end, 84
  and global bond market, 74
  and immunization, 43

bullet structures (continued)
  intermediate credit, 84
  maturity, 74
  structure trades, 77
  in US credit markets, 82–83
"bums," in bond indexes, 14–15
buy-and-hold investors, constraints for, 79
buy-side research, 231

C
CAC 40 (index), 176, 183
callable structures, 83, 84
  structure trades, 77
  and US corporate bond market, 83
  in US investment-grade credit markets, 83
call options, covered, 122
Canada
  currency hedging, 133, 134
  equity indexes, 176
  equity real rates of return, 164
  government bond index returns, 128
  pension fund equity allocations, 163
  Quebec independence movement, 88
capital gains, 210
cap rate, 122
cap risk, 42
caps
  fee, 223
  and floating rate, 42
  hedging with options, 122
  interest rate for, 122
Carril, Peter J., 91
cash flow matching strategies, 48–52
  applications of, 51–52
  cash flow analysis for, 50
  as dedication strategy, 30
  extensions of basic strategy, 51
  multiple liability immunization vs., 50
  symmetric, 51
cash flows
  analysis of, 50
  immunization strategies for general, 46–47
  present value distribution of, 20–21
  secondary trade and reinvestment of, 77–78
CBOT. see Chicago Board of Trade
cell-matching technique, 18
Central Europe. see specific countries
certificates of deposit, 120
CFA Centre for Financial Market Integrity, 207
CFA Institute, 207
cheapest-to-deliver (CTD) issue, 115
Chicago Board of Trade (CBOT), 115, 116
Chicago Mercantile Exchange (CME), 182
Citigroup World Government Bond Index, 14
classical single-period immunization
  and active bond management strategies, 40–41
  assumptions of, 37
  characteristics of, 31
  duration and convexity of assets and liabilities, 41–42
  extensions of, 37–45
  risk minimization for immunized portfolios, 42–45
  and risk–return tradeoff, 40
  and shifts in interest rates, 37–40
  and shifts in time horizon, 39–40
  types of risk, 42
classic relative-value analysis, 70–72
CME. see Chicago Mercantile Exchange
Coca-Cola, 186
Code of Ethics (CFA Institute), 207
collars, hedging, 122
collateral, for repurchase agreements, 109, 110
collateralized debt obligations, 133n.6
combination matching, 51
combination strategies, for fixed-income portfolios, 106
commercial paper, 120
completeness funds, 220–221
confidence interval, 44
consistent growth investment style, 188
constraints
  for buy-and-hold investors, 79
  of long-only investing, 207–208
  on secondary trade, 78–79
consultants, pension fund, 185
contingent claims risk, 42
contingent immunization, 40
contracts
  futures
    defined, 115
    equity index, 182–183
    interest rate, 115–120
  guaranteed investment, 31–33
contrarian investment style, 187
conversion factors, for interest rate futures, 115
convexity
  of assets/liabilities, 41–42
  of benchmark bond indexes, 21
convexity adjustment, for benchmark bond indexes, 18, 20
core investment style, 188–189
core-plus fixed-income portfolios, 137
core-satellite portfolios, 217–220
corporate bonds
  and sector-rotation trades, 76
  and spread duration, 21
correlation of returns, for government bond indexes, 128–129
costs
  sell disciplines based on, 210
  transaction
    of dedication strategies, 52
    and immunized portfolios, 52
    and indexed portfolios, 25, 178
country beta, 131
covered call options, 122
Crabbe, Leland, 92
credit analysis, for global portfolio management, 87
credit barbell strategy, 86
credit bond portfolio management. see global credit bond portfolio management
credit curve analysis, for global portfolio management, 86–87

credit-default swaps
  credit relative-value analysis for, 70
  for fixed-income portfolio management, 127–128
  and spread analysis, 80
credit-defense trades, 76
credit derivatives, 123
credit events, 127
credit forwards, spread, 124–127
credit options, 123–124, 126–127
credit protection sellers, 123
credit risk
  benchmark bond index selection, 11
  and fixed-income portfolio management, 123–128
  and spread duration, 36
credit spread forwards, 124–126
credit spread options, 124, 126–127
credit spread risk, 123
credit spreads, 86–87
credit-upside trades, 75–76
cross hedging
  currency, 133
  duration, 118–119
CTD issue. see cheapest-to-deliver issue
currency-hedged instruments, 132
currency hedging, cross hedges in, 133
currency risk
  defined, 129
  hedging of, 132–136
    comparing hedged returns, 134
    with forward contracts, 134–136
    interest rate parity, 132
  and international bond investing, 129
currency swaps, 68. see also interest rate swaps
curve-adjustment trades, 77
cushion spread, 40

D
DAX 30
  composition and characteristics, 176
  stock index futures, 183
debt
  collateralized debt obligations, 133n.6
  emerging market
    analysis of, 79–80, 138–139
    and growth/maturity of market, 137–138
    and international bond investing, 137–139
    risk and return characteristics, 138
dedication strategies, 29–48
  cash flow matching strategies, 48–52
    applications, 51–52
    cash flow analysis for, 50
    extensions of basic strategy, 51
    multiple liability immunization vs., 50
  and classes of liabilities, 30
  immunization strategies, 30–48
    classical single-period immunization, 31–33
    dollar duration in, 34–35
    duration and convexity of assets/liabilities, 41–42
    example, 36–37
    extensions of classical immunization, 37–45

Index

for general cash flows, 46–47
multiple liability immunization, 45–46
rebalancing immunized portfolios, 33
return maximization for immunized portfolios, 47–48
risk in, 42–45
spread duration in, 35–36
target return for, 33–34
time horizon for, 34
and total return/accumulated value, 31–33
total return and yield curve of immunized portfolios, 39
value and interest rate of immunized portfolio, 38
yield curve of immunized portfolios, 39
monitoring of, 52
optimization of, 51
security selection for, 51
transaction costs of, 52
default risk
in credit curve analysis, 86
defined, 26
for emerging market debt, 138, 139
and indexed portfolio costs, 26
and repurchase agreements, 110–111
delivery, repurchase rate and, 110
delivery options, 116
delta, 121
Denmark, 164
derivatives. *see also specific types, e.g.:* options
credit, 123
and global bond market, 73
derivatives-based semiactive equity investing, 211, 213
derivatives-enabled strategies, 111–128
and alternative measures of dispersion, 113
bond variance and duration, 114
with credit risk instruments, 123–128
credit forwards, 124–127
credit options, 123–124
credit swaps, 127–128
with interest rate futures, 115–120
duration hedging, 118–120
duration management, 116–118
and interest rate risk, 111–112
with interest rate swaps, 120–121
and asset/liability management, 121
dollar duration of, 120
with options, 121–122
bond options and duration, 121–122
portfolio hedging, 122
deteriorating fundamentals sell discipline, 210
Dialynas, Chris, 92
direct quotation, currency, 132
discounts, forward, 132
dispersion, alternative measures of, 113
diversification
and bond indexed portfolios, 11
and DJIA history, 175
indexed portfolios, 181
in value-weighted/float-weighted indexes, 170
DJIA. *see* Dow Jones Industrial Average

dollar, Australian, 132–133
dollar, US
Australian dollar vs., 132–133
and government bond index returns, 129
dollar duration, 112
calculation of, 34
in immunization strategies, 34–35
of interest rate swaps, 120
rebalancing based on, 35
dollar value of a basis point (DV01), 34n.26
Dow Jones & Co., 232, 236
Dow Jones Corporate Bond Index, 14
Dow Jones Industrial Average (DJIA)
composition and characteristics, 175, 176
price weighting, 170
Dow Jones Wilshire indexes, 200
down-from-cost sell discipline, 210
downgrade risk, 123
due diligence questionnaire, for portfolio managers, 141–143
duration
of assets and liabilities, 41–42
and benchmark bond index selection, 18, 20–21
bond, 114, 121–122, 130–131
dollar, 34–35, 112, 120
effective, 18, 26
of equities in fixed-income portfolios, 109
functional, 39
key rate, 20–21, 23
Macaulay, 34n.27
portfolio
immunized time horizon, 34
international bond investing, 130–131
multiple liability immunization, 45
and portfolio holdings, 111–112
return maximization for immunized portfolios, 47
and tracking risk, 23
quality-spread, 23
rate, 20
sector, 23
spread, 21, 23, 35–36
duration hedging, 118–120
duration management
and fixed-income portfolio management, 116–118
international bond investing, 130–131
DV01. *see* dollar value of a basis point
Dynkin, Lev, 91

E

earnings momentum investment style, 188
Eastern Europe. *see specific countries*
ECNs. *see* electronic communication networks
economic growth, of emerging markets, 137–138
economic sectors, 87–88
economic surplus, 41
effective duration, 18, 26
efficient frontiers, of managers, 214, 215
efficient markets theory, 184

EFP. *see* Exchange of Futures for Physicals
electronic communication networks (ECNs), 74
Ellis, Charles D., 167
EMBI+. *see* Emerging Markets Bond Index Plus
EMBI Global Core Index, 14
EMBI Global Index (EMBIG), 14
emerging market debt (EMD)
analysis of, 79–80, 138–139
and growth/maturity of market, 137–138
and international bond investing, 137–139
risk and return characteristics, 138
emerging markets, growth/maturity of, 137–138
Emerging Markets Bond Index Plus (EMBI+), 138
e-mini S&P 500, 182–183
enhanced indexing, 25–27. *see also* semiactive equity investing
as equity investment approach, 166
by matching primary risk factors, 9–10
semiactive equity investing, 211–213
by small risk factor mismatches, 10
Enron, 79
equal-weighted indexes, 169–171, 173–174
equities. *see also specific types*
allocation of, 163, 200–201
duration of, 109
industry classification of, 231–232
inflation's effects on, 163–164
large-cap, 170
real rate of returns, 164–165
small-cap, 205
equitization
defined, 211n.58
of market-neutral long–short portfolios, 207
equity index futures, 182–183
equity investment styles, 184–204
advantages of, 190
based on market capitalization, 189–190
growth, 185–186, 188
in holdings-based style analysis, 190–191, 196–199
identifying, 190–199
indexes based on, 199–202
market-oriented, 188–189
in returns-based style analysis, 191–196, 199
and style boxes, 202–203
and style drift, 203–204
value, 185–188
equity portfolio management
about, 162
active equity investing, 184–210
equity styles, 184–204
long–short investing, 205–210
sell disciplines, 210
socially responsible investing, 204–205
trading frequency, 210
equity investment approaches in, 165
passive equity investing, 166–184
with indexes, 168–177
investment vehicles, 175, 178–184

equity portfolio management (*continued*)
  for portfolios of managers, 214–221
    alpha and beta separation, 221
    completeness funds, 220–221
    core-satellite portfolios, 217–220
    and pension fund's performance objectives, 218–219
  practice problems, 235–241
  research
    buy- vs. sell-side, 231
    and industry classification, 231–232
    top-down vs. bottom-up approaches, 230
  role of equity portfolios, 163–165
  selecting securities for, 230–232
  semiactive equity investing, 211–213
    derivatives- vs. stock-based, 211, 213
    Fundamental Law of Active Management, 212
  solutions to problems, 242–245
equity portfolio managers
  fixed-income vs., 141
  selecting, 222–230
    fee proposals, 229–230
    fee structures, 223
    finding suitable candidates, 222
    past performance, 222
    questionnaires for, 223–229
equity portfolios, role of, 163–165
equity total return swaps, 183–184
ETFs. *see* exchange-traded funds
euro(s), 129
Eurobonds, 73, 83
Eurodollars, 115
Europe. *see also specific countries*
  credit market, 80
  emerging market debt, 137, 139
  government bond index returns, 129
  indexed portfolio regulation, 181
  sector rotation, 87, 88
European Central Bank, 129
European Union, 181
event risk, 21, 87–88
excess returns, 135
Exchange of Futures for Physicals (EFP), 183
exchange-traded funds (ETFs)
  in indexed portfolios, 175, 178–179
  and market-neutral long–short portfolios, 207
  and uptick rule, 183
exposures. *see* risk exposures
exposure weighting, 118
Exxon, 171–174

F
factor exposures, 111, 119
federal funds rate, 120
Federal Reserve, 76
fee caps, 223
fees
  ad valorem fees, 223, 229–230
  assets under management, 223
  and bond indexed portfolios, 10
  performance-based, 223, 229–230
Ferket, Peter, 91
Financial Times Stock Exchange (FTSE), 200
Finland, 164

fixed-income portfolio management, 5–63, 105–157. *see also* global credit bond portfolio management
  about, 6
  with benchmark bond indexes, 7–29
    active strategies, 27–29
    classification of strategies, 9–10
    indexing (pure and enhanced), 10–27
    and monitoring/adjusting portfolio, 29
  cash flow matching strategies, 48–52
  combination strategies, 106
  dedication strategies, 29–48
    cash flow matching strategies, 48–52
    and classes of liabilities, 30
    immunization strategies, 30–48
    monitoring of, 52
    optimization of, 51
    security selection for, 51
    transaction costs of, 52
  derivatives-enabled strategies, 111–128
    and alternative measures of dispersion, 113
    bond variance and duration, 114
    with credit risk instruments, 123–128
    with interest rate futures, 115–120
    and interest rate risk, 111–112
    with interest rate swaps, 120–121
    with options, 121–122
  framework for, 6–7
  international bond investing, 128–139
    active vs. passive management, 129–131
    breakeven spread analysis, 136–137
    currency risk, 131–136
    emerging market debt, 137–139
  leverage, 107–111
    effects of, 107–109
    and portfolio returns/yields, 107–109
    and repurchase agreements, 109–111
  with liabilities, 29–52
  practice problems, 55–60, 145–152
  solutions to problems, 61–63, 153–157
fixed-income portfolio managers, 139–143
  criteria for, 140–141
  due diligence questionnaire, 141–143
  historical performance of, 140
  selection of equity managers vs., 141
fixed-income portfolios
  core-plus, 137
  hedging of, 122
fixed-rate corporate bonds, 76
fixed-rate payers, 120
float adjustment
  for float-weighted index, 170
  for value-weighted index, 170
floating-rate bonds (floaters)
  corporate, 76
  perpetual, 70
floating-rate payers, 120
floating supply of shares, issue's, 169
float-weighted indexes, 170, 173
floors, 122
Ford Motor Company, 75
Ford Motor Credit, 81
foreign bonds, 131. *see also* global credit bond portfolio management; international bond investing

forward contracts (forwards)
  credit spread, 124–127
  hedging currency risk with, 134–136
forward discounts, 132
forward hedging, 133–136
France
  equity indexes' composition/characteristics, 176
  equity real rates of return, 164
  government bond index returns, 128
free float, of shares, 169
front-end bullets, 84
FTSE. *see* Financial Times Stock Exchange
FTSE 100 Index, 236
  composition and characteristics, 176
  long–short investing, 208–210
  stock index futures, 183
FTSE Global Government Bond Index, 14
FTSE International Ltd, 232
full replication approach
  and bond index investability, 14
  for fixed-income portfolio management, 9
  for passive investing, 179–180
functional duration, 39. *see also* key rate duration
Fundamental Law of Active Management, 212
futures (futures contracts)
  defined, 115
  equity index, 182–183
  interest rate, 115–120
    duration hedging, 118–120
    duration management, 116–118
  options on, 121
  price of, 115

G
General Electric, 175
General Motors, 75
Germany
  equity indexes' composition/characteristics, 176
  equity real rates of return, 164
  government bond index returns, 128
  international bond investing, 149
GIC. *see* guaranteed investment contract
GICS. *see* Global Industry Classification Standard
glamour stocks, 187
global credit bond portfolio management, 65–102
  asset allocation and sector rotation, 87–88
  credit analysis, 87
  credit curve analysis, 86–87
  history of, 65–68
  liquidity and trading analysis, 74
  practice problems, 91–97
  primary market analysis, 73–74
    and market-structure dynamics, 73
    and product structure, 74
  relative-value analysis, 68–72
    classic, 70–72
    and definition of relative value, 70
    methodologies, 72

Index

secondary trade rationales, 75–79
  and cash flow reinvestment, 77–78
  for credit-defense trades, 76
  for credit-upside trades, 75–76
  for curve-adjustment trades, 77
  for new issue swaps, 76
  for sector-rotation trades, 76
  for structure trades, 77
  and trading constraints, 78–79
  for yield/spread pickup trades, 75
solutions to problems, 98–102
spread analysis, 79–82
  alternative spread measures, 79–80
  swap spreads, 80–81
  tools, 81–82
structural analysis, 82–85
  bullet structures, 83–84
  callable structures, 84
  putable structures, 85
  sinking fund structures, 85
total return analysis, 72
Global Industry Classification Standard (GICS), 232
Google, 186
government bond indexes, total returns of, 128–129
"Great Spread-Sector Crash," 73, 84
growth-at-a-reasonable price investment style, 189
growth investment style, 185–186, 188
  consistent, 188
  indexes with, 199–201
  and Microsoft, 186
  sell disciplines, 210
  value vs., 185–186
guaranteed investment contract (GIC), 31–33

H
hedged returns, 134
hedge ratios, 118–120
hedging. *see also* currency hedging
  with credit default swaps, 127
  cross, 118–119, 133
  of currency risk, 132–136
  duration, 118–120
  of fixed-income portfolios, 122
  forward, 133–136
  hedged vs. unhedged returns, 134
  inflation, 163–164
  proxy, 133
high-water mark, 223
high yield investment style, 187–188
historical performance, fixed-income portfolio managers', 140
holdings-based style analysis, 190–191, 196–202
horizon matching, 51
HWM. *see* high-water mark
Hyman, Jay, 91

I
IBM, 87, 186
immunization strategies, 30–48
  and accumulated value, 31–33
  active/immunization combination, 106
  classical single-period, 31–33, 37–45
    and active bond management strategies, 40–41
    assumptions of, 37
    characteristics of, 31
    duration and convexity of assets and liabilities, 41–42
    extensions of, 37–45
    risk minimization for immunized portfolios, 42–45
    and risk–return tradeoff, 40
    and shifts in interest rates, 37–40
    and shifts in time horizon, 39–40
    types of risk, 42
  contingent, 40
  defined, 30
  dollar duration in, 34–35
  duration and convexity of assets/liabilities in, 41–42
  example, 36–37
  for general cash flows, 46–47
  multiple liability immunization, 40, 45–46, 50
  rebalancing immunized portfolios, 33
  and return maximization, 47–48
  risk in, 42–45
  spread duration in, 35–36
  target return for, 33–34
  time horizon for, 34
  and total return, 31–33, 39
  value and interest rate of immunized portfolio, 38
  yield curve of immunized portfolios, 39
immunized time horizon, 34
income risk, 11
indexed portfolios, 175, 178–184
indexes
  based on equity style, 199–202
  benchmark bond, 7–29
    active strategies, 27–29
    classification of strategies, 9–10
    indexing strategies, 11–27
    monitoring/adjusting portfolio with, 29
  composition and characteristics of, 174–177
  equal-weighted, 169–171, 173–174
  float-weighted, 170, 173
  investability, 13–17
  passive equity investing with, 168–177
    benchmark index selection, 171–174
    composition and characteristics of major indexes, 174–177
    index weighting choices, 168–174
  price-weighted, 168–170, 172
  selecting benchmark, 11–13, 171–174
  style, 185
  value-weighted, 169, 170, 172–173
indexing
  with benchmark bond indexes, 11–27
    enhanced indexing, 25–27
    investability of indexes, 13–17
    reasons for using, 10–11
    risk exposures with, 17–21
    selection of benchmark for, 11–13
    and tracking risk, 22–25
  defined, 165
  enhanced, 25–27, 165
  as equity investment approach, 165
  by matching primary risk factors, 9–10
  semiactive equity investing, 211–213
  by small risk factor mismatches, 10
  for equity investments, 165
  pure bond, 9
index weighting
  and bond index investability, 14–15
  for passive equity investing, 168–174
industry classification, of equities, 231–232
Industry Classification Benchmark, 232
inflation hedges, assets as, 163–164
information, efficiency of, 166
information coefficient, 212
information ratio, 166
institutional portfolios, indexing, 179
Intel, 171–174
interest rate futures
  duration hedging with, 118–120
  in duration management strategies, 116–118
  in fixed-income portfolio management, 115–120
interest rate parity (IRP), 132
interest rate risk
  in benchmark bond index selection, 18
  and fixed-income portfolio management, 111–112
  and immunization, 42
  and putable structures, 85
interest rates
  in benchmark bond index selection, 18
  cap, 122
  in classical single-period immunization, 37–40
  and international bond investing, 130–131
  prime rate, 120
  and repurchase agreements, 111
  and value of immunized portfolio, 38
interest rate swaps, 120–121
interest rate swap spreads, 80, 81
intermediate credit bullets, 84
Internal Revenue Code, 181
international bond investing, 128–139
  active vs. passive management, 129–131
  breakeven spread analysis, 136–137
  currency risk, 131–136
    hedging of, 132–136
    interest rate parity, 132
  emerging market debt, 137–139
    analysis of, 138–139
    and growth/maturity of market, 137–138
    risk and return characteristics, 138
International Monetary Fund, 137
investability, bond index, 13–17
investment-grade credit bonds
  credit spread, 86–87
  market for, 82–83
  returns, 67
  Sharpe ratio, 68
investment styles, 184–204
  advantages of, 190
  based on market capitalization, 189–190
  blend, 188–189
  consistent growth, 188
  contrarian, 187
  core, 188–189
  earnings momentum, 188

investment styles (*continued*)
  growth, 185–186, 188
    consistent, 188
    indexes with, 199–201
    and Microsoft, 186
    sell disciplines, 210
    value vs., 185–186
  growth-at-a-reasonable price, 189
  high yield, 187–188
  in holdings-based style analysis, 190–191, 196–199
  identifying, 190–199
  indexes based on, 199–202
  low P/E, 187
  market-oriented, 184, 188–189
  and portfolio characteristics, 197–198
  in returns-based style analysis, 191–196, 199
  and style boxes, 202–203
  and style drift, 203–204
  style rotator, 189
  value, 185–188
    defined, 184
    growth vs., 185–186
    Microsoft and, 186
    sell disciplines, 210
investor constraints, for buy-and-hold investors, 79
investors
  benchmark of, 219
  buy-and-hold, 79
  large-cap equity, 189–190
  micro-cap equity, 189
  mid-cap equity, 189, 190
  small-stock, 189
Ireland, 164
IRP. *see* interest rate parity
Italy, 164

J
Japan
  currency hedging, 134
  equity indexes' composition/characteristics, 176
  equity real rates of return, 165
  government bond index returns, 128
  international bond investing, 149
  pension fund equity allocations, 163
JP Morgan, 14, 15

K
key rate duration
  and benchmark bond index selection, 20–21
  and tracking risk, 23

L
large-cap equities, 170
large-cap equity investors, 189–190
Latin America, 137, 139. *see also specific countries*
Lehman Brothers, 66n.1
Lehman Brothers Equal-Weighted Corporate Bond Index, 96
Lehman Brothers Global Government Bond Index, 96
Lehman Brothers Selected Municipal Bonds Index, 96

Lehman Brothers US Corporate Bond Index, 95–96
Lehman Brothers US Investment-Grade Credit Bond Index, 83
leverage
  effects of, 107–109
  in fixed-income portfolio management, 107–111
  in long–short investing, 206
  and portfolio returns/yields, 107–109
  and repurchase agreements, 109–111
liabilities
  classes of, 30
  convexity of, 41–42
  fixed-income portfolio management with (*see* dedication strategies)
  multiple liability immunization, 40, 45–46, 50
liability framework risk, 11
liability matching, 7
LIBOR. *see* London Interbank Offered Rate
life insurance, 31–33
linear programming, 44
liquidity
  and full replication, 180
  and global credit bond portfolio management, 74
London Interbank Offered Rate (LIBOR), 120, 183
London Stock Exchange, 176
long-only constraint, 207–208
long–short investing, 205–210
  equitizing a market-neutral long–short portfolio, 207
  long-only constraint, 207–208
  and market structure, 209–210
  price inefficiency on short side of market, 206–207
  short extension strategies, 208–209
long–short portfolios, market-neutral, 207
low P/E investment style, 187

M
Macaulay duration, 34n.27
McDonald's, 171–174
Malkiel, Burton, 167
managers, efficient frontiers of, 214, 215. *see also* portfolio managers
market capitalization, 189–190
market-neutral long–short portfolios, 207
market-oriented investment styles, 184, 188–189
market-oriented with growth bias (investment style), 189
market-oriented with value bias (investment style), 189
markets. *see also* emerging markets
  credit, 80–81
  structure of, 73, 209–210
market value risk, 11
Markowitz mean-variance framework, 128
matrix pricing, 13
maturity
  of bullet portfolios, 74
  of emerging markets, 137–138

  term to, 110
  ultra-long, 84
maturity variance, 44
mean-reversion analysis, 81–82
measurable benchmarks, 15n.12
medium-term notes (MTN), 73
Merck, 171–174
Mexico
  debt, 137
  financial crisis, 137
Michelin, 232
micro-cap equity investors, 189
Microsoft
  equity market data, 171–174
  free-float adjustments, 169n.10
  growth vs. value stock, 186
mid-cap equity investors, 189, 190
Middle East, 137, 139
misfit risk, 219–220
monitoring
  of dedication strategies, 52
  of portfolios, 29
Moody's Investor Services, 139
Morgan Stanley Capital International (MSCI)
  equity styles, 200
  Global Industry Classification Standard, 232
  growth/allocation criteria and rebalancing rules for indexes, 200
  index composition and characteristics, 177
  stock categorization by, 236
Morningstar
  equity styles, 200
  growth/allocation criteria and rebalancing rules for indexes, 200
  style box, 202
MSCI. *see* Morgan Stanley Capital International
MSCI International All Country World Index (MSCI ACWI), 163, 177, 238–239
MSCI World ex-Australia Index, 218–220
MSCI World Growth Index, 235
MSCI World Index, 177
MSCI World Value Index, 235
MTN. *see* medium-term notes
multifactor model technique, 18, 181
multifunctional duration, 39. *see also* key rate duration
multiple liability immunization
  about, 45–46
  cash flow matching strategies vs., 50
  defined, 40

N
NAICS. *see* North American Industry Classification System
National Investor Relations Institute, 207
negative skewness, 138
Netherlands
  equity real rates of return, 165
  government bond index returns, 128
  pension fund equity allocations, 163
new issue swaps, 76
New Zealand, 165

Index

Nikkei 225 Index
  composition/characteristics, 176
  price-weighting of, 170
  stock index futures on, 183
Nikkei Stock Average, 176
nominal spread, 36, 79
normal portfolio, as benchmark, 191
North American Industry Classification System (NAICS), 232
Norway, 165
notional principal amount, 120

O

OAS. see option-adjusted spread
objectives, of pension funds, 218–219
130/30 short extension strategies, 208–209
opportunity costs, sell disciplines based on, 210
optimization
  of dedication strategies, 51
  of indexed portfolios, 180–182
option-adjusted spread (OAS)
  and spread analysis, 79–80
  and spread duration, 36
options. see also specific types, e.g.: call options (calls)
  binary credit, 123–124, 126–127
  bond, 121–122
  covered calls, 122
  credit, 123–124, 126–127
  fixed-income portfolio management with, 121–122
  on futures, 121
  on physicals, 121
  protective puts, 122
  quality, 116
  timing, 116
  wild card, 116
owned benchmarks, 15n.12

P

pairs trade, 206
passive equity investing, 166–184
  equity index futures, 182–183
  equity total return swaps, 183–184
  indexed portfolios, 175, 178–184
  with indexes, 168–177
    benchmark index selection, 171–174
    composition and characteristics of major indexes, 174–177
    index weighting choices, 168–174
  portfolio construction for, 182
passive management
  bond market index as benchmarks for, 9
  of equity investments, 165
  for international bond investing, 129
payoffs, credit spread forward, 124–126
pension fund consultants, 185
pension funds
  equity allocations of, 163
  performance objectives of, 218–219
  portfolios of managers for, 214–217
percent yield spread analysis, in spread analysis, 82
performance, of portfolio managers, 140
performance-based fees, 223, 229–230

perpetual floaters, 70
physicals, options on, 121
Pohang Iron & Steel, 87
political risk
  and emerging market debt, 139
  and sector rotation, 88
portable alpha, 206, 221
portfolio duration
  and holdings, 111–112
  for immunized portfolios, 45, 47
  and immunized time horizon, 34
  and international bond investing, 130–131
  and tracking risk, 23
portfolio managers
  equity
    fixed-income vs. equity managers, 141
    portfolios of, 214–221
    questionnaires for, 223–229
    selecting, 222–230
  fixed-income, 129–131, 139–143
    criteria for, 140–141
    due diligence questionnaire, 141–143
    equity vs. fixed-income managers, 141
    historical performance of, 140
portfolio trades, 182
present value distribution, of cash flows, 20–21
price(s)
  futures, 115
  growth-at-a-reasonable price investment style, 189
  stale, 13
price inefficiency, 206–207
price risk, 118
price value of a basis point (PVBP), 34n.26
price-weighted indexes, 168–170, 172
pricing, matrix, 13
primary market analysis, 73–74
primary risk factors, for bonds, 9
prime rate, 120
program trades, 182
protective puts, 122
proxy hedging, 133
pure bond indexing, 9
putable structures, 85
  structure trades, 77
  in US investment-grade credit markets, 83
put options (puts), protective, 122
PVBP (price value of a basis point), 34n.26

Q

quality options, 116
quality-spread analysis, 82
quality-spread duration, 23
Quebec independence movement, 88

R

range forwards. see collars
rate duration, 20
real rate of returns, equities, 164–165
rebalancing
  based on dollar duration, 35
  based on equity styles, 199–201

and benchmark bond indexes, 25
of immunized portfolios, 33
rebalancing ratio, 35
rebound effect, 79
reference entities, 127
reflective of current investment opinions (term), 15n.12
Regulated Investment Company (RIC) diversification, 181
regulations, indexed portfolio, 181
reinvestment risk, 43–44
relative strength indicators, 188
relative value, 70
relative-value analysis
  classic, 70–72
  and definition of relative value, 70
  in global credit bond portfolio management, 68–72
  methodologies, 72
repurchase agreements, 109–111
research
  buy-side, 231
  sell-side, 206–207, 231
  top-down vs. bottom-up, 70, 230, 231
return(s)
  active, 166
  on borrowed funds, 108
  correlation of, 128–129
  in currency hedging, 134, 135
  and emerging market debt, 138
  excess, 135
  on funds invested, 108
  hedged, 134
  of immunized portfolios, 31–33, 39–40, 47–48
  and leverage, 107–109
  real rate of, 164–165
  total
    and accumulated value, 31–33
    defined, 28
    of government bond indexes, 128–129
    of immunized portfolios, 31–33, 39–40
    total returns analysis, 28, 72
    and yield curve, 39
  unhedged, 134
returns-based style analysis
  example, 201, 202
  holdings-based style analysis vs., 199
  identifying investment style with, 190–196
RIC diversification. see Regulated Investment Company diversification
Richards, Thomas M., 15
risk. see also specific types, e.g.: market equity risk
  active, 166, 215–216, 219–220
  basis, 118
  and benchmark bond index selection, 11, 17–25
  cap, 42
  contingent claims, 42
  credit, 11, 36, 123–128
  credit spread, 123
  currency, 129
  default
    in credit curve analysis, 86
    defined, 26
    for emerging market debt, 138, 139

risk (*continued*)
   and indexed portfolio costs, 26
   and repurchase agreements, 110–111
   downgrade, 123
   of emerging market debt, 138
   event, 21, 87–88
   in immunization strategies, 42–45
   of immunized portfolios, 42–45
   income, 11
   with indexing strategies for benchmark bond indexes, 17–21
   interest rate
     in benchmark bond index selection, 18
     and fixed-income portfolio management, 111–112
     and immunization, 42
     and putable structures, 85
   liability framework, 11
   market value, 11
   misfit, 219–220
   political, 88, 139
   price, 118
   primary risk factors for bonds, 9
   reinvestment, 43–44
   shortfall, 78–79, 113
   spread, 18, 21
   tracking, 22–25, 166
   true active, 219–220
   yield curve, 18
risk-controlled active investing, 211–213. *see also* semiactive equity investing
risk exposures
   and fixed-income portfolio management, 111–112
   issuer, 21
   weighting of, 118
Russell 1000 Growth Index, 192–194
Russell 1000 Index, 177, 237
Russell 1000 Value Index, 192–194
Russell 2000 Growth Index, 192–194
Russell 2000 Index
   composition and characteristics, 177
   indexed portfolios, 180
   and liquidity, 175
   portfolio construction with, 182
Russell 2000 Value Index, 192–194
Russell 3000 Index, 176, 237
Russell Investments, 200
Russell Midcap Growth Index, 195, 196
Russell Midcap Value Index, 195, 196
Russell Top 200 Growth Index, 195, 196, 221
Russell Top 200 Value Index, 195, 196
Russia
   debt default, 138
   emerging market debt, 136–138
   political instability, 88

S
Samuelson, Paul, 167
scenario analysis, 28–29
Scotia Capital Universe Bond Index, 26–27
seasonality, of secondary trading, 79
secondary offerings, 165
secondary trade, 75–79
   and cash flow reinvestment, 77–78
   constraints on, 78–79
   for credit-defense trades, 76
   for credit-upside trades, 75–76
   for curve-adjustment trades, 77
   for new issue swaps, 76
   rationales for, 75–79
   for sector-rotation trades, 76
   for structure trades, 77
   and trading constraints, 78–79
   for yield/spread pickup trades, 75
sector duration, 23
sector-rotation trades, 76
sectors, economic, 87–88
securities
   lending of, 178
   selection of
     for dedicated strategies, 51
     for equity portfolios, 230–232
   transfer of, 110
   US Treasury, 115, 116
sell disciplines, active equity investing, 210
sell-side research, 206–207, 231
semiactive equity investing, 165, 211–213
   derivatives- vs. stock-based, 211, 213
   and Fundamental Law of Active Management, 212
semiactive management, 165
semivariance, 113
settlement date, 115
Sharpe, William F., 167, 185, 191
Sharpe ratio, 68
Sharpe style weights, 191
short extension strategies, 208–209
shortfall risk, 78–79, 113
short positions, 206
Siegel, L., 14
Singapore, 149
sinking fund structures, 83, 85
skewness, negative, 138
small-cap equities, 205
small-stock investors, 189
socially responsible investing (SRI), 204–205
Sony, 186
South Africa, 165
Southeast Asia, 137, 139. *see also specific countries*
S&P 500 Index
   composition and characteristics, 177
   float weighting, 169
   futures on, 182–183, 221
   indexed portfolios, 180
   mutual fund expense ratios, 178
   passive equity investing, 167
   portfolio trades, 182
Spain, 165
S&P/Citigroup 500 Growth Index, 195
S&P/Citigroup 500 Value Index, 195
S&P/Citigroup World indexes, 201
specified in advance (term), 15n.12
S&P MidCap 400 Index, 169
spread analysis
   alternative spread measures, 79–80
   global credit bond portfolio management, 79–82
   swap spreads, 80–81
   tools, 81–82
spread duration, 21
   benchmark bond index selection, 21
   in immunized portfolios, 35–36
   and tracking risk, 23
spread risk, 18, 21
spreads
   credit, 86–87
   cushion, 40
   interest rate swap, 80
   nominal, 36, 79
   option-adjusted, 36, 79–80
   static, 36
   strike, 123
   swap, 80–81
   for "vol" sectors, 79–80
   yield, 82, 119–120
   yield/spread pickup trades, 75
   zero-volatility, 36
S&P SmallCap 600 Index, 169, 175
S&P TSX Composite, 176
SRI. *see* socially responsible investing
stale prices, 13
Standard & Poor's
   emerging market debt, 139
   Global Industry Classification Standard, 232
Standards of Professional Conduct (CFA Institute), 207
static spreads, 36
stock-based semiactive equity investing, 211, 213
stock index futures, 182–183
stocks, glamour, 187. *see also* equities
"story" disagreement, 78–79
stratified sampling, 18, 180–181
strike spreads, 123
structural analysis
   bullet structures, 83–84
   callable structures, 84
   global credit bond portfolio management, 82–85
   putable structures, 85
   sinking fund structures, 85
structure trades, 77
style analysis, for fixed-income manager selection, 140
style box, 202–203
style drift, 203–204
style indexes, 185
style rotator (investment style), 189
style weights, 191
substitution, 210
Sumitomo, 87
supply, credit spreads and, 73
supranationals, 73
surplus, economic, 41
swaps
   asset, 84
   credit-default, 70, 80–81, 127–128
   currency, 68
   equity total return, 183–184
   interest rate, 80, 81, 120–121
   new issue, 76
   total return, 183–184
swap spreads, 80–81
Sweden, 165
Switzerland
   equity real rates of return, 165

Index

government bond index returns, 128, 129
pension fund equity allocations, 163
symmetric cash flow matching, 51

T
tactical asset allocation, 184
target returns, for immunized portfolios, 33–34
target value, of guaranteed investment contract, 31–33
taxes
  and benchmark bond index selection, 11–12
  for equity total return swaps, 183–184
  and sell disciplines, 210
tax-exempt bonds, 12n.7
Taylor, Christopher, 91–92
term to maturity, repurchase agreements, 110
Texas Utilities, 87
tick (term), 183n.28
Tierney, David E., 15
time horizons, immunized, 34
timing options, 116
Tokyo Stock Exchange, 176
top-down research approaches, 70, 224, 230, 231
TOPIX
  alpha and beta separation, 221
  composition and characteristics, 176, 177n.a
  float weighting for, 169
  as pension fund benchmark, 214
  stratified sampling for, 180
Toronto Stock Exchange, 176
total returns
  and accumulated value, 31–33
  defined, 28
  of government bond indexes, 128–129
  for immunized portfolios, 31–33, 39–40
  and yield curve, 39
total returns analysis, 28, 72
total return swaps, 183–184
Toyota, 180
tracking risk
  and benchmark bond indexes, 22–25
  defined, 166
  interpreting and reducing, 24–25
  and spread duration, 24
trades
  basket, 182
  credit-defense, 76
  credit-upside, 75–76
  curve-adjustment, 77
  pairs, 206 (see also long–short investing)
  portfolio, 182
  program, 182
  sector-rotation, 76
  structure, 77
trading
  frequency of, 210
  in secondary market, 75–79
trading analysis, for global credit bond portfolio management, 74

transaction costs
  of dedication strategies, 52
  and immunized portfolios, 52
  and indexed portfolios, 25–26, 178
Treasury spot curve, 33
true active risk, 219–220
twist, yield curve, 18

U
UCITS. *see* Undertakings for Collective Investment in Transferable Securities
ultra-long maturities, 84
unambiguous benchmarks, 15n.12
underlying (term), 115
Undertakings for Collective Investment in Transferable Securities (UCITS), 181
unhedged returns, 134
United Kingdom
  equity indexes' composition/characteristics, 176
  equity real rates of return, 165
  government bond index returns, 128, 129
  international bond investing, 149
  pension fund equity allocations, 163
United States
  credit market, 81
  equity indexes' composition/characteristics, 175–177
  equity real rates of return, 165
  government bond index returns, 128, 129
  indexed portfolio regulation, 181
  international investing, 149
  investment-grade credit bonds, 67, 68, 82–83, 86–87
  pension fund equity allocations, 163
  sector rotation, 87, 88
  swap spreads, 80–81
US agency benchmark curve, 80
US dollar
  Australian dollar vs., 132–133
  and government bond index returns, 129
US Treasury bills
  interest rate futures on, 115
  as interest rate swap benchmark, 120
  in semiactive equity investing, 211
US Treasury bonds
  credit assets vs., 66
  fixed-income portfolio management with, 56–57
  interest rate futures on, 115
  and macroeconomic influences on credit spreads, 72
  and spread duration, 21, 36
US Treasury notes, 115, 116
US Treasury securities, interest rate futures on, 115, 116
US Treasury spot curve, 33, 80
US Treasury yield curve, 80, 81
up-from-cost sell discipline, 210
uptick rules, 183

V
valid benchmarks, 15–16
valuation-level sell discipline, 210
value. *see also* relative-value analysis
  accumulated, 31–33
  dollar value of a basis point, 34n.26
  of immunized portfolios, 31–33, 38
  present value distribution of cash flows, 20–21
  price value of a basis point, 34n.26
  relative, 70
  target, 31–33
value at risk (VAR), 113
value investment style, 185–188
  defined, 184
  growth vs., 185–186
  Microsoft and, 186
  sell disciplines, 210
Value Line Arithmetic Composite Index, 176
value-weighted indexes, 169, 170, 172–173
Vanguard Admiral class shares, 179
Vanguard Group, Inc., 167, 179
Vanguard Mid-Cap Growth Fund, 202–203
van Leeuwen, Erik, 91
VAR. *see* value at risk
variance
  and bond duration, 114
  Markowitz mean-variance framework, 128
  maturity, 44
  semi-, 113
"vol" sectors, spread measures for, 79–80

W
Wal-Mart Stores
  equity market data, 171–174
  free-float adjustments, 169n.10
Wells Fargo, 166–167
wild card options, 116
World Bank, 73
WorldCom, 76
Wu, Wei, 91

Y
yield beta, 120
yield curve management, 130
yield curve risk, 18
yield curves
  in benchmark bond index selection, 18
  for discounting liabilities, 34
  of immunized portfolios, 39
  and indexed portfolio costs, 25
  and total return of immunized portfolios, 39
  Treasury, 80, 81
  twists in, 18
yields
  and duration hedging, 119–120
  high yield investment style, 187–188
  and leverage, 107–109
yield spread, 82, 119–120

Z
zero-volatility spread, 36